COMPARATIVE REGIONAL INTEGRATION

The International Political Economy of New Regionalisms Series

The International Political Economy of New Regionalisms Series presents innovative analyses of a range of novel regional relations and institutions. Going beyond established, formal, interstate economic organizations, this essential series provides informed interdisciplinary and international research and debate about myriad heterogeneous intermediate level interactions.

Reflective of its cosmopolitan and creative orientation, this series is developed by an international editorial team of established and emerging scholars in both the South and North. It reinforces ongoing networks of analysts in both academia and think-tanks as well as international agencies concerned with micro-, meso- and macro-level regionalisms.

Comparative Regional Integration
Theoretical Perspectives

Edited by
FINN LAURSEN

ASHGATE

Published by
Ashgate Publishing Limited
Gower House
Croft Road
Aldershot
Hampshire GU11 3HR
England

Ashgate Publishing Company
Suite 420
101 Cherry Street
Burlington, VT 05401-4405
USA

Ashgate website: http://www.ashgate.com

British Library Cataloguing in Publication Data
Comparative regional integration : theoretical
    perspectives. - (The international political economy of new
    regionalisms series)
    1. International economic integration - Congresses
    2. Regionalism (International organization) - Congresses
    3. International relations - Congresses
    I. Laursen, Finn
    337.1

Library of Congress Cataloging-in-Publication Data
Comparative regional integration : theoretical perspectives / edited by Finn Laursen.
        p. cm. -- (The international political economy of new regionalisms series)
    Conference papers.
    Includes bibliographical references and index.
    ISBN 0-7546-3261-X -- ISBN 0-7546-4086-8 (pbk.)
        1. International economic integration--Congresses. 2. Regionalism (International
organization)--Congresses. 3. Regionalism--Congresses. 4. International
relations--Congresses. 5. Security, International--Congresses. I. Laursen, Finn. II. Series.

HF1418.5.C656 2004
337.1--dc22   2003060972

ISBN 0 7546 3261 X (Hbk)
ISBN 0 7546 4086 8 (Pbk)

Printed and bound in Great Britain by MPG Books Ltd, Bodmin, Cornwall

Contents

PART IV: CONSTRUCTIVIST PERSPECTIVES

PART V: NEOFUNCTIONALIST AND HISTORICAL
INSTITUTIONALIST PERSPECTIVES

PART VI: CONCLUDING COMMENTS

List of Figures and Tables

Figures

Tables

Notes on Contributors

Svetlozar A. Andreev is a Ph.D. student at the European University Institute, Florence, Italy.

Susana Borrás is Associate Professor at the Department of Social Sciences at Roskilde University, Denmark. Her research interests are centred on the EU policy process and governance patterns, with special focus on political economy. Her latest publication is the book *The innovation policy of the EU* published by Edward Elgar.

M. Leann Brown is Associate Professor of Political Science at the University of Florida, USA. She is a former Fulbright European Union Research Fellow and author of a book entitled *Developing Countries and Regional Economic Cooperation*. Her current research interests include organizational learning in the European Union, and the role of scientific experts in EU environmental processes.

Scott Cooper is Assistant Professor of Political Science at Brigham Young University, Provo, Utah. His research is in the field of International Political Economy with special attention to patterns of regional monetary cooperation worldwide.

Peter M. Dennis is currently a researcher at the Washington, D.C.-based Advisory Board Company. He has spent the past few years working in international development and continued his studies on legal institutions and regional economic organizations at the New York University School of Law in the Fall of 2002.

Michael Kluth is Associate Professor at the Department of Social Sciences at Roskilde University, Denmark. He has previously worked on various aspects of European co-operation including labour market integration and European innovation policy. His current research interests are in the area of institutional political economy in the emerging markets of Latin America, Asia and Eastern Europe.

Finn Laursen is Professor of International Politics at the University of Southern Denmark where he also directs the Centre for European Studies. He is a graduate of political science from Aarhus University, Denmark. He did his Ph.D. at the University of Pennsylvania, Philadelphia, USA (1980). He has been a research fellow at the European University Institute, Florence (1977-80), Princeton University, New Jersey (1980-81), and Woods Hole Oceanographic Institution, Massachusetts (1984-85). Earlier appointments include Odense University, Denmark (1981-84), the London School of Economics (1985-88) and the European

Institute of Public Administration, Maastricht (1988-95). He was Director of the Thorkil Kristensen Institute for East-West Studies, Esbjerg (1995-1999). His books include *Superpower at Sea: US Ocean Policy* (Praeger, 1982) and *Small Powers at Sea: Scandinavia and the New International Marine Order* (Nijhoff, 1993). Edited works include *The Political Economy of European Integration* (Kluwer, 1995) and *The Amsterdam Treaty: National Preference Formation, Interstate Bargaining and Outcome* (Odense University Press, 2002). Together with Sophie Vanhoonacker he edited *The Intergovernmental Conference on Political Union* (Nijhoff, 1992) and *The Ratification of the Maastricht Treaty* (Nijhoff, 1994).

Andrés Malamud completed his Ph.D. at the Department of Social and Political Sciences of the European University Institute in Florence. He is now a Researcher at CIES (Research Center of Sociology) in Lisbon. He is on leave from his position as Assistant Professor of political science at the University of Buenos Aires. His current research interests include political institutions and regional integration.

Walter Mattli is Associate Professor of political science and a member of the Institute of War and Peace Studies at Columbia University. He received his Ph.D. from the University of Chicago and has taught at Columbia since 1995. He is the author of *The Logic of Regional Integration: Europe and Beyond* (Cambridge UP, 1999) and editor of *Governance and International Standards Setting* (Journal of European Public Policy, 2001). He has published articles on European legal integration, comparative regional integration, international commercial dispute resolution, and globalization and international governance. His new book project is titled *The Politics of International Standards Setting*. Smaller projects concern transatlantic relations and EU enlargement. He has been a Forum and Jean Monnet Fellow at the European University Institute in Florence (1997-98), a Fellow at the Center for International Studies at Princeton University (2000-01), and a Fellow at the Wissenschaftskolleg (Institute for Advanced Studies) in Berlin (2002-03). In 1995 he was awarded the Helen Dwight Reid Award of the American Political Science Association.

Andrea Oelsner is a Ph.D. student of International Relations at the London School of Economics and Political Science, UK. She received her MSc degree in International Relations from the same university. Her current research interests include processes of regional integration, regional politics in South America, and theories of peace.

Michelle Pace is subject lecturer in contemporary global studies and European society and thought at SOAS, University of London. She is also research associate at the Europe in the World Centre, University of Liverpool. She received her MA degree in International Studies from the University of Warwick (1995) and her Ph.D. from the Centre for European Studies Research, University of Portsmouth (2001). Her research interests include the politics of identity in the Mediterranean area, discourse analysis, European-Mediterranean relations and the Euro-Mediterranean Partnership.

José Raúl Perales is a Ph.D. student at the Department of Political Science, University of Michigan, Ann Arbor, Michigan, USA. Currently, he is also Advisor on International Economic Policy at the Corporation for the Development of Puerto Rican Exports (Promoexport), a government agency in the Department of Economic Development in San Juan, Puerto Rico.

Rafael Sánchez is a British citizen, originally from El Salvador. Because of the civil war, he and his family left El Salvador and settled in Costa Rica in the 1980s, where he finished his BA and a Licentiate degree in International Economic Relations at the *Universidad Nacional*. He got his MA in Politics of International Resources and Development at the University of Leeds, UK (1994) and his Ph.D. in International Relations from Sheffield University (2001) with a thesis on Central American Integration. Currently, he is doing research for the Open University on the role and interests of Mexico within the North American Free Trade Agreement (NAFTA). His research interest also includes the European Union-Latin American relations.

Brock Taylor is pursuing a joint MPP/JD degree from Duke University and Harvard Law School. His research specialization is Middle Eastern history and politics.

Douglas Webber is Professor of Political Science at INSEAD (European Institute of Business Administration) and has been stationed at its Asian campus in Singapore since 1999. He has published widely on German politics and foreign policy and European integration. He recently edited two books, *The Franco-German Relationship in the European Union* (Routledge, London, 1999) and *New Europe, New Germany, Old Foreign Policy? German Foreign Policy Since Unification* (Frank Cass, London, 2001).

Preface

In the Call for Papers issued towards the end of 2000, we stated that we were interested in papers applying various integration theories to case studies. We specifically mentioned the possibility of applying Andrew Moravcsik's liberal intergovernmentalism to other integration schemes than the EU. In his book *The Choice for Europe* (Cornell University Press, 1998), pp. 494-6, Andrew Moravcsik suggested such possible use.

We further mentioned Walter Mattli's book *The Logic of Regional Integration: Europe and Beyond* (Cambridge University Press, 1999) as another interesting framework that could be applied. Mattli put emphasis on the role of leadership in a process of integration.

We suggested that realist and neo-realist writings have found it difficult to explain European integration. This led to a question concerning the role of security issues in a process of integration.

Finally we asked whether we need to go beyond rationalist approaches to understand regional integration. A special issue of the *Journal of European Public Policy* (Vol. 6, No 4, 1999) discussed "The Social Construction of Europe." How do systemic interactions affect identity? Should social constructivist theories be applied more systematically in integration studies?

We received 30 papers in response to our call, which were presented in Odense 25-26 May 2001. Afterwards it was decided that some of them had dealt with theoretical issues in such a way that they deserved to be published together in one volume. Various feedbacks from the participants, especially some useful suggestions from Scott Cooper, helped the editor see how the chapters could be arranged to produce a book with various theoretical perspectives on integration.

All participants at the Odense symposium are thanked for their contributions to some very interesting discussions. And those authors selected for this book are thanked for their cooperation in revising their chapters for publication. We trust the book will be a contribution to an ongoing scholarly debate.

Acknowledgements

This book is based on selected contributions to a conference on Comparative Regional Integration, which took place at the Centre for European Studies at the University of Southern Denmark, Odense, Denmark, 25 - 26 May 2001. Special thanks go to Jean Monnet Professor Jørgen Drud Hansen, director of the Centre at the time, for his cooperation.

The project was organised in cooperation with the Danish Society for European Studies. Thanks also go to Jean Monnet Professor Morten Kelstrup, president of the Association at the time, for his cooperation.

The Danish Institute of International Affairs, Copenhagen, gave financial support to the conference and so did the Faculty of Social Sciences of the University of Southern Denmark. Their support is gratefully acknowledged.

Dorrit Andersen-Alstrup, secretary for the Centre for European Studies, is thanked for her excellent support in connection with the organisation of the conference, and Vibeke Pierson, secretary at the Department of Political Science, is thanked for her diligent help and linguistic assistance during the editorial process. My student assistant Laura Lund Olsen was also a great help in connection with the conference, and Tonny Lundgren Rasmussen produced the index.

Finally, thanks are due to Professor Timothy Shaw, general editor of this series of books, for his encouragement and advice.

Odense, April 2003
Finn Laursen

List of Abbreviations

ABACC	Brazilian-Argentine Agency for Accounting and Control of Nuclear Materials
AFTA	ASEAN Free Trade Area
AIA	ASEAN Investment Area
ANEC	European Association of Consumer Representation in Standardization (Association de Normalisation Européenne pour les Consommateurs)
APEC	Asia-Pacific Economic Cooperation
APT	ASEAN Plus Three
ARF	ASEAN Regional Forum
ASEAN	Association of Southeast Asian Nations
ASEM	Asia-Europe Meeting
CACM	Central American Common Market
CAP	Common Agricultural Policy
CCJ	Central American Court of Justice
CEECs	Central and Eastern European Countries
CEN	European Committee for Standardization (Comité Européen de Normalisation)
CENELEC	European Committee for Electrotechnical Standardization (Comité Européen de Normalisation Eléctronique)
CEPAL	Economic Commission for Latin America
CESDP	Common European Security Defence Policy
CET	Common External Tariff
CFSP	Common Foreign and Security Policy
CNEN	National Commission of Nuclear Energy
COMECON	Council for Mutual Economic Cooperation (CMEA)
EAEG	East Asian Economic Grouping
EC	European Community
ECB	European Central Bank
ECJ	European Court of Justice
ECOMOG	ECOWAS Cease-Fire Monitoring Group
ECOWAS	Economic Community of West African States
ECSC	European Coal and Steel Community
EEC	European Economic Community
EFTA	European Free Trade Association
EMP	Euro-Mediterranean Partnership
EMS	European Monetary System
EMU	European Economic and Monetary Union
EOTC	European Organization for Testing and Certification
EPC	European Political Co-operation

ETSI	European Telecommunications Standardization Institute
ETUC	European Trade Union Confederation
EU	European Union
EVSL	Early Voluntary Sectoral Liberalization
FDI	Foreign Direct Investment
FIESP	Federation of Industrialists of São Paulo
FMLN	Farabundo Marti guerillas
FTAA	Free Trade Area of the Americas
GAC	General Affairs Council
GATT	General Agreement on Tariffs and Trade
GCC	Gulf Cooperation Council
GIC	Gulf Investment Corporation
GMP	Global Mediterranean Policy
IGC	Intergovernmental Conference
IMF	International Monetary Fund
LAFTA	Latin American Free Trade Association
LAIA	Latin American Integration Association
MENA	Middle East and North Africa
MERCOSUR	Mercado Común del Sur
MNC	Mediterranean Non-Member Countries
NAFTA	North American Free Trade Agreement
NALADISA	Standard Commercial Classification of the Latin American Integration Association
NATO	North Atlantic Treaty Organization
NMP	New Mediterranean Policy
NPFL	National Patriotic Front of Liberia
NPT	Nuclear Non-Proliferation Treaty
NTBs	Non-Tariff Barriers to Trade
OAMCE	Organisation Africaine et Malagache de Coopération Economique
OAU	Organization of African Unity
ODECA	Organisation of Central American States
OECD	Organization for Economic Cooperation and Development
PAECA	Central American Economic Action Plan
PARLACEN	Central American Parliament
PHARE	Programme of Community Aid to the Countries of Central and Eastern Europe
PICAP	Integration and Cooperation Program
PICE	Programme for Integration and Economic Cooperation
PTA	Preferential Trade Area
QMV	Qualified Majority Vote
RDF	Rapid Deployment Force
RMP	Renewed Mediterranean Policy
RSC	Regional Security Complex
SCCC	Common System of Accounting and Control
SDOs	National Standards Developing Organizations

SEA	Single European Act
SG-SICA	General Secretariat of SICA
SICA	System of Central American Integration
SICA-CC	Consultative Committee of SICA
SIECA	Central American Secretariat for Economic Integration
SMC	Standing Mediation Committee
SMEs	Small and Medium-sized Enterprises
TP	Tegucigalpa Protocol
TUTB	European Trade Union Technical Bureau for Health and Safety
UIA	Argentine Industrial Union
UN	United Nations
UNCTAD	United Nations Conference on Trade and Development
UNU/WIDER	United Nations University/World Institute for Development Economics Research
WTO	World Trade Organization

PART I
Introduction

Chapter 1

Theoretical Perspectives on Comparative Regional Integration

Finn Laursen

Introduction

Theories of integration have mainly been developed to explain European integration. Europe was the region of the world, where regional integration started in the early 1950s with the European Coal and Steel Community (ECSC) in 1952. Ernest Haas theorized this experience in *The Uniting of Europe* (1958). The main theoretical contribution was the concept of spillover. Later Lindberg used this concept to study the early years of the European Economic Community (EEC), which started its existence in 1958 (Lindberg, 1963). These early theories are usually referred to as neo-functionalist theories.

There were some efforts to apply these neo-functionalist theories to integration in other parts of the world, especially in Latin America (Haas, 1961; Haas and Schmitter, 1964; Haas, 1967).

The integration process in Europe experienced a crisis in the mid-1960, when General de Gaulle instructed his ministers not to take part in meetings of the EEC Council. In the Luxembourg Compromise in January 1966, the then six members of the European Communities (EC) agreed to disagree. The French insisted that decisions by a qualified majority vote (QMV) could not take place, when a Member State opposed a decision because of important national interests.

The nature of common institutions has remained a controversial issue in Europe, but Europe has gone further in creating effective common institutions than other regions in the world.

Some neo-functionalists tried to modify the theory to take account of the events in Europe in the mid-60s. This included Lindberg and Scheingold in *Europe's Would-Be Polity* (1970) and J. S. Nye in *Peace in Parts* (1971). But many students of European integration started stressing the 'logic of diversity' and the more intergovernmental aspects of the EC (e.g. Hoffmann, 1965; Taylor, 1983).

The early rich theoretical discussions about European integration petered out during the 1970s and early 1980s. But as the European integration process got a new momentum from the mid-1980s, with the Single European Act (SEA) and the Single Market programme, scholars started taking a theoretical interest in

3

European integration again. Some argued that neo-functionalism still had explanatory power (e.g. Laursen 1990, Tranholm-Mikkelsen 1991). Others looked for new ways to explain the phenomenon.

The main alternative was intergovernmentalism, which put emphasis on the role of the member states. Andrew Moravcsik developed 'liberal inter-governmentalism' during the 1990's to explain the process of integration in Europe, suggesting the combination of a liberal theory to explain national preference formation and an intergovernmental theory of interstate bargaining to explain substantive outcomes (Moravcsik, 1991, 1993). Later he added a third stage, institutional choice, where pooling and delegation of sovereignty are mainly seen as a way to create 'credible commitments' (Moravcsik, 1998).

During the 1990s, in parallel with the IR debate concerning rationalist approaches vs. social constructivist approaches, it has also been claimed that we need a social constructivist approach to understand European integration (e.g. Checkel, 1999; Marcussen et al., 1999). In the following we shall take a closer look at some of these approaches and theories.

The Concept of International Integration

When early theories of integration were developed, there was much discussion in the literature on how to define the concept. It was, for instance, discussed whether integration refers to a process or to an end product. Of course the two can be combined. Integration could then be defined as a process that leads to a certain state of affairs. Karl Deutsch, for instance, defined integration as 'the attainment, within a territory, of a "sense of community" and of institutions and practices strong enough and widespread enough to assure, for a "long" time, dependable expectations of "peaceful change" among its population.' When a group of people or states have been integrated this way, they constitute a 'security community.' Deutsch and his collaborators used another term, amalgamation, to refer to 'the formal merger of two or more previously independent units into a single larger unit, with some type of common government' (Karl W. Deutsch et al., 1957, pp. 5-6). These distinctions led to a simple two-by-two table (see Table 1.1).

On the bases of empirical studies Deutsch and his collaborators made conclusions about the conditions of creating security communities and arriving at amalgamated security communities. The cases included the USA (break-up of union during the Civil War and reunion afterwards), the UK (union with Scotland, break-up of union with Ireland), German and Italian unifications in 19th century, the Habsburg Empire (long preservation and dissolution in 1918), Norway-Sweden (union in 1814, separation in 1905) and the gradual integration of Switzerland that was completed in 1848 (Ibid., pp. 16-17). The conclusion was that nine conditions were essential for an amalgamated security-community:

1. mutual compatibility of main values
2. a distinctive way of life
3. expectations of stronger economic ties or gains

4. a marked increase in political and administrative capabilities of at least some participating units
5. superior economic growth on the part of at least some participating units
6. unbroken links of social communication, both geographically between territories and sociologically between different social strata
7. a broadening of the political elite
8. mobility of persons, at least among the politically relevant strata, and
9. a multiplicity of ranges on communication and transaction (Ibid., p. 58).

Table 1.1 Integration and amalgamation according to Karl Deutsch

	Non-Amalgamation	**Amalgamation**
Integration	*Pluralistic Security-Community* Example: Norway-Sweden today	*Amalgamated Security-Community* Example: USA today
Non-Integration	*Not Amalgamated Not Security-Community* Example: USA-USSR during Cold War	*Amalgamated but not Security-Community* Example: Habsburg Empire 1914

Source: Karl W. Deutsch et al. (1957, p. 7).

For a pluralistic security-community, on the other hand, only two or three conditions were considered essential:

1. compatibility of major values relevant to political decision-making
2. the capacity of the participating political units or governments to respond to each other's needs, messages, and actions quickly, adequately, and without resort to violence
3. mutual predictability of behaviour (which however is closely related to the second condition) (Ibid., pp. 66-67).

Deutsch's concept of a pluralistic security community has kept intriguing social scientists and has remained relevant for understanding regional integration in the world. Amalgamation goes beyond the examples of regional integration studied in this book, although in the case of the EU one could ask whether the process is approaching amalgamation, a kind of pre-federal order.

As mentioned, most early efforts to study regional international integration concentrated on the European case, especially the European Coal and Steel Community (ECSC) and the European Economic Community (EEC). In Ernst Haas's classical study of the ECSC, *The Uniting of Europe*, integration was defined as

... the process whereby political actors in several distinct national settings are persuaded to shift their loyalties, expectation and political activities to a new center whose institutions possess or demand jurisdiction over the pre-existing national states (Haas, 1958, p. 16).

In Leon Lindberg's study of the early EEC, *The Political Dynamics of European Economic Integration*, integration was defined without reference to an end point:

... political integration is (1) the process whereby nations forgo the desire and ability to conduct foreign and key domestic policies independently of each other, seeking instead to make *joint decisions* or to *delegate* the decision-making process to new central organs; and (2) the process whereby political actors in several distinct settings are persuaded to shift their expectations and political activities to a new center (Lindberg, 1963, p. 6).

Lindberg considered his own concept of integration more cautious than that of Haas. Central to it was 'the development of devices and processes for arriving at collective decisions by means other than autonomous action by national governments' (Ibid., p. 5).

Some concepts of integration applied in studies of the European Communities (EC) may be too specific, if we want to conduct comparative studies. Clearly, the process of European integration within the EC has gone further than integration in other regional settings. A relatively loose definition may be better for comparative studies. However, it seems fair to say that collective decision-making is an important aspect of all regional integration efforts. This collective decision-making can cover a varying number of functional areas (scope). The decision-making process can be more or less efficient and the common institutions established can be more or less adequate (institutional capacity).

What then explains changes in functional scope and institutional capacity of regional integration efforts? This is the central question in integration theory. Ernst Haas developed the concept of spillover, which was also applied by Lindberg. According to Lindberg

... 'spillover' refers to a situation in which a given action, related to a specific goal, creates a situation in which the original goal can be assured only by taking further actions, which in turn create a further condition and a need for more action, and so forth (Lindberg, 1963, p. 10).

Haas saw the EEC as spillover from the ECSC. He talked about 'the expansive logic of sector integration.' He predicted that the process would continue in the EEC. Liberalization of trade within the customs union would lead to harmonization of general economic policies and eventually spillover into political areas and lead to the creation of some kind of political community (Haas, 1958, p. 311).

When the European integration process experienced a crisis in the mid-1960s, however, many scholars concluded that Haas' early theory had been too deterministic. This included Haas himself, who now admitted that he had not foreseen 'a rebirth of nationalism and anti-functional high politics.' A revised theory would have to take account of 'dramatic-political' aims of statesmen such as General de Gaulle (Haas, 1967).

In a much-quoted article, Stanley Hoffmann argued that the national situations and role perceptions were still rather diverse within the EC. In general he argued:

> Every international system owes its inner logic and its unfolding to the *diversity* of domestic determinants, geo-historical situations, and outside aims among its units (Hoffmann, 1966, p. 864).

So, he contrasted the logic of integration with the logic of diversity. The latter sets limits to the degree to which the 'spillover' process can operate. 'It restricts the domain in which the logic of functional integration operates to the area of welfare.' Hoffmann advanced the suggestion that 'in areas of key importance to the national interest, nations prefer the certainty, or the self-controlled uncertainty, of national self-reliance, to the uncontrolled uncertainty' of integration (Ibid., p. 882).

Early Comparative Studies

In a study where Haas compared regional integration in Europe with integration in other regions of the world, he suggested that one should study the environments in which the processes take place to understand the differences. He listed three sets of 'background' factors, which he considered important. The first factor was *social structure*. Here Western Europe is dominated by pluralism, i.e. the existence of 'articulate voluntary groups, led by bureaucratized but accessible elites.' The second factor was *economic and industrial development*. Here Western Europe has a high degree of industrialization and urbanization. The third factor was *ideological patterns*. Here there is a certain degree of homogeneity in Western Europe. According to Haas, 'integration proceeds most rapidly and drastically when it responds to socio-economic demands emanating from an industrial-urban environment, when it is an adaptation to cries for increasing welfare and security born by the growth of a new type of society.' On the other hand, 'countries dominated by a non-pluralistic social structure are poor candidates for participation in the integration process' (Haas, 1961).

In a study of Latin American integration with Philippe Schmitter 'the *size and power of the units* joining in the economic union' as well as 'the *rate of transaction among the participants*' were added to the background conditions of pluralism and elite complementarity. Haas and Schmitter further included two conditions at the time of union, namely *governmental purposes* and *powers of the union*. Next they added three process conditions, namely *decision-making style, rate of transaction* and *adaptability of governments*. This added up to a total of nine variables. The EEC scored high on most of these factors, while the Latin American Free Trade Association (LAFTA) scored mixed to low (Haas and Schmitter, 1964). This might explain the different fates of these two integration efforts. The COMECON, incidentally, also scored low to mixed on most of these factors, with the exception of rate of transaction and elite complementarity (see Table 1.2).

Table 1.2 The Haas-Schmitter predictions about economic unions (1964)

	EEC	EFTA	OECD	COM-ECON	East African Common Market	West African Federation	West Indian Feder-ation	Central American Common Market	LAFTA
BACKGROUND CONDITIONS									
1. Size of Units	Mixed	Low	Low	Low	Mixed	Low	Low	High	Mixed
2. Rate of transactions	High	Mixed	Mixed	High	Low	Low	Low	Low	Mixed
3. Pluralism	High	High	High	Mixed	Low	Low	Low	Mixed	Mixed
4. Elite complementarity	High	Mixed	Mixed	High	Mixed	High?	High?	Mixed	Mixed
Total Judgment	High	Mixed	Mixed	Mixed+	Mixed-	Low+	Low+	Mixed	Mixed
CONDITIONS AT TIME OF ECONOMIC UNION									
5. Governmental purposes	High	Low	Low	Mixed	Low	Mixed	Mixed	Mixed	Low
6. Powers of union	High	Low	Low	Low	High	Low?	Low?	Low	Low
Total Judgment	High	Low	Low	Low	Mixed	Mixed	Mixed?	Mixed-	Low
PROCESS CONDITIONS									
7. Decision-making style	Mixed	Mixed	Low	Mixed	Mixed	?	?	Low	Mixed
8. Rate of transaction	High	High	Mixed	High	Low	Low	Low	Mixed	Mixed
9. Adaptability of governments	High	High	Mixed	Mixed	Low	Low	Low	?	Mixed
Total Judgment	High	High	Mixed	Mixed	Low	Low	Low	Mixed?	Mixed
CHANCES OF AUTOMATIC POLITICIZATION	Good	Fairly good	Possible-doubtful	Possible-doubtful	Doubtful	Poor?	Poor?	Possible	Possible-doubtful

Source: Haas and Schmitter, 1964 (after 1966 ed.). We have left out the Organisation Africaine et Malagache de Coopération Economique (OAMCE).

There were other studies of comparative regional integration in the 1960s and 1970s, but they were not so theoretical in approach as those by Haas and Schmitter.

Adapting Neo-functionalism

To the extent that European integration has often been seen as a kind of model for integration efforts in other parts of the world, it may be worthwhile to include a few remarks about the European process.

Reference was made to the crisis in the EC in the mid-60s. The feeling that early theory had seen the process as too automatic led to various efforts to reformulate integration theory. The effort by Lindberg and Scheingold in their book *Europe's Would-Be Polity* deserves special mention (Lindberg and Scheingold, 1970). Lindberg and Scheingold now studied the EC as a political system, where inputs in the form of demands, support and leadership are transformed into outputs in the form of policies and decisions. They added three integration mechanisms to that of spillover already developed by Haas, namely (a) *log-rolling and side-payments*, i.e. bargaining exchanges designed to 'gain assent of more political actors to a particular proposal or package of proposals,' (b) *actor socialization*, i.e. the process whereby the 'participants in the policy-making process, from interest groups to bureaucrats and statesmen, begin to develop new perspectives, loyalties, and identifications as a result of their mutual interactions,' and (c) *feedback*, which mainly refers to the impact of outputs on the attitudes and behaviour of the public at large. If the public finds the output from the system good and relevant, support for the system is expected to increase.

Lindberg and Scheingold see integration as a political process with both demand and supply factors determining the process. On the demand side various domestic groups have expectations and lobby the governments for certain outcomes. On the supply side, coalition formation and leadership are seen as central aspects of the process. To get decisions through the system you must have the support of various groups and individual decision-makers. This is where the role of the independent Commission was seen as important in the EC. The Commission can actively try to build coalitions to overcome national resistance to new policies and decisions, i.e. exercise supranational leadership.

How would the EC's new momentum associated with the completion of the Internal Market in the EC during the years 1987-92 fit in with Lindberg and Scheingold's revised neo-functionalist theory of international integration? Quite well, one could argue. The EC was gradually expanding its scope, developing new policies to complement early policies, including technology, environment and monetary policies. The Internal Market project was partly due to feedback processes. The originally chosen approach of harmonization to overcome non-tariff barriers to trade (NTBs) had produced too few results. A new approach was necessary. Industry made demands. The Commission of Jacques Delors contributed with leadership. Also, the Single European Act (SEA) adopted in 1986 introduced qualified majority voting (QMV) as the rule to complete the Internal Market. The practice of unanimity, which had become the rule after the Luxembourg Compromise in January 1966, had contributed to a slow-down or even halting of the process of integration. Further, the negotiation process of the Intergovernmental Conference (IGC), which negotiated the SEA in 1985, had its own dynamics of linkages and bargaining exchanges (log-rolling and side-payments). Thus, we find some of the major mechanisms and dynamics singled out by second-generation neo-functionalist theoreticians such as Lindberg and Scheingold well represented in a catalogue of explanatory factors (Laursen, 1990).

However, one can argue that converging national interests were important or even decisive. This included changes in domestic politics in some of the Member States, in particular in France under President Mitterrand (Moravcsik, 1991). Maybe neo-functionalists had not studied domestic politics sufficiently? Maybe they exaggerated the role of supranational institutions?

Among efforts to revise early neo-funtionalism we should also mention J.S. Nye's *Peace in Parts* (1971). Nye discussed the following seven process mechanisms: external actors, rising transactions, functional linkages, deliberate linkages, regional group formation, elite socialization and identitive appeal (Ibid., pp. 64-75). Especially the involvement of external actors brought in a factor to which the early neo-functionalists had paid insufficient attention. As was the case in Lindberg and Scheingold's systemic model, Nye's revised model included demand for integration from groups – as well as opposition to integration from other groups – and supply from decision-makers responding to pressures and mechanisms, and the model also included feedback loops.

Neo-functionalist-inspired studies of European integration still exist. There are scholars putting emphasis on supranational institutions (Sandholz and Stone Sweet, 1998) and multi-level governance (Marks, Hooghe and Blank, 1996). There are various new institutionalist approaches to integration studies (Pollack, 1996, Schneider and Aspinwall, 2001). One of these approaches is Pierson's historical institutionalism, according to which gaps emerge in member states' control and these gaps are difficult to close. Factors creating these gaps include the autonomous actions of EC institutions, the restricted time horizons of political decision makers, unanticipated consequences and shifts in policy preferences of governments. The gaps are difficult to close because of the reluctance of supranational actors, institutional barriers to reform and various costs of change. A key concept in this literature is path dependency (Pierson, 1996).

Game-Theoretic Perspectives

Regional integration efforts can be seen as an effort to overcome a fundamental problem in the system of classical international relations, namely that of defection. According to classical international law states are sovereign. They do not have to accept supranational authorities. They can of course conclude agreements with other states, bilaterally or multilaterally; but once they find that conditions have changed, they are no longer bound by such agreements. International lawyers refer to this as the *rebus sic stantibus* rule. And it is the state itself which determines whether conditions have changed. Obviously the rule of law in international relations is different from the rule of law which we find domestically in civilized countries.

International agreements and cooperation efforts can be fragile and unstable as long as they are based on the classical notion of sovereignty and rules of international law.

Modern game theory discusses this in a formal deductive fashion. The famous Prisoners' Dilemma game illustrates the situation where individually rational actors, e.g. states, arrive at sub-optimal outcomes if they act independently. Further, the theory shows that agreements, which should realize optimal outcomes, will often be unstable because actors will be tempted to cheat or defect from the cooperative agreement to realize outcomes that are better for themselves in the short run (Brams, 1975; Stein, 1990; Taylor, 1987).

Actor B

		Co-operation	Defection
Actor A	Co-operation	3,3	1,4
	Defection	4,1	2,2

Source: Stein, 1982.

Figure 1.1 Prisoners' Dilemma

The Prisoners' Dilemma can be depicted as a dilemma between co-operation and defection. In its simplest version there are two actors, A and B. Each has to decide between two possible strategies. The values in the matrix are the payoffs for A and B respectively. So the first value is the outcome for Actor A, and the second value is for Actor B. In a one-shot game A is expected to choose the defection strategy because the payoff will be best irrespective of what B decides. The same goes for B, and the collective outcome will be 2,2, which is sub optimal (or Pareto inferior). The optimal outcome, 3,3, can be reached through co-operation, but will be unstable because each actor can gain by defecting (or cheating). It may therefore take a good international regime, possibly including sanctions in order to avoid defection.

Post-war efforts at international cooperation among industrialized countries in the economic area can be seen as a response to the protectionism – and beggar-thy-neighbour policies – of the 1930s. Free trade is not easy to realize because of the temptation to cheat. The states tried to liberalize trade through the General Agreement on Tariffs and Trade (GATT) – now part of the World Trade Organization (WTO). Yet trade conflicts and protectionist measures have remained important aspects of relations among the industrialized countries (Grieco, 1990; Conybeare, 1987; Gilpin, 1987).

The experience of the EC is instructive in this respect. The EC is first of all a customs union, which should realize free trade among its members (and introduce a common tariff towards third countries). But once the customs union was in place in 1968, it gradually became clear that a customs union is not sufficient to realize free trade. Member States could continue to protect their national industries through non-tariff-barriers to trade (NTBs). Some of these were technical barriers to trade like different national standards for products (Pelkmans and Winters, 1988).

A number of curious cases followed. Many of these eventually were taken to the European Court of Justice (ECJ). There were cases like the French alcoholic drink *Cassis de Dijon*, which could not be exported to Germany because it did not have the alcohol content required by German law; pasta which could not be exported to Italy because it was made of soft wheat instead of durum wheat; bread that could not be exported to the Netherlands because it did not have the salt content required by Dutch law, etc., etc. The ECJ played an important role in stopping this kind of 'defection' and in enunciating the principle of 'mutual recognition of standards.'

The Internal Market project can be seen as a renewed effort to overcome Prisoners' Dilemma situations. There were demands from economic groups in the Member States and the EC institutions played a role. The Commission under President Jacques Delors played a leadership role. In the Single European Act (SEA) the Member States also accepted the use of qualified majority voting (QMV) to complete the Internal Market.

These elements of an independent Commission and QMV add up to what could be called supranationality (Keohane and Hoffmann, 1990). The Commission is an independent European body; it is there to represent and further European interests. National interests are represented in the Council (of Ministers); but to the extent that QMV is accepted in the Council, no single member can stop the adoption of measures they do not like. One of the problems of traditional intergovernmental cooperation, and the concomitant rule of unanimity, is that the slowest members will determine the speed. Under such form of cooperation one should expect decisions to be based on the lowest common denominator. The EC, on the other hand, has created institutions that should facilitate the 'upgrading of the common interest' (Haas, 1961).

Reference was made to the important role of the ECJ. Community law is different from traditional international law. It has primacy if it conflicts with national law; and much EC legislation has direct effect (Louis, 1990).

If we compare the EC with other regional integration organizations some of these institutional differences become apparent. None of the other regional schemes have created independent supranational bodies like the EC Commission; none of them have accepted anything resembling Community law and real limits on their sovereignty in the form of binding majority decisions (see also Feld and Boyd, 1980; Jamar, 1982). In the EC there has been a pooling and delegation of sovereignty. According to Moravcsik this is done to ensure 'credible commitments' (Moravcsik, 1998).

Integration is not only about getting optimal outcomes, however. There are also issues of distribution in integration processes. The game that can illustrate this is the coordination game known as Battle of the Sexes. Whereas the question about efficiency is the question of reaching the Pareto-frontier, the question of distribution is where you end up on the Pareto-frontier. An element of power enters the equation. Whereas liberal institutionalists scholars have looked at efficiency, realists and neo-realists have emphasized the question of power (Krasner, 1991, Little, 1997). In the integration literature especially Mattli has emphasized the importance of a leader who plays the role of a regional paymaster. Such leader can help solve problems of distributional inequities which will often be part of the integration process (Mattli, 1999a and 1999b).

Actor B

		Mountains	Ocean
	Mountains	3,4	0,0
Actor A			
	Ocean	0,0	4,3

Source: Krasner, 1991.

Figure 1.2 The Battle of the Sexes

The Battle of the Sexes (Figure 1.2) is often illustrated by a couple going on holiday. What happens if the male partner prefers the mountains and the female partner prefers to go to the beach? If the greater part of the holiday is spent in the mountain the male partner will have won the little power game. This game can also be illustrated as different points on the Pareto frontier (see Figure 1.3), where 3½, 3½ is the perfect compromise.

In the following we shall take a closer look at two recent contributions to integration theory, namely the contributions by Moravcsik and Mattli. Both suggest models that are rather simple and useful for understanding regional integration.

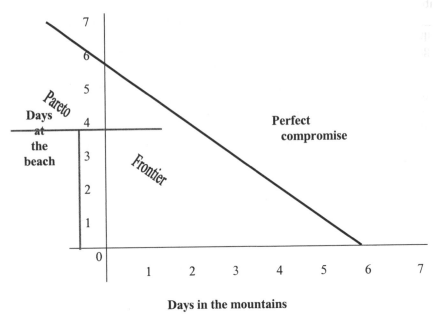

Source: Little, 1997.

Figure 1.3 Pareto Frontier

Liberal Intergovernmentalism

The liberal intergovernmental framework is summarized in Table 1.3. The model is simple and could be used to structure studies of integration in other parts of the world than Europe.

The first stage in the model is to try to explain national preferences. The central question asked by Moravcsik here is whether it is economic or geopolitical interests that dominate. The answer based on major decisions in the European integration process is that economic interests are the most important ones (Moravcsik, 1993, 1998).

The second stage, interstate bargaining, seeks to explain the efficiency and distributional outcomes. Here two possible explanations of agreements on substance are contrasted: asymmetrical interdependence or supranational entrepreneurship. Moravcsik arrives at the answer that asymmetrical interdependence has the most explanatory power.

Table 1.3 International cooperation: A rationalist framework

Stages of Negotiation	National Preference Formation	Interstate Bargaining	Institutional Choice
Alternative independent variables underlying each stage	What is the source of underlying national preferences?	Given national preferences what explains the efficiency and distributional outcomes of interstate bargaining?	Given substantive agreement, what explains the transfer of sovereignty to international institutions?
	Economic interests or Geopolitical interests?	Asymmetrical interdependence or Supranational entrepreneurship?	Federalist ideology or Centralized technocratic management or More credible commitment?
	↓	↓	↓
Observed outcomes at each stage	Underlying national preferences →	Agreements on substance →	Choice to delegate or pool decision-making in international institutions

Source: Moravcsik (1998), p. 24.

The third stage explores the reasons why states choose to delegate or pool decision-making in international institutions. Delegation in the EU refers to the powers given to the Commission and the European Court of Justice. Pooling of sovereignty refers to the application of majority decisions. To explain institutional choice, Moravcsik contrasts three possible explanations: Federalist ideology, centralized technocratic management or more credible commitment. The answer is that states delegate and pool sovereignty to get more credible commitment.

The brief overview given here cannot do justice to the richness of the analysis of European integration in *The Choice for Europe*. Using theories of decision-making, negotiations and international political economy in an elegant combination has allowed Moravcsik to construct a simple framework for the study of international cooperation, including international integration.

In the last chapter in *The Choice for Europe,* Moravcsik suggests that his study has implications for International Relations theory in general and that it could be used to study regional integration in other parts of the world than Europe. In a brief discussion he mainly looks at regional trade dependency as the underlying factor explaining the demand for integration.

He noticed that intra-regional trade in relation to GDP is much higher in Europe than in North America and East Asia. Concerning intra-industry trade, which is considered conducive to trade liberalization, Europe is ahead of North America and East Asia. But intra-industry trade is quite high in North America, too. This produces a ranking, where one should expect most demand for integration in Europe, followed by North America and with East Asia on a third place. Moravcsik summarizes:

> Bringing together these simple indicators... the political economy theory predicts very strong pressures for trade liberalization in Europe, more moderate pressure in North America, and very little pressure in East Asia. This is indeed what we observe (Moravcsik, 1998, p. 495).

He goes on to say 'geopolitical theories have difficulty explaining this outcome.' He does admit, 'these data are more suggestive than conclusive.' But, he says, 'they do suggest that the primacy of political economy observed in postwar Europe is not just a contingent fact about Europe but a generalization about postwar industrial nations' (Ibid., p. 496).[1] He finishes the discussion by saying that "the comparative political economy of regionalism deserves more intensive study, beginning with the assumption that Europe and other regions face similar challenges and opportunities."

Mattli's Contribution

In Moravcsik's brief discussion of comparative regionalism emphasis is on the demand side. Walter Mattli has dealt with regional integration from a comparative perspective, comparing European experiences with experiences in other regions of the world. He also emphasizes the importance of supply factors, especially 'the presence of an undisputed leader among the group of countries seeking closer ties:'

> Such a state serves as a focal point in the coordination of rules, regulations, and policies; it may also help to ease distributional tensions by acting as regional 'paymaster' (Mattli, 1999a, p. 14).

---

[1]   In a footnote Moravcsik makes the following statement: 'Although we can reject objective geopolitical circumstances as the source of preferences, we cannot entirely dismiss the role of ideas. Yet until ideas are clearly measured and more precisely theorized, claims for the importance of ideology and ideas cannot be more than speculative' (fn 26, ibid., p. 496).

Successful integration depends both on demand from market actors and supply from political actors. Willingness to supply integration 'depends on the payoff of integration to political leaders' (Ibid., p. 13). On the supply side both "commitment institutions" (such as the Commission and ECJ in Europe) and an institutional leader are considered important. In the German *Zollverein* the role of regional paymaster was played by Prussia. It is argued that Germany has played such a role in the EU. A central question on the supply side is how to overcome collective action problems associated with both Prisoners' Dilemma and coordination games. There must be mechanisms to deal with the temptation of defection as well as distributional inequities.

Looking at integration in different regions of the world over time Mattli finds two puzzles:

1. Why have so many attempts at integration failed while a few have been crowned with success?
2. What explains when outsiders seek to become insiders? (Outsiders can become insiders either by joining an existing economic union or by creating their own regional group) (Mattli, 1999a, p. 41).

Once an integration scheme starts, it will have external effects (externalities) because of discriminatory policies among the insiders. Outsiders may face trade and investment diversion, which will create a demand for joining (the first integrative response) or create an alternative scheme (the second integrative response). In Europe, EFTA was an example of the second response in 1960. But eventually most EFTA countries joined the EC/EU, examples of the first integrative response.

Table 1.4 Outcomes of integration schemes

| | | (Uncontested) regional leadership | |
		Yes	No
(Potential) market gains from integration	**Relatively significant**	3 EU NAFTA EFTA (until 1973)	2 EFTA (after 1973) APEC MERCOSUR
	Relatively insignificant	2 CACM (until 1969)	1 CACM (after 1969) ASEAN ECOWAS LAFTA Andean Pact

Success rate: 3 highest
1 lowest

Source: Adapted from Mattli (1999a), p. 66.

Some integration schemes outside Europe, it is argued, can be seen as second integration responses to developments in Europe. The creation of the EEC in 1958 was a factor behind the Latin American Free Trade Association (LAFTA) in 1960. Later, 'efforts to deepen integration through the Single European Act raised fears of a "Fortress Europe," triggering a veritable tidal wave of integration projects throughout the world in the late 1980s.' However, 'none of the projects of the second integrative response type is guaranteed automatic success.' It all depends on whether the conditions are met. On the supply side, absence of leadership can cripple integration (example the Andean Pact) and unwillingness to address distributional issues (such as in LAFTA) can undermine the prospects for integration (Ibid., pp. 63-64).

Mattli has illustrated the varying outcomes of integration in a figure that we reproduce in slightly shortened form (Table 1.4). Leaving out some of the integration schemes studied by Mattli, we note that he has given the EU, NAFTA and EFTA until 1973 the highest success rate (1973 was the year the UK and Denmark left EFTA to join the EC). The lowest success rate is given to the Central American Common Market (CACM) after 1969, ASEAN, the Economic Community of West African States (ECOWAS), LAFTA and the Andean Pact (as well as the Carribbean Community and the Arab Common Market, which we have not included in the table). In the middle groups we find two contemporary schemes, the Asia Pacific Economic Cooperation Forum (APEC) and Mercosur.

The Mattli framework for studying regional integration also has the clear advantage of simplicity, singling out a small number of variables as decisive for the success of integration. It pays equal attention to demand and supply factors. Among the things suggested by the scheme is the problem of leadership for schemes like Mercosur and APEC, despite the presence of significant potential market gains from integration. Can and will Brazil be a leader in Mercosur? Can and will Japan – or the United States – be a leader in APEC? We also note that Mattli does not see great prospects of integration among ASEAN countries, despite renewed integration efforts from 1992.

One could ask whether it is useful – and methodologically correct – to compare integration and cooperation schemes as diverse as those studied by Mattli. Obviously a scheme including four South American countries like Mercosur is very different from NAFTA, a scheme including more than 20 countries on both sides of the Pacific Ocean. Despite the differences, however, both schemes try to create freer trade among the participating states, and it seems to us that one must look at both economic demand factors as well as the capacity of political leaders and systems to produce such freer trade to understand economic integration.

Social Constructivist Critiques

In International Relations (IR) theory the 1980s witnessed a great debate between neo-realists and neo-liberal institutionalists (Baldwin, 1993). Neo-realists, emphasizing relative gains, were rather sceptical about international cooperation (Grieco, 1990). Neo-liberal institutionalists, emphasizing absolute gains from cooperation, were more optimistic about international cooperation. But, during the debate, it became clear that the two sides shared a number of basic positions: states as primary actors, the usefulness of assumptions of rationality, and the importance of relative capabilities or power of states.

In the late 1980s and early 1990s, a critique set in from various sides. New reflectivist approaches emerged as alternatives to the rationalist approaches. The fact that the mainstream approaches had failed to predict the end of the Cold War was part of the reason for this changing mood of IR. Especially neo-realists had made predictions about the continuation of bipolarity in the mid and late 1980s just before the revolutionary changes in 1989. And then there were neo-realists who predicted that the EU and NATO would decline after the end of the Cold War and that Europe would revert to unstable multipolarity (Mearsheimer, 1990). Such predictions may have underestimated the role of institutions in Europe (Keohane and Hoffmann, 1993). Although the EU may face some problems of democratic legitimacy, the process of integration has continued to deepen and widen, expanding the functional scope, pooling sovereignty further through the Maastricht, Amsterdam and Nice treaties. After the 4th enlargement in 1995, it is preparing the next enlargements with Central and Eastern European countries (CEECs), which will unite most of Europe under a common integration scheme.

In 1992 Alexander Wendt told scholars 'Anarchy is What States Make of It' (Wendt, 1992). This was obviously a very different way of looking at matters, compared with the way neo-realists had explained and predicted international politics from international anarchy and relative capabilities of states (Waltz, 1979).

A number of younger European scholars now started wondering whether the dominant approaches to the study of European integration were too rationalistic and paid too little attention to how interaction affects interests and identity. A special issue of the *Journal of European Public Policy* explored the issue in 1999 (Christiansen, Jørgensen and Wiener, 1999). Moravcsik was invited to contribute. He asked whether something was rotten in the state of Denmark, referring also to the 'Copenhagen school' in security studies: '...the force of continental constructivist theories appears to radiate outward from the Danish capital, where it is the hegemonic discourse' (Moravcsik, 1999, p. 669). His judgment was harsh: 'Hardly a single claim in this volume is formulated or tested in such a way that it could, even in principle, be declared empirically invalid' (ibid., p. 670). Most of the contributors to the volume were criticized for not advancing testable theories. Based on his own research, Moravcsik claimed that ideas are transmission belts for interests and indeed rather epiphenomenal. The authors did not take alternative theories seriously enough to test them. 'Constructivism prevails by default rather than by surmounting the challenge of honest empirical validation' (ibid., p. 676).

Among those criticizing liberal intergovernmentalism we also find Marlene Wind, who said that

> ... important institutional elements such as the evolution and change of norms, ideas and historically produced codes of conduct – discursive as well as behavioural, are completely expelled from analysis (Wind, 1997, p. 28).

She further criticizes Moravcsik for underestimating the role of the Commission and personalities. 'The member states are far from "in control" of the process,' she says (Ibid., p. 30).

When it comes to applying social constructivism to integration in other parts of the world we have to mention Richard Higgott, who suggests that comparative analysis of EU and East Asia allows us to refine dominant neo-liberal institutionalist approaches and see the utility of alternative 'constructivist' applications (Higgott, 1998).

Higgott argues that there has been a 'convergence in the dominant ideas system underwriting policy change in both Europe and the Asia-Pacific' towards a form of neo-liberal ideology. This was the case with the Internal Market programme in Europe as well as 'market-led open regionalism' in Asia. Referring to Susan Strange, who saw both the EU and APEC as responses to globalization which produce a desire to respond collectively to certain problems, he argues that rationalist approaches ignore the ideational dimensions of the process:

> Ideational approaches allow us to see the extent to which regime building is influenced by ideology, beliefs and knowledge, and especially the evolution of consensual knowledge positions among crucial actors (Higgott, 1998, p. 45).

Higgott argues 'In a regional context, questions of regional awareness and regional identity become important factors' (Ibid., p. 46). Further, 'a constructivist analysis alerts us to the possibility that systemic regional interaction may transform identity' (Ibid., p. 56).

The role of ideas and emerging regional identities clearly remain factors to be explored further in comparative regional integration studies.

This introduction has not been able to mention all existing studies of regional integration. The Brookings Institution in Washington, D.C. had a project on 'Integrating National Economies: Promise and Pitfalls' during the 1990s that produced some useful books (e.g. Haggard, 1995; Kahler, 1995a; Lawrence, 1996). Recent studies include the works from a major project, 'The New Regionalism', under the United Nations University/World Institute for Development Economics Research (UNU/WIDER). Björn Hettne, András Inotai and Osvaldo Sunkel directed this work (1999, 2000a, 2000b, 2000c, 2001). No less than five volumes have been published, including a number of useful chapters on various regionalisms in different parts of the world, *inter alia* relating regionalism to development issues and security. We should also mention a special issue of *Third World Quarterly*, edited by Marianne H. Marchand, Morten Boas and Timothy M. Shaw dealing with regionalism in the third world (1999).

Clearly the new wave of integration efforts from the end of the 1980s and early 1990s has sparked new interest in the phenomenon of regional integration and other manifestations of regionalism. This book is yet another contribution to the ongoing analysis and theoretical debate.

Overview of Contributions to This Volume

The contributions to this volume explore various aspects of regional integration in different parts of the world. They have all been selected for their contribution to the theoretical debate. We start with a section on governmentalist perspectives. Rafael Sánchez (Chapter 2) analyses the process of reform of Central American integration within an intergovernmentalist perspective. Emphasis is placed on the governments' preferences and actions. According to this perspective integration occurs as a result of intergovernmental bargaining and asymmetrical co-operation.

In Chapter 3 Andrés Malamud contrasts the Mercosur with the EU, asking how the former has been able to advance integration without the supranational institutions of the latter. The answer given is that Mercosur integration can be partly explained by domestic institutional settings, especially presidential democracy.

In Chapter 4 José Raúl Perales looks at the supply side of integration, using Mercosur as a case. The main proposition is that Mercosur is an attempt by political elites in Argentina and Brazil to gain credibility for their trade policies and to recast the role of the private sector in the economies of these countries.

Then follows a section on power perspectives starting with Chapter 5 in which Scott Cooper and Brock Taylor review the realist applications to economic regionalism by means of a case study of economic cooperation in the Persian Gulf: the Gulf Cooperation Council (GCC). The chapter examines balance-of-threat theory as an explanation for the GCC. It is shown that this realist theory does not provide a complete explanation for the timing or form of the GCC. A better understanding of the GCC is achieved when internal threats to the governing regimes, and not just external threats, are considered.

In Chapter 6 Douglas Webber analyses the ups and downs of regionalism in East Asia and Asia Pacific. The principal regional organizations in this part of the world, ASEAN and APEC, are widely seen to be crisis-stricken. At the same time, East Asia is witnessing the emergence of a new, as yet embryonic body, ASEAN Plus Three (APT). Webber discusses the roots of the perceived decline of ASEAN and APEC and the origins of the rapid rise of APT. It is argued that the Asian financial crisis exposed the structural weaknesses of ASEAN and APEC, both of which are handicapped by the political and economic diversity of their member states and the absence of a benevolent dominant state or coalition of states. The APT, however, is likely to exhibit similar structural weaknesses.

The next chapters present constructivist perspectives. In Chapter 7 Michelle Pace applies a 'discursive-constructivist' approach to the Mediterranean 'region'. An analysis of the EU discourses on the Mediterranean – in particular its Euro-Mediterranean Partnership (EMP) – reveals practices that give this area a fixed meaning. The resulting Mediterranean is just one of the many 'others' in Europe's self-identification process.

In Chapter 8 Andrea Oelsner deals with the changes in the Argentine-Brazilian relationship since the late 1970s. The focus is principally on the dramatic transformation in this relationship, which, after decades of rivalry and hostility, is resulting in the emergence of a security community and in parallel changes in their mutual perceptions. It is argued that the conditions originally listed by Karl Deutsch as contributing to developing a security community – and hence to common identification – viz. mutual compatibilty of major values, mutual responsiveness and mutual predictability of behaviour, are present.

In Chapter 9 Susana Borrás and Michael Kluth analyse two recent events in Mercosur and the EU, the macro-economic crises in Brazil and Argentina and the constant loss of value of the euro against the US dollar after its launch in 1999. Both events have put pressure on the institutionalised order of the regional arrangements. The theoretical framework applied combines institutionalism and social constructivism, trying to accommodate a perspective on ideational/cognitive factors without undermining the explanatory value of interests. To understand the continuity of regional arrangements in times of instability, it is argued, we need to bring in the cognitive-ideational dimension.

In Chapter 10 Peter M. Dennis and M. Leann Brown apply neo-functionalist concepts of spillover to analyse the development of ECOWAS. Faced with mounting disorder in Liberia, most West African states desired and preferred outside intervention by the UN, OAU or international powers such as the United States. This assistance was not forthcoming. The only actors with the interests and wherewithal to undertake the mission were Nigeria and a Nigeria-led ECOWAS. It was clear to political and economic leaders across the region that achieving integration and growth was contingent on military security in the region.

In Chapter 11 Svetlozar A. Andreev applies historical institutionalism to understand the EU's eastern enlargement process. Both path dependency, with emphasis on initial conditions, and major external shocks help us understand the process. These shocks include the collapse of communist rule in Eastern Europe (1989-91) and the Kosovo conflict (1998-99). The latter demonstrated some of the shortcomings of the initial policies of enlargement.

Finally, the book includes concluding comments by Walter Mattli and Finn Laursen.

References

Anderson, Jeffrey J. (ed.) (1999), *Regional Integration and Democracy: Expanding on the European Experience*, Rowman & Littlefield, Lanham.

Bach, Daniel C. (ed.) (1999), *Regionalisation in Africa: Integration and Dis-integration,* James Currey, Oxford; Indiana University Press, Bloomington and Indianapolis.

Baldwin, David A. (ed.) (1993), *Neorealism and Neoliberalism: The Contemporary Debate*, Columbia University Press, New York.

Baldwin, Richard E. (1997), 'The Causes of Regionalism', *The World Economy*, Vol. 20(7), pp. 865-888.

Beach, Derek (2002), 'Negotiating the Amsterdam Treaty: When Theory Meets Reality', in Finn Laursen (ed.), *The Treaty of Amsterdam: National Preference Formation, Interstate Bargaining and Outcome*, Odense University Press, Odense, pp. 593-637.

Beeson, Mark and Jayasuriya, Kanishka (1998), 'The political rationalities of regionalism: APEC and the EU in comparative perspective', *The Pacific Review*, Vol. 11(3), pp. 311-336.

Beuter, Rita and Tsakaloyannis, Panos (eds) (1987), *Experiences in Regional Cooperation*, European Institute of Public Administration, Maastricht.

Bowden, Sharon and Elling, Martin (1991), 'In the Shadow of 1992: Developing Country Efforts at Economic Integration', *Harvard International Law Journal*, Vol. 32, pp. 537-552.

Brams, Steven J. (1975), *Game Theory and Politics*, The Free Press, New York.

Checkel, Jeffrey T. (1999), 'Social Construction and Integration', *Journal of European Public Policy*, Vol. 6(4), pp. 545-60.

Christiansen, Thomas, Jørgensen, Knud Erik and Wiener, Antje (eds) (1999), 'The Social Construction of Europe', Special Issue of *Journal of European Public Policy*, Vol. 6(4).

Conybeare, John A.C. (1987), *Trade Wars: The Theory and Practice of International Commercial Rivalry*, Columbia University Press, New York.

Deutsch, Karl W. (1954), *Political Community at the International Level: Problems of Definition and Measurement*, Doubleday and Co., New York.

Deutsch, Karl, et al. (1957), *Political Community and the North Atlantic Area: International Organization in the Light of Historical Experience*, Princeton University Press, Princeton, N.J.

Eliassen, Kjell A. and Monsen, Catherine Børve (2000), 'Institutions and Networks: A Comparison of European and Southeast Asian Integration', in Erik Beukel et al. (eds), *Elites, Parties and Democracy. Festschrift for Professor Mogens N. Pedersen*, Odense University Press, Odense, pp. 49-74.

Fawcett, Louise and Hurrell, Andrew (eds.) (1995), *Regionalism in World Politics: Regional Organization and International Order*, Oxford University Press, Oxford.

Feld, Werner J. and Boyd, Gavin (eds) (1980), *Comparative Regional Systems: West and East Europe, North America, The Middle East, and Developing Countries*, Pergamon Press, New York.

Gamble, Andrew and Payne, Anthony (eds.) (1996), *Regionalism & World Order*, Macmillan, Houndsmills.

Ganesan, N. (1995), 'Testing neoliberal institutionalism in Southeast Asia', *International Journal*, Vol. 50 (Autumn), pp. 779-804.

Gauhar, Altaf (ed.) (1985), *Regional Integration: The Latin American Experience*, Third World Foundation, London.

Gilpin, Robert (1987), *The Political Economy of International Relations*, Princeton University Press, Princeton.

Grieco, Joseph M. (1990), *Cooperation among Nations: Europe, America, and Non-Tariff Barriers to Trade*, Cornell University Press, Ithaca and London.

Grugel, Jean (1996), 'Latin America and the Remaking of the Americas,' in Andrew Gamble and Anthony Payne (eds), *Regionalism and World Order*, Macmillan, London, pp. 131-167.

Haas, Ernst B. (1958), *The Uniting of Europe: Political, Social, and Economic Forces 1950-1957*, Stanford University Press, Stanford.

Haas, Ernst B. (1961), 'International Integration: The European and the Universal Process,' *International Organization*, Vol. 15(4), pp. 366-392.

Haas, Ernst B. (1967), 'The Uniting of Europe and the Uniting of Latin America,' *Journal of Common Market Studies*, Vol. 5, pp. 315-343.

Haas, Ernst B. and Schmitter, Philippe C. (1964), 'Economics and Differential Patterns of Political Integration: Projections about Unity in Latin America', *International Organization*, Vol. 18(4), Also in *International Political Communities. An Anthology*, Anchor Books, Garden City, N.Y, 1966, pp. 259-299.

Haggard, Stephan (1995), *Developing Nations and the Politics of Global Integration*, The Brookings Institution, Washington, D.C.

Harris, Stuart (1993), 'Economic Cooperation and Institution Building in the Asia-Pacific Region', in Richard Higgott, Richard Leaver, and John Ravenhill (eds), *Pacific Economic*

Relations in the 1990s: Cooperation or Conflict? Lynne Rienner, Boulder, CO, pp. 271-298.

Hettne, Björn, Inotai, András and Sunkel, Osvaldo (eds) (1999), *Globalism and the New Regionalism,* Macmillan, Houndsmills.

Hettne, Björn, Inotai, András and Sunkel, Osvaldo (eds) (2000a), *National Perspectives on the New Regionalism in the North,* Macmillan, Houndsmills.

Hettne, Björn, Inotai, András and Sunkel, Osvaldo (eds) (2000b), *National Perspectives on the New Regionalism in the South,* Macmillan, Houndsmills.

Hettne, Björn, Inotai, András and Sunkel, Osvaldo (eds) (2000c), *The New Regionalism and the Future of Security and Development,* Macmillan, Houndsmills.

Hettne, Björn, Inotai, András and Sunkel, Osvaldo (eds), (2001), *Comparing Regionalisms: Implications for Global Development,* Palgrave, Houndsmills.

Higgott, Richard (1993a), 'Economic Cooperation: Theoretical Opportunities and Practical Constraints', *The Pacific Review,* Vol. 6(2), pp. 103-117.

Higgott, Richard (1993b), 'Competing Theoretical Approaches to International Cooperation: Implications for the Asia-Pacific', in Richard Higgott, Richard Leaver and John Ravenhill (eds), *Pacific Economic Relations in the 1990s: Cooperation or Conflict?* Lynne Rienner, Boulder, CO, pp. 290-311.

Higgott, Richard (1995), 'Economic co-operation in the Asia Pacific: a theoretical comparison with the European Union', *Journal of European Public Policy,* Vol. 2(3) (September), pp. 361-83.

Higgott, Richard (1998), 'The international political economy of regionalism: the Asia-Pacific and Europe compared', in William D. Coleman and Geoffrey R.D. Underhill (eds), *Regionalism and Global Economic Integration: Europe, Asia and the Americas,* Routledge, London, pp. 42-67.

Higgott, Richard and Richard Stubbs (1995), 'Competing conceptions of economic regionalism: APEC versus EAEC in the Asia Pacific', *Review of International Political Economy,* Vol. 2(3) (Summer), pp. 516-35.

Hoffmann, Stanley (1966), 'Obstinate or Obsolete? The Fate of the Nation-State and the Case of Western Europe', *Daedalus,* Vol. 95 (Summer), pp. 862-915.

Hoffmann, Stanley (1982), 'Reflections on the Nation-State in Western Europe Today', *Journal of Common Market Studies,* Vol. 21 (September-December), pp. 21-37.

Hosli, Madeleine O. and Saether, Arild (eds) (1997), *Free trade agreements and customs unions: Experiences, challenges and constraints,* European Institute of Public Administration, Maastricht.

Hosona, Akio (1996), 'APEC and NAFTA: Regionalism, Open Regionalism and Globalism', *Journal of International Political Economy,* Vol. 1(1) (March), pp. 71-84.

Jacob, Philip E. and Toscano, James V. (eds.) (1964), *The Integration of Political Communities,* J.P. Lippincott Company, Philadelphia.

Jamar, Joseph (ed.) (1982), *Intégrations régionales entre pays en voie de développement,* De Tempel, Tempelhof, Bruges.

Kahler, Miles (1995a), *International Institutions and the Political Economy of Integration,* The Brookings Institution, Washington, D.C.

Kahler, Miles (1995b), 'A World of Blocs: Facts and Factoids', *World Policy Journal,* Vol. 12(1) (Spring), pp. 19-27.

Katzenstein, Peter J. (1996), 'Regionalism in Comparative Perspective', *ARENA Working Papers,* Vol. 96(1).

Keohane, Robert O. (1984), *After Hegemony: Cooperation and Discord in the World Political Economy,* Princeton University Press, Princeton.

Keohane, Robert O. (1989), *International Institutions and State Power: Essays in International Relations Theory,* Westview, Boulder, CO.

Keohane, Robert O. and Hoffmann, Stanley (1990), 'Community politics and institutional change' in William Wallace (ed.), *The Dynamics of European Integration,* Pinter Publishers, London, pp. 276-300.

Keohane, Robert O. and Hoffmann, Stanley (eds) (1991), *The New European Community: Decisionmaking and Institutional Change,* Westview Press, Boulder, CO.

Keohane, Robert and Hoffmann, Stanley (1993), *After the Cold War: International Institutions and State Strategies in Europe 1989-1991,* Harvard University Press, Cambridge, MA.

Keohane, Robert O. and Nye, Joseph S. (1977), *Power and Interdependence: World Politics in Transition,* Little, Brown and Company, Boston.

Krasner, Stephen D. (1991), 'Global Communications and National Power: Life on the Pareto Frontier', *World Politics,* Vol. 43 (April), pp. 336-66.

Laursen, Finn (1990), 'Explaining the EC's New Momentum', in Finn Laursen, ed., *EFTA and the EC: Implications of 1992,* European Institute of Public Administration, Maastricht.

Laursen, Finn (1991), 'Comparative regional economic integration: the European and other processes,' *International Review of Administrative Sciences,* Vol. 57, pp. 515-526.

Laursen, Finn (1992), 'Explaining the Intergovernmental Conference on Political Union,' in Finn Laursen and Sophie Vanhoonacker, eds, *The Intergovernmental Conference on Political Union,* European Institute of Public Administration, Maastricht, pp. 229-248.

Laursen, Finn (1994), 'The Not-So-Permissive Consensus: Thoughts on the Maastricht Treaty and the Future of European Integration', in Finn Laursen and Sophie Vanhoonacker (eds), *The Ratification of the Maastricht Treaty,* Nijhoff, Dordrecht, pp. 295-317.

Laursen, Finn (1995), 'On Studying European Integration: Integration Theory and Political Economy', in Finn Laursen (ed.), *The Political Economy of European Integration,* Kluwer, The Hague, pp. 3-29.

Laursen, Finn (1997), 'European Integration and Trade Regimes: From the European Economic Area to the "Europe" Agreements', in Madeleine O. Hosli and Arild Saether (eds), *Free trade agreements and customs unions,* European Institute of Public Administration, Maastricht, pp. 267-291.

Laursen, Finn (2002), 'Explaining and Evaluating the Amsterdam Treaty: Some Concluding Remarks', in Finn Laursen (ed.), *The Amsterdam Treaty: National Preference Formation, Interstate Bargaining and Outcome,* Odense University Press, Odense, pp. 639-655.

Lawrence, Robert Z. (1996), *Regionalism, Multilateralism, and Deeper Integration,* The Brookings Institution, Washington, D.C.

Lindberg, Leon N. (1963), *The Political Dynamics of European Economic Integration,* Stanford University Press, Stanford.

Lindberg, Leon N. and Scheingold, Stuart A. (1970), *Europe's Would-Be Polity: Patterns of Change in the European Community,* Prentice-Hall, Inc., Englewood-Cliffs, N.J.

Lindberg, Leon N. and Scheingold, Stuart A. (eds) (1971), *Regional Integration: Theory and Research,* Harvard University Press, Cambridge, MA.

Little, Richard (1997), 'International Regimes', in John Baylis and Steve Smith (eds), *The Globalization of World Politics: An Introduction to International Relations,* Oxford University Press, Oxford, pp. 231-247.

Louis, Jean-Victor (1990), *The Community Legal Order,* Office for Official Publications of the European Communities, Luxembourg.

Mansfield, Edward D. and Milner, Helen V. (1999), 'The New Wave of Regionalism', *International Organization,* Vol. 53(3), pp. 589-628.

Marchand, Marianne H., Boas, Morten and Shaw, Timothy M. (eds) (1999), 'The Political economy of new regionalism', special issue of *Third World Quarterly,* Vol. 20(5) (October), pp. 897-1070.

Marcussen, Martin et al. (1999), 'Constructing Europe: The Evolution of French, British, and German Identities', *Journal of European Public Policy,* Vol. 6(4), pp. 614-33.

Marks, Gary, Hooghe, Lisbett and Blank, Kermit (1996), 'European Integration from the 1980s: State-Centric v. Multi-Level Governance', *Journal of Common Market Studies*, Vol. 34(3), pp. 341-378.

Mattli, Walter (1999a), *The Logic of Regional Integration: Europe and Beyond*, Cambridge University Press, Cambridge.

Mattli, Walter (1999b), 'Explaining regional integration outcomes', *Journal of European Public Policy*, Vol. 6(1) (March), pp. 1-27.

Mearsheimer, J. (1990), 'Back to the Future: Instability After the Cold War', *International Security*, Vol. 15(1).

Milner, Helen (1998), 'Regional economic co-operation, global markets and domestic politics: a comparison of NAFTA and the Maastricht Treaty', in William D. Coleman and Geoffrey R.D. Underhill (eds), *Regionalism and global economic integration: Europe, Asia and the Americas*, Routledge, London, pp. 19-41.

Mittelman, James H. (1996), 'Rethinking the "New Regionalism" in the Context of Globalization', *Global Governance*, Vol. 2, pp. 189-213.

Moravcsik, Andrew (1991) 'Negotiating the Single European Act: National interests and conventional statecraft in the European Community', *International Organization* 45(1), pp. 19-56.

Moravcsik, Andrew (1993), 'Preferences and Power in the European Community: A Liberal Intergovernmental Approach', *Journal of Common Market Studies*, Vol. 31(4), pp. 473-523.

Moravcsik, Andrew (1998), *The Choice for Europe*, Cornell University Press, Ithaca.

Moravcsik, Andrew (1999), 'Is something rotten in the state of Denmark? Constructivism and European integration', *Journal of European Public Policy*, Vol. 6(4), pp. 669-81.

Moravcsik, Andrew and Kalypso Nicolaïdis (1999), 'Explaining the Treaty of Amsterdam: Interests, Influence, Institutions', *Journal of Common Market Studies*, Vol. 37(1) (March), pp. 59-85.

Mulat, Teshome (1998), 'Multilateralism and Africa's Regional Economic Communities', *Journal of World Trade*, Vol. 32(4), pp. 115-138.

Ng'ong'ola, Clement (1999), 'Regional Integration and Trade Liberalisation in Africa', *Journal of World Trade*, Vol. 33(1), pp. 145-171.

Nicoll, Davidson, Echeverria, Luis and Peccei, Aurelio (eds) (1981), *Regionalism and the New International Economic Order*, Pergamon Press, New York.

Nye, Joseph S., Jr. (1968), 'Comparative Regional Integration: Concepts and Measurement', *International Organization*, Vol. 22(4), pp. 855-80.

Nye, Joseph S., Jr. (1970), 'Comparing Common Markets: A Revised Neo-Functionalist Model', *International Organization*, Vol. 24(4), pp. 796-835.

Nye, J.S. (1971), *Peace in Parts: Integration and Conflict in Regional Organization*, Little, Brown and Company Boston.

O'Brian, Robert (1995), 'North American Integration and International Relations Theory', *Canadian Journal of Political Science*, Vol. 28(4) (December), pp. 693-724.

Page, Sheila (2000), *Regionalism among Developing Countries*, Macmillan, Houndsmills.

Pelkmans, Jacques and Winters, Alan (1988), *Europe's Domestic Market*, Royal Institute of International Affairs, London:.

Pentland, Charles (1973), *International Theory and European Integration*, Faber and Faber Limited, London.

Pierson, Paul (1996), 'The Path to European Integration: A Historical Institutional Analysis', *Comparative Political Studies*, Vol. 29(1), pp. 123-163.

Pollack, Mark A. (1996), 'The New Institutionalism and EC Governance: The Promise and Limits of Institutional Analysis', *Governance*, Vol. 9(4) (October), pp. 429-458.

Risse-Kappen, Thomas (1996), 'Collective Identity in a Democratic Community: The Case of NATO', in Peter J. Katzenstein, ed., *The Culture of National Security: Norms and Identity in World Politics*, Columbia University Press, New York, pp. 357-399.

Rosamond, Ben (2000), *Theories of European Integration*, Macmillan, Houndsmills.

Sandholtz, Wayne (1993), 'Choosing Union: Monetary Politics and Maastricht', *International Organization*, Vol. 47(1), pp. 1-39.

Sandholtz, W. and Stone Sweet, A. (eds) (1998), *European Integration and Supranational Governance*, Oxford University Press, Oxford.

Schmitter, Philippe C. (1969), 'Three Neofunctionalist Hypotheses about International Integration', *International Organization*, Vol. 23(1), pp. 161-166.

Schmitter, Philippe C. (1970), 'A Revised Theory of Regional Integration', *International Organization*, Vol. 24(4), pp. 836-868.

Schneider, Gerald and Aspinwall, Mark (eds) (2001), *The rules of integration: Institutionalist approaches to the study of Europe*, Manchester University Press, Manchester.

Schulz, Michael, Söderbaum, Fredrik and Öjendal, Joakim (eds) (2001), *Regionalization in a Globalizing World: A Comparative Perspective on Forms, Actors and Processes*, Zed Books, London and New York.

Smith, Peter H. (ed.) (1993), *The Challenge of Integration: Europe and the Americas,* North-South Center Press, Miami, FL.

Stein, Arthur (1982), 'Coordination and Collaboration in an Anarchic World', *International Organization*, Vol. 36(2), pp. 299-324.

Stein, Arthur A. (1990), *Why Nations Cooperate: Circumstance and Choice in International Relations*, Cornell University Press, Ithaca and London.

Taylor, Michael (1987), *The possibility of cooperation*, Cambridge University Press, Cambridge.

Taylor, Paul (1983), *The Limits of European Integration*, Columbia University Press, New York.

Telò, Mario (ed.) (2001), *European Union and New Regionalism: Regional actors and global governance in a post-hegemonic era,* Ashgate, Aldershot.

Tranholm-Mikkelsen, Jeppe (1991), 'Neo-functionalism: Obstinate or Obsolete? A Reappraisal in the Light of the New Dynamism of the EC', *Millennium: Journal of International Studies*, Vol. 20(1), pp. 1-22.

Tussie, Diane (1998), 'In the whirlwind of globalization and multilateralism: the case of emerging regionalism in Latin America', in William D. Coleman and Geoffrey R.D. Underhill (eds), *Regionalism and global economic integration: Europe, Asia and the Americas*, Routledge, London and New York, pp. 81-96.

Urata, Shujiro (1998), 'Regionalization and the Formation of Regional Institutions in East Asia', in Kiichiro Fukasaku, Fukunari Kimura and Shujiro Urata (eds), *Asia and Europe: Beyond Competing Regionalism*, Sussex Academic Press, Brighton, pp. 13-44.

Waltz, Kenneth N. (1979), *Theory of International Politics*, Reading, MA: Addison-Wesley.

Wendt, Alexander (1992), 'Anarchy Is What States Make of It', *International Organization*, Vol. 46, pp. 394-419.

Wincott, Daniel (1995), 'Institutional Interaction and European Integration: Towards an Everyday Critique of Liberal Intergovernmentalism', *Journal of Common Market Studies*, Vol. 33(4) (December), pp. 597-609.

Wind, Marlene (1997), 'Rediscovering Institutions: A Reflectivist Critique of Rational Institutionalisme', in Knud Erik Jørgensen (ed.), *Reflective Approaches to European Governance*, Macmillan Press, Houndsmills, pp. 15-35.

Winters, L. Alan (1997), 'What Can European Experience Teach Developing Countries About Integration?' *The World Economy*, Vol. 20(7), pp. 889-912.

Wionczek, Miguel (1970), 'The Rise and Decline of Latin American Economic Integration', *Journal of Common Market Studies*, Vol. 9(1), pp. 49-66.

Young, Oran (1991), 'Political leadership and regime formation: on the development of institutions in international society', *International Organization,* Vol. 45(3) (Summer), pp. 281-308.

Young, Soogil (1994), 'Globalism and regionalism: complements or competitors?' in Ross Garnaut and Peter Drysdale (eds), *Asia Pacific Regionalism: Readings in International Economic Relations*, Harper Educational Publishers, Pymble, NSW, pp. 179-193.

PART II
Governmentalist Perspectives

Chapter 2

Rebuilding the Central American Bloc in the 1990s: An Intergovernmentalist Approach to Integration[1]

Rafael Sánchez

Introduction

In the 1990s, following the success of the Esquipulas peace process to end the civil wars, the Central American governments turned their attention to rebuilding and redefining integration. This chapter looks at the process of reorganising regionalism in Central America as a result of strategies pursued by the governments in order to boost both the process of regional integration and the internationalisation of the economies of the region. This reorganisation of regionalism includes the reform of the Central American Common Market (CACM), and the reshaping of the process of integration in general, with the establishment of SICA (System of Central American Integration) in 1991. The focus of the chapter is on the process of institutional reform, bargaining and the strategic interactions of the member states of the CACM (Costa Rica, Guatemala, El Salvador, Honduras and Nicaragua) which led to the re-launch of regionalism in the 1990s under SICA. The main contentions put forward here are:

1. That the rebuilding of regionalism in Central America reflects governments' preferences constrained domestically by their political economy (distributional conflicts) and externally by global pressures and the desire of the governments to integrate their countries into the world economy.

---

[1] The Central American bloc refers to a group of states made up of Costa Rica, El Salvador, Guatemala, Honduras and Nicaragua. These states got their independence from Spain in 1821 and since then have been linked together in different processes of integration. These include, among others, the Organisation of Central American States (ODECA) created in 1951 and the Central American Common Market (CACM) created in 1960. In 1991 these five states created the System of Central American Integration (SICA) which includes Panama and Belize, but the latter does not participate in economic integration under the CACM.

2. In the rebuilding of regionalism, governments' preferences and interests remain a central feature, which determines the scope and reach of integration. But the external dependence of the region also instigates pressures on the interstate bargaining for integration.

3. Although the governments embrace integration within the context of open regionalism and globalisation, there still exists a conceptual divide within the region. As a result, variable geometry, rather than a solid and far-reaching process, defined the nature of integration in the 1990s. This divide seriously undermines the pursued goal of integrating the region effectively into the world economy.

The Impact of Security Concerns on Integration

It may seem paradoxical that although the military conflicts of the 1980s exacerbated disintegration in Central America, they also created some conditions for the reinvention of regionalism in the 1990s. Politically, the rise of the left and the turning of Central America's crisis into an East-West conflict meant that previous 'high politics', such as the border dispute and political rivalry between El Salvador and Honduras, lost political importance. The guerrillas were the only significant enemies. Some of these threatened the survival of the military regimes. Therefore, co-operation on security matters became a high politics necessity for the governments.

Increasingly, the governments viewed themselves as part of a regional 'security complex' in the sense put forward by Buzan (1991), which implies that they recognised their interdependence on security matters and the need to reinforce co-operation on security and economic matters. This forced the Honduran and Salvadorian governments to resolve their political and territorial differences by negotiations. Preventing the success of the Farabundo Marti guerrillas (FMLN) became a national security interest of both governments, which dictated the need for co-operation (see López Contreras, 1984, pp. 105-108). The outcome was the Peace Treaty of 30 October 1980, when the states recognised part of their common border and agreed to submit to international adjudication for the remaining areas on which there was still disagreement.

The peace treaty converted El Salvador, Honduras and Guatemala into a sub-regional bloc, which not only involved military, but also economic and trade-related co-operation. The three states began to co-ordinate their security policy as early as May 1980 (see Dunkerley, 1982, p. 164, Schulz and Schulz, 1994, p. 60). By 1986 these states were moving into full economic co-operation, originally through joined developmental programmes at 'El Trifinio', a cross border natural and populated resource involving the three states (SIECA, 1990, p. 96). This was followed by a trilateral trade agreement in 1987 when the governments sought to strengthen their economic relations grounded on neo-liberal principles. The agreement fell outside the CACM. Costa Rica and Nicaragua were not invited to join (Latin American Monitor: Central America, June 1987, p. 424). Bypassing the CACM appears to have been intentional in order both to bring in Honduras which remained outside the CACM, and to avoid annoying the Reagan administration, which opposed reviving the common market for both ideological and political reasons. This trade agreement created the conditions for Honduras' return to the region's economic and political arrangements. It formed the basis for the creation by these states of the North Triangle area in 1992 (El Salvador, Guatemala and Honduras) and the formal re-incorporation of Honduras to the CACM in the same year.

The Contribution of the Esquipulas Process[2]

However, it was the Esquipulas process (1986-1990) that became the instrument through which the governments would gradually rebuild Central American regionalism, enhancing macroeconomic co-operation, particularly after 1990. Under the Esquipulas process, and within it the so-called Arias Peace Plan,[3] the governments began to move away from the political and ideological fragmentation brought about by the cold war. The Arias Plan operated as a political pact among the governments allowing the reestablishment of political and economic co-operation region wide. One of the main contributions of the Esquipulas process consisted of rebuilding integration understood as policy co-ordination. In the same way that the trade agreement of 1987 helped bringing Honduras back to the CACM, the Esquipulas process brought Nicaragua back into the regional process of negotiation and policy making (Rouquié, 1994, p. 283).

The willingness of the Sandinistas to introduce democratic reforms as established in the Peace Plan increased the level of trust among the governments. Esquipulas was efficient as a conflict resolution mechanism and as a system of policy co-ordination. The creation of the presidential summit as the main and regular decisional body, and the embracing of the principle of simultaneity in the

---

[2] A detailed analysis of the significance of the Esquipulas Peace Process for integration is presented in Chapter 5 of my Ph.D.-thesis entitled: 'Peace Negotiations and the Process of Reform of the Central American Common Market in the 1990s: An Inter-governmentalist Approach to Integration', England, University of Sheffield, July 2002.

[3] The Esquipulas process was initiated in 1986 by the Guatemalan president Marcos Vinicio Cerezo following the virtual collapse of the Contadora's Group in attaining peace in the region. The Esquipulas process was strengthened when in 1987 President Oscar Arias of Costa Rica launched a peace plan aimed at seeking a negotiated solution to the civil wars and political divisions in Central America. The Arias Plan defied the US foreign policy of intervention in Central America and became the basis for the solution of the conflicts based on intergovernmental bargaining.

implementation of regional decisions, produced by the end of the decade a great sense of political integration in the region of 1980 (see Arias Sánchez, 1992, p. 80). Bilateral differences between governments were properly diffused through collective bargaining among the Presidents. The reestablishment of integration as policy co-ordination enabled the governments to establish a process of political co-operation,[4] which let them work together in the process of rebuilding and reforming integration in the 1990s.

Thus, the new regionalism in Central America has not been a spontaneous process brought about by the end of the cold war or by the US turn towards regionalism as stressed by some authors (e.g., Hettne, 2000, p. xvii, Bhagwati, 1994, p. 150). These factors, however, have operated as catalysts creating pressures for integration in the region. The main explanation for the resumption of integration in the 1990s has to be found in the integrationist tradition of the region, the political co-operation under the Esquipulas process of negotiation, and in the increasing level of political and economic convergence among the states (Sanahuja, 1998, p. 20). International agreement, as Moravcsik argues (1993, p. 487) 'requires that the interest of dominant domestic groups in different countries converge'. In Central America there has been an increase in the level of regionness and convergence. This increased level of convergence, however, is limited to the realms of politics and economics.

On the political side, the advance of the process of democratisation instigated by the Esquipulas process led to the idea of presenting the region as 'a region of peace, freedom, democracy and co-operation' (Declaración de Puntarenas, December 1990; Protocolo de Tegucigalpa, 1991, Art. 3). The region seems to have consolidated the transition from authoritarianism to democracy. There still remain differences regarding the level of democratisation in the region, ranging from a well-consolidated democratic system in Costa Rica to really fragile democracies in the other states.[5] However, the democratic legitimacy of the governments is no longer questioned. As Luis Guillermo Solis argues (interviewed by the author, 24 April 1998) 'for some time the region has enjoyed a democratic normality. There has been a profound change in the way power is distributed and no one is thinking of killing opposition leaders or impeding the participation of the left in the political process, which has had a positive impact on integration'.

On the economic side, the implementation of neo-liberal economic policies in all the states has favoured the convergence and openness of the economies. The convergence of macroeconomic policy preferences is considered to be a precondition for the revival of integration and furthering unification (Moravcsik, 1993, p. 482, Aron, 1954, p. 314). With the end of the civil wars, and the arrival in

---

[4] Political co-operation in a regional context, as Laffan (1992, p. 151) applies it to Europe, 'deals with the ways and means by which the member states harmonise their views on world politics and speak with one voice in the external arena and on major world issues'.

[5] For a good discussion of diversity in Central America, see Goma and Font (1996).

power in 1989 and onwards of neo-liberal governments, a profound change took place in the region in terms of economic policy. These governments were all sympathetic to the implementation of policies of structural adjustment required to stabilise and boost economic growth (Latin American Monitor, September 1989, p. 698; April 1990, p. 768; March 1991, p. 876).

As a result of these policies, the level of convergence of the economies of the region increased considerably during the decade of the 1990s. This convergence of policy preferences became the basis for co-ordinating the macroeconomic policies through the adoption of PAECA (Central American Economic Action Plan) in June 1990 and provided the basis for the re-launch of integration under the System of Central American Integration (SICA). As a result of both political and economic convergence, intra-regional trade has since 1991 shown an extraordinary recovery after a decade of stagnation and decline as shown in Table 2.1.

Table 2.1 Central America: Intra-regional trade. Value of imports. (Current US Dollars)

Year	Value	Year	Value
1983	896.6	1990	750.4
1984	814.9	1991	861.7
1985	601.1	1992	1,123.1
1986	530.8	1993	1,204.7
1987	587.7	1994	1,411.4
1988	600.8	1995	1,712.8
1989	738.0	1998	2,200.*

Source: CEPAL, 1995a, p. 13, Table no. 7. SIECA*. 1999.

The Resumption of Integration in the 1990s

In June 1990 at the presidential summit held in Antigua, Guatemala, the process of rebuilding and reforming the Central American integration within a new regionalist conception formally began. Although the aim was to rebuild integration and to form and consolidate a 'Central American Economic Community', the purpose of integration would not be regional cohesiveness or community building, but integration to the world economy (Declaración de Antigua, Numerals 24, 26). In this sense, integration becomes an 'association' purposively organised by the governments to pursue the external integration where the possibilities of growth of the region are supposed to lie.[6] It is, as Lizano argues (1994, p. 3) 'a return to the

---

[6]   I am drawing this qualification of integration as association based on a distinction made by Raphael (1970, pp. 33-34). For Raphael an association has two characteristics. First,

old outward model of integration that prevailed from the 19th century to the 1950s'. Integration in the 1990s, therefore, took the form of *'open regionalism'*. This implies combining external openness with regional reciprocity (preferential treatment to regional partners) (CEPAL, 1995b, p. 4). There is no longer incompatibility between regional integration and globalisation. Both doctrines are embraced by this new conception of open regionalism.

It is possible to identify two aims pursued by the new regionalism in Central America. First, it is intended as a means to negotiate preferential access to external markets and to attract FDI, new technologies and aid for the economic reconstruction of the region (see Grugel, 1995, pp. 215-216). Second, it is promoted as 'an arrangement to increase the comparative advantages of the region by means of creating scale economies and encouraging economic competition with states of similar size, multinational firms and other regional blocs' (Francisco Sorto, interviewed on 18 March 1998, San Salvador).

The force behind the re-launch of regionalism in Central America in the 1990s was the governments themselves. Integration fundamentally reflects governments' preferences constrained by domestic and external pressures. The re-launch of integration was grounded on the governments' concerns with the economic decline and marginalisation of the states from the world economy (trade and investment) and its implications in terms of consolidating peace and democracy in the region (Declaración de Montelimar, 1990).

Thus, the pressure for new regionalism in Central America largely came from within the region. However, it has not been as spontaneous as suggested by some theorists of new regionalism (Bull, 1999, p. 958). Hettne (1997; 2000) assumes the existence of a strong participation of diverse social actors along side the state which feel the need for co-operation to deal with the new challenges brought about by globalisation. Central American new regionalism fits the pattern identified by Gamble and Payne (1996, p. 253), in that there has been little popular involvement or influence in the process. It is a government's reaction first of all to the need for rebuilding and reforming its domestic economies in order to overcome economic decline and to adapt them to the international restructuring taking place in the world economy.

With the exception of big business groups, the role of non-governmental actors is indeed limited. Even if participation from civil society organisations exists it is, according to Luis G. Solis, 'limited to SICA's Consultative Committee which is entirely controlled and led by the governments' (Luis G. Solis, interviewed on 24 April 1998, Costa Rica). To the extent that social participation is emerging in the region it tends to operate as a counteracting force to the intergovernmental paradigm of integration, skewing its trade and neo-liberal orientation (see De la Ossa, 1996, pp. 42, 55; Rivera, 1995, pp. 236-238). Most social forces oppose the governments' paradigm of integration because it does not represent their interests.

---

the members of the group must have a specified common purpose or set of common purposes. Second, they must be organised for the pursuit of that purpose.

They favour a process of integration which embraces the social dimension which in their view should include social security, a social charter, sustainable development and economic democracy (Rivera, 1995, pp. 232-233; De la Ossa, 1996, p. 56).

Thus, new regionalism in Central America takes the form of what De la Ossa terms the 'official integration', which is a neo-liberal regionalism carried out by the governments and heavily concentrated on trade, foreign investment and external integration (De la Ossa, 1994). It is the governments guided by their own interests and the neo-liberal ideology that have been the leading cause of this form of integration.

The Impact of Structural Factors

The structural dependence of the region is also a major factor pressing the governments for this fashion of neo-liberal integration. The central concern emerging from the dependence of the region has to do with avoiding its exclusion from the global economy and the trend of building regional blocs for trade and investment. This is what largely accounts for the governments' preference for external integration, which tends to undermine the efforts at regional building. Thus, although the process of rebuilding integration in Central America is grounded on domestic and regional preferences and quite in line with established evolutionary patterns in Latin American integration (see Rosenthal, 1991, p. 63), it was also a clear attempt by the governments to avoid exclusion from the world economy. It was an attempt to avoid being pushed further down the periphery.[7] This does not substantially contradict the intergovernmental contention regarding the process of decision making which tends to concentrate on the domestic political economy of the states and the intergovernmental bargaining (see Moravcsik, 1993, pp. 515, 517). However, it brings about the need to strengthen the impact of external factors in the interstate bargaining when dealing with developing regions (see Nye, 1965, p.683; 1970, p.811).

The main external change, as far as Central America is concerned, consisted of a shift in the strategic interests of both the United States (US) and the European Union (EU). With the end of the cold war, US interests shifted away from security-led regionalism (Mittelman and Falk, 2000, p. 175). As a result, Central America lost importance within the new American and European geo-economics. The interests of these external actors concentrated increasingly on 'the larger countries of Latin America, but emphasising economic problems created by the debt crisis' (Varas, 1995, p. 282). Other US interests such as the environment, democracy, labour, and drug trafficking did not give Central America any political lever vis-à-vis the US or the EU.

---

[7] For the analysis of regionalism in developing countries as a strategy to avert being left in the periphery, see Hettne, 1997, p. 156; Grugel and Hout, 1998b).

Trade and the drug trafficking became a major concern of both the US and the EU in the 1990s (Payne, 1996), placing the attention on the biggest states of the region and on the Andean Group. Reforming Central American integration was therefore an attempt to reengage both the US and the EU in Central American affairs. Particularly, the governments would use it to demand the extension of the benefits enjoyed by Mexico within NAFTA (North American Free Trade Agreement) and the Andean countries in the EU. These are the so-called NAFTA and Andean parities both in the US and the EU markets. The Central American governments view themselves as having lost out on the concessions granted to Mexico and the Andean states by the US and the EU, respectively, and spent the decade of the 1990s demanding the extension of the benefits.

The reinvention of regionalism was reinforced following the crisis faced by export agriculture (EXA) since 1989, and considerable losses in economic aid and market privileges, especially from the US and the EU during the 1990s (see LAM: Central America, October 1990, p. 821; LAM: Central America, March 1990, pp. 748-749; November, 1990, p. 832). Thus, there was a perception that reinventing regionalism was the answer to these new challenges and to gain or even maintain preferential access in both the US and the EU markets.

To the extent that both the US and the EU impact heavily on Central American development, it is possible to agree with Grugel (1995, p. 207) who argues that the Central American states can only pursue a *'reactive regionalism'*. In other words, because they are small and peripheral states, they cannot play the card of *'strategic regionalism'* or even that of free trade in international relations because this involves structural power and reciprocity, two conditions that small and peripheral states normally lack. Should they pursue these strategies, they would be hurt by international competition. This, however, does not prevent the governments from embracing regionalism as a strategy to deal with their economic problems and as a way of building a kind of regional governance to head off the challenges generated by globalisation. Regional integration is one way of dealing with the problem of a sub-optimal size of states in terms of territory, population, financial and natural resources (see Olafsson, 1998, p.24).

These concerns led the Presidents at their summit in Montelimar, Nicaragua, in April 1990 to shift their attention from conflict resolution towards economic integration, a task designed to be the focus of the summit at Antigua. Conscious of the importance of rebuilding and enlarging the integration to head off external pressures and to realise domestic gains, the Presidents formally invited Panama to apply for membership and participate actively in the process (Declaración de Montelimar, April 2-3, 1990). The move towards integration was reinforced following the US rejection of pursuing negotiations with each state to participate in the Enterprise for the Americas and NAFTA. It was this rejection which led Costa Rica to re-evaluate its geo-economic interests within the region, forcing it to get back to the integration agenda.[8] Integration in the 1990s, as Castillo argues (1993, p. 389) became 'a condition for the survival of the states of the region'. Therefore, no government could ignore it.

Deepening of Integration: A Contentious and Convoluted Process

From 1990 to 1993 with the adoption of PAECA, the Tegucigalpa and the Guatemalan Protocols, the governments reinvented the Central American integration. The rebuilding of integration, which the governments carried out through presidential summits and the adoption of regional instruments, such as the above mentioned, was the outcome of an intergovernmental bargaining forged by the success of the Equipulas process and by external concerns. This bargaining responded primarily to the interests and preferences of the larger states (El Salvador, Guatemala and Costa Rica), leading to a political compromise. The Tegucigalpa Protocol (TP) adopted on December 1991 created the System of Central American Integration (SICA) as the new institutional framework of Central American Integration, which was based on a reform of the Organisation of Central American States (ODECA).

Reforming ODECA, instead of getting into a deeper integration as originally intended with the Central American Parliament (PARLACEN) in 1986, underlined the concern of the governments with sovereignty. The intergovernmentalist hypothesis regarding institutional building argues that governments create institutions in order to ease the intergovernmental bargaining and co-operation as well as to increase their leverage and autonomy vis-à-vis domestic groups which might not be supporters of integration and other governmental policies (Moravcsik, 1993a, p. 507; Putnam, 198, pp. 454-456). This hypothesis neatly fits the process of institutional building carried out in Central America in the 1990s. The institutional building set out in the region aimed at facilitating the governmental process of decision making. The institutions and bodies created were reduced to the role of secretariats of the presidential summits and the meetings of ministers and other governmental bodies. This is clearly the case with the General Secretariat of SICA (SG-SICA) (CEPAL, 1997, p. 36). The reasons underlying this are, first of all, the unwillingness of the governments to transfer sovereignty to regional institutions and a divergent interest regarding the level of regionness required. There was also the fact of governments' preference for market arrangements as opposed to economic planning. As the minimalist or small state had become a national preference of both governments and business interests, the integration's institutions could not escape this rationale.

---

[8] Costa Rica was negotiating a bilateral agreement with the US in order to access the Enterprise for the Americas Initiative launched by President George Bush, but was forced to embrace regionalism following rejection by the US of the bilateral track.

There have not been moves towards supra-nationality. Although the reach of integration was expanded with the inclusion of new issues, there has not been a transfer of competence to regional institutions so as to enable them to operate as supranational bodies. This is a major difference, for instance, between the re-launch of regionalism in Central America and in the EU in the 1990s. In the EU, the move towards deeper integration, through the Single European Act, the Maastricht Treaty and further agreements, brought about greater pooling of sovereignty and transfer of competence to regional institutions (delegation) (Nugent, 1993, pp. 42-45). In Central America, rather, the move has been towards creating a sense of order within the system, simplifying the institutional milieu and pooling sovereignty on issues of common interest only.

Under SICA the governments have sought to create some level of interconnectedness of the decision-making process within a systemic perspective. The system has been structured to ensure the governments' control of the process of integration. As such it is composed of the following bodies:

1. The Presidents' Summit.
2. The Council of Ministers.
3. The Executive Committee, and
4. The General Secretariat.
   (Tegucigalpa Protocol, Art. 12).

The Presidents' Summits and the Council of Ministers are the most important bodies of SICA. The former has a wide range of responsibilities including defining and leading Central America's regional politics, harmonising the foreign policy of the states, approving reforms, and admitting new members (TP: Art. 15). Regarding the Council of Ministers, its main function is to follow up and ensure the implementation of the decisions adopted by the Presidents (TP: Art. 16).

The Foreign Secretaries are the most important within the Council. They are the real carriers of the process of integration, as they constitute the principal co-ordinating organ of SICA. They represent the region in external relations, execute the presidents' decisions, recommend the admission of new SICA members, and are responsible for democracy and the security complex of the region. Jointly with the Economic Ministers, they define the strategy of the region for its external integration (TP: Art. 20). Finally, they are the link with the presidents. Any proposal submitted to the presidents has to be channelled though them (TP: Art. 17).

The Executive Committee and the General Secretariat of SICA (SG-SICA) are considered the permanent bodies of SICA. The former consists of states' representatives appointed by the Foreign Secretaries. SG-SICA is the highest administrative authority of SICA and represents SICA externally. It is politically dependent on the central bodies and under authorisation by these it can negotiate international accords, especially, technical and financial agreements. Its main function, however, is to act as a Secretariat for the Presidents and Council meetings and implement their decisions (TP: Art. 26). In practice, however, SG-SICA has been uneasy performing such a central function and has been de facto overtaken by the so-called 'Protempore Secretariat' (the equivalent of the Presidency in the European Community) shared on a rota basis by the Foreign Secretaries (CEPAL, 1997, p. 36, Cerdas, 1998, p. 259).

The TP also includes the Meeting of Vice-presidents, PARLACEN, the Central American Court of Justice (CCJ) and SICA's Consultative Committee (SICA-CC) as part of SICA. The inclusion of PARLACEN and the CCJ gave rise to a form of discontent, which for a long while obstructed the Costa Rican and Guatemalan ratification process of the Tegucigalpa Protocol. This discontent together with other contentious issues have made the prospect for structuring a coherent regional bloc slim. The conflict of interest is grounded on two factors: the unwillingness of Costa Rica and Guatemala to compromise on sovereignty and the desire of the former to emphasise its external integration.

While supporting the widening of integration, particularly Costa Rica has opposed deepening and supranationality. Having a more consolidated economic and political system than its neighbours, Costa Rica seems to perceive that it 'may have far less to gain by economic integration' than the other states of the region (Davis, Gabel and Coleman, 1998, p. 94). As a result, this state is more interested in negotiating its external integration rather than granting credible commitment to the deepening of integration within SICA. That is why Costa Rica rejected signing the CCJ and PARLACEN. During the conservative government of Rafael Angel Calderón (1990-1994), Costa Rica also refused to sign the Tegucigalpa and Guatemalan Protocols because of opposition within the government to deeper integration. It was only when the Partido Liberación Nacional (Social Democratic Party) took over the government under José Figueres Olsen (1994-1998) on a more committed agenda to integration that Costa Rica ratified such instruments (not PARLACEN and the CCJ) and went along with the integration efforts.

As with Guatemala, the country is committed to deepening integration under the North Triangle Area and CA-4 (Central America-4), where it is trade dependent, but has refused supranationality and the surrender of national control on other region-wide arrangements, particularly on trade disputes and institutional reform. To a large extent, this reflects the government's preference for PARLACEN as the core of the system of integration instead of SICA, where it attempted to pursue regional leadership.[9] But it also reflects a crisis of the Esquipulas process (a

---

[9]   This preference in based on the fact that it was Guatemala, which in 1986 proposed the establishment of PARLACEN as a system of integration. PARLACEN would have a double purpose. First, to reassert the Guatemalan leadership in the region. Second, to stand as the highest institution within the integration system. The politics of Central American integration was supposed to be defined in PARLACEN. The Guatemalan project was overshadowed following President Oscar Arias's success in leading the political process of the region under his peace plan which provided the basis for the settling of the military conflicts of the 1980s, especially in Nicaragua and El Salvador. As Costa Rica did not support the far-reaching nature of PARLACEN as a system of

regionally oriented one) as a result of increasing pressures from globalisation and the need to promote the external integration, which seems to be depriving Central American regionalism from needed regional content and cohesion (see Bull, 1999, pp. 957-958).

To a large extent, the preference of SICA (widening) over PARLACEN (deepening), as mentioned, came as a result of Costa Rica's disagreement with the latter owing to this state's preference for intergovernmental co-operation as opposed to supranationality. The governments understand that integration is the way forward to respond to the challenges brought about by globalisation, which led them to a compromise involving reforming and re-conceptualising integration, but they disagreed on the scope of it. Thus, although as Lizano argues (1994, p. 4) the governments no longer question the convenience of openness and external integration, which they pursue by different means, the states of the North Triangle (El Salvador, Guatemala, Honduras and Nicaragua) have a preference for a quick and far-reaching integration, strengthening regional cohesion. These states have committed themselves to consolidating the free trade regime and the economic union, allowing the free movement of goods and factors of production, e.g. capital and labour.

Costa Rica has found it difficult to engage at this level of regionness with the other states, first, because of the fear of losing sovereignty, but also owing to divergence in the level of social development among the states. Costa Rica is the most developed state of the region. In Costa Rica's perspective, for deeper integration to go ahead, 'the social conditions in the other states must be improved, including labour conditions, and changes in the legislation. While convergence in the social conditions of the countries does not exist, Costa Rica cannot support or adhere to political union' (Patricia Solano, interviewed on 21 April 1998, Costa Rica).

Costa Rica, therefore, does not support the deepening of integration, which could lead to political or economic union (see Davis et al., 1998, p. 91). This is why it has avoided participating in regional arrangements, which could compromise its sovereignty and national interest, including a mechanism to resolve trade disputes within the domain of the CCJ being negotiated since 1998. On this issue Costa Rica favours a technical instrument operating outside integration.[10] Costa Rica has also been active in further promoting the reform of regional institutions. The aim is to prevent SICA from turning into an EU like bureaucratic arrangement

---

integration, the institution lost the primacy that it originally was intended to have within integration.

[10] As stated by Amparo Pacheco, Director of Department of Commercial Treaties, Foreign Trade Ministry, inter-viewed by the author on 9 December 1999, San José, Costa Rica. The reason underlying such opposition is the belief that placing the mechanism under integration will obstruct the process because the governments could reject an outcome that would not serve their interests.

with regional institutions based in a single country from which decisions could be imposed on the country.

Institutional Reform

In the period 1994-1998, as a result of President Figueres' greater commitment to integration, the move towards institutional reform and political integration showed an unqualified importance. Figueres' commitment strengthened the Liberal-Morazanic bloc led by El Salvador.[11] Facing isolation, the conservative government of Alvaro Arzú in Guatemala also supported the cause of institutional reform whose aim was to transform San Salvador into the Brussels of Central America.

Under a new institutional reform agreed by the presidents during a summit in Panama in July 1997, all the integration institutions had to be located in El Salvador under the SICA system. The different sectors under integration such as the Central American Common Market (CACM), tourism, social and security had to be placed under SICA's framework as subsystems of it. Their Secretariats, including SIECA, had to be moved to San Salvador in order to establish an integrated system. Pressed by Costa Rica, the Presidents also agreed to reduce the size, privileges and immunities of the bureaucracy in some regional institutions, especially PARLACEN and the CCJ. The other governments accepted Costa Rican demands on regional reform in exchange for Costa Rican support for integration in other areas such as political integration and the consolidation of SICA as a regional system.

It is important to point out that despite this move towards further integration, the governments were in no way compromising their sovereignty. In Panama the Presidents were categorical when they stated that the institutional reform was in pursuit of the consolidation of the Central American Community. But this had to be done 'without diminishing the autonomy, specificity and the constitutional order of the states' (Panama Declaración de Panamá, July 12, 1997). Keeping sovereignty is a condition for integration and consensus or unanimity is the rule under the Tegucigalpa and Guatemalan Protocols (Arts. 14 and 52). The move was, therefore, to consolidate the Central American integration as a community of nations or more properly, as a confederation of sovereign states. Reforming institutions in Central America has always been a complicated and unpredictable issue. Despite the

---

[11] The Liberal bloc is made up of El Salvador, Honduras and Nicaragua. I am grateful to Luis Guillermo Solis who talked to me about the survival of the traditional divide in the region between 'the liberal-Morazanist bloc' made up of the above mentioned states, and 'the conservative' one by Guatemala and Costa Rica. These political forces currently compete in the remaking of the Central American integration. According to Solis, the liberal-Morazanist bloc consolidated its influence in the period 1994-98 following the election of Armando Calderón Sol in El Salvador, Carlos Reina in Honduras and Arnoldo Alemán in Nicaragua and the willingness of the Figueres administration in Costa Rica to follow the integrationist agenda.

willingness of governments to bargain on this issue in a given moment, there is no guarantee, for the reasons mentioned below, that they will succeed in the long run.

Following the Panama Summit, the governments attempted during 1997 and 1998 to correct the shortcomings of the institutional framework. In February of 1998 the governments were negotiating the adoption of a 'single treaty'. This treaty sought to simplify the institutional framework of the region.[12] 'In 90 articles, the single treaty incorporates all the treaties and instruments that have been accumulated since the integration process began'.[13] It comprises areas ranging from 'preserving the democratic system and the security of the region, its social and cultural values, the environment and the economic integration and a commitment to accelerate it' (Eduardo Ayala Agrimaldi, interviewed on 10 March 1998, San Salvador).

The treaty sought to create a unified General Secretariat under SICA. As mentioned, it is intended that all branches of Central American integration as well as technical and specialised institutions currently dispersed throughout the region would be placed under a single administration within SICA. The aim was to provide a 'better level of co-ordination for the whole system of integration' (Eduardo Ayala Agrimaldi, interviewed on 10 March 1998, San Salvador). The treaty was a bold move in the fashion of Maastricht, but it failed to be adopted. Four reasons account for this political failure:

1. Change of government in Costa Rica in May 1998. While Figueres was supporting and leading the institutional reform in 1997 and also signed the Managua Declaration on political integration of September 1997, the conservative administration of Miguel Angel Rodríguez, which succeeded Figueres, did not support it. The Rodríguez administration thought that the single treaty 'would take away legitimacy from the system. It would bureaucratise it. It would turn it anti-democratic and it would make it less attractive for states which would lose institutions currently located in their territories' (Carlos M. Echeverría, interviewed on 17 December 1999, Costa Rica). The triumph of Rodrigues in Costa Rica allowed for the temporary activation of the conservative bloc Costa Rica-Guatemala. Both governments

---

[12]   The basic proposals for reform were put forward by SICA in the document entitled 'Lineamientos para el Fortalecimiento y Racionalizacion de la Institucionalidad Regional', presented to the presidents in Panama in July 12, 1997. The document was based on an earlier version adopted by a High Level Group of Government Representatives in February and March 1997, under the title 'Propuesta para el Fortalecimiento y la Racionalización de la Institucionalidad Regional Centroamericana'.

[13]   Elber Durán, Department of Information, SICA, interviewed by the author on 10 March 1998, San Salvador. The information regarding the content of the single treaty was provided in interviews to the author by Elber Duràn from SICA and Eduardo Ayala Agrimaldi, Deputy Minister of Economics of El Salvador. At the time when the interviews were carried out, the single treaty was in an early stage of negotiation. It had not yet been released to the public. For this reason it was not possible to obtain a copy.

expressed discontent with the idea of removing regional institutions from their territories, despite the original commitments.

2. Hurricane Mitch. As a result of the damage caused by Mitch in October 1998, the governments changed the regional agenda from integration to reconstruction. Reconstruction became the priority and most efforts at regional co-operation focused on reconstruction. As a result, the single treaty and other integration matters were ignored. 'For a long while the governments did not talk of integration together. 'It was no longer a matter of urgency whether SIECA left or stayed in Guatemala' (Patricia Solano, interviewed on 14 December 1999, Costa Rica). Because of the devastating effect of Mitch, the attention of the governments concentrated, from the first quarter of 1999, on international assistance, bypassing the regional agenda on integration.

3. Bureaucratic competition. Both regional bureaucrats as well as some governments' departments were unhappy with the institutional rearrangement because it sidelined them in the regional decision-making process. According to Carreras, the Ministers of Economics have been reluctant to consolidate SICA at the expense of SIECA, which inevitably implied lowering their political position within integration. SIECA's bureaucrats also disliked the idea of been deposed from their historical role as the institutional core of the process of integration (Rodrigo Carreras, interviewed on 2 April 1998, Costa Rica). The impact of institutions and bureaucratic politics on the interstate bargaining has not received sufficient attention in the intergovernmental theory of integration. To some extent this constitutes a shortcoming of the theory.

4. The rise of border conflicts. Intergovernmentalism rightly argues that high politics is likely to disrupt the patterns of regional co-operation and integration. The politics of regional integration, as Joseph Nye argues (1970, p. 819) is not only the politics of co-operation but also the politics of status and, therefore, of rivalry between states. Thus, governments would be concerned not only about how much they might gain from integration in terms of welfare, but also how much they might forgo in terms of status in international relations which would inevitably have an impact on the process of integration. In Central America the major conflict occurred in November 1999 when the Honduras Parliament ratified a border treaty with Colombia in the Caribbean Sea. Nicaragua objected to the treaty because, in it, Honduras recognised sovereignty rights to Colombia, on areas which Nicaragua had been disputing with both countries. As a reprisal, Nicaragua imposed a 35 percent surcharge on Honduran goods and pursued a demand against the latter state in the CCJ. Although both governments avoided exiting from integration, the process of integration had been quite severely affected. A border difference also took place between Nicaragua and Costa Rica, while the Honduran-Salvadorian border difference lurks unresolved despite the resolution by the International Court of Justice in 1992.

The combined impact of natural disasters, change of governments, bureaucratic politics and border disputes, have adversely affected intra-regional co-operation since 1999 and strengthened the cause for unilateral action. This has reinforced the pursuit of unilateral and bilateral actions of some states such as Costa Rica, with its efforts at consolidating its external integration, and El Salvador which has sought to consolidate its relations with its neighbour on a more bilateral basis. The Central American integration, therefore, reached a plateau in 1998 and entered into a period of concern and instability from the end of 1999, a situation not yet overcome.

Conclusion

In the 1990s, Central American integration was rebuilt as a new regionalism. The aim of integration is no longer to protect infant industries or even to create a Central America Union, but to create economic competition among the states and to incorporate the region into the world economy. It is also a strategy through which the governments seek to negotiate or even maintain preferential access to external markets, particularly in the US and the EU. By increasing the level of regionness in areas such as trade, macroeconomic stability, and democracy, the governments seek to increase their bargaining power in their negotiations with other trading partners and multinational businesses in order to avoid being excluded from the new international restructuring.

The new regionalism is, among other things, an arrangement to promote the competitiveness of the economies of the region. In the face of an increasingly globalised economy, enlarging the markets through integration has become a condition of survival, especially for small economies. In the period 1990-1993, this realisation brought the Central American governments to accelerate the process of reform of the CACM and the institutions of integration. The end of the cold war favoured the building of democratic governance and the peaceful resolution of conflicts in the region, but it also eroded the strategic importance of the region as the interests of the US and the EU have shifted towards economically important regions. In the face of exclusion from globalisation, the governments upheld the banner of integration as a strategic imperative (Lizano cited in: Sanahuja, 1998, p. 23).

The process of rebuilding integration, however, is not free of contradiction. The main problem is that integration taken as a trampoline for external competitiveness does seem to undermine regional cohesion. Integration is only one means to achieve the external objective. In the search for their external integration the governments have tried different ways ranging from unilateralism to joint action, in most cases at the expense of regional cohesion, which underlines the hollowness of the Central American bloc. Thus, although the governments have presented integration as a new regionalism in the sense that it goes beyond trade to include other issues, the centrality of trade and concerns with external integration have undermined regional cohesion and regionness. Regional cohesion is also undermined by the increasing impact of high politics conflicts between the states. In this respect, SICA and other regional arrangements do not guarantee that the region will move in bold steps towards an enduring process of regionalisation. The system reflects the preferences and interests of the governments and works as a compromise, where some governments press for cohesion and deepening integration, while Costa Rica looks outwards, favouring its external integration. The result has been variable geometry, where the states move at different speeds and at different levels of commitment. But the move is not always forward. There does not seem to be a way to escape this trend in the process of integration unless the governments willingly accept some constraints on their sovereignty and give credible commitment to integration. The challenge for Central America is, therefore, how to reach a balance between the need for inward and outward integration or how to use integration in both senses for the promotion of sustainable development in the region.

References

Arias Sánchez, Oscar (1993), 'El Proceso de Paz como premisa para el proceso de integración', in Olga Marta Sánchez and Jaime Delgado (eds.), *Una Contribución al Debate: Integración Regional*, Flacso-UNA, 1ˢᵗ Ed., San José, pp. 77-101.

Aron, Raymond (1954), *The Century of Total War*, Derek Verschoyle, London.

Bhagwati, Jagdish (1994), 'Regionalism and Multilateralism: an overview', in Ross Garnaut and Peter Drysdale (eds.), *Asia Pacific Regionalism: Readings in International Economic Relations*, Harper Education Publishers, 1ˢᵗ Ed., Australia, pp. 145-166.

Biersteker, Thomas J. (1990), 'Reducing the Role of the State in the Economy: A conceptual Explanation of IMF and World Bank Prescriptions', *International Studies Quarterly*, Vol. 34, pp. 477-492.

Biersteker, Thomas J. (1992), 'The Triumph of Neoclasical Economics in the Developing World: Policy Convergence and Bases of Governance in the International Economic Order', in James N. Rosenau and Ernst-Otto Czempiel (eds.), *Governance Without Government: Order and Change in World Politics*, Cambridge University Press, Cambridge, 1ˢᵗ Ed., pp. 102-131.

Bull, Benedicte (1999), 'New Regionalism in Central America', *Third World Quarterly*, Vol. 20(5), pp. 957-970.

Bulmer-Thomas, Victor (1988), *Studies in the Economics of Central America*, Macmillan Press, Cambridge.

Busch, Marc L. and Milner, Helen V. (1994), 'The Future of International Trading System: International Firms, Regionalism, and Domestic Politics', in Richard Stubbs and Geoffrey R.D. Underhill (eds.), *Political Economy and the Changing Global Order*, Macmillan, London, 1ˢᵗ Ed., pp. 259-276.

Buzan, Barry (1991), *People States and Fear: An Agenda for International Security Studies in the Post-cold War Era*, Lynne Rienner Publishers, USA.

Cáceres, Luis R. and Irvin, George (1989), 'The Reconstruction of the CACM and European Cupertino', in George Irvin and Stuart Holland (eds.), *Central America: the Future of Economic Integration*, Westview Press, London, 1ˢᵗ Ed., pp. 163-185.

Castillo, Carlos M. (1993),'Una Agenda Centroamericana para la integración', in Olga Marta Sánchez and Jaime Delgado (eds.), *na Contribución al Debate: Integración Regional,* Flacso-UNA, San José, 1ˢᵗ Ed., pp. 389-395.

Catalán, Aravena, O. (1997), 'The Revitalization of the Central American Common Market', *Journal of Political Economy,* Vol. 26(4), Winter, pp. 37-55.

CEPAL (1995a), *El Regionalismo Abierto en Centroamérica: El Desafío de Profundizar y Ampliar la Integración,* LC/MEX/L.261, Mexico, D.F.

CEPAL (1995b), *Informe de la Reunión Extraordinaria de Consulta del Comité de Cooperación Económica del Istmo Centroamericano* (CCE), LC/MEX/-CCE/L.421, Mexico, D.F.

CEPAL (1997), 'Diagnostico de la Institucionalidad Regional Centroamericana', in Carlos Sojo (ed.), *Centroamérica: La Integración que no Cesa,* Cuaderno de Ciencias Sociales, no. 103, Flacso, San José, pp. 15-54.

Cerdas, Rodolfo (1992), *El Desencanto Democrático: Crisis de Partidos y Transición Democrática en Centroamérica y Panamá,* Rei, San José.

Cerdas, Rodolfo (1998), 'Las Instituciones de Integración en Centroamérica', in Victor Bulmer-Thomas, (ed.), *Centroamérica en Reestructuració,* Flacso, San José, 1ˢᵗ Ed., pp. 245-276.

Consejo Monetario Centroamericano (1995), *Situación Económica de los Países Centroamericanos en 1994,* San José.

Corte Centroamericana de Justicia: *Memoria. Managua:* from 12 October 1994 to 12 October 1995.

Davis, Charles L. et al. (1998), 'Citizen Response to Regional Integration in the Americas: The Cases of Costa Rica and El Salvador', *Studies in Comparative International Development,* Vol. 33(2), Summer, pp. 88-109.

Declaración de Antígua, Guatemala, 15-17 de junio de 1990, in Ennio Rodríguez et al. (1991), *El Desafío del Desarrollo Centroamericano,* Euned, San José, 1ˢᵗ Ed., pp. 233-244.

Declaración de Montelimar, Nicaragua, 2-3 de abril 1990, *Revista Centroamericana de Administración Pública,* nos. 22-23, pp. 140-144.

Declaración de Panamá, 12 de Julio de 1997, in Carlos Sojo (ed.), *Centroamérica: La Integración que no Cesa,* Flacso, San José, 1ˢᵗ Ed., pp. 11-14.

Declaración de Puntarenas, Costa Rica, 17 de diciembre de 1990, *Pensamiento Centroamericano,* Vol. XLVI, Enero-Marzo, 1991, pp. 72-78.

De la Ossa, Alvaro (ed.) (1994), *El Sistema de la Integración Centroamericana: Crítica de la Visión Oficial,* Fundación Friedrich Ebert, San José.

De la Ossa, Alvaro (1996), La Integración Social: Nuevas Rutas Hacia la Discordia', in Alvaro de la Ossa, (ed.), *La Integración Social: Nuevas Rutas Hacia la Discordia,* Fundación Friedrich Ebert/ Fundación Centroamericana por la Integración, San José, 1ˢᵗ Ed., pp. 25-142.

De la Ossa, Alvaro (1997), 'La Revision Oficial de la Institucionalidad de la Integracion: Otro Paso mas en el Ajuste Neo-Liberal'?, in Carlos Sojo (ed.), *Centroamérica: La Integración que no Cesa,* Flacso, San José, pp. 91-98.

Dunkerley, James (1982), *The Long War: Dictatorship & Revolution in El Salvador,* Junction Books, London.

Dunkerley, James (1994), *The Pacification of Central America: Political Change in the Istmus, 1987-1993,* Verso, London-New York.

El Diario de Hoy, digital, August 20, 2000.

Gamble, Andrew and Payne, Anthony (eds.) (1996), *Regionalism & World Order,* Macmillan Press, London.

Goma, Richard and Font, Joan (1996), 'Political Change and Socioeconomic Policies in Central America: Patterns of Interaction', *Third World Quarterly*, Vol. 17(4), pp. 737-751.

Grugel, Jean (1995), 'El Nuevo Regionalismo en las Americas: Las Opciones de Centroamerica despues de NAFTA', *Sintesis: Revista de Ciencias Sociales Iberoamericana*, no. 25, pp. 205-221.

Grugel, Jean (1996), 'Latin America and the Remaking of the Americas', Andrew Gamble and Anthony Payne (eds.), *Regionalism & World Order,* Macmillan Press, London , 1st Ed, pp. 131-167.

Grugel, Jean (1998a), 'State and Business in Neo-Liberal Democracies in Latin America', *Global Society*, Vol. 12(2), pp. 221-235.

Grugel, Jean and Hout, Wil (eds.) (1998b), *Regionalism Across the North-South Divide,* Routledge, London.

Grupo de Representantes de Anto Nivel de los Gobiernos Centroamericanos (1997), 'Propouesta para el Fortalecimiento y la Racionalización de la Institucionalidad Regional Centroamericana', in Carlos Sojo (ed.), *Centroamérica: La Integración que no Cesa,* Flacso, San José, 1st Ed., pp. 55-80.

Hettne, Bjorn (1993), 'Neo-Mercantilism: The Pursuit of Regionness', *Cooperation and Conflict*, Vol. 28, pp. 211-232.

Hettne, Bjorn (1997), 'El Nuevo Regionalism', *Relaciones Internacionales*, no. 73, pp. 155-162.

Hettne, Bjorn (2000), 'The New Regionalism: A Prologue', in Bjorn Hettne et al. (eds.), *National Perspectives on the New Regionalism in the North*, Vol. 2, Macmillan Press, London, 1st Ed., pp. xv-xxix.

Hoffmann, Stanley (1965), 'The European Process at Atlantic Crosspurposes', *Journal of Common Market Studies*, Vol. 3(2), pp. 85-101.

Hoffmann, Stanley (1966), 'Obstinate or Obsolete? The Fate of the Nation-State and the case of Western Europe', *Daedelus*, Vol. 95(2), pp. 862-915.

Hoffmann, Stanley (1982), 'Reflections on the Nation-State in Western Europe Today', *Journal of the Common Market Studies*, Vol. XXI(1, 2), pp. 21-37.

Hurrell, Andrew (1992), 'Latin America in the New World Order: A Regional Bloc of the Americas'?, *International Affairs*, Vol. 68(1), pp. 121-139.

Hurrell, Andrew (1995a), 'Explaining the Resurgence of Regionalism in World Politics', *Review of International Studies*, Vol. 21(4), pp. 331-358.

Hurrell, Andrew (1995b), 'Regionalism in the Americas', in Louise Fawcett and Andrew Hurrell (eds.), *Regionalism in World Politics,* Oxford University Press, Oxford, 1st Ed., pp. 250-282.

IILA/BID, (1991), *El Proceso de Integracion en America Latina*, Buenos Aires.

Keohane, Robert O. (1984), *After Hegemony: Cooperation and Discord in the World Political Economy*, Princeton University Press, Princeton.

Keohane, Robert O. and Hoffmann, S. (eds.) (1991), *The New European Community: Decisionmaking and Institutional Change*, Westview Press, Boulder.

Laffan, Brigid (1992), *Integration and Cooperation in Europe,* Routledge, London and New York.

La República, June 18, 1990.

Latin American Monitor: Central America, June 1987.

Latin American Monitor: Central America, September 1989.

Latin American Monitor: Central America, March 1990.

Latin American Monitor: Central America, April 1990.

Latin American Monitor: Central America, October 1990.

Latin American Monitor: Central America, November 1990.

Latin American Monitor: Central America, March 1991.

Lizano, Eduardo (1994), 'Centroamérica y el Tratado de Libre Comercio de América del Norte', *Integración Latinoamericana*, Año. 19(204), pp. 3-14.

López Contreras, Carlos (1984), *Las Negociaciones de Paz: Mi Punto de Vista*, Tegucigalpa.

Lusztig, Michael (1998), 'The Limits of Rent Seeking: Why protectionists become free traders', *Review of International Political Economy*, Vol. 5(1), Spring, pp. 38-63.

Mansfield, Edward D. and Milner, Helen V. (1999), 'The New Wave of Regionalism', *International Organisation*, Vol. 53(3), Summer, pp. 589-627.

Ministerio de Relaciones Exteriores: *Memoria 1992*, San Salvador.

Ministerio de Relaciones Exteriores: *Memoria 1993*, San Salvador.

Mittelman, James H. and Falk, Richard (2000), 'Sustaining American Hegemony: The Relevance of Regionalism'?, in Bjorn Hettne et al. (eds.), *National Perspectives on the New Regionalism in the North,* Macmillan Press, London , 1st Ed., pp. 173-193.

Moravcsik, Andrew, (1991), 'Negotiating the Single European Act', in Robert O. Keohane and Stanley Hoffmann (eds.), *The New European Community: Decisionmaking and Institutional Change*, Westview Press, Boulder, 1st Ed., pp. 41-84.

Moravcsik, Andrew (1993), 'Preferences and Power in the European Community: A Liberal Intergovernmentalist Approach', *Journal of Common Market Studies*, Vol. 31(4), pp. 473-524.

Moravcsik, Andrew (1995), 'Liberal Intergovernmentalism and Integration: A Rejoinder', *Journal of the Common Market Studies*, Vol. 33(4), pp. 611-628.

Moravcsik, Andrew (1998), *The Choice for Europe*, Cornell University Press, Ithaca.

Muñoz G, Mercedes (1994), La Seguridad de Costa Rica Hoy', in Luis Guillermo Solis Rivera and Francisco Rojas Aravena (eds.), *De la Guerra a la Integración: La Transición y la Seguridad en Centroamérica*: Flacso-Chile/Fundación Arias para la Paz y el Progreso Humano, San José, 1st Ed., pp. 38-72.

Nugent, Neill (1993), 'The European Dimension', in Patrick Dunleavy et al. (eds.), *Developments in British Politics 4,* Macmillan Press, London , 1st Ed., pp. 40-68.

Nye, Joseph S. (1968), 'Comparative Regional Integration: Concept and Measurement', *International Organization,* Vol. 22, pp. 855-880.

Nye, Joseph S. (1970), 'Comparing Common Markets: A Revised Neo-Functionalist Model', *International Organization,* Vol. 24, pp. 796-835.

ODECA (1962), *Charter of the Organisation of Central American States.* San Salvador.

Olafsson, Bjorn G. (1998), *Small States in the Global System: Analysis and Illustrations from the case of Iceland*, Ashgate Publishing Limited, England.

Palacios L, Juan J. (1995), 'El Nuevo Regionalismo Latinoamericano: El futuro de los Acuerdos de Libre Comercio', *Comercio Exterior*, Vol. 45(4), pp. 295-302.

Payne, Anthony (1996), 'The United States and its Enterprise for the Americas', in Andrew Gamble and Anthony Payne (eds.), *Regionalism & World Order,* Macmillan Press, London, 1st Ed., pp. 93-129.

Pensamiento Centroamericano, Vol. XLV(208), julio-septiembre, 1990, pp. 81-87.

Phillips, Nicola (2000), 'The Future of the Political Economy of Latin America', in Richard Stubbs and Geofrey R.D. Underhill (eds.), *Political Economy and the Changing Global Order,* Oxford University Press, Canada, 2nd Ed., pp. 284-293.

Protocolo al Tratado General de Integracion Económica Centroamericana, October 29, (1993), *Integracion Latinoamericana*, Vol. 18(196), pp. 104-110.

Protocolo de Tegucigalpa (1992), in SICA (ed.), *Secretaria General del Sistema de la Integracion Centroamericana.* San Salvador, pp. 3-26.

Putnam, Robert D. (1988), 'Diplomacy and Domestic Politics: The Logic of Two-Level Games', *International Organization*, Vol. 42(3), Summer, pp. 427-460.

Raphael, D.D. (1970), *Problems of Political Philosophy*, Macmillan, London.

Rivera, Rolando (1995), 'Concertación Social e Integración Regional: ?Una Nueva Forma de Participación Social?', in Klaus D. Tangermann (ed.), *Ilusiones y Dilemas de la Democracia en Centroamérica*, Flacso, San José, 1st Ed, pp. 207-261.

Robson, Peter (1998), *The Economics of International Integration*, Routledge, London.

Rosenthal, Gert (1991), 'Un Informe Crítico a 30 Años de Integración en América Latina', *Nueva Sociedad*, no. 113, pp. 60-65.

Rosenthal, Gert (1995), 'El Regionalismo Abierto en la CEPAL', *Pensamiento Ibero-americano*, no. 26, pp. 47-65.

Rouquié Alain (1994), *Guerras y Paz en America Central*, Fondo de Cultura Económica, México.

Sanahuja, José A. (1997), 'Integración Regional en América Central, 1990-1997: Los Limites del Gradualism', *America Latina Hoy*, no. 17, pp. 43-57.

Sanahuja, José A. (1998), 'Nuevo Regionalismo e Integración en Centroamérica 1990-1997', in José Antonio Sanahuja and José Angel Sotillo (eds.), *Integración y Desarrollo en Centroamérica*, IUDC/UCM, Madrid, 1st Ed., pp. 13-58.

Sánchez, Rafael A. (2002), *Peace Negotiations and the Process of Reform of the Central American Common Market in the 1990s: An Intergovernmentalist Approach to integration*, Ph.D.-dissertation, University of Sheffield, England.

Sandholtz, Wayne and Zysman, John (1989), '1992: Recasting the European Bargain', *World Politics*, Vol. 42(1), pp. 95-128.

Schmitter, Philippe C. (1970), 'Central American Integration: Spill-over, Spill-around or Encapsulation?', *Journal of Common Market Studies*, Vol. IX(1), pp. 1-48.

Schulz, Donald E. and Sundloff Schulz, Deborah (1994). *The United States, Honduras, and the Crisis in Central America*, Westview Press, Boulder.

SG-SICA-ICAP (1996), Anuario Institucionalidad Regional: Sistema de la Integración Centroamericana (SICA), San Salvador.

SICA (1997a), *Lineamientos para el Fortalecimiento y Racionalización de la Institucionalidad Regional*, Panamá, 12 de Julio.

SICA (1997b), Unión Centroamericana: Un Compromiso ante el Mundo, Vol. 1, Sica El, Salvador.

SIECA (1990), *Hacia Una Estrategia de Integracion Para el Desarrollo de Centroamerica*, Guatemala.

SIECA (1999), *Avances de la Integración Económica Centroamericana 1995-1998*, May 1999, Digital Information, Guatemala.

Soto Acosta, Willy (1990), 'Costa Rica: La Integracion Centroamericana como Mecanismo de Reforzamiento del Estado-Nacional (Una Hipotesis)', *Annales Des Pays D' Amerique Centrale Et Des Caraibes*, no. 9, pp. 45-69.

Varas, Augusto (1995), 'Latin America: Towards a New Reliance on the Market', in Barbara Stallings (ed.), *Global Change, Regional Response: The New International Context of Development*, Cambridge, University Press, Cambridge, 1st Ed., pp. 272-308.

Varas, Augusto and Tulchin, Joseph (1994), 'Presentacion', in Luis Guillermo Solis Rivera and Francisco Rojas Aravena (eds.), *De la Guerra a la Integracion: La Transición y la Seguridad en Centroamérica*, Flacso-Chile, San José, 1st Ed., pp. I-VI.

Vicepresidencia de Guatemala (1986), 'Proyecto del Tratado Constitutivo del Sistema Parlamentario Centroamericano', *Panorama Centroamericano: Pensamiento y Acción*, no. 2, Abril-Junio, pp. 21-25.

Interviews

Eduardo Ayala Agrimaldi, Deputy Economics Minister, 10 March 1998, San Salvador, El Salvador.

Rodrigo Carreras, Deputy Foreign Secretary, 2 April 1998, San José, Costa Rica.

Elber Durán, Deputy at Department of Communication, SICA, 10 March 1998, San Salvador, El Salvador.

Carlos Manuel Echeverría, Chief of Staff, Foreign Office, 17 December 1999, San José, Costa Rica.

Amparo Pacheco, Director of Deparment of Commercial Treaties, Ministry of Foreign Trade, 9 December 1999, San José, Costa Rica.

Patricia Solano (first interview), Director of Integration, Foreign Office, 21 April 1998, San José, Costa Rica.

Patricia Solano (second interview) Director of Integration, Foreign Office, 14 Dcecember 1999, San José, Costa Rica.

Luis Guillero Solis, Chief of Staff, Foreign Office, 24 April 1998, San José, Costa -Rica.

Francisco Sorto, Director at the Department of Integration, Foreign Office, 18 March 1998, San Salvador, El Salvador.

Chapter 3

Presidentialism and Mercosur: A Hidden Cause for a Successful Experience[*]

Andrés Malamud

'El Mercosur es una historia exitosa'
Adalberto Rodriguez Giavarini, Argentine Foreign Minister, October 2001

Introduction

The consolidation of European unity since the signing of the Treaty of Maastricht in 1992, along with the contemporary mushrooming of integrating regions all around the world, illustrate a significant new phenomenon. This is the way most nation-states are choosing, at the turn of the century, to deal with new challenges that risk placing their previous positions in jeopardy. Some of the larger regional entities are the North Atlantic Free Trade Agreement (NAFTA), the Association of South-East Asian Nations (ASEAN), and the Common Market of the South (Mercosur or Mercosul). All of these initially – if not as maximum aspiration – aimed at becoming free trade zones, in order to increase both their intra-regional trade and investment flows and the competitive position of their member countries *vis-à-vis* the global markets. Notwithstanding these common goals, some of the newly created regions have attempted to go further, Mercosur being the most ambitious in this respect.

Mercosur was formally created in 1991, when previous agreements between Argentina and Brazil were expanded and Paraguay and Uruguay joined these countries in the venture. Later on, Bolivia and Chile were accepted as associate

[*] This chapter constitutes a part of an ongoing broader research. I owe much stimulus and advice to Philippe Schmitter and Stefano Bartolini. I would also like to thank Félix Peña and Marcelo Oviedo for their early comments on some of the ideas herein presented.

53

members, and other South American countries expressed their wish to apply. Mercosur has now reached the customs union stage – albeit not completely – and is sketching the blueprint for its enlargement to the rest of the sub-continent, while deepening the scope and level of the integration itself. As the uppermost sign of the ambitious aims of the project, an increasing number of informal talks concerning monetary unification took place in 1998 and 1999. Shortly afterwards, the Brazilian crisis of 1999 triggered a heated discussion on the need to take a jump forward instead of delaying or setting back the integration process; however, the aftermath of the subsequent devaluation of the Real is still evolving in 2001.

According to most of the literature concerning regionalization, based mainly on the European case, the goal of creating a common market and, furthermore, an economic union, implies sooner or later the setting up of regional institutions. These are supposed to deal with the two main dilemmas of collective action, i.e. the decision-making processes and the resolution of controversies. To date, however, Mercosur has not built any significant institutional structure, whether supranational or not.[1] Its decisions are taken through purely intergovernmental mechanisms, requiring unanimity in every case. The only decision-making organization consists of three regional bodies made up of either member states' public officials or nationally appointed technicians with low-level responsibilities, and a minimum Secretariat located in Montevideo (see figure 3.1). A limited dispute settlement system provides for an *ad hoc* mechanism of arbitration, but this has been called on only three times in a decade. Furthermore, neither direct effect nor any supremacy of the community law exist – even the term 'community law' does not fit the legal structure of Mercosur, since regional rules should be internalized by every member country through its own domestic procedures before coming into force. These features were purposefully advanced since the foundational stages, in order to clearly distinguish between the political direction and an eventual bureaucratic direction that could threaten the project.[2] In contrast, the European Union has developed a complex structure of multilevel governance, combining supra-nationalism with intergovernmentalism, unanimity with majority rule, and the supremacy of community law with the principle of subsidiarity (Hix, 1994; Schmitter, 1996; Sandholtz and Stone Sweet, 1998). It features a powerful Court of Justice that has been crucial in furthering integration, a Parliament whose members are directly elected by the European peoples, and an executive Commission with substantial autonomy – among other institutions. By and large, the European Union exhibits a highly institutionalized, and increasingly bureaucratized, shape.

---

[1] Some public officials openly aim at a 'pooling' of sovereignty rather that at any supranational arrangement (author's interview with the then Argentine undersecretary of foreign trade Félix Peña, August 1998). However, not even this lesser form of delegation has been achieved so far.

[2] Author's interview with former Argentine foreign minister Dante Caputo, September 1999.

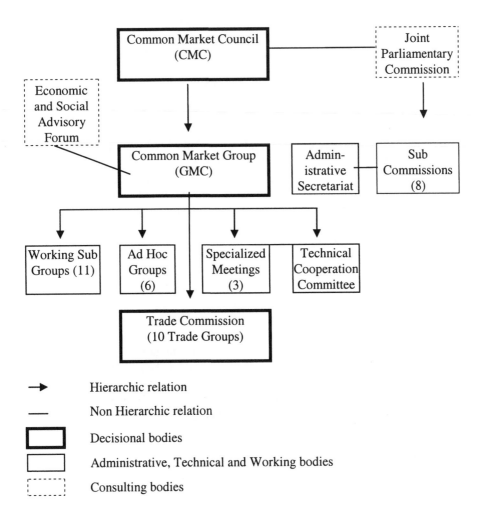

Figure 3.1 Mercosur institutional structure

As for Mercosur, a great deal of political and technical debate has been fostered in some member countries with regard to the need to establish common institutions. Government officials, professional associations – especially lawyers' –, academics, producers, and some other groups have postulated the necessity of supranational institution-building, especially focusing on the creation of a Court of Justice of Mercosur (Calceglia, 1998; Oviedo, 1998; Rocha Filho, 1999).[3] Some have also

---

[3]   In Argentina, the 1999-2001 government coalition (the *Alianza*) had issued public declarations along the same line while in the opposition (*Clarín*, 9-3-1999). Previously,

argued that the Mercosur development would follow the European model, but neither the former claims nor the latter expectations have come true. Nonetheless, the progress in the indicators of integration – such as commercial interdependence, investment flows, policy coordination, and business strategies – is apparent to observers, and has puzzled most analysts and actors.

This chapter attempts to sketch this perceptible mismatch between the ambitious aims proclaimed by Mercosur – whether through official documents or public statements by its architects and rulers – and the scarce development of regional institutions. I will advance a main hypothesis in order to account for this novelty – namely successful integration without significant regional institutions. My claim is that this process has not grown out of an institutional limbo, but was upheld by other kinds of institutions that are less visible than the supranational ones. In short, I will argue that the coexistence of progress in integration with a minimum set of regional institutions has been possible due to the local shape of one national institution, that of the executive format. This chapter suggests that a specific type of executive format, namely presidentialism, has managed to act as a functional equivalent to regional institutions.

Brief Antecedents

Although the first steps were taken in 1979, under military presidencies in both Argentina and Brazil, the current integration process can be reckoned as beginning in the 1980s, when democratic regimes were inaugurated in the region. Democracy would consequently become one of the main goals as well as an indispensable condition of support for the agreements reached (Schmitter, 1991; Hurrell, 1995; Lafer, 1997; Fournier, 1999). The turning point was the Argentine-Brazilian Integration Act (*Acta para la Integración Argentino-Brasileña*), endorsed in July 1986 in Buenos Aires, which established the Integration and Cooperation Program (*Programa de Integración y Cooperación Argentino-Brasileño - PICAB*) and can be seen indeed as the embryo of Mercosur.[4] This move was substantially due to the role the newly appointed democratic presidents had decided to play in the regional scenario. Arguably, neither the globalization pressures nor the democratization process as such would have been sufficient to overcome the secular distrust

---

two then top government officials (*Partido Justicialista*) had made clear their position to the contrary, stating that no stronger institutionalization was needed for the time being (Andrés Cisneros and Jorge Campbell, '*El Mercosur no necesita de la burocracia para crecer*', *Clarín*, 18-5-1999).

[4]   Both presidents had already signed the *Declaración de Iguazú* in 1985, expressing their 'strong will to accelerate the process of bilateral integration.'

between Argentina and Brazil, including as it did military cooperation and the mutual inspection of their nuclear installations.[5]

In 1988, during the same presidential tenures, the Treaty on Integration, Cooperation and Development (*Tratado de Integración, Cooperación y Desarrollo*) was signed. Conceived of as the culmination of a process of mutual recognition and confidence building, it instead turned out to be a crucial step into the next phase of the new relationship. During the period between the signature of the PICAB and the creation of Mercosur in 1991, a versatile institutional arrangement was settled in order to keep the process working. Its main features were the direct participation of top officials in the negotiations, under the coordination of the Foreign Ministries; the meeting of a six-monthly presidential summit; the high profile of bilateral diplomatic channels, especially the ambassadors in every capital; and the nonexistence of common bodies integrated by independent experts (Peña, 1998a). Most of these characteristics, imprinted by maximum pragmatism and flexibility, were maintained along the further stages of the process despite the establishment of some formal structures.

Mercosur has later changed what was a free-trade zone among its member countries into a customs union, with a long-term goal of becoming a common market. Such an organization constitutes one of the most developed forms of regional integration, only transcended by an economic union. Beyond this broad substantive classification, it should be noted that the framework adopted so far is distinctive of the region, different to any previous or contemporaneous experience. As observed by Peña (1998b, p. 2), Mercosur is *'un caso de regionalismo abierto en el marco de la Organización Mundial de Comercio,...un proceso de integración original que no sigue necesariamente una metodología similar a la empleada en Europa.'*

The most evident successes of Mercosur have been a notable increase in intra-regional trade, accompanied by a parallel increase in extra-regional trade (Informe Mercosur N° 3, 1997, p. 7; Bouzas, 1998, p. 219); a significant increase of direct foreign investment in the countries of the region (Secretaría de Relaciones Económicas Internacionales de la República Argentina, 1996, p. 14); and a growing international interest in Mercosur, both by investors and by governments and technicians or *técnicos* (Nofal, 1997). The combination of the first indicators (growth of intra-regional and extra-regional trade) indicates that trade creation surpassed trade diversion (see Table 3.1) – thus contradicting the pessimistic visions of some World Bank reports (Yeats, 1997). The other indicators show how Mercosur opened its way through the global economy, becoming a target of greater interest for businesses and impinging on the strategies of enterprises and governments from outside the area. Both the largest economies of Mercosur, Argentina and Brazil, are reckoned as global traders, and therefore any restoration of the policies of economic closure would harm rather than benefit them.

---

[5] Along with the main Treaty the presidents signed a Joint Declaration on Nuclear Policy (*Declaración Conjunta sobre Política Nuclear*). For further developments on nuclear cooperation, see Hirst and Bocco (1989).

Furthermore, the region's new orientation made that its constituent countries be seen under a new light. As it was put in *The Economist*, 'in just five years Mercosur has already done much to help its members feature on the world's map for the new century' (Reid, 1996, p. 30).

Table 3.1 Mercosur trade (imports) 1985-1996: creation, not diversion

	U$S millions			Percentage of variation		
	1985	1990	1996	1990-85	1996-90	1996-85
Intra-Mercosur	1.848	4.241	17.060	129.5%	302.3%	823.2%
Extra-Mercosur	17.418	25.061	67.370	43.9%	168.8%	286.8%
Total	19.266	29.302	84.430	52.1%	188.1%	338.2%

Source: Nofal (1997, p. 74).

The Particular Development of Mercosur

To account for the emergence of an integrating region is not the same as to explain its further progress (Haas, 1964). On the contrary, many approaches would argue that any concession on sovereignty can be seen as the consequence of a contingent necessity, brought about by a temporary weakness in the nation-state power which is urged to be overcome. Consequently, no subsequent progression can be expected from regional agreements – states do not go bankrupt, it is said; nor do they commit suicide, delivering their sovereign powers to other entities if they can avoid it. Other theories stress instead the feedback effect of the first moves towards integration, whether it be called spillover or not. However, none of these theories attempts to allocate the same causes to the origin and the continuation of an integration process.

While the factors that set off a process are not necessarily equal to those that keep it going, other variables likely to have a relevant impact on both stages may either change or hold. Many were ignored or at best taken for granted in the first theorizing efforts to grasp the move towards integration in Europe; among the most significant was the democratic condition of the contracting states. Later studies (Karl, 1989; Schmitter, 1991) demonstrated that this neglected factor was not trivial but crucial. Further research has been conducted in order to appraise the extent to which domestic regimes impinge upon international cooperation and regional integration (Putnam, 1988; Schmitter, 1991; Russell, 1992; Remmer, 1994; Moravcsik, 1997). Yet the main distinction was made between democratic and authoritarian rule, somehow overlooking the differences within each type of regime. In this respect, as long as the homogeneity of these types was presumed, the kind of democracy – whether presidential or parliamentary, consociational or majoritarian – was ignored. Lately, new democracies and new regions, increasingly widespread over the last decade, allow – or indeed demand – us to test the accuracy of such an assumption.

In order to understand the reasons for the creation of Mercosur and its progress, many theories on integration may be considered. It is worthwhile reviewing the more plausible of them, while offering empirical evidence in each case to check their applicability.

Intergovernmentalism has a strong case to make, Moravcsik being its main defender. He applies 'an alternative theory of foreign economic policy' (1998, p. 6) to explain the emergence of integrative efforts. In this approach, economic interdependence is seen as a strong condition for integration. The working mechanism consists in the impact that increasing exchange has on the capability of single states to individually manage higher levels of complex interaction. Export dependence and intra-industry trade are, thus, reckoned to generate the strongest pressures for trade liberalization, which in turn is the main cause of integration. Although Moravcsik recognizes that the empirical data 'are more suggestive than conclusive' (1998, p. 496), he argues against geopolitics as an alternative explanation, and especially against regional particularities as a reasonable basis for explaining regional integration. Table 3.2 shows the data supporting the political economy hypothesis, by showing that Europe is the most natural region to embrace integration, and Pacific Asia the least likely to set off a similar process.

Table 3.2 Regional trade dependence of Germany, United States, and Japan as a proportion of GNP, 1958 and 1990

	Intra-Regional Trade/GNP (1960)	Intra-Regional Trade/GNP (1990)	Intra-Industry Trade/Regional Trade (1980s)
Germany (vis-à-vis EC6 then EC12)	6%	21%	66%
United States (vis-à-vis Canada & Mexico)	1%	2%	60%
Japan (vis-à-vis Northeast Asia, ASEAN and India)	2%	3%	25%

Source: Moravcsik (1998, p. 495).

However, intergovernmentalists do not provide additional reasons for the further development of integration. According to their standpoint, each decision regarding integration is seen as independent from any preceding agreement. States would face a 'blank' situation whenever they engaged in negotiations for reaching an international accord, and the goal to grant new 'credible commitments' is not thought to build accumulative constraints for autonomous state action. To be sure, intergovernmentalists do not deny constraints derived from increasing interdependence; rather, their core argument is that states stay in control and all key decisions are intergovernmental.

With regard to origin and development, neofunctionalism may be considered the opposite of intergovernmentalism: neofunctionalists do not fully explain the starting up of an integration process, but advance a hypothesis on the causes for further expansion. Their central mechanism, spillover, departs from either or both the extension of the area scope and the deepening of the authority level required to sustain the process once initiated (Schmitter, 1969; 1971). Increasing technical necessities are seen as demanding further intervention and regulation over wider areas, in turn generating new necessities. Unlike sheer functionalism, neo-functionalism accords a role to politics: supranational bargaining and interest group lobbying influence the dynamics of integration, being crucial factors for the reproduction of the spillover logic. In short, the principle is that what fosters the process is, in due time, fostered through feedback, therefore keeping the wheel spinning. The logical corollary of this continuing movement approach is that the cessation of the expansion would jeopardize the process.

The neofunctional approach stresses the interaction between integration and institutions, rather than that between interdependence and integration (as intergovernmentalism does). However, its supporters do not deny the same basic sequence: both theories agree on the order of precedence, in spite of underlining different dyads according to their theoretical assumptions and heuristic goals.[6]

Neotransactionalism, to give a label to an extensively developed but so far unnamed theory (Sandholtz and Stone Sweet, 1998), draws centrally on neofunctionalism. It consequently highlights the 'inherent expansionary' nature of integration processes, sustained 'by means of policy feedback' (1988, p. 25), and the role of supranational organization. However, it does not dismiss the power of national governments and the primacy of intergovernmental bargaining in a number of areas. The relation stressed by this theory is that between interdependence – called exchange – and institutions – the process of institutionalization is included. Integration as a voluntary state policy is therefore seen as an intermediary transmission level, a sort of crossing point between the actions carried out by transnational transactors and the institutional channels that are developed in their wake and in turn regulate them. Briefly, increasing transnational transactions make the first move, the consequent demands for facilitating and regulating the

---

[6]   The discussion on whether the label of theory fits these theoretical stands, or rather approach (Schmitter, 1996) or framework (Moravcsik, 1998), would do better, is not relevant here.

transnational transactors and the institutional channels that are developed in their wake and in turn regulate them. Briefly, increasing transnational transactions make the first move, the consequent demands for facilitating and regulating the transnational society give rise to an institution-building process, and the new institutions keep the cycle going and growing.

The first grand theory that calls into question the sufficiency of the three-stage sequence – i.e. interdependence, integration and institutionalization – has come to be called neoidealism. Drawing on the thought of Kant ([1795] 1985), it not only focuses on inter-state relations but also on intra-state structures and processes. According to this theory, the type of political regime influences the kind of link that countries may develop with one another. Moreover, the coincidence of one of these types – namely democracy – in two or more countries has shown to have dramatic effects, one of the most important of which is the impracticability of war (Schmitter, 1991). It is true that other theories had also recognized the importance of societal actors and their subnational or transnational links; none of them, however, had emphasized these points so strongly, nor considered the relevance of the political regime as such.

Empirical evidence is frequently displayed in order to prove that democracy accounts for cooperation among countries that feature such a regime, and even for integration (Schmitter, 1991; Sorensen, 1992; Dixon, 1994). In contrast, other studies call into question the very tenets of neoidealism with statistical data (Remmer, 1994). What is surprising is that both assertions, despite their opposition, are defended with evidence derived from the Southern Cone. Furthermore, not only is it difficult to verify the neoidealist hypotheses, but their claim to explain the causes of cooperation/integration is also incomplete: as intergovernmentalism, they account for the origin but not for the subsequent steps of integration. Nevertheless, the crucial novelty of this approach is to add a stage at the beginning while simultaneously keeping the rest of the sequence untouched.

However, none of these theories explains Mercosur. According to the data shown in Table 3.3, the sequence of interdependence-integration-institutions simply did not take place. Instead, as can be seen in Table 3.4, interdependence had been declining for some years by the time the first steps toward integration were taken, and only started to rise from then on (Hurrell, 1995; Nofal, 1997; Peña, 1998a). It is also noteworthy that regional institutions came into being as mere intergovernmental fora, where national representatives were constrained to reach unanimity as the only means to take a decision.

The evidence eloquently shows, in the first place, that interdependence was not a precondition for integration in the case of Mercosur. Furthermore, the largest Mercosur economy Brazil – hardly exceeds at present one third of Germany's figures in the 1960s. So relevant for the objection of major integration theories as it could appear, such a claim is just half of the news. The remaining half goes beyond the mere invalidation of the causal relation between interdependence and integration, turning it upside-down: in the Southern Cone, the moves toward integration actually brought about increasing interdependence (see Tables 3.3 and 3.4 for the data, and Figure 3.2 for a comparative theoretical framework).

**Table 3.3 Regional trade dependence of Mercosur countries as a proportion
of GDP, 1986 and 1997**

	Intra-regional trade/GDP (1986)	Intra-regional trade/GDP (1997)
Argentina	1.5%	5.1%
Brazil	0.9%	2.4%
Paraguay	11.0%	24.5%
Uruguay	12.5%	14.7%

Source: Own elaboration, from data of the World Bank report (1997) for GDP and INTAL
databases for intra-Mercosur trade. Uruguay's small increase is due to the large
augment of its GDP along the decade, not to stagnant trade. Data regarding
Paraguay are not highly reliable.

Table 3.4   Interdependence between Argentina and Brazil, 1980-1996

	Exports (in M $)	Imports (in M $)	Exchange (in M $)
1980	765	1.072	1.837
1985	496	612	1.108
1990	1.423	718	2.140
1996	6.615	5.326	11.941

Source: Nofal (1997, p. 67).

Having put into question the mainstream theories on integration, which underline
interdependence as the determining variable, it is now necessary to examine the
role played by the institutional variables at their two levels: national and regional.
While the former is considered either irrelevant or independent depending on the
theory used, the latter is always reckoned as dependent on the other variables.
There is little to say in this exposition about regional institutions: Mercosur
countries have been regularly and consciously reluctant to set up any kind of
institutional arrangement that could restrain national sovereignty. And they have
certainly succeeded in this respect. Although the building of regional institutions
has been verified only in the European Union thus far, many authors have used this
case to elicit conclusions and generalize hypotheses (Deutsch, 1957; Mitrany, 1975;
Haas, 1961, 1964, 1975; Sandholtz and Stone Sweet, 1998; Moravcsik,

1998). Some form of institution building was, therefore, believed to be a logical consequence – and a support means – of regional integration. However, the region coming right behind the European experience – in terms of accomplished stages of integration – contradicts this inference.

The many approaches to the rationale of Mercosur's emergence draw either on external or internal causes. The former stress in general the pressures coming from the globalization of trade and investment flows – since regional inter-dependence cannot be seen as a cause for Mercosur, as shown above –, and in particular those rising from the costs that NAFTA threatens to impose on non-cooperating and isolated countries in the western hemisphere (Bouzas, 1996). The internal causes involve instead more heterogeneous sources, ranging from regime change – democratization (Schmitter, 1991) – to economic change – from inward to outward looking economies (Foders, 1996). Regarding the nature rather than the source of the process, Hurrell arguably claims that 'the first moves towards regional co-operation were essentially political' (1995, p. 253; also Peña, 1996). Yet they were due to a shared sense of vulnerability rather than strength on the part of the newly established regimes.

Be it cause, consequence, or feedback effect, as the political movements that fostered the emergence of Mercosur got stronger the region was definitely becoming a 'pluralistic security community' (Deutsch, 1957). The most stunning effects were the nuclear agreements and the cooperation on security and defense policies.[7] These decisions were certainly an output of the confidence-building measures practiced by the incoming democratic authorities, but also of the new vision they shared about the ongoing changes 'out there' in the world. Therefore, to allocate the causes exclusively to one level, either external or internal, would not capture the whole picture.

Besides the factors that led to the integration in the first place, and kept up the momentum of the process later on, there is one element omnipresent throughout the history of Mercosur: the high profile of national presidents. The role performed by these agents was not casual, but responded to the very logic of the region. As a key actor of the negotiations put it, the flexibility of the *diplomacia presidencial* manifested a clear political motivation and *'comprensión frente a las dificultades coyunturales de los socios'*, proof of the *'lógica política'* rather than *'jurídica'* of the integration (Peña, 1996; see also de Núñez, 1997). Unlike the European Union case, no Court of Justice was at work more or less subtly to sustain and deepen the integration, nor were day-to-day politics adding to an increasing regional power.

The relevant role of presidents to keep integration from stalling is an outstanding characteristic of Mercosur. However, it is even more bewildering that it has also proved decisive in the other crucial stage of integration, i.e. its origin.

---

[7] 'The 1990 Declaration on a Common Nuclear Policy created a system of jointly monitored safeguards and opened the way for full implementation of the Tlatelolco Regime' (Hurrell, 1995, pp. 259-260). In addition to nuclear cooperation, military spending and arms imports started to decline steadily after democratization in all of Southern Cone countries, and augmented the decreasing rhythm since 1990 on.

While it could be said that the development shows no sign of completion so far, and the next stages may observe a diminution in the presidential importance, it is still true that without the presidents' action neither the initial impulse nor the crucial crises solution would have been accomplished (Peña, 1996). A more accurate appraisal of the difference between presidents as individuals and presidentialism as an institution is developed in the next section.

Another particular feature displayed by Mercosur, concerning its flexibility as well as its informal complexity, is the contrast between its public, or state-driven political inspiration and its private microeconomic implementation (Lafer, 1997, p. 261). This brings us to the role played by firms, interest groups and, in the language of a theory, transnational actors. In Europe these actors are recognized for having sought common institutions, in order to reduce the costs of information and transactions through single rules (Streeck and Schmitter, 1991; Sandholtz and Stone Sweet, 1998). They believed that the uncertainty and sub-optimal outcome of multiple national institutions would hinder the realization of the customs union and, later, the consolidation of the single market. Today, the economic union would be unthinkable without supranational institutions.

The reality of Mercosur is still far from that of the European Union. On the contrary, national businesses in the Southern Cone are used to the, so to speak, 'institutional deficit' already prevalent in their countries – although some maintain that Mercosur deficit is not institutional but 'normative'.[8] Such a reality had accustomed them to addressing directly the core of the decision-making power in the case of necessity, instead of going through the less trustworthy institutional channels. As far as the political regime was concerned, this aspect was called 'other institutionalization' rather than institutional deficit (O'Donnell, 1996). Nevertheless, what matters here is that national regime institutions were already perceived as ineffective when it came to taking rapid decisions and solving problems fairly. From this perception about domestic institutions to a similar one regarding possible regional institutions there was a short distance, meaning that the only reliable authorities would be the same ones that resolved problems at home: the presidents. Figure 3.2 shows what inter-presidential dynamics fostering regional integration would look like. Paraphrasing O'Donnell (1994), it is not only metaphoric but heuristically useful to derive that, from delegative democracies, Mercosur might have engendered a 'new regional animal': delegative integration.

---

[8]   Author's interview with Norberto Moretti, Secretary of the Brazilian Embassy in Buenos Aires, September 1999 (see also Baptista, 1999).

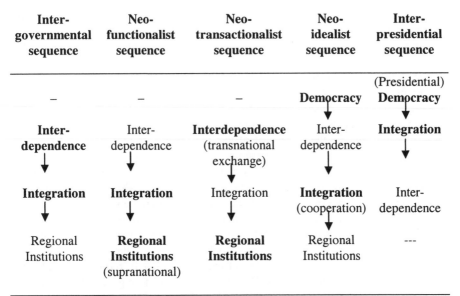

Inter-governmental sequence	Neo-functionalist sequence	Neo-transactionalist sequence	Neo-idealist sequence	Inter-presidential sequence
				(Presidential)
–	–	–	**Democracy** ↓	**Democracy** ↓
Inter-dependence ↓	Inter-dependence ↓	**Interdependence** (transnational exchange) ↓	Inter-dependence ↓	**Integration** ↓
Integration ↓	**Integration** ↓	Integration ↓	**Integration** (cooperation) ↓	Inter-dependence
Regional Institutions	**Regional Institutions** (supranational)	**Regional Institutions**	Regional Institutions	---

Note: The core relation (dyad of variables) for each theory is marked in bold letters.

Figure 3.2 Integration theories: sequence of phases and core relations

National Institutions and the Performance of Mercosur

As noted above, Mercosur was born as a consequence of certain national processes underwent in Brazil and Argentina: re-democratization, the removal of old hypotheses of conflict between the two neighboring countries, and a new, more outwardly oriented, economic profile. It is worth underlining that Argentina exhibited the most radical changes, since Brazilian political transition, foreign policy definition, and economic restructuration had started much earlier, in the 1970s. At any rate, Alfonsín and Sarney headed a process of rapprochement signed by their personal and political high profile.

South American presidentialism has been sharply distinguished in the literature from its historical model, American presidentialism. The latter was originally conceived of and later developed as a regime of separation of power, whereas the former is better defined as a 'centralized decision-making arrangement' (Cheibub y Limongi, 2000) or a 'concentrationist subtype of presidentialism' (Malamud, 2001). This categorization stems from both formal and informal institutions. Among the formal institutions, Mainwaring and Shugart (1997) stress the degree of legislative power endowed to the presidents and their capacity to rule over the cabinet without parliamentary interference – what adds up to the constitutive features of presidentialism, i.e. independent origin and survival. Among informal institutions are worth noting the political practices that favor particularistic exchanges and the personalization of power, which O'Donnell (1994; 1996) has termed 'delegative.'

Upheld by the institutional characteristics of South American presidentialism, the new presidents accomplished a crucial role for setting off the integration project. This 'presidential protagonism' was an institutional side-effect more than a purely personal one, as theoretically supported by other studies. Lijphart, for instance, asserts that American presidents compensate their institutional limitations in other areas by stressing their direct link to foreign policy. Therefore, 'the general pattern is that, during their terms of office, they tend to direct more and more of their attention and energy toward foreign policy issues' (1994, p. 102). Danese (1999), following Barilleaux, goes further in appraising the phenomenon, as he distinguishes five areas of the decision-making process where it is possible to assess the performance of chief executives regarding foreign policy. [9]

In the Southern Cone, the pattern described was reinforced by the new democratic regimes. As observed by Silva, in Sarney's Brazil 'the process of democratization has produced a major 'politicization' of the Foreign Ministry' (Silva, 1989, p. 94). In Argentina the effect was similar in terms of presidential involvement, but in contrast with Brazil – where the foreign policy defined in Itamaraty was upheld without significant breaks since 1971 – the new regime improved the country's historically erratic line. For the first time in sixty years, it was recognized that the 'central coordination of international relations within one ministry has given Argentina's foreign policy a higher degree of coherence and predictability. However, the power of decision is still concentrated too much in the hands of president Alfonsín and his minister of foreign affairs, Dante Caputo' (Silva, 1989, p. 91). This feature continued with the subsequent presidency. The strong role played by the *cancilleres* stresses the political dimension of the process – as opposed to its economic dimension – without shadowing the predominant position of the presidents.

Whereas Mercosur was intentionally created and kept as an intergovernmental process, the actual feature of the region appears to be its extreme type: let us call it 'inter-presidentialism'. As an analyst has pointed out:

> el proceso del Mercosur está, a nuestro juicio, bajo el signo de un apriorismo ejecutivista y tecnocrático, que los partidos y las representaciones parlamentarias han tolerado, hasta el presente (Pérez Antón, 1997, p. 19).

---

[9] The five areas are (a) foreign policy formulation and direction, (b) organization and constitution of foreign policy teams, (c) administration and supervision of foreign policy (especially in case of crisis), (d) skill to build and maintain consensus around foreign policy, and (e) accomplishment (Barilleaux, 1985, p. 114; Danese, 1999, p. 394).

This unique aspect brought about a kind of spillover that is not the one predicted by the neo-functionalist theories, but a different one driven from above.[10]

What distinguishes Mercosur from similar processes of integration is the celerity of its development as well as the exiguousness of the norms that rule the process (Pérez Antón, 1997, pp. 16-7). Both traits, velocity and political action regardless of the presence of regulations, are characteristics of Latin American presidentialism.[11] The beneficial paradox of the Southern Cone novelty is, thus, that the national and regional levels converge now towards a minimum and flexible institutionalization. Whereas past failures of democracy and integration in Latin America were attributed to deficit or excess of formal institutionalization respectively, at present an equilibrium has apparently been reached – as shown by the persistence of Mercosur despite the recent turbulence, brought about by the Brazilian devaluation and the simultaneous recession in both of the largest partners (Peña, 1999).

Another lasting – and sometimes misleading – attribute of Mercosur is decentralized bargaining as a basic mechanism. Once the bulk of a given bargain has been done, presidents exert a decisive influence to get their preferred outcome – sometimes even in contradiction with the proposals drafted by the national negotiators. As unified and authoritative actors, they can capitalize better on their resources facing a spread arena with many low-authority protagonists than a narrow one with fewer but stronger players. A last peculiarity favoring presidential power, especially of the largest countries, is that there are no overlapping cleavages in the region as there are in Europe. Instead, the axis Argentina-Brazil catches all the attention while in the European Union this is divided among the opposition between, say, Germany and France, the big and the small countries, the Nordic and the Southern, the supranational and the intergovernmental, and the like. Lane and Maeland (1998) have proved how, depending on decision rules, the more the members the less the power each one wields; in Europe, larger numbers concur with cross-cutting cleavages to diffuse power, whereas in Mercosur these conditions are radically different.

Two recent examples further illustrate the issues at stake. In chronological order, the first case refers to the management of the crisis set off by the Brazilian devaluation of 1999. The second case points at the resolution of a bitter dispute over the incorporation of sugar to the free trade area, which by mid-2000 seriously jeopardized the Argentine-Brazilian relations – thus Mercosur itself.

---

[10] There have been other processes of integration in Latin America in which the presidents have played some role (e.g. the Andean Group and the Central American Common Market). However, their performances have been far less impressive than that of Mercosur, and presidential intervention – as a crucial factor of support for integration – has been to a much more limited extent.

[11] This point is usually acknowledged (for instance, Shugart and Carey, 1992; O'Donnell, 1994; and Carey and Shugart, 1998) and is further developed in Malamud (2000).

Throughout 1998, the Brazilian economy was under heavy external pressure. In January 1999, its authorities made the decision to devaluate their currency, the Real. As a consequence, relative prices against Brazilian partners in Mercosur were halved, and Brazilian exports became more competitive, thus creating the perception of a threatening 'invasion' to the other Mercosur domestic markets. In July, the effects of the Brazilian devaluation led the Argentine government, pressed by domestic interests, to impose restrictions on Brazilian imports – a measure that went against regional agreements. The controversy heated up, and both foreign ministers Di Tella and Lampreia recommended their presidents not to get involved in a matter that could not result in any gain to them – as differences seemed irreconcilable and Mercosur was considered dead and buried by many analysts. Nonetheless, president Menem arranged with Cardoso to fly to Brasilia directly from the United States, where he was attending a meeting. The two presidents got together against the advice of their foreign ministers, one of whom was informed of the meeting only when the Secretary General of the Argentine presidency had already arranged it. The outcome of the summit was remarkably positive, since an agreement was reached that reduced the previous tension and reinstated the continuity of the integration scheme.

As for the debate about sugar trade regulations, it has been one of the most sensitive areas of Mercosur since its very inception, having needed a special treatment – as also happened with the automobile industry – and the establishment of an *Ad Hoc Group* under the jurisdiction of the GMC. The asymmetry between the larger countries of Mercosur is unequivocal in this matter: Brazil is the first world exporter of sugar, and subsidizes its production in order to develop combustibles derived from cane alcohol, whereas Argentina's lesser volume of production adds up to the fact that many provincial economies of the poor Northwest subsist exclusively from the production of sugar. Consequently, there have always been significant social actors and interest groups that advance their demands before both congress and the executive, and legislators have been especially receptive to such demands (Vigevani, Mariano and Oliveira, 2000). This situation led to an outbidding of measures, countermeasures, threats and retaliations throughout the last decade, mainly addressed from each congress to one another. In November 1997, only the official visit of president Menem to Brazil helped ease the tension caused by the disputes between the two congresses, providing a temporary resolution for the crisis (Seixas Corrêa, 1999). The Gordian knot, however, was to be cut by the Argentine executive three years later: in September 2000, president De la Rúa vetoed a bill just passed by the congress that established the protraction of the protection regime until 2005; simultaneously, he signed a resolution instituting the same provision! Closely analyzed, there is no contradiction: in this way, the Argentine president met a promise made to his Brazilian counterpart that would make possible for the presidents to conclude a new arrangement – without the restriction of having to revoke a law – as soon as the conditions for it were favorable.[12] The refusal by the presidents to leave open the field for a two level game – which would have improved their bargaining positions *vis-à-vis* each other, by way of claiming domestic pressures to sustain each other's arguments – speaks eloquently of the decisive role they have played to keep Mercosur going.

Conclusion

This chapter outlines the original development and operation of Mercosur as opposed to those that would be expected by most theories of regional integration. Moreover, Mercosur differs widely from the European Union in that the former does not present a pattern of increasing institutionalization at a supranational level, but progresses through inter-governmental mechanisms, in a more politicized, as opposed to institutionalized, shape. The hypothesis advanced here suggests that the above could be partially explained by the domestic institutional settings that the member countries feature in either case. Executive format is thus addressed in order to appraise whether presidential democracies have been able to back up a successful regional-building process in a novel way. The conclusion is that national, as opposed to supranational, institutions can provide effective bases for regional integration.

The perspectives for the forthcoming years seem to be quite stable for Mercosur – provided that it does not dilute into a Free Trade Area of the Americas (FTAA). Only the enlargement towards medium-sized countries such as Chile may dissipate the risk of a 'diarchy of authority'; but this is not likely to happen soon. With respect to the internal organization, as one of the main specialists on the region has put it

> o modelo intergovernamental deverá assim ser mantido e o futuro de curto e médio prazo do Mercosul dependerá da capacidade de negociação de diferenças mais do que da identificação de interesses comuns (Hirst, 1995, p. 195).

In other words, as the negotiation over different positions has had no higher and, thus far, more suitable channel than the inter-presidential one, the operation and inner dynamics of Mercosur are not expected to change in the foreseeable future. This is not to say that presidentialism will be positive for regional integration any time anywhere; but, in the absence of regional institutions, it is plausible to assert – *ex post* – that it was a necessary condition for Mercosur to succeed.

---

[12] Clarín, 5-9-2000, 'De la Rúa firmó una resolución y vetó una ley. El azúcar, protegido hasta el 2005'.

References

Baptista, Luis Olavo (1999), 'La agenda futura del Mercosur: Pautas viables para un desarrollo institucional', *Archivos del Presente,* Vol. 17, pp. 153-163.

Barilleaux, Ryan J. (1985), 'Evaluating Performance in Foreign Affairs', in George C. Edwards III et al. (eds.), *The President and Public Policy Making,* Pittsburgh.

Bartolini, Stefano (1998), 'Exit Options, Boundary Building, Political Structuring. Sketches of a Theory of Large-Scale Territorial and Membership 'Retrenchment/ Differentiation' Versus 'Expansion/Integration' (With Reference to the European Union),' *SPS WP, European University Institute,* Vol. 98(1).

Bouzas, Roberto (1996), 'El Regionalismo en el Hemisferio Occidental: Nafta, Mercosur y Después,' *Desarrollo Económico. Revista de Ciencias Sociales,* 36 (Número Especial).

Bouzas, Roberto (1998), 'El Mercosur Frente al Nuevo Milenio,' *Comunidad Andina y Mercosur. Desafíos Pendientes de la Integración en América Latina,* AAVV, Ministerio de RREE de Colombia/Corporación Andina de Fomento, Bogotá, pp. 217-234.

Calceglia, Inés M. (1998), *Integración: El Desafío de las Instituciones. Reflexiones Sobre el Tribunal Internacional, El Activismo Judicial y el Déficit Democrático. Proyecciones y Aplicabilidad para Mercosur,* La Ley, Buenos Aires.

Carey, John M. and Shugart, Soberg (1998), *Executive Decree Authority,* Cambridge University Press, Cambridge.

Cavarozzi, Marcelo (1998), 'La Integración sin Instituciones,' *Comunidad Andina y Mercosur. Desafíos Pendientes de la Integración en América Latina,* AAVV, Ministerio de RREE de Colombia/Corporación Andina de Fomento, Bogotá, pp. 3-16.

Cheibub, José Antonio and Limongi, Fernando (2000), 'Where is the Difference? Parliamentary and Presidential Democracies Reconsidered,' *XVIII World Congress of Political Science, IPSA,* Québec City, August 1-5.

Danese, Sergio (1999), *Diplomacia Presidencial. História e crítica,* Topbooks, Rio de Janeiro.

de Núñez, Alberto (1997), 'La diplomacia presidencial', *Archivos del Presente,* Vol. 3(10), pp. 133-139.

Deutsch, Karl (1957), *Transnational Community and the North Atlantic Area: International Organization in the Light of Historical Experience,* Princeton University Press, Princeton.

Dixon, W.J. (1994), 'Democracy and the Peaceful Settlement of International Conflict,' *American Political Science Review,* Vol. 88, pp. 14-32.

Fawcett, Louise and Hurrell, Andrew (1995), *Regionalism in World Politics. Regional Organization and International Order,* Oxford University Press, Oxford.

Ferrer, Aldo (1997), *Hechos y Ficciones de la Globalización. Argentina y el Mercosur en el Sistema Internacional,* FCE, Buenos Aires.

Foders, Federico (1996), 'Mercosur: A New Approach to Regional Integration?' *The Kiel Institute of World Economics, Kiel Working Paper,* 746.

Fournier, Dominique (1999), 'The Alfonsín Administration and the Promotion of Democratic Values in the Southern Cone and the Andes,' *Journal of Latin American Studies,* Vol. 31, pp. 39-74.

Haas, Ernst B (1958), *The Uniting of Europe. Political, Social, and Economic Forces, 1950-1957,* Stanford University Press, Stanford.

Haas, Ernst B. (1961), 'International Integration: The European and the Universal Process', *International Organization,* Vol. 15, pp. 366-93.

Haas, Ernst B. (1964), *Beyond the Nation-State. Functionalism and International Organization,* Stanford University Press, Stanford.

Haas, Ernst B. (1975), *The Obsolescence of Regional Integration Theory,* University of California, Berkeley.

Hirst, Monica (1995), 'A Dimensão Política do Mercosul: Especificidades Nacionais, Aspectos Institucionais e Actores Sociais,' in Guilherme d'Oliveira Martins et al. (eds.), *A Integração Aberta: Um Projecto da União Europeia e do Mercosul,* Instituto de Estudos Estratégicos e Internacionais, Lisboa, pp. 173-197.

Hirst, Monica and Bocco, Héctor E. (1989), 'Cooperação Nuclear e Integração Brasil-Argentina,' *Contexto Internacional,*Vol. 9.

Hix, Simon (1994), 'The Study of the European Community: The Challenge to Comparative Politics,' *West European Politics,* Vol. 17(1).

Hurrell, Andrew (1995), 'Regionalism in the Americas,' in Louise Fawcett and Andrew Hurrell (eds.), *Regionalism in World Politics. Regional Organization and International Order,* Oxford University Press, Oxford.

Instituto para la Integración de América Latina y el Caribe (INTAL) (1996-1997), 'Informe MERCOSUR,' 1-3 ed., Banco Interamericano de Desarrollo, Buenos Aires.

Kant, Immanuel ([1795] 1985), *La Paz Perpetua,* Editorial Tecnos, Madrid.

Karl, Terry (1989), 'Hegemons and Political Entrepreneurs: Dependence, Democratization, and Cooperation in the Americas,' *Paper Presented at the Seminar on 'The New Inter-dependence in the Americas,' The Americas Program,* Stanford University, Stanford.

Lafer, Celso (1997), 'Relaçoes Brasil-Argentina: Alcance e Significado de Uma Parceria Estratégica,' *Contexto Internacional,* Vol. 19(2), pp. 249-265.

Lane, Jan-Erik and Maeland, Reinert (1998), 'Constitutional Analysis - The Power Index Approach,' Unpublished.

Lijphart, Arend (1994), 'Presidentialism and Majoritarian Democracy. Theoretical Observations,' in Juan J. Linz and Arturo Valenzuela (eds.), *The Failure of Presidential Democracy,* Johns Hopkins University Press, Baltimore.

Mainwaring, Scott and Shugart, Matthew Soberg (1997), *Presidentialism and Democracy in Latin America,* Cambridge University Press, Cambridge.

Malamud, Andrés. (2000), 'Chief Executives and Integration Processes. Toward a Research Agenda,' *XVIII World Congress of Political Science, IPSA,* Québec City, August 1-5.

Malamud, Andrés (2001), 'Presidentialism in the Southern Cone. A Framework for Analysis,' *SPS WP. European University Institute,* Vol. 01(1).

Mitrany, David (1975), *The Functional Theory of Politics,* London School of Economics and Political Science, London.

Moravcsik, Andrew (1997), 'Taking Preferences Seriously: A Liberal Theory of International Politics,' *International Organization,* Vol. 51(4), pp. 513-53.

Moravcsik, Andrew (1998), *The Choice for Europe. Social Purpose and State Power From Messina to Maastricht,* Cornell University Press, Ithaca, New York.

Nofal, María B. (1997), 'Las Grandes Asignaturas Pendientes en el Mercosur,' *Boletín Informativo Techint Separata,* Vol. 292.

O'Donnell, Guillermo (1994), 'Delegative Democracy,' *Journal of Democracy.*

O'Donnell, Guillermo (1996), 'Otra Institucionalización,' *La Política. Revista de Estudios sobre el Estado y la Sociedad,* Vol. 1.

Oviedo, Marcelo (1998), 'Mercosur y los Tribunales Nacionales: Desregulación, Re-Regulación y la Cuestión de la Corte Común,' unpublished, European University Institute, Florence.

Peña, Félix (1996), 'La Construcción del Mercosur. Lecciones de Una Experiencia,' *Archivos del Presente,* Vol. 2(4).

Peña, Félix (1998a), 'El Desarrollo Institucional del Mercosur,'*Comunidad Andina y Mercosur. Desafíos Pendientes de la Integración en América Latina,* AAVV, Ministerio de Relaciones Exteriores de Colombia y Corporación Andina de Fomento, Bogotá, pp. 95-114.

Peña, Félix (1999a), 'El Mercosur y las Negociaciones del ALCA,' *Regular e democratizar o sistema global. Uma parceria para o século XXI,* Instituto de Estudos Estratégicos e Internacionais, S. João do Estoril, Cascais, Principia, pp. 59-74.

Peña, Félix (1999b), 'Ni tiempo de funerales ni de "Tudo bem"', *Archivos del Presente,* Jul-Sep, Vol. 5(17), pp. 35-48.

Pérez Antón, Romeo (1997), 'El Contexto Político e Institucional del Mercosur,' *Além do Comércio. Ampliar as Relações Europa-Mercosul,* Instituto de Estudos Estratégicos e Internacionais, Lisboa, pp. 9-43.

Putnam, Robert (1988), 'Diplomacy and Domestic Politics: The Logic of Two-Level Games,' *International Organization,* Vol. 42(3), pp. 427-60.

Reid, Michael (1996), 'A Survey of Mercosur,' *The Economist,* Vol. 341.

Remmer, Karen L. (1998), 'Does Democracy Promote Interstate Cooperation? Lessons From the Mercosur Region,' *International Studies Quarterly,* Vol. 42, pp. 25-52.

Rocha Filho, Almir Porto da (1999), 'Mercosul: Institutional Structure, Dispute Settlement System and a Supranational Court,' *Minerva Program,* Spring.

Russell, Roberto (1992), 'Type of Regime, Changes of Government and Foreign Policy: The Case of Argentina (1976-1991),' *FLACSO, Documentos e Informes De Investigación,* Vol. 127.

Sandholtz, Wayne and Stone Sweet, Alec (1998), *European Integration and Supranational Governance.* Oxford: Oxford University Press.

Schmitter, Philippe C. (1969), 'Three Neo-Functional Hypotheses About International Integration,' *International Organization,* Vol. 23(1), pp. 161-166.

Schmitter, Philippe C. (1971), 'A Revised Theory of Regional Integration,' *Regional Integration: Theory and Research* (eds.), Leon N. Lindberg and Stuart A. Scheingold, Harvard Universtity Press Cambridge, Massachusets, pp. 232-264.

Schmitter, Philippe C. (1991), 'Change in Regime Type and Progress in International Relations,' in Emanuel Adler and Beverly Crawford (eds.), *Progress in Postwar International Relations,* Columbia University Press, New York.

Schmitter, Philippe C. (1996), 'Examining the Present Euro-Polity With the Help of Past Theories,' in Gary Marks, Fritz W. Scharpf, Philippe C. Schmitter, and Wolfgang Streeck (eds.), *Governance in the European Union,* Sage Publications, London, pp. 1-14.

Secretaría de Relaciones Económicas Internacionales de la República Argentina (1996), 'El Mercosur: Regionalismo Abierto o Un *"Building Bloc"*?' *Boletim De Integração Latino-Americana,* Edição Especial.

Seixas Corrêa, Luiz Felipe (1999), 'La visión estratégica brasileña del proceso de integración,' in Jorge Campbell (ed.), *Mercosur. Entre la Realidad y la Utopía,* CEI-Nuevohacer, Buenos Aires, pp. 229-272.

Shugart, Matthew S. and Carey, John M. (1992), *Presidents and Assemblies. Constitutional Design and Electoral Dynamics,* Cambridge University Press, New York.

Silva, Patricio (1989), 'Democratization and Foreign Policy: the Cases of Argentina and Brazil,' in Benno Galjart and Patricio Silva (eds.), *Democratization and the State in the Southern Cone. Essays on South American Politics*, CEDLA, Amsterdam.

Sorensen, G. (1992), 'Kant and Processes of Democratization: Consequences for Neorealist Thought,' *Journal of Peace Research*, Vol. 29, pp. 397-414.

Streeck, Wolfgang and Schmitter, Philippe C. (1991), 'From National Corporatism to Transnational Pluralism: Organized Interests in the Single European Market,' *Politics and Society,* Vol. 19.

Vigevani, Tullo, Mariano, Karina L. Pasquariello, and Oliveira, Marcelo Fernandez de (2000), 'Democracia e atores políticos no Mercosul,' unpublished, São Paulo.

Yeats, Alexander (1997), 'Does Mercosur's Trade Performance Raise Concerns About the Effects of Regional Trade Arrangements?' *World Bank.*

Chapter 4

A Supply-Side Theory of International Economic Institutions for the Mercosur

José Raúl Perales

Introduction

This chapter proposes a theoretical framework for understanding the formation and the development of the Mercosur. Its main proposition is that the Mercosur is an attempt by political elites in Argentina and Brazil to gain credibility for their trade policies and to recast the role of the private sector in the economies of these countries. The theoretical framework through which this perspective will be explored is based on a theory of international economic institutions that underscores the supply-side of institutional formation. The supply of an international institution, in this sense, emphasizes how politicians create organizations based on common rules and sanctioning procedures so that they may attain important policy goals that would have been impossible without the instruments and mechanisms an international institution could provide.[1] In this sense, the goals of Argentine and Brazilian politicians throughout the evolution of the Mercosur have been essentially domestic: to gain political credibility for major economic reform programs (in light of a history of unstable economic policy-making) and to recast the role of the private sector to suit the needs of open economies.

The supply aspect of international economic institutions has not received adequate attention from international relations (IR) scholars. Most work in the field usually emphasizes how governments create these institutions in reaction to opportunities or constraints offered by the international economic environment (such as globalization, increased economic interdependence, changes in global markets, and financial shocks) or in response to the demands of powerful domestic economic interests (such as exporters, bankers, or import-substituting industrialists). In both cases, government choices are constrained by the

---

[1]   Although in the literature they refer to different entities, the terms 'organization' and 'institution' here are used interchangeably (unless otherwise specified) given that the matter under discussion is the formation and development of an international body containing an organic treaty, a secretariat, a membership, and an internationally recognized legal presence.

preferences and the behavior of strategic actors, either in the international system or in the domestic scenario. While such constraints help define the context in which political negotiation and bargaining takes place, too much attention to this aspect of institution formation fails to explain how politicians can transform the preferences of these actors through institutions. In the case of domestic actors in particular, politicians may use international institutions to signal information about policy intentions, new agendas, and changes in decision-making 'styles'; and to create new material conditions through which the private sector will refocus its preferences and its links to the government. For Brazil and Argentina in the early 1990s, the formation of the Mercosur represented an attempt to achieve these objectives, as will be argued in the following pages.

This chapter will be divided as follows. First the main points of theoretical work on international institutions will be summarized in order to derive specific claims about how these institutions emerge and develop. Then what kind of behavior should be expected of international institutions in the Mercosur region will be discussed. Next the applicability of these theories to the Southern Cone will critically be evaluated, and what is missing from theoretical accounts of institution formation will be explained. Finally, a supply-side theory of international institutions will be proposed accounting for the observed behavior of Mercosur governments.

The Emergence and Development of International Economic Institutions – Existing Approaches at the International Level

While many international relations scholars typically focus on the question of whether institutions 'matter' or not (Martin and Simmons, 1998), most studies share the assumption that institutions contribute to the solution of collective action or contractual problems among states in an anarchic international system. Under the guise of 'regime theory', the study of international institutions has been dramatically influenced during the last twenty years by the literature on transaction economics. Studies have demonstrated how international institutions, regarded in a broader sense than just international organizations or bureaucracies, reduce the transaction costs of interstate cooperation by providing a set of common rules (thus helping to stabilize state preferences) and information to members of the agreement, and by monitoring compliance (thus reducing the chance of defection) (Oye, 1986, Keohane, 1984).

Scholarly attention has shifted in the last ten years to how institutions achieve these objectives. The mere presence of an international institution does not warrant interstate cooperation nor does it prevent states from cheating. Thus the choice of organizational structure (membership requirements, governing bodies, voting rules) and of rules of enforcement (dispute settlement mechanisms, sanctioning procedures) of most international institutions has assumed a central position in scholarly analyses of the sustainability of institutionalized cooperation.[2]

---

[2] See Koremenos, Lipson, and Snidal (2001).

The choice of institutional structure as such has been approached as a response to the collective action problem states face when they seek to cooperate. Two important sources of this collective action problem have been identified in the literature. The first is the strategic context of negotiation. International cooperation involves shared costs and has distributional consequences that may leave some states in a superior position relative to their partners (the classical relative gains problem identified in the literature on international cooperation).[3] Since states are concerned about how cooperation will affect their relative position in the international system, they will not engage in sustained cooperation for long-term benefits when the risk of cheating or free riding by any member of the club will result in greater costs to those who abide by the rules (and thus a relative disadvantage vis-à-vis its partners or other states in the system). The institutionalized form of cooperation among states facing this kind of dilemma usually involves substantial delegation to a third party – a supranational authority, for instance – with monitoring and sanctioning capacity (Hamlet 2000). Institutional rules (for instance, decision-making procedures and vote distribution among members) will thus reflect the type of contractual problem member states confront.

In her study on the rational choice of multilateralism, Lisa Martin (1993) proposes an instrumental approach to the formation of multilateral institutions based on the strategic dilemmas posed by different cooperation problems (collaboration, coordination, assurance, and persuasion). According to Martin, each type of cooperation problem involves a particular strategic context that institutionalized cooperation must address. State preferences over the shape and character of international institutions will reflect the strategic requirements of these situations. For instance, states facing a collaboration problem, where they must strike a policy balance and eschew their dominant strategy (the typical Prisoner's Dilemma), will seek to create international institutions emphasizing the maintenance of negotiated agreements (since each state possesses an incentive to defect from cooperation and obtain immediate rewards). This requires a certain degree of institutional centralization, so that extensive information about state behavior, careful monitoring, and formal sanctioning procedures will reduce state incentives to cheat. According to Martin, a formal organization with a clear mandate and procedural rules will satisfy the requirements of such strategic context.[4]

---

[3] Powell (1991) and Snidal (1991). To be sure, the relative-absolute gains debate has usually assumed a single equilibrium for international cooperation under the logic of a single-shot game (as in the basic Prisoner's Dilemma). The problem with this assumption is that, given an interdependent world, cooperation among multiple actors with divergent preferences leads to different equilibriums, thus exacerbating the distributional dilemma of international cooperation. See Morrow (1994).

[4] Martin also notes that, although multilateral organizations may help cooperation among states facing a collaboration problem, the norms of multilateralism (in other words, multilateralism as an institution) may actually hinder cooperation. Two characteristics

In this 'functional' perspective, the shape of an international institution will be determined by the type of strategic problem its creation was intended to solve (thus making some organizations more bureaucratically 'dense' or autonomous than others). Moreover, each of these strategic contexts is sensitive to specific exogenous circumstances, thus leading to modifications in the international institution. For instance, collaboration regimes will be more susceptible to changes of government or any sort of political instability that would lead to shorter time horizons or to a change in the information available about other states' behavior. This, in turn, would lead to pressures for bargaining and renegotiation of rules and procedures within the international institution.

Similarly, Yarbrough and Yarbrough (1992) contend that the fear of skirmishing or opportunistic behavior by any member of an international agreement bears a direct influence over the shape of an international institution. In their assessment of the organizational structure of free trade, the authors point out that when the cost of retaliation to opportunistic behavior is high and the shadow of the future is a concern, states will seek to build a trading system based on multilateral norms (if there is an international hegemony or third party enforcement); 'minilateral' norms, such as customs unions and other preferential trading agreements (if there is no clear hegemony and third party enforcement is restricted); or bilateral norms (if there is no third party enforcement, thus making the agreement self-enforcing). Although minilateral and bilateral agreements may seem as suboptimal arrangements in terms of the aggregate world economy, by solving the contractual problem of international cooperation, according to Yarbrough and Yarbrough these agreements actually introduce efficiency gains from relation-specific investment that offset the losses in world output.[5]

A second source of collective action problems for states pertains to issue-specific matters, where differences in national preferences over courses of action affect cooperation and, thus, lead to particular institutional configurations. For instance, the Single European Act (SEA) of 1986 and the ensuing internal market of the European Community (EC) has been regarded as a compromise between Britain and Denmark, on one hand, and France and Germany on the other (Garrett, 1992). Both sets of countries wanted greater competitiveness and economies of scale, but the United Kingdom preferred a substantial deregulation of economic activity across the entire EC, including automatic recognition of national standards

---

ascribed to multilateralism – indivisibility (where negotiated items are equally applicable to all states) and diffuse reciprocity (where members abide by generalized rules of equal obligation) – can present problems for sustaining cooperation. These two features of multilateral arrangements encourage free riding, since no member can be legally excluded from the benefits generated by the collaborative arrangement. It is for this reason that Martin, as well as other authors, claims that states tend to move away from these two norms of multilateralism during the implementation of negotiated bargains.

[5]   On the suboptimality of preferential trading agreements, see Bhagwati (1996), (1990), and Krugman (1993). On the relationship between customs unions and efficiency costs, see Kemp and Wan (1976).

for goods and services, while France and Germany objected to deregulation in key sectors, such as finance and industrial policy. Moreover, deepening the common market presented less developed countries in the EC (such as Greece and Ireland) with the possibility of severe economic dislocations resulting from further opening of their domestic markets. In this sense they advocated a more interventionist internal market than did France and Germany. Although the final structure of the internal market avoided specifying how the EC would control the process of deregulation, the introduction of qualified majority voting in several policy areas in the Council of Ministers (thus eliminating the unanimity rule, a major impediment to deregulation) reflects a compromise that accommodates the interests of all bargaining sides.[6]

Perhaps nowhere have different state preferences mattered more clearly in the formation of international institutions than in the creation of the Bretton Woods international monetary system. The architects of Bretton Woods shared a common view about the causes of the interwar monetary crisis; they also agreed on the need to have a multilateral payments system, stable exchange rates, and full employment (Bordo, 1993). The clash between British and American views over the appropriate institutional framework for the post-war international monetary system was based on different national concerns. The United States was particularly interested in the creation of a multilateral payments system that would avoid some of the pitfalls of bilateralism and regionalism (such as the British Commonwealth Preference system established in 1931), as had happened during the interwar years. In this sense, it favored the creation of an international fund to which deficit countries could appeal in case of a balance of payments problem by selling their own currency (whose value had been fixed par value to a value in gold) for the currency of a surplus country.

The British, on the other hand, wanted greater freedom to pursue full employment policies without much preoccupation about balance of payments. Their proposal for an international monetary system (the Keynes Plan) placed greater emphasis on the availability of international liquidity, the provision of which would be guaranteed through an international central bank, where members would run overdrafts in an international currency (called *bancor*) that would be transferred to the credit of surplus countries (Bordo, 1993). In the end, the British compromised their aspirations for the overdraft system and the amount of international liquidity set up in the system. However, the general view among analysts has been that the ensuing international institution – the IMF – was a

---

[6] A similar problem emerged during the negotiation of the European Monetary Union and the Treaty of Maastricht. Most European countries favored budgetary restraints, price stability, and responsible monetary policies in general, especially after the recessionary episodes of the 1980s. However, Germany favored a strong, independent central bank for Europe that would ensure such price stability and the proper functioning of market mechanisms across the Union. Britain and France, on the other hand, favored a less independent central bank, in the sense that such an institution, especially some of its fiscal requirements, would curtail their ability to check unemployment (Dyson and Featherstone, 1999).

compromise between the United States and Britain, facilitated in great measure by the privileged economic, political, and military position of the United States after the war (Bordo, 1993, Ikenberry, 1993, Eichengreen, 1992).

State preferences mattered in the formation of both the Bretton Woods system and the SEA only to the extent that relatively powerful states were able to exert their influence in the negotiation process in order to shape the institutional outcome. While representing a compromise among participants, the SEA was completed only after it became clear for Britain that its insistence on deregulation and openness would push France and Germany into forming a free trade area among them and create a 'two-speed' Europe that would hurt British interests in the Community (Dyson and Featherstone, 1999; Garrett, 1992; Moravcsik, 1991). Similarly, the international monetary arrangement negotiated at Bretton Woods involved a substantial British concession on some key points that could only happen as a result of American pressure and its hegemonic financial position at the conclusion of World War II. In this sense, the argument about different national preferences over institutionalized cooperation lies in how strong states exert their influence during the formation of rules and principles of international behavior. If this logic is correct, the presence of a relatively strong power – a hegemony – among a group of countries involved in a cooperative framework ought to lead to an institutional outcome that reflects the interests of said hegemony (Grieco, 1997; Moravcsik, 1991; Keohane, 1984).

The Emergence and Development of International Economic Institutions – Existing Approaches at the Domestic Level

Domestic politics is an essential factor for understanding how international economic institutions are formed and developed. The most fundamental reason for this assertion is that the norms and rules of international institutions involve distributive costs that affect domestic groups in different ways. Domestic actors will therefore have an incentive to influence how these norms and rules are drafted, negotiated, and implemented.

Scholarly analyses of this topic have usually centered on the specific role different domestic groups play, especially in terms of institutional formation phases (proposal, negotiation, ratification, implementation), the receptiveness of these domestic audiences to outcomes in each of these phases, and the mechanisms through which domestic audiences transform their preferences into outcomes. In political economic terms, under an assumption of interest-maximization, asset-holders will try to influence government policies that bear direct relevance to the returns on their assets. Their ability to organize effectively toward this goal is determined by a variety of circumstances, but in terms of incentives to act collectively, most important among these are the intensity with which policy will affect the rates of return to their assets, how dependent on public policy is their asset's rate of return, and the ease with which said assets can be employed in other activities (Frieden, 1991).

Increased economic interdependence and exposure to the international economy present domestic actors with further incentives to influence policy decisions on matters such as trade barriers and exchange rates, where policy decisions have the most direct effect on the prices of assets. The problem with internationalization is not just how different sectors will benefit from different types of policies, but also how the speed with which changes in global prices will be transmitted at the domestic level (Frieden and Rogowski, 1996). Different sectors and industries will have specific interests and preferences over the rate and the mechanisms for trade liberalization, depending on characteristics such as international competitiveness and increasing returns to scale. In this sense, lowering trade barriers and deregulating capital markets would be in the interest of export-oriented producers and holders of mobile assets. Conversely, raising tariffs and imposing capital controls would be in the interest of owners of fixed assets or producers for the domestic market. Yet in spite of incentives to lobby in order to limit the extent to which a government reduces trade barriers and other controls on international economic transactions, Frieden and Rogowski note that increases in global trade affect all states, even those where governments introduce barriers or other policy distortions. The reason is that the gap between domestic and international prices would become larger with any surge in global trade. Political conflict over trade policy will increasingly reflect this tension, especially in terms of the level of liberalization, and how it is to be pursued.

From this perspective, an international economic institution such as a preferential trade area (PTA) would emerge as a political equilibrium between domestic winners and losers from international trade. A preferential trade area permits the negotiation of commercial liberalization such that winners from tariff reductions – for instance, industries with mobile assets that can achieve economies of scale in a regional context – will receive benefits from liberalization, while potential losers – owners of immobile assets or factors of production – will continue receiving some degree of protection (Milner, 1997b). We should expect to see these cleavages reflected in some of the operational characteristics of the organization, such as in tariff reduction schemes and rules of origin.[7]

Yet how domestic political conflict over trade liberalization will manifest itself is a matter of debate among scholars, since the specification of a group's preferences does not automatically mean that political action will ensue. It is not entirely clear what kind of coalition would emerge in terms of winners and losers from trade (whether in terms of sectors, factors, or firms), especially when the relevant cleavage is in itself a point of disagreement. In the case of developed economies, where most of the theoretical work on this debate has taken place, the contemporary explosion of intra-industry trade (above 60 per cent of all

---

[7] In this sense, even if a state joins a multilateral organization such as the WTO, domestic cleavages and sectoral demands would still make politicians willing to negotiate a PTA that, although compatible with the multilateral system, affords them the opportunity to compensate losers from international trade. See Fernandez and Portes (1998) and Pahre (1998).

commercial activities for most developed countries) and of stock market capitalization makes some of these distinctions even harder to establish.[8] Such tendencies may also be found in the developing world, especially in Latin America, where the attraction of foreign direct investment (both through privatizations and new enterprises) has sought precisely to establish the kind of intra-industry links (both regionally and with advanced economies) that characterize much of contemporary global production.

Collective action problems pose additional challenges, especially because domestic political arrangements and institutions may facilitate some types of coalition formation over others, irrespective of who wins and loses from international trade. For instance, Alt et al. (1996) note that if policy-making institutions make it easy for small-scale lobbying to affect the course of trade policy (for instance, if legislative committees have substantial decision-making power; see also Martin, 2000), then the need for broad-based coalitions involving multiple sectors or factors might not be present at all. Similarly, political institutions where the costs of lobbying are substantial (for instance, large electoral districts; Verdier, 1994) might reduce the incentives for collective action and coalition formation. Power-sharing arrangements between executives and legislatures (Milner 1997a; Milner and Rosendorff, 1997), especially where preferences vary substantially between branches, agencies, and even committees, may also make a difference on the formation of international trade institutions or agreements. Finally, to the extent that the degree of party discipline allows predictions about policy proposals or voting patterns, differences in party affiliation of key policy-makers may affect the feasibility of some international bargains and of institutional solutions (Verdier, 1994, Epstein and O'Halloran, 1996).

The questions, then, seem to be just who the relevant coalition is, as well as how mobilization of a protectionist coalition will affect the formation of international economic institutions. Following the Ricardo-Viner model of trade policy formation, Frieden (1991) answers the first question by looking at asset specificity. Some factors or assets are specific to particular locations and uses, such as steel mills or a highly trained automobile worker. As stated above, it is therefore expected that owners of such factors will have an intense preference over policies that affect the survival of their enterprise. These people will have incentives to lobby for policies that increase their rates of return to their assets. Incentives should be directly proportional to the specificity of said assets. However, according to Frieden, their ability to act collectively will depend also on the level of industry

---

[8]   Global stock market capitalization reached \$35 trillion in 2000, or 110 per cent of the global GDP. In the United States alone, almost 50 per cent of all Americans own shares (*The Economist*, March 10, 2001). In this sense, workers' interests might become closer to those of managers, especially in those firms that are internationally competitive.

concentration, so that political pressure becomes easier; and on the costs of entry, so that free-riding behavior can be kept to a minimum.[9]

From this perspective, the formation of an international economic institution such as a PTA will be opposed by any concentrated industry with highly specific assets. This would be the case whenever decisions about trade policy are made at the highest possible level of government. If any such industry can mobilize effectively, it will either block the negotiations leading to trade liberalization among a group of countries, or pressure governments to negotiate institutional rules so that their industry will have a separate liberalization protocol from all other sectors or industries. Alternatively, said industry may be rewarded with some type of subsidy (such as a tax exemption or some other form of credit), or even be excluded from the PTA altogether.

Recognizing this potential for mobilization and contestation, politicians should therefore avoid any type of negotiation for a PTA (or the implementation of any trade liberalization program) when they are facing elections, since such a politically sensitive time may lead to intense opposition from organized, disaffected owners of specific assets. Conversely, governments should pursue PTAs when the owners of specific assets derive concrete benefits from institutionalized trade liberalization, such as reduction of demand for goods from countries outside the PTA (the infamous trade diversion argument), or increased productive efficiency as a result of economies of scale (Fernandez and Portes, 1998).

A recent account of the progress in European integration illustrates some of the points about international institutions and domestic politics made so far. According to Moravcsik (1998), changes in the global economy during the 1980s created a set of challenges and opportunities for European producers such that the most powerful ones would stand to gain from deeper intra-industry trade on the Continent. In order to facilitate such trade, European governments needed to reduce bureaucratic and political obstacles to the movement of capital and investment across national borders, especially in light of the European Community's (EC) stated goal of creating a single European market. Thus the stage was set for negotiations leading to the creation of a single currency and other measures of macroeconomic coordination (Treaty of Maastricht). National preferences over the contours of such coordination, themselves the result of national bargains struck between powerful producers and ruling coalitions, naturally varied among members of the EC. Interstate bargaining ensued to solve distributional conflicts created as a result of the costs of coordinating policies (for instance, adjustments to inflation targets, reduction of fiscal deficits, and other macroeconomic policies that affect the chances of successful macroeconomic coordination). Such bargaining logically followed the power structure of the European Community, with larger countries (notably France and Germany) setting

---

[9]   Alternatively, owners of specific assets could diversify their portfolios to more mobile sectors, as has been the recent case of various international industrial conglomerates. With diversification, the cost/benefit analysis behind trade policy preferences may change towards a less protectionist stance. See Schonhardt-Bailey (1991).

the parameters of the negotiation, especially through vetoes, credible threats, and side payments. When countries could not strike a particular bargain, authority was explicitly delegated to the supranational authority (the European Commission) so that individual governments could be forced to cooperate on the basis of their international commitments. Perceiving the potential benefits of such enforcement, influential producers shifted much of the focus of their lobbying activities to Brussels.

International and Domestic Approaches to the Formation of International Economic Institutions and the Mercosur

In order to derive implications from international and domestic theories of international institutions to explain the formation of the Mercosur, a brief note should be made regarding the political and economic environment in the Southern Cone during the late 1980s and early 1990s. The role of historical developments has been a frequent starting point in many accounts of European integration, especially the legacy of conflict between two key members of the European Union – France and Germany – and how institutionalized economic interdependence was regarded as the solution for making any further conflict between these two countries unthinkable (Mattli, 1999). According to some analysts, important political transformations and processes such as the creation of the EU should therefore be examined in their proper historical dimension, in order to understand the impact of path-dependence on both decisions and institutions (Pierson, 1996, 2000). Applying this logic to the Southern Cone, the emergence of the Mercosur in 1991 ought to be considered in light of a background of collapsing economies following the unraveling of the debt crisis, the transition to and consolidation of democratic governance, the repeated failure of regional integration in Latin America, and a historical rivalry between Argentina and Brazil.

Several points may help to illustrate the domestic and international scenario confronting Southern Cone leaders during this period. The early 1990s brought substantial political and economic restructuring throughout much of Latin America, especially in Argentina and Brazil, where military dictatorships gave way to democratically elected governments, in a context of extreme economic emergency. In the case of Brazil, amid fiscal crisis and bouts of hyperinflation, a new constitution was enacted in 1988. It provided for a decentralization of policy-making functions and important legal restrictions on the federal government (especially the executive branch), a reflection of the achievements of state and local politicians during the process of democratization. Accordingly, the federal government's capacity to bargain would become substantially diminished, while at the same time budgetary provisions required sizeable financial transfers from an increasingly indebted federal government to states and municipalities. Given the fragmented structure of the Brazilian political party system (where coalitions are usually short-lived), legislative majorities required major economic reforms, such as reducing the fiscal deficit, became almost unattainable under the new constitution. The result was an exclusionary policy-making style, in which the executive repeatedly surprised economic agents and political actors by announcing new plans and changes in macroeconomic policy direction in lieu of deep economic restructuring (Sola, 1994; Kinzo, 1993).

Meanwhile, a Peronist government returned to power in Argentina after an early election in 1989, the result of a crisis of governability that combined a collapsing economy, social unrest, and political deadlock. For many years, economic policy in Argentina had been the by-product of political competition among several powerful sectors and groups, who regarded control of the state as the prize through which the benefits of growth and prosperity would be distributed (Smith et al., 1994b; Palermo and Novaro, 1996). When the debt crisis of the 1980s threw the Argentine economy into a recessionary spiral involving deep episodes of hyperinflation and devaluation, a weakly-institutionalized democratic government responded by implementing emergency packages and programs (for instance, the *Plan Primavera*) that reflected political demands from important peak associations, such as the Argentine Industrial Union (UIA). Pacting became the norm for economic policy, since it was regarded as the only way to combine 'democracy plus stability'.[10] Although politically expeditious from the standpoint of President Raúl Alfonsín, these pacts further restrained the ability of the Argentine government to take the necessary measures for restructuring the economy, for it became almost impossible to distribute the burden of macroeconomic adjustment without some massive reaction and civil unrest. Thus, politically untenable plans gave way to new plans that shifted the focus attention (and consequently the distributive costs of adjustment) to an ever-changing array of measures, including price and wage controls and exchange rate fluctuations. The Peronist opposition utilized each new plan to undermine the current administration and improve its chances of seizing power. Indeed, the result was a presidential election in May 1989, seven months before its scheduled time.

Amid this seemingly turbulent scenario, formal attempts at bilateral economic cooperation between Brazil and Argentina had been launched in 1986, when both countries signed a trade accord (the Integration and Economic Cooperation Program – PICE) that focused on sectoral reductions of trade tariffs and other restrictions. Most of the goods included in this accord were capital goods. The underlying assumption was that by reducing tariffs on specific 'spearhead' sectors, competitiveness would increase so that an eventual dismantling of all tariff restrictions would be gradually achieved. Given the political and economically unstable environment in both countries, this gradual approach was the avenue policy-makers thought would liberalize trade without imposing abrupt adjustment costs on producers. In addition, it was expected that this program would lead to a symmetric trading relationship between Brazil and Argentina characterized by intra-industrial, rather than inter-industrial, specialization (Campbell, 1999). The gradualist approach floundered, however, precisely because of extremely unstable and unpredictable macroeconomic conditions in both countries. An already

---

10 This expression was actually a phrase the Argentine government used to refer to the *Plan Austral*, one of the first economic emergency packages of the new democratic government, launched in June 1985.

skeptical private sector gave little importance to trade agreements when previous attempts at regional integration and trade liberalization (especially in the late 1970s) had failed miserably.

Under these circumstances, how can we explain the emergence of an international economic institution such as Mercosur? In the late 1980s and early 1990s, Brazil and Argentina had several strategic incentives for engaging in economic cooperation. Both countries were negotiating debt rescheduling programs with the International Monetary Fund and private banks. While international lenders had been able to agree on a common response to the debt crisis of the 1980s (the so-called Paris Club), the world's largest debtors failed to act collectively to meet this crisis. Given the similarities in their debt portfolios, some type of policy coordination between Brazil and Argentina would have led to a common bargaining strategy before international creditors – in effect, setting the bases for a debtors club. Indeed, out of this experience, macroeconomic coordination became one of the explicit goals of the Mercosur integration process.

Brazil and Argentina had already been cooperating in other international areas of common interest. Both countries, as well as Uruguay (later to become the third member of Mercosur), counted among the founders of the Cairns Group of agricultural producers within the GATT system in 1986. In 1985 the two signed the Iguazú Declaration, which set a nuclear cooperation program that effectively ended any possibility of a nuclear arms race in the Southern Cone. That same year they formed the Contadora Support Group (together with Peru and Uruguay), whose purpose was to find a peaceful solution to armed conflict in Central America. Together with the Contadora Group (Panama, Colombia, Venezuela, and Mexico), their association later became the Permanent Mechanism for Consultation in 1986, otherwise known as the Rio Group, or G8.

The strategic context of the relationship between Brazil and Argentina in the early 1990s resembles the set-up of a collaboration game such as the Prisoner's Dilemma, in which the governments of both countries face similar problems (collapsing economies, domestic political instability and uncertainty, foreign debt negotiations and rescheduling, lack of progress in multilateral trade talks) and would stand much to gain from abandoning individual economic strategies in favor of a common policy framework (for instance, by reducing the externalities generated by unilateral trade and monetary policies). Information about the other government's intentions and strategies, however, presented a problem, because uncertainty was such a pervasive feature of the political context in the region at that historical moment. Moreover, as we saw before, neither government was credible regarding their economic policy announcements, which posed a further challenge for cooperation because their actions could not be reliable guides to their future behavior (Morrow, 1999). The solution to this cooperation problem would seem to be third-party enforcement through an international organization with clear rules and explicit sanctioning and monitoring capabilities (in this case, the Mercosur). By delegating power to such an organization, each government would be signaling its commitment to a common strategy and thus reinforcing international cooperation. Similarly, under such an autonomous organization, political changes within each country would have less overall effect in the pattern of international cooperation because if a new government unsuccessfully demanded renegotiation of institutional rules, defection would be heavily punished.

Given that interstate collaboration involves distributional costs and multiple institutional possibilities, as well as fears of delegating too much authority to the international institution, it is expected that the organic structure of the institution (bureaucratic divisions, governing bodies, voting procedures) should reflect a specific equilibrium, reached either through bargaining and negotiation, imposition by the strongest state among members, or both. For Mercosur, this equilibrium had to reflect several considerations: 1) the incentives to defect from cooperation were quite strong, given the time inconsistency problem of economic policy-making in most of the members of the group;[11] and 2) Brazil's size (both geographically and economically), in particular how to manage an asymmetrical relationship between the regional hegemony, a regional contender (Argentina), and two small countries (Uruguay and Paraguay).

Strategic theories of international institution formation would suggest that, given these conditions, cooperation among Southern Cone countries should take the form of a strong, independent institution to which substantial policy-making authority is delegated (such that collective action problems originating from political uncertainty and the incentive to defect can be reduced). In terms of a PTA such as Mercosur, this would involve features such as a full-fledged secretariat and an authoritative, independent dispute settlement mechanism. The secretariat can act as an institutional 'watch-dog' by providing clear information about national positions, assisting in member sanctioning, and linking issues in order to advance the process of regional economic integration (Hamlet, 2000). The dispute settlement mechanism would lead to procedural transparency and better enforcement of regional rules. Moreover, the organic structure and functions of the institution would reflect the preferences of the largest member -Brazil. Considering its economic circumstances in the early 1990s as an economic reform laggard (Smith et al., 1994b), a customs union involving Brazil in the role of dominant power would show a tendency towards a relatively higher common external tariff (CET) than what the smaller, more market-oriented countries in the group would prefer, as well as a variety of escape clauses, such as a list of exempted products from the CET (especially those in which Brazil has some degree of regional competitiveness, such as technology-intensive products). Finally, in order to reduce the political effects of asymmetry, each member of the Mercosur must have one vote in the decision-making body of the organization, in this case the Common Market Group and the Trade Commission.

---

[11] The problem of defection from economic cooperation under conditions of macroeconomic instability is closely related to an observation many economists make regarding trade liberalization, such as that envisioned under a customs union like MERCOSUR. The implementation of free trade policies should follow a successful economic stabilization program to avoid additional adjustment costs resulting from the natural effects of an open economy on the real value of the currency. See Canitrot and Junco, 1993.

From a domestic perspective, the volatile environment of Southern Cone politics in the late 1980s and early 1990s meant that almost all social sectors at that time were effectively mobilized and exerted pressures for economic policies that would offer specific rewards, especially in Argentina. PTAs were among the alternatives politicians negotiated as part of their economic packages; indeed, the first agreements signed in 1986 reflect the dynamics of such sectoral demands. Regarding a more open and inclusive trade regime such as a customs union, however, it must be noted that the benefits of free trade tend to be quite dispersed and may take longer to become evident, while the costs are usually concentrated and immediate. In this sense, domestic demands for institutionalized economic cooperation between Argentina and Brazil would seem most improbable unless such cooperation could lead to tangible gains for key economic players, particularly concentrated industries with highly specific assets. More specifically, sectors organized into peak associations with a clear hierarchy should be more capable of forming a blocking coalition to free trade initiatives, or at least negotiate substantial concessions so that they might be excluded from lower tariffs or a CET.

The level of industry concentration and organization in Argentina and Brazil reflects the presence of several major industrial conglomerates in strategic sectors, as well as firms and sectors effectively organized into powerful associations. For instance, in the case of Argentina, 30 out of 58 categories of capital goods under the Standard Commercial Classification of the Latin American Integration Association (NALADISA) exhibited a 75 per cent concentration index among the four largest producers by the time the first commercial agreements with Brazil were signed in 1986 (Porta and Fontanals, 1987). Considering such a high index, it is not surprising that when the Argentine government launched its privatization program between 1990 and early 1991, the major beneficiaries were six of the country's largest industrial conglomerates (Techint, Exxel, Soldati, Macri, Pérez Companc, and Astra) (Margheritis, 1999, Peres, 1998). Although industry concentration levels in capital goods were not as high in Brazil, several other manufactured products, such as transport material and rubber products, had concentration indices of 50 per cent and higher, while the overall average for all manufactures reached 38 per cent (Frieden, 1991). Regarding the prospects of international economic cooperation between Argentina and Brazil, these figures suggest that a major opening to international trade, especially in terms of its effects on areas such as the price of inputs, investment incentives, and competition regulations, should generate enough incentives for a concentrated group of powerful industrialists to act collectively and resist such changes.

Indeed, political bargaining over reforms had been a persistent feature of economic policy-making in Argentina and Brazil throughout the 1980s. Much of this bargaining took place between policymakers and peak associations as well as specific industries (particularly in the case of Argentina, where the previous experience with economic orthodoxy and trade liberalization imposed by the military dictatorship in the 1970s led to catastrophic losses in industrial output). Organized groups such as the Argentine Industrial Union (UIA) and the Federation of Industrialists of São Paulo (FIESP) were able to steer the course of various programs by threatening to 'exit' from productive investment, although their ability to offer inputs in terms of policy formulation (especially in the case of Brazil) was substantially smaller (Schneider 1997). Recently restored democratic governments in turn responded through the classical corporatist and clientelistic networks that for many decades had been such an important feature of interest representation in Southern Cone politics (Hagopian, 1998, 1996). According to Hagopian, corporatist arrangements with the UIA re-emerged as a result of a law restoring legal status to that organization in late 1984. In Brazil, however, the military had substantially eroded corporatist networks, so that when democracy returned in 1985, no single peak association was able to represent the interests of the business community. In this sense, clientelistic networks through members of Congress became the practice. Considering the pervasiveness of both corporatist and clientelistic networks in the region, their manifestation in the organizational structure of an economic policy bargain such as Mercosur is to be expected, in the shape of institutionalized fields for concertation between the government, the private sector, and other organized actors such as unions.

In sum, the combination of international and domestic insights into the formation of international economic institutions leads to the following 'prescription' for the Mercosur region. Four neighboring countries facing similar economic and political challenges enter into an agreement so that they will reap the benefits of sustained cooperation. Domestic political uncertainty, and consequently time inconsistent policies, presents a problem that can be resolved through strong third-party enforcement; in this case, a strong international institution with some degree of supranational authority and independent monitoring power. Considering Brazil's relative size in the region, the organizational make-up of the ensuing institution will tend to favor Brazil's interests. Yet since the two largest member states (Argentina and Brazil) are facing domestic political pressures from groups of organized producers with asset-specific interests, the regional bargain will include institutionalized fields for corporatist negotiation (as well as less formal clientelistic networking). This continuous bargaining will lead to an eschewed trade liberalization regime characterized by an escalated tariff regime and several special provisions for politically sensitive sectors.

These elements are summarized in Table 4.1.

Table 4.1 Theories of international cooperation and the choice of institutional structure in the Mercosur

	Conditions	*Cooperation problem*	*Institutional solution*	*Predicted outcome in the Mercosur*
International approaches	Strategic context	Collaboration problem	Strong third party enforcement	Secretariat with substantial functions for monitoring and enforcing rules. Independent dispute settlement mechanism
	National interests	Collaboration and distribution problem	Preferences of the strongest state should prevail	Brazil's organizational preferences should prevail
Domestic approaches	High asset specificity and industry concentration	Protectionism	Tariff breaks per sector; product exemptions, escape clauses	'Escalated' tariff regime, including lists of exceptions and special provisions for specific sectors
	Strong organizational capacity	Hostages	Corporatist bargaining and clientelistic networking at national and international levels	'Supranational' lobbying. Quasi-corporatist arrangements established in the organizational structure

Mercosur and Theories of International Cooperation – a Critical Assessment

The empirical record seems to confirm some of the predicted outcomes for the institutional design of the Mercosur. Indeed, Mercosur has often been described as an 'imperfect' customs union containing several gaps in the implementation of its common external tariff, the completion of free trade among members of the group, and the application of special regimes to its two smallest members (Uruguay and Paraguay). Its tariff structure is an escalated system divided into three categories (raw materials, semi-manufactures and industrial inputs, and fully processed goods) that apply differently to each of Mercosur's members, with Brazil obtaining the highest average tariff (see Table 4.3). Overall, the CET, taken as a production-weighted sum of the politically optimal tariffs for each country, reflects the proportional size of Brazil's total output within the group: 70 per cent of all Mercosur's production (Olarreaga and Soloaga, 1998). Looking at the entire productive platform of member countries, the sectors with the highest effective rate of tariff protection are passenger cars, trucks, and buses; electrical materials; electronic equipment; the dairy industry; beverages and food products; textiles; and plastic products (Laird, 1997). Surprisingly enough, several of these sectors are also among the most organized in Mercosur countries, at least at the time when the Treaty of Asunción was signed in 1991 and when the CET provisions were negotiated in 1994. Of particular relevance in this sense are automobiles (which have a separate commercial protocol from the customs union), and electronic equipment and electrical materials (part of the first sectoral agreements between Brazil and Argentina in 1986, some of which are also under a separate protocol).

Table 4.2 Tariff escalation and tariff ranges in the Mercosur, 1995 and final (2006) (Percentages)

Product and processing	Argentina	Brazil	Paraguay	Uruguay	Average	Final
1st stage of processing (raw materials)	6.3	6.4	6.2	6.1	6.3	6.3
Semi-processed (semi-manufactures and industrial inputs)	9.3	9.3	9.0	8.6	9.1	9.4
Fully processed goods	12.0	14.7	10.2	13.1	12.5	13.3

Source: Laird (1997).

Similarly, elements of corporatist contacts between governments and the private sector can be seen in different parts of the Mercosur, although their overall influence on policy decisions is not proportional to the importance of business within national economies or to its ability to organize and lobby. The Treaty of Asunción in 1991 created eleven working subgroups under the Common Market Group, the 'executive arm' of the Mercosur. These subgroups have been in charge of dealing with all technical aspects regarding negotiations over the form and extent of economic integration in the region, especially between 1991-1994, when the CET was being designed. Private entrepreneurs have actively participated in many of the subgroups. Moreover, in 1995, as a result of the Ouro Preto Protocol, several sectoral committees were set up in each of the member states of the Mercosur. Their purpose was to establish concerted action between government, business, and labor in order to propose policies that would lead to regional harmonization and a deepening of the integration process. These sectoral committees report directly to the executive branch of each member state, which then takes the committees' recommendations to the Common Market Group and the Common Market Council. An Industrial Council of the Mercosur, comprising peak associations of industrialists from all member states, acts as a transnational lobby for the private sector, although it was not officially recognized until 1994. Finally, sectoral, intra-industry agreements have always been encouraged, since it is considered that closer transnational business relations lead to a faster pace of regional integration.

Nevertheless, Mercosur remains a feeble, shallow international institution, extremely dependent on intergovernmental bargaining for its functioning. While a small secretariat exists in Montevideo, its duties are merely clerical (at best an information center for business and government officials) and its resources are quite limited. There is no supranational authority such as a court of justice or regional legislature that can enforce agreements or monitor compliance. Although the Brasilia Protocol of 1991 established a dispute settlement mechanism, it has been used only on few occasions, the first time in 1997. Disputes among member states are usually settled through the personal intervention of presidents, ministers, or other officials of the executive branch of member states. In spite of persistent recommendations for further institutionalization of the Mercosur in order to deepen the process of integration (Laird, 1997, Bouzas, 1996), politicians in all member states repeatedly refuse this alternative, calling it an 'unnecessary bureaucratization' that does not fit with Mercosur's goals of faster integration through political will and direct bargaining.[12] What can explain this attitude toward institutionalization among these politicians?[13]

To be fair, regional economic bureaucracies have a sour history in Latin America. Throughout the 1960s and 1970s grandiose institutions purporting to create a Latin American common market failed catastrophically, mostly due to the fact that they lacked proper grounding in the economic and commercial reality of most countries at the time. Until the 1990s, intra-regional trade had always been extremely scarce in Latin America. Under the import substitution model of development, negotiations for tariff reductions among groups of countries basically sought to expand markets for protected industries, thus making these early integration efforts part of industrial policy programs rather than genuine trade agreements. When productivity floundered, the benefits of international trade could not be materialized because of piecemeal agreements containing provisions that still afforded inefficient sectors substantial protection over domestic markets. The process of economic integration stalled and regional bureaucracies became useless

---

[12]   The most eloquent exponent of this perspective is Carlos S. Menem, former president of Argentina, who even wrote a book on the subject, entitled *¿Qué es el Mercosur?* (Menem, 1996).

[13]   Deeper institutionalization was originally proposed by the smaller members of Mercosur, especially Argentina and Uruguay, as a mechanism for containing the overwhelming weight of Brazil. However, in spite of the strong European influence in many leaders' conception of the end goal of regional integration in the Southern Cone, their calls for a stronger institution never resembled anything like an independent supranational institution.

drags on national budgets. Thus, when Mercosur was launched in 1991, following an abrupt turn toward market-oriented economic policies throughout the region, shallow institutionalization could very well have been a further expression of the political rupture with the institutions of the old import substitution economic model.

The persistence of corporatist policy networks in the Mercosur, however, casts doubts on the extent to which politicians actually broke off with the 'old model'. If anything, Mercosur seems to be taking these traditional structures of domestic interest representation and shifting them to the transnational scene, just as it is trying to create a new regulatory regime for trade policy-making in Argentina and Brazil. This apparent contradiction casts doubts on the feasibility of strong third-party enforcement in the Mercosur, as predicted by traditional theories of international institutions, even considering the strategic context in the region.[14] Deepened economic cooperation and interdependence between Brazil and Argentina, although moving through stop-and-go patterns not entirely unlike those witnessed in Europe between the 1960s and 1980s, reached unprecedented levels by the mid-1990s (as measured by the percentage increase in intra-regional trade), much faster than any observer had expected (Reid, 1996). Such relative success, in spite of leaders' opposition to a supranational bureaucracy, is indicative that executive preferences over economic policy making, including the shape of international cooperation, played a more complex role in the formation and development of the Mercosur than the almost residual function accorded to the executive in traditional theories of international institutions. What is missing, in this sense, is a supply-side theory of the process, in which executive preferences and political entrepreneurship constitute the source of institutionalized cooperation.

A Supply Side Theory of the Mercosur

As we have seen before, critical economic conditions in the late 1980s and early 1990s presented leaders in the Southern Cone with the major challenge of restructuring their economies along market-oriented principles. One of the most important aspects of this new setting was trade liberalization, a move that had been substantially opposed by the private sector when it was first attempted in the orthodox experiments of the 1970s, and had remained a problematic matter since. Especially in the case of Argentina, absence of capital, low productivity, technological lags, as well as gains from protectionism (such as industrial concentration and oligopolistic behavior in the case of industrial conglomerates), informed trade policy preferences throughout much of the private sector. While the

---

[14] Even in Europe, where successful models of corporatist governance had sustained a delicate economic balance and permitted small states such as Austria and Sweden to adjust to changes in the international economic order, the apparent incompatibility of their corporatist structures with supranational institutions will soon become a challenge for national and regional policy-makers. On the logic of European corporatist arrangements, see Katzenstein (1985).

crisis inflicted losses to entrepreneurs, their willingness to consider some degree of economic openness did not make them receptive to an encompassing trade liberalization program, as political leaders purported to accomplish (Weyland, 1996). The problem for politicians in this sense, then, laid in finding ways to change the preferences of the private sector.

Politicians not only had to deal with a relatively unreceptive private sector, but also with a credibility problem that affected the implementation of their economic policy announcements. As we had seen before, post-authoritarian governments in the Southern Cone confronted the debt crisis and the virtual collapse of their national economies with limited resources and policy instruments. At the same time the new political elites needed to consolidate democratic governance and handle demands from mobilized sectors that were seeking effective participation after years of repressive governments. The result of this particular combination, in terms of economic policy, was time inconsistency: a leader would announce a plan or strategy to stave off the crisis, but pressures from society and from the opposition made some of the tougher parts of the economic programs politically untenable. Decision-makers would compromise; the most immediate aspects of the crisis would be temporarily relieved (especially the rise in consumer prices), only to return more violently as soon as the structural causes of the economic emergency (such as fiscal deficits or balance of payments problems) re-emerged. Politicians would then respond with new plans and emergency measures. Private actors, realizing politicians' predicament, anticipated policy failure (especially inflation and exchange rate targets) and acted accordingly, spending massively now to avoid future currency depreciation and consumer price hikes. Prices would respond to the upsurge in demand and inflationary pressures would set in, thus making policy failure a self-fulfilling prophecy. The hyperinflationary emergency cycle would start again.

By the early 1990s, the need for a new regulatory framework leading to a different, less uncertain policy-making setting became a crucial piece of the economic reform puzzle for the newly elected governments of Brazil and Argentina. In this sense, the goals of politicians were twofold: to create a different bargaining scenario with the private sector, as well as to change entrepreneurs' policy preferences. In order to break the time inconsistency trap decision-makers needed to establish the credibility of their commitments to reform, while at the same time maintain some flexibility and discretion over the course of reform programs. In monetary affairs discretion was one of the sources of the hyperinflationary cycle, since printing money (often without proper reserves to back it up) was always an option whenever demands for redistributive policies after hikes in consumer prices reached conflictive levels.[15] Politicians solved the problem of discretion by explicitly tying their hands through fixed exchange rates (a currency board in Argentina in 1991 and a crawling peg system in Brazil in 1994). These policies, in addition to investment deregulation and privatization,

---

[15]   In Argentina the problem of monetary discretion was compounded by the fact that the governments in that country had typically financed their budget deficits and overall spending by printing money, as well as external borrowing.

were meant to kill inflation and attract foreign capital, yet they also put pressure on several domestic producers, particularly owners of specific assets who would now face foreign competition.

If the government tied its hands with respect to monetary policy, newly disaffected entrepreneurs could find a space for extracting concessions from the government in trade policy, where the opportunity costs of lobbying against reform would be considerably smaller. Across-the-board trade liberalization would introduce further incentives for such lobbying activities, especially since openness would undermine the relative benefits of sectoral agreements. Reformist governments, anticipating this reaction, needed to reduce business opposition, especially in the long run, as economic restructuring gained momentum. In this sense, the logic of forming an international trade institution lay in the benefits of reciprocal commercial concessions (Pahre, 1998), so that the distributive costs of tariff reductions could be somewhat diminished and private support for the reforms might be secured. Moreover, by linking trade reform to an international bargain (Lohmann, 1997), leaders would be reinforcing the credibility of their commitments to economic openness. Recalling the strategic scenario in the Southern Cone during this period, this would be a further reason to eschew individual trade reform strategies in favor of a common framework.

In this sense, the emergence of the Mercosur in 1991 and its deepening in 1994 coincide with the launching of two major economic reforms in Argentina and Brazil: the Convertibility Plan and the *Real* Plan (see Table 4.3). The choice of a customs union over other forms of PTAs conforms to the commitment problem these governments were facing: the CET leads to stronger policy coordination among countries, thus reducing the incentives for unilateral action. The international rules and constraints of a customs union create the sort of stable political environment that leads to fairly stable predictions about trade policy behavior. This would substantially reduce the time consistency problem of Argentine and Brazilian economic policy-making. While it may seem that a strong, independent international institution ought to be the best way to demonstrate credibility of policy commitments (both domestic and international), for the two largest countries in the Mercosur a 'weak' institution that depends heavily on executive control is actually the best outcome.[16] It affords leaders a macroeconomic instrument with which to bargain and build 'institutionalized' linkages to the private sector based on a policy framework in which the executive proposes the rules of the game, while the private sector is accorded a minor technical role. This is especially true in the case of Brazil, where communication channels between the government and business were substantially eroded (to the disadvantage of the executive) at the onset of its economic reform program (Hagopian, 1998).

---

[16] Cooperation between Brazil and Argentina would remain possible under a weak institution as the three necessary conditions for sustained international cooperation – repeat play, issue linkage, and reputation – would still be present (Mattli, 1999; Lohmann, 1997).

This approach to the origins of Mercosur leads to several important conjectures regarding its development. An interesting observation on the deepening of integration in the Southern Cone is that it tends to occur whenever there is a deep macroeconomic crisis (in at least one of the larger members) that creates a new bargaining 'game' between governments and business (see Table 4.3). This observation conforms to expectations about institutional development given the explanation for Mercosur presented in this study, particularly in terms of the credibility of government commitments to trade reform. Bearing in mind how the articulation of executive preferences and their relationship to business determined institutional choice in the Mercosur, a more systematic analysis of its development must look at the role of the executive throughout the process.

Table 4.3 International and domestic policy linkages in the Southern Cone

	1991 *Treaty of Asunción* *(Mercosur founded)* *March 26*	*1994* *Ouro Preto Protocol* *(Institutional configuration of* *the customs union)* *Ratified December 17*
Argentina	Convertibility Law (Currency board) March 24	'Tequila' effects of the Mexican devaluation of the peso (December 1994-March 1995) Constitutional reform
Brazil	Collor II Plan (Recession, forced devaluation, tariff cuts, orthodox measures) February 1991-October 1992	*Real* Plan (Crawling peg currency regime) June 1993-March 1994 Presidential election

Decree authority was one of the most readily available tools executives in Brazil and Argentina used to circumvent intractable obstacles to their economic reform programs. These decrees were politically validated under a category labeled 'necessity and urgency', which allowed the executive to implement measures regarding taxes, duties, salaries, and privatizations, without congressional approval, even if any of these measures involve circumventing the constitution (Carey and Shugart, 1998). In the case of Brazil, the collective action problem of obtaining legislative support for any economic reform measure, and the institutional difficulty in building prolonged coalitions, led presidents Fernando Collor and Itamar Franco to resort to this practice. In this sense, the use of decrees reflected a problem in executive-legislative relations resulting from the 1988 Constitution rather than the whims of overpowered presidents. In the case of Argentina, President Carlos Menem's use of decrees served to build presidential authority under intense economic pressures and a potential crisis of governability.

In both cases, however, some economic reform policies moved forward under the leadership of empowered presidents who were able to take advantage of political opportunities and institutional resources to advance their agendas.

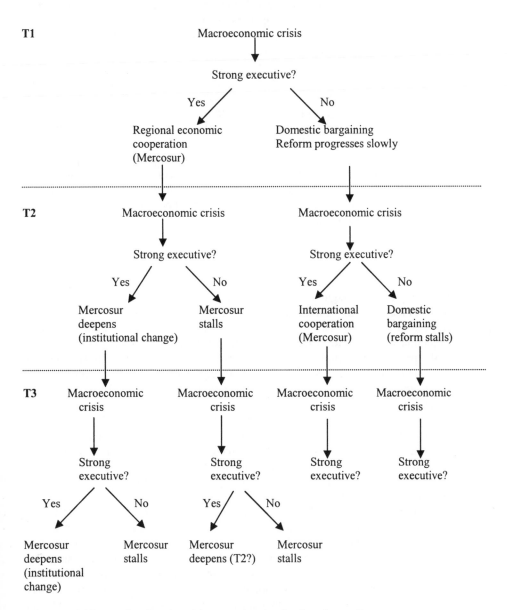

Figure 4.1 The path of regional integration in the Southern Cone

In view of how Mercosur reflects some of these presidential prerogatives, as well as the importance of executive-level bargaining among member states, changes in the power of presidents should have repercussions in the pace of regional integration in the Southern Cone. In this sense, weak presidencies or waning presidential authority in Argentina or Brazil should result in a slowdown of the integration process. While a macroeconomic crisis may set the stage for a new round of regional negotiations (especially as the economies of Argentina and Brazil grow more interdependent), the context of domestic bargaining, in terms of how proactive presidents are in setting the terms of the policy debate and pushing their agendas, will determine whether such regional bargaining will occur. Presidents with a strong support coalition (in terms of party discipline, in the case of Argentina, or winning coalitions in Congress, in the case of Brazil) should be able to bargain internationally more effectively and thus deepen Mercosur when economic crises occur. This conjecture about international cooperation is consonant with analysts who have observed that economic reforms are deeper around the time of elections, be those presidential or mid-term, since they offer winners the opportunity of recasting coalitions in support of their policy programs (Hagopian, 1998; Remmer, 1993).

Conclusion

This chapter has sought to provide a supply-side theory of the formation and development of the Southern Cone Common Market (Mercosur). Its main proposition has been that the Mercosur constitutes an attempt by political elites in Argentina and Brazil to gain credibility for their trade policies and to recast the role of the private sector in the economies of these countries. The framework through which this proposition has been explored focuses on the supply-side, an area often neglected in the study of international economic institutions. 'How' institutions matter (Martin and Simmons, 1998) has typically been defined in terms of a relationship between the type of cooperation problem states face, or in terms of the challenges governments face (both domestic and international), and the political 'solutions' most convenient for the situation. Thus, one is presented with a demand-side view of international institutions, whereby the creation and the development of an institution can frequently be determined as the aggregation of interests of the parties concerned.

This detracts from a deeper understanding of an important characteristic of international institutions: as international bargains, they may be subject to – or conditioned by – the power of their creators. Politicians may create an international institution to solve myriad problems, but also to introduce political or economic changes at the domestic level that would otherwise be less viable (Gourevitch, 1978). Considering how the 'functional' aspects of international institutions have received much of the attention in scholarly work on the subject, it would seem appropriate to expand our notion of functionality to incorporate political entrepreneurship as an agent that sets the tone for the creation and development of international institutions. As evidenced by the case of the Mercosur, institutions may become instrumental in signaling the political intentions of a reformist government; in the crafting of political coalitions supporting trade liberalization; and in the creation of domestic links such as neo-corporatist arrangements between the state and the private sector.

References

Alt, James A., Frieden, Jeffry, Gilligan, Michael, Rodrik, Dani and Rogowski, Ronald (1996), 'The Political Economy of International Trade: Enduring Puzzles and an Agenda for Inquiry,' *Comparative Political Studies*, Vol. 29, pp. 689-717.

Bates, Robert (1997), *Open-Economy Politics: The Political Economy of the World Coffee Trade*, Princeton University Press, Princeton, NJ.

Bouzas, Roberto (1996), 'La agenda económica del MERCOSUR: Desafíos de política a corto y mediano plazo,' *Integración y Comercio* (INTAL-BID), Vol. 1, pp. 64-85.

Campbell, Jorge (ed.) 1999), *MERCOSUR: entre la realidad y la utopía*, Buenos Aires: Centro de Economía Internacional / Nuevohacer – Grupo Editor Latinoamericano.

Carey, John M. and Shugart, Matthew Soberg (eds.) (1998), *Executive Decree Authority*, Cambridge University Press, New York.

Dyson, Kenneth and Featherstone, Kevin (1999), *The Road to Maastricht: Negotiating Economic and Monetary Union*, Oxford University Press, New York.

Eichengreen, Barry (1992), *Golden Fetters: The Gold Standard and the Great Depression 1919-1939*, Oxford University Press, New York.

Epstein, David and O'Halloran, Sharyn (1996), 'The Partisan Paradox and the U.S. Tariff, 1877-1934,' *International Organization*, Vol. 50, pp. 301-324.

Fernández, Raquel and Portes, Jonathan (1998), 'Returns to Regionalism: An Analysis of Nontraditional Gains from Regional Trade Agreements, *The World Bank Economic Review*, Vol. 12(2), pp. 197-220.

Frieden, Jeffrey (1991), *Debt, Development, and Democracy: Modern Political Economy and Latin America, 1965-1985*, Princeton University Press, Princeton, NJ.

Frieden, Jeffrey, and Rogowski, Ronald (1996), 'The Impact of the International Economy on National Policies: An Analytical Overview,' in Keohane and Milner (eds.), *Internationalization and Domestic Politics*, Cambridge University Press, New York.

Garrett, Geoffrey (1992), 'International Cooperation and Institutional Choice: The European Community's Internal Market,' *International Organization*, Vol. 46, pp. 533-560.

Gourevitch, Peter (1996), 'Squaring the Circle: The Domestic Sources of International Cooperation,' *International Organization*, Vol. 50(2), pp. 349-373.

Gourevitch, Peter (1986), *Politics in Hard Times: Comparative Responses to International Economic Crises*, Cornell University Press, Ithaca, NY.

Gourevitch, Peter (1978), 'The Second-Image Reversed: International Sources of Domestic Politics,' *International Organization*, Vol. 32, pp. 881-912.

Grieco, Joseph (1997), 'Systemic Sources of Variation in Regional Institutionalization in Western Europe, East Asia, and the Americas,' in Edward Mansfield and Helen Milner (eds.), *The Political Economy of Regionalism*, Columbia University Press, New York.

Hagopian, Frances (1996), *Traditional Politics and Regime Change in Brazil*, Cambridge University Press, New York.

Hagopian, Frances (1998), 'Negotiating Economic Transitions in Liberalizing Polities: Political Representation and Economic Reform in Latin America,' Harvard University, Weatherhead Center for International Affairs, Cambridge, MA.

Hamlet, Lawrence (2000), 'Cooperation Problems, Secretariat Solutions: States, International Secretariats, and the Politics of Institutional Design,' Paper presented at the 41st Annual Convention of the International Studies Association.

Keohane, Robert O. (1984), *After Hegemony: Cooperation and Discord in the World Political Economy*, Princeton University Press, Princeton, NJ.

Kinzo, Maria D'Alva G. (ed.) (1993), *Brazil: The Challenges of the 1990s*, Institute of Latin American Studies (University of London) and British Academic Press, London.

Koremenos, Barbara, Lipson, Charles, and Snidal, Duncan (2001), 'The Rational Design of International Institutions,' *International Organization*, Vol. 55, pp. 761-800.

Laird, Sam (1997), 'MERCOSUR: Objectives and Achievements,' Presented at the Third Annual World Bank Conference on Development in Latin America and the Caribbean, Montevideo, (June 29 - July 1).

Lohmann, Susanne (1997), 'Linkage Politics,' *Journal of Conflict Resolution*, Vol. 41(1), pp. 38-67.

Margheritis, Ana (1999), *Ajuste y reforma en Argentina (1989-1995): la economía política de las privatizaciones*, Nuevohacer/Grupo Editor Latinoamericano, Buenos Aires.

Martin, Lisa (1993), 'The Rational State Choice of Multilateralism,' in Ruggie (ed.), *Multilateralism Matters: The Theory and Praxis of an Institutional Form*, Columbia University Press, New York.

Martin, Lisa and Simmons, Beth (1998), 'Theories and Empirical Studies of International Institutions,' *International Organization*, vol. 52, pp. 729-758.

Mattli, Walter (1999), *The Logic of Regional Integration: Europe and Beyond.* Cambridge, Cambridge University Press, UK.

Menem, Carlos (1996), *¿Qué es el MERCOSUR?*, Editorial Ciudad Argentina, Buenos Aires.

Milner, Helen (1997a), *Interests, Institutions, and Information: Domestic Politics and International Relations*, Princeton, Princeton University Press, NJ.

Milner, Helen (1997b), 'Industries, Governments, and Regional Trade Blocs,' in Edward Mansfield and Helen Milner (eds.), *The Political Economy of Regionalism*, Columbia University Press, New York.

Milner, Helen V. and Rosendorff, Peter (1997), 'Democratic Politics and International Trade Negotiations: Elections and Divided Government as Constraints on Trade Liberalization,' *Journal of Conflict Resolution*, Vol. 41(1), pp. 117-146.

Moravcsik, Andrew (1991), 'Negotiating the Single European Act: National Interests and Conventional Statecraft in the European Community,' *International Organization*, Vol. 45, pp. 19-56.

Moravcsik, Andrew (1998), *The Choice for Europe: Social Purpose and State Power from Messina to Maastricht*, Ithaca, NY: Cornell University Press.

Morrow, James D. (1994), 'Modeling the Forms of International Cooperation: Distribution vs. Information,' *International Organization*, Vol. 48, pp. 387-423.

Morrow, James D. (1999), 'The Strategic Setting of Choices: Signaling, Commitment, and Negotiation in International Politics,' in David A. Lake and Robert Powell (eds.), *Strategic Choice and International Relations*, Princeton, NJ: Princeton University Press.

Olarreaga, Marcelo and Soloaga, Isidro (1998), 'Endogenous Tariff Formation: The Case of MERCOSUR,' *The World Bank Economic Review*, Vol. 12(2), pp. 297-320.

Oye, Kenneth (ed.) 1986), *Cooperation Under Anarchy*, Princeton University Press, Princeton, NJ.

Pahre, Robert D. (1998), 'Reactions and Reciprocity: Tariffs and Trade Liberalization from 1815 to 1914,' *Journal of Conflict Resolution*, Vol. 42, pp. 467-492.

Palermo, Vicente and Marcos, Novaro (1996), *Política y poder en el gobierno de Menem*, Facultad Latinoamericana de Ciencias Sociales / Grupo Editorial Norma, Buenos Aires.

Peres, Wilson (ed.) 1998), *Grandes empresas y grupos industriales latinoamericanos*, Siglo Veintiuno Editores / CEPAL, México.

Pierson, Paul (1996), 'The Path to European Integration: A Historical Institutionalist Analysis,' *Comparative Political Studies,* vol. 29, pp. 123-163.

Pierson, Paul (2000), 'Increasing Returns, Path Dependence, and the Study of Politics,' *American Political Science Review* 94, pp. 251-268.

Porta, Fernando and Fontanals, Jorge (1987), 'La integración Argentina-Brasil en bienes de capital: perfil de sectores y empresas vinculados a la primera negociación,' Presidencia de la Nación, Secretaría de Planificación, Buenos Aires.

Powell, Robert (1991), 'Absolute and Relative Gains in International Relations Theory,' *American Political Science Review,* Vol. 85, pp. 1303-1321.

Reid, Michael (1996), 'Remapping South America: A Survey of MERCOSUR,' *The Economist,* 12 October 1996.

Remmer, Karen L. (1993), 'The Political Economy of Elections in Latin America, 1980-1991,' *American Political Science Review,* Vol. 87, pp. 393-407.

Schneider, Ben Ross (1997), 'Big Business and the Politics of Economic Reform: Confidence and Concertation in Brazil and Mexico,' in Sylvia Maxfield and Ben Ross Schneider (eds.), *Business and the State in Developing Countries,* Cornell University Press, Ithaca, NY.

Schonhardt-Bailey, Cheryl (1991), 'Specific Factors, Capital Markets, Portfolio Diversification, and Free Trade: Domestic Determinants of the Repeal of the Corn Laws,' *World Politics,* Vol. 43, pp. 545-569.

Smith, William C., Acuña Carlos and Gamarra, Eduardo A. (eds.) (1994b), *Democracy, Markets, and Structural Reform in Latin America: Argentina, Bolivia, Brazil, Chile, and Mexico,* North-South Center, University of Miami / Transaction Publishers, Miami, FL.

Snidal, Duncan (1991), 'Relative Gains and the Pattern of International Cooperation,' *American Political Science Review,* Vol. 85, pp. 701-727.

Sola, Lourdes (1994), 'Gobernabilidad, reforma fiscal y democratización, Brasil en una perspectiva comparada,' *Desarrollo Económico,* Vol. 33(132), pp. 483-514.

Verdier, Daniel (1994), *Democracy and International Trade: Britain, France and the United States, 1860-1990,* Princeton University Press, Princeton, NJ.

Weyland, Kurt (1996), 'Risk Taking in Latin American Economic Restructuring: Lessons from Prospect Theory,' *International Studies Quarterly,* Vol. 40, pp. 185-208.

Yarbrough, Beth V. and Yarbrough, Robert M. (1992), *Cooperation and Governance in International Trade: The Strategic Organizational Approach,* Princeton University Press Princeton, NJ.

PART III
Power Perspectives

Chapter 5

Power and Regionalism: Explaining Regional Cooperation in the Persian Gulf

Scott Cooper and Brock Taylor*

Introduction

Scholars of the first wave of postwar regional economic cooperation focused almost exclusively on neo-functionalist theories based on institutional spillover from one issue area to the next (Haas, 1958; 1961; Haas and Schmitter, 1964; Nye, 1968; Schmitter, 1969; Lindberg and Scheingold, 1971). But with the widely acknowledged failure of neo-functionalist explanations, the second wave of regional cooperation has been studied from much more diverse theoretical vantage points (Haas, 1976; Mansfield and Milner, 1999).

This chapter highlights one strand of that theoretical revival: the insertion of realism into the debate. A number of scholars have focused on power distributions to explain the origins of particular regional efforts. For example, several authors have pointed to *global power disparities* as a leading cause of regionalism. Grieco (1999) and Crone (1993) focus on the hegemonic power of the United States after World War II; they explain the pattern of regional economic cooperation in Europe and Asia as a function of contrasting U.S. security interests in the two regions. On the other hand, Krasner's enduringly controversial Hegemonic Stability Theory (1976) links regionalism with *weakening* global hegemony. He uses regionalism as an indicator of declining economic openness, and argues therefore that regionalism is more likely as a reaction to hegemonic decline.

Other authors focus on *regional power disparities* rather than on the global system. For example, Mattli (1999) proposes that beneficial regional cooperation is only achieved when there is a benevolent regional leader to 'supply' cooperation; the leader's role includes creating a focal point solution and resolving distributional issues by the use of side payments. Contesting Mattli's assumption of mutually beneficial cooperation, Gruber (2000) argues that powerful regional states can structure the

* We express appreciation to Hein Goemans, Quinn Mecham, and Wade Jacoby for helpful comments. An earlier version of this chapter was presented at the International Studies Association convention in February 2001.

choice of regional institutions in such a way that weaker states have little choice but to join, even though they would be better off with the status quo. He uses this model to assert that the pattern of European and North American economic cooperation resulted from the ability of powerful states to institutionalize their preferences at the expense of weaker partners. Grieco (1996) suggests the opposite possibility: weak states may structure regional cooperation in order to bind stronger partners. He too analyzes the West European case, but concludes that the deepening of regional monetary institutions in the 1990s was driven in large part by the desires of weaker states like France and Italy to increase their voice vis-á-vis Germany within regional institutions.

Other scholars point out an additional possibility within regions: weak states may actively avoid and even undermine regionalism in order to reduce the coercive power of strong states. For example, Cooper (1999, ch. 7) argues that regional currencies are unlikely in regions where one state predominates, because weaker states will be concerned about their bargaining power within regional institutions. And in an innovative argument, Grieco (1997) suggests that weak states are especially concerned about *changes* in regional power distributions. That is, weak states in regions with a stable balance of power have little to fear from increased institutionalization, but regional economic cooperation is unlikely when power distributions are changing. Insecure, weak states prevent regionalism because they fear locking themselves into long-term relations with stronger states where the bulk of the relative gains will accrue to, and perhaps be misused by, their stronger partners.

In short, there is no single widely accepted realist theory of the link between power and regional economic cooperation, but rather a proliferation of contradictory hypotheses. Many of these theories purport to explain the same cases, but do so in dramatically different ways. As a result, current realist theory fails to provide a generalizable explanation for regional cooperation.

We hope to contribute to the development of a more generalizable explanation by turning to the well-developed literature on alliances. Alliance theory, after all, has been widely used to explain patterns of regional security cooperation. In our opinion, the time has come to see what light it might shed on other kinds of regional cooperation.

Joanne Gowa (1994) explicates the crucial theoretical link between what was once called the 'high politics' of alliances and the 'low politics' of economic cooperation. She shows that security cooperation and economic cooperation are functionally linked. When economic ties correspond to alignment patterns, the benefits of trade for states are two-fold. Most obviously, states reap all the direct benefits of free trade predicted by modern economic theory, and can convert those economic gains into political power. But states also reap 'security externalities' from their allies' economic gains. Allies' benefits from trade increase their wealth, therefore increasing the economic base of their power, and often their military spending too. And having more powerful allies increases each state's overall security. Thus, as Jacob Viner (1929) suggested, there is good reason to believe that security alignments and economic cooperation will go hand in hand. Regional economic cooperation might then be a substitute for, a complement to, or a steppingstone toward regional security cooperation. The alliance literature and the regional economic cooperation literature, too long analytically separate, should begin to merge.

As a first step in that direction, the remainder of this chapter applies Stephen Walt's well-known and highly developed balance-of-threat theory (1987) to the issue of regional *economic* cooperation. Walt uses case studies of alignment patterns in the modern Middle East to show that states balance not simply against rising powers, but against rising threats. Powerful states do not provoke a balancing coalition unless they are perceived as threatening. Applied to regional economic cooperation, Walt's argument suggests that economic blocs are likely to coalesce to counter external threats. Regional cooperation would be driven more by threats outside the bloc than dynamics within the bloc.

Rather than attempting a comprehensive empirical test of realism and regionalism, we choose a single compelling case: the formation of the Gulf Cooperation Council (GCC) in 1981 by Saudi Arabia and its five smaller Persian Gulf neighbors, Kuwait, Bahrain, Qatar, the United Arab Emirates, and Oman. Despite its recent origins, the GCC exhibits the most extensive economic cooperation in the Middle East region. Among other achievements it has eliminated customs duties on intra-regional products and harmonized external tariff schedules by setting a common minimum tariff level. The GCC has also fully integrated its capital markets. The GCC also has some alliance functions (enough that it has commonly been described in the security literature as an alliance) although these have been weakly implemented. In sum, the Gulf Cooperation Council is an interesting mix of trade and investment cooperation with weak security cooperation (Chawla, 1991, pp. 71-77; UNCTAD 1996, pp. 83-86; Twinam, 1992; Tripp, 1995, pp. 293-95; Zahlan, 1989, pp. 135-40; Peterson, 1988, pp. 169-70; Priess, 1996).

We choose to focus on the GCC because it is a most likely case for realism. It should easily be explained by realist theories because of the high salience of military and security issues in the Middle East region in general and the Gulf of the 1980s in particular. If realism cannot explain patterns of regional cooperation in the 'dog eat dog' world of the modern Middle East, it is hard to believe that it can provide a generally convincing explanation for regionalism.[1] It is also a most likely case for Walt since the Middle East is the crucible in which he successfully tested his balance-of-threat theory and because the GCC shares many alliance characteristics. Walt himself specifically describes the GCC as a balancing alignment 'intended to limit potential pressure from both Iran and the Soviet Union' (1987, p. 270).

In partial support of Walt, we find that the formation of GCC economic cooperation *was* powerfully affected by the rising Iranian threat to the Gulf. But we show that balance-of-threat theory mischaracterizes the mechanism for GCC cooperation. Iran's primary threat to the Gulf states was internal rather than external.

The Gulf Cooperation Council was formed roughly two years after the Iranian revolution brought a territorially revisionist regime to power in Iran. But, upon closer inspection, balance-of-threat theory fails to explain either the *timing* or the *nature* of GCC cooperation. When Gulf cooperation began in 1981, Iran was on the defensive in its war with Iraq and in no position to militarily threaten the Gulf states. More importantly, the GCC was far more effective at economic cooperation directed at

---

[1] Of course, the theory might still be useful in specific cases of regionalism even if it failed to provide a general explanation.

reducing domestic unrest than at external security cooperation. The GCC did create a weak security alliance, but implementation was largely superficial even before the Gulf War. In addition to economic cooperation, the GCC has paid more attention to intelligence cooperation to reduce domestic dissent.

The Gulf Cooperation Council can be better explained by looking at the *internal* security threats to these regimes. Steven David (1991) points out that Third World governments are at least as likely to be deposed by internal opposition as by external powers. For this reason, regional economic cooperation is more likely to be directed at maintaining internal stability than dealing with external challenges. We show that religious minority groups – i.e., Shiites in Sunni-dominated Gulf states – posed a real threat to Gulf regimes in the aftermath of the Iranian revolution. Emboldened by the example and propaganda of Iran, Shiite minorities in the Gulf states became increasingly assertive in pushing for political change. Thus, the timing of the GCC's formation in 1981, only two years after the Iranian revolution, is more closely related to the *domestic* threats facing GCC regimes than to an external Iranian military threat.

Once we understand the essentially domestic nature of the threat to GCC monarchs, we understand the choice of issue areas for cooperation. Political coordination created greater unity, thereby enhancing regime legitimacy in member states. Investment and trade cooperation within the GCC was particularly important because economic effects would be felt most by restive domestic groups. Increased sharing of intelligence about political dissidents directly improved regime security and was, not surprisingly, an early achievement within the GCC framework.

Military cooperation, on the other hand, has been very limited because it does not really enhance – and may even compromise – regime stability. The key to understanding the GCC is that the greatest threat was not spillover from the Iran-Iraq War or direct Iranian invasion, but the spread of internal unrest. Military integration was therefore superfluous to the organization's core goals. In fact, strong military cooperation might actually have *reduced* regime security because a powerful centralized military organization could undermine Gulf regimes (Quinlivan 1999).

In sum, we argue that the timing and the specific form of GCC cooperation – trade, investment, and intelligence cooperation but only weak alliance functions – are best explained by a theory focusing on internal threats.

An important caveat should be emphasized here. Although balance-of-threat theory's apparent failure to explain the most likely case of the Gulf Cooperation Council casts doubt on the generalizability of the theory as an explanation of regional economic cooperation, we are not proving the domestic threat theory. Further refinement and testing is obviously necessary.

To advance our arguments, the first section maps the level of GCC cooperation by issue area. The second section presents the balance-of-threat explanation for the GCC as well as its limitations. The third traces the internal fault lines of the Gulf states and shows how revolutionary Iran threatened to disrupt governments' foundations. The fourth section demonstrates how the formation of the Gulf Cooperation Council reduced the regimes' internal vulnerability. Both the timing and form of the GCC reflected this internal security dynamic.

GCC Cooperation by Issue Area

In any analysis of regionalism, the number of officially proclaimed accomplishments exceeds the number of actual accomplishments, usually by a wide margin. The Gulf Cooperation Council is no exception. For that reason, this study looks carefully not only at agreements, but at the level of implementation of those agreements. Once we ignore the agreements that have never been fulfilled, the overall picture that emerges is of a hybrid economic and security organization, although progress has been greater on the economic front.

Military Integration

The six Gulf states have repeatedly pledged to come to each other's aid in case of outside attack. This policy of 'self-reliance' is what most differentiates this regional grouping from more typical regional economic agreements. As a result, the hybrid GCC is at least partially an alliance – even though its leaders have often disavowed the term 'alliance' in order to make the grouping less troubling for more powerful neighbors (Ramazani, 1988, pp. 2-3, 35, 67; Christie, 1987, pp. 18-19; Barnett and Gause, 1998, p. 169).

At the same time, the six states have done relatively little to boost their stated commitment into substantive military cooperation. Initial goals in this area were relatively high: linked air and naval defenses, joint training, and military exercises all leading to an integrated, regional military force (Peterson, 1988, p. 203). However, progress towards those goals has been minimal.

Probably the most noteworthy development was regional military exercises in 1983 and 1984, known as Peninsula Shield. These exercises also led to greater coordination in training procedures and additional bilateral military exercises. However, they did not lead to regular, regional military exercises (Ramazani, 1988, pp. 60-68; Nakhleh, 1986, pp. 39-46; Peterson 1988, pp. 203-5).

In another much-heralded endeavor, GCC members agreed to create a small Rapid Deployment Force (RDF), based in Saudi Arabia. While in principle this involved closer and more routine military cooperation than the Peninsula Shield military exercises, the RDF had no regular troops, only the promise of troops that could be called up in an emergency. Even at its full strength of two brigades, the RDF would be more of a 'trip-wire' or symbol than a credible deterrent. Oman has proposed a much more substantial joint force of about 100,000 soldiers, but discussion of this proposal has been repeatedly postponed (Ramazani, 1988, pp. 64-67; Peterson, 1988, pp. 205; Mainuddin, Aicher, and Elliot, 1996, p. 42; Dunn, 1993).

Another area of potential cooperation involves sharing air defense information, especially after Saudi Arabia obtained AWACS planes from the United States. But proposals for creating an integrated air defense system did not lead to agreement.

Overall, while GCC military cooperation has been noticeable, it has never been substantial. Although often viewed primarily as an alliance, GCC states have been willing to endorse military cooperation only at the margins – a Rapid Deployment Force that exists mainly on paper, sporadic military exercises, ad hoc information sharing, and so on. Repeated calls for true military integration have been rebuffed. And in the aftermath of the Gulf War, Gulf states have turned increasingly to western alliances instead of strengthening the GCC (Mainuddin, Aicher, and Elliot, 1996; Tetreault, 1996; Dunn, 1993; Ahady, 1994).

Domestic Security

Similar outcomes are visible in the area of countering domestic subversion and terrorism. A key accomplishment in this area was expanding the exchange of information on political dissidents. Another early priority was a series of bilateral security accords involving Saudi Arabia and every other GCC state except Kuwait. These bilateral agreements involve intelligence sharing, coordination of training, border cooperation, and provisions for extradition of criminals. At least one plot against the Bahraini government was reportedly prevented as a result of this cooperative framework (Ramazani, 1988, pp. 33-42; Twinam, 1987, pp. 37-38; Nakhleh, 1986, p. 39; Ispahani 1984, p. 160).

Kuwait was extremely hesitant to sign a bilateral agreement with Saudi Arabia and delayed plans for multilateral cooperation for many years. In 1987, GCC members did agree to coordinate a broad range of intelligence activities, but Kuwaiti concerns about its sovereignty in general and potential Saudi interference in particular significantly constrained the range of cooperative efforts agreed to by the entire membership (Peterson, 1988, pp. 207-9; Ramazani, 1988, pp. 35-38; Twinam, 1987, p. 38; and Tetreault, 1996, p. 24).

Foreign Policy

The Gulf Cooperation Council has also served a role in coordinating member states' foreign policies. In this area, the GCC can best be seen as a forum for discussions — there is neither an independent secretariat driving discussions nor any rule-bound procedure for reaching agreement. But the process of military and economic cooperation launched in 1981 has been accompanied by many efforts to forge consensus among the six in order to gain strength in larger political disputes and negotiations. For example, in the 1980s GCC states worked to coordinate responses to the Iran-Iraq War, mediated a longstanding dispute between member Oman and non-member South Yemen, and attempted to contain territorial conflicts between Bahrain and Qatar. In the aftermath of the Gulf War, much of the GCC's attention has obviously turned to Iraq, but intra-GCC territorial issues have also been a frequent concern. Perhaps the best indicator of the GCC's weakness in the area of foreign policy is that, after two decades of discussions, the GCC has still not resolved the Bahrain-Qatar or Saudi Arabia-Qatar territorial disputes (Ramazani, 1988, pp. 118-29; Peterson, 1988, pp. 119-41; Rathmell, 1997; N. Jaber, 1992a; 1992b; Ispahani, 1984; Barnett and Gause, 1998, 183-84).

Trade

Despite its recent origins, the GCC exhibits the most extensive economic cooperation in the Middle East region. Its most notable achievement is the complete elimination of intra-regional customs dutiesВan accomplishment with few parallels in the history of Third World regionalism. Nearly as important was the move to harmonize external tariff schedules by setting a common minimum tariff level of 4% and a maximum of 20%. While this tariff band falls somewhat short of a common external tariff, it has dramatically reduced variation in tariff rates. Much of the remaining variation involves luxury goods. As a result of this market integration, intra-GCC trade increased from 3% of total trade in 1980 to 8% in 1990 (International Monetary Fund, 1997; Ramazani, 1988, pp. 102-3; Peterson, 1988, p. 151, pp. 159-63; UNCTAD, 1996, p. 84).

The GCC has also greatly increased labor mobility within the region. The ability of GCC citizens to travel and work in other member states has been significantly increased and professionals are now allowed to register and practice throughout the region (Ramazani, 1988, pp. 100-1; Peterson 1988, p. 160; UNCTAD 1996, p. 84; Lawrence 1996, Table A-2).

Taken together, these efforts show a sustained effort by GCC states to create a fully integrated common market. Very few regional economic institutions in the Third World have ever approached this level of trade liberalization. Although GCC market integration does not compare favorably with trade cooperation in industrialized Europe or North America, it does hold its own in comparison with other relatively successful Third World efforts.

Finance

One of the most visible economic accomplishments of the GCC has been the Gulf Investment Corporation (GIC), created in 1982. With paid-in capital of $540 million, the GIC is charged with investing for long-term industrial and agricultural development in member states. Areas of special concern include petrochemicals, light manufacturing, and livestock (Peterson, 1988, pp. 151-52, 176; Ramazani, 1988, p. 100; UNCTAD, 1996, p. 85).

Important results have also been achieved in loosening restrictions on capital mobility. GCC citizens have increased ability to own land and property in other member states. And capital markets in member countries have been substantially integrated, including the right of citizens of one country to own corporate shares in other countries (Ramazani, 1988, p. 101; Lawrence, 1996, Table A-2; M. Jaber, 2000, p. 23).

For those who see the GCC as primarily a military alliance, the lack of solid progress on the security dimension is hard to explain, and the extensive range of economic cooperation is perhaps even more confusing. The Unified Economic Agreement of June 1981 is not only one of the GCC's earliest common projects, but also probably the most fully implemented (Christie, 1987, p. 20). At the same time, the pledge of mutual defense, the establishment of training exercises, and the creation of a joint force (however small) point to the existence of an organization that goes beyond the typical regional trade grouping.

Balance-of-Threat Theory and Regional Cooperation in the Gulf

It is hard to imagine a world region more suited to realist analysis than the Middle East. Conflict and violence are recurrent themes in the politics of the region, rivalries are bitter and very apparent, and state survival is acknowledged to be a salient concern for most states. For these reasons, the Middle East constitutes a most likely case for realism. If realism is going to be a general explanation for regionalism, it should apply in the Middle East. If realism falls short in this region, it is unlikely to be widely applicable to patterns of regionalism around the worldBalthough it could still be useful in specific cases.

The most plausible realist explanation for the formation of the GCC is Stephen Walt's balance-of-threat theoryBwhich is not surprising given Walt's extensive efforts to demonstrate the theory's applicability to the Middle East (1987). Walt studies the pattern of alignments within the Middle East from 1955 to 1979 to show that balancing is more likely than bandwagoning, but that states balance against perceived threats, rather than against the most powerful states. States perceived as hostile or offensively threatening bring about balancing coalitions.

In addition to being a most likely case for realist theories generally, the Middle East is a fair test case for Walt's balance-of-power theory. While Walt does not set out to create a theory of regional economic cooperation, he does explicitly characterize the GCC as the product of increasing regional threats: 'The council was designed as a vehicle for enhanced *economic and security* cooperation, intended to limit potential pressures from both Iran and the Soviet Union' (1987, p. 270; italics added). Balance-of-threat theory would suggest that the Gulf states faced increasing external threats after 1971 because of the political vacuum created by the British military withdrawal. But the threat escalated dramatically in 1979 with the Iranian revolution and the installation of a regime with revisionist territorial goals. The large Iranian military could not only threaten the small Gulf states but also try to intimidate Saudi Arabia with its muscle. As a result, according to the theory, the Gulf states banded together in an effort to prevent Iran from intimidating or attacking them one by one. The GCC could then be seen as a collective defense agreement that blended economic, political, and security cooperation to create a united front in dealings with a suddenly threatening Iran.

The difficulty for balance-of-threat theory is that, while Iran did pose a threat to Gulf states, the theory cannot effectively explain the timing or nature of the response to the Iranian threat. Iranian military capabilities actually declined after the revolution due to the chaos of the transition and the lack of access to spare parts for military equipment purchased from the U.S. under the Shah (Barnett and Gause, 1998, p. 170). Iran did not become a real military threat until September 1981, when they launched their first successful offensive against Iraq. By this time the GCC had already been in existence for almost half a year (Ramazani, 1988, p. 10).

Balance-of-threat theory also fails to explain the nature of the GCC response. It fails to explain the hybrid nature of the GCC and, in fact, mischaracterizes the GCC as primarily an alliance (Priess 1996, p. 152). Support for this characterization is based on the Peninsula Shield military exercises, increased military spending, the regional Rapid Deployment Force, and intelligence sharing (Ibid., pp. 152-53). As noted in Section I though, actual regional military integration has been low. After the first two years, military exercises were primarily bilateral rather than regional (Peterson 1988, p. 204). The Rapid Deployment Force is more symbolic than real, consisting in essence of a headquarters staff and promises of troops (Ramazani, 1988, p. 67). GCC Defense Ministers did agree to $30 billion of combined defense expenditures, but in practice there has been no 'indication that acquisition patterns have been guided by a central plan', nor is there evidence that 'arms acquisition programs in the member states have been heavily influenced by considerations of GCC compatibility or interoperability' (Peterson, 1988, pp. 202, 209). And intelligence sharing has targeted potentially disloyal or subversive domestic groups and individuals, rather than Iranian military forces.

Thus, the types of military integration we typically observe in an alliance are only weakly present in the Gulf Cooperation Council. If the GCC was 'best described as an alliance,' it would be little more than a paper tiger, a set of declarations on self-reliance lacking any substance.

Moreover, viewing the GCC as primarily an alliance misses the significant economic cooperation that has occurred among the Gulf states. As discussed in Section I, the GCC has pursued meaningful economic cooperation, including dismantling internal trade barriers, harmonizing external tariffs, jointly funding intra-regional investment, increasing labor and capital mobility, and coordinating communications networks. If the GCC is primarily an alliance, why has it been more successful in pursuing economic integration than military integration? Why spend more time on capital mobility than military coordination?

Iranian Threat to Gulf Regimes' Internal Stability

Focusing on domestic threats gives us a much clearer picture of the internal security mechanism behind the GCC's creation in 1981. The year 1979 represents a traumatic turning point in the Gulf. After revolutionary forces toppled the Shah's regime in Iran, Iranian clerics, eager to export their Islamic Revolution, quickly became a serious threat to ruling elites throughout the Gulf. These revolutionary Shiite clerics embraced expansionist ideologies and adopted a policy of intimidation toward neighboring Gulf states. 'In 1979 Islam with Iran as its stand-bearer appeared irresistible and irrepressible, an incipient tidal-wave' (Chubin, 1990, pp. 73-74).

Although most Gulf monarchs viewed the prospect of military invasion by Iran as unlikely, a more frightening prospect was the domestic security threat of militant Shiites inspired by Iranian rhetoric. Although Shiite Muslims represent a minority of the total population of most Gulf states, Table 5.1 shows that the number of Shiites within these states is much higher in terms of their percentage of citizens.[2] Shiites are clearly a significant community in Qatar, Bahrain, the United Arab Emirates, and to a lesser extent Kuwait. But they are a substantial concern even in Saudi Arabia because Saudi Shiites are concentrated in the oil-rich Hasa province, where they constitute a majority of the population. Similarly, Shiites within the U.A.E. are concentrated in the crucial emirate of Dubai and compose a significant economic community there.

Table 5.1 Shiite muslims in the Gulf

	Shiites as Percentage of Total Population	Shiites as Percentage of Citizen Population
Iran	92	95
Bahrain	49	72
Qatar	22	80
U.A.E.	12	41
Kuwait	9	23
Oman	6	7
Saudi Arabia	4	5

Source: Ramazani (1988, p. 200).

Despite the large number of Shiites scattered throughout the Gulf states, the Gulf kingdoms are ruled by Sunni regimes, 'whose attitudes toward Shiism vary from cold indifference to acute hostility' (Hiro, 1988, p. 36).[3] After the Iranian revolution, fear of internal instability caused by Shiite revolt rose among Gulf monarchs (Ramazani, 1986, 32). Iran dismissed ruling Gulf monarchies as little more than 'tribes with flags.' This religious and ideological mandate licensed Iranian clerics to meddle with other Gulf states' domestic affairs, ultimately hoping to spread the Islamic Revolution throughout the Muslim world. Iran's clerics targeted socioeconomic cleavages in the smaller and militarily weaker Gulf states in order to undermine social cohesiveness, religious unity, and above all, the regimes' Islamic legitimacy (Goldberg, 1990, p. 161). Thus, the Islamic Revolution in Iran constituted one of the most serious challenges to these regimes in the twentieth century.

Political fragility in the Gulf states stems largely from the inability of the ruling classes to meet mass demands for a better standard of living and for more political participation. Many socioeconomic problems were created as a result of rapid economic growth and these socioeconomic problems were accentuated among Shiite populations. Literacy among Shiites is much lower than national averages. On the whole Shiites were overlooked during the heavy investment in education during the 1970s. Unskilled Shiites compose an abnormally large percentage of the unemployed in

---

[2]   Other estimates suggest the Shiite population of these states is even higher.

[3]   The only exception is Oman, whose monarch belongs to the Ibadi school within the Kharaji sect, which is neither Sunni nor Shiite.

the Gulf, especially among citizen populations. For example, unemployment among Bahraini Shiites is reportedly over 30 percent, more than double the rate in the entire population. Those Shiites fortunate enough to find work were normally under-employed, filling low paying, unskilled, manual labor positions (Bahry, 1997, pp. 49-51; Ramazani, 1986, p. 53; McNaugher, 1984, p. 6; Abir, 1988, p. 17; Cobban, 1981, p. 7).

Compounding this economic cleavage – and partially as a result of it – Gulf Shiites are traditionally politically repressed. Many Gulf Shiites consider themselves economically and politically disadvantaged, second-class citizens. As just one example, Shiites are virtually excluded from the Bahraini army or interior ministry, which are considered too important; interestingly, both institutions are instead staffed largely by foreigners (Al-Haj, 1996, p. 559; Bahry, 1997, p. 43, pp. 50-51; Ramazani, 1986, p. 34).

The Islamic Revolution in Iran accentuated these problems. After the Iranian revolution, Gulf Shiites owed their secular allegiance to their respective governments, but they also owed spiritual allegiance to and looked for spiritual guidance from Iran's top leader, the Ayatollah Khomeini. By playing upon the religious loyalties of poor Shiite populations within Gulf states, Iranian clerics seriously threatened domestic conditions within Gulf regimes (Doelling, 1979; Korany, 1984, p. 250; Khashan, 1997, p. 164).

Because many poorer Shiites linked societal injustices with deviations from Islamic teachings, only a return to Islamic values could rectify societal injustices. Many Shiites viewed the implementation of Islamic law at the social level as a 'gateway to a more egalitarian society' (Shah, 1980). In short, many Shiites came to harbor a worldview in which economic and political justice would only be achieved within a theocratic Islamic Republic.

In the wake of the Iranian revolution, leading Iranian clerics identified Hasa, Saudi Arabia's Eastern province, and Bahrain as areas where 'Shiite brothers' were being oppressed and needed assistance (Goldberg 1990, p. 159). Tehran viewed Saudi Shiites as 'an ideal conduit for the export of the revolution . . . [and] as a direct subversive instrument which could be used to undermine Saudi authority' (Ibid., p. 160). Concentrated in Saudi Arabia's crucial oil region bordering the Gulf, Hasa Shiites became a valuable tool for undermining the House of Saud's legitimacy.

Iranian clerics used radio broadcasts to urge Shiites in Saudi Arabia to revolt against their 'oppressors' and engaged in propaganda campaigns among Shiites in Hasa and pilgrims in Mecca, calling for the overthrow of Gulf monarchies. Iranian propaganda, including leaflets and cassette recordings, began circulating in Hasa during the summer of 1979. In early November 1979, about 90,000 demonstrators took to the Saudi Arabian streets, defying the government ban on the religious commemoration of Imam Hussein's martyrdom. The ensuing riots produced the deaths of both Shiites and Saudi Arabian soldiers. 'This was the first real political challenge posed by the Shiites of Hasa since the establishment of Saudi Arabia, and it was no coincidence that it surfaced just ten months after the revolution in Iran' (Goldberg, 1990, p. 160; Hindy, 1980; Korany, 1984, p. 252; Ramazani 1986, p. 40).

During 1979's annual pilgrimage to Mecca, Iranian pilgrims organized political demonstrations and passed out political propaganda to potentially subversive Saudi groups. Later that month, protesting Saudi Arabia's 'deviation from the "true Islamic path,"' the Mahdist Muslims, a group closely associated with Iranian Shiites, seized the Grand Mosque of Mecca. The mosque siege was actually a coup attempt, similar to the takeover in Iran. It began as militant Islamists stormed the Grand Mosque in an attempt to take members of the royal family hostage and proclaim an Islamic government. It took almost two weeks of bloody fighting for Saudi security forces to oust the Islamist attackers. Many surmise that 'the seizure of the Grand Mosque might have been made in response to . . . calls from Ayatollah Ruhollah Khomeini . . . for a general uprising by fundamentalist Muslims in the Middle East.' The attack severely threatened the Wahhabis' religious legitimacy. The House of Saud's inability to control the belligerent behavior of Islamist pilgrims was a 'major source of embarrassment for the Kingdom's status as guardians of the Holy Shrines' (Goldberg 1990, pp. 159-65; Taubman, 1979, A5; Hindy, 1980; Korany, 1984, p. 272).

A related revolt occurred in February 1980. Shiite oil workers in Hasa, motivated by revolutionary propaganda from Iran, violently sought to stop the extraction of oil reserves, demanding a greater share of revenues from oil sales to relieve the sufferings of Shiite oil workers (Ramazani 1986, p. 40; Goldberg 1990, p. 165). Thus, by targeting Saudi Arabia's 'oppressed' Shiite minority, Iranian clerics disrupted domestic tranquility in Saudi Arabia and threatened the political and religious legitimacy of the ruling elite.

Bahrain, with the highest concentration of Shiite Muslims outside Iran, was extremely affected by Iranian interference. Radio broadcasts and other political propaganda urged Bahraini Shiites to overthrow the existing regime and replace it with an Islamic Republic patterned after the Iranian model. The calls to revolt produced four political demonstrations between August and September 1979 in which Shiites protested government repression and called for the establishment of a more Islamic government. The largest demonstration included about 1,400 Shiite activists, who took to the streets waving Khomeini pictures and calling for a the creation of an Islamic republic. These Shiite uprisings presented a real threat to the Bahraini ruling class. Indeed, as a result of the Shiite strikes, Bahraini government officials curtailed the consumption of alcohol and suspended many nightclub shows for the duration of Ramadan (Hindy, 1980; *U.S. News and World Report,* 1984; Doelling, 1979).

Perhaps the most viable threat posed by Iran toward Bahrain was its support for the Islamic Front for the Liberation of Bahrain, a militant Islamist faction based in Tehran. This revolutionary organization trained professional saboteurs in Iran who were later held responsible for a December 1981 coup attempt in Bahrain (Ramazani, 1986, p. 50; Bahry, 1997, p. 45; *Associated Press,* 1981).

The United Arab Emirates' native Shiite population, concentrated in the emirate of Dubai, was also highly influenced by Iranian actions. Dubai benefitted enormously from trade with Iran. Additionally, most of the U.A.E.'s oil wells are offshore, susceptible to Iranian attack. The U.A.E's vulnerability to Iran became clear after the 'unofficial' visit of the powerful Iranian cleric, Ayatollah Sadekh Khalkali. Following Ayatollah Khalkali's visit, the emirates of Abu Dhabi and Dubai quickly regulated the consumption of alcohol and shut down the emirates' thriving nightclub industry (Cordesman, 1984, p. 13; Hiro, 1988; Doelling, 1979).

Kuwaiti rulers, fearing Shiite uprisings and facing rising Islamist sentiment, deported a militant Shiite activist along with his family in 1979. The activist allegedly incited other Muslims to turn against the ruling government (Doelling, 1979; Ghabra, 1997, pp. 60-61). Demonstrating his government's fear of Shiite uprising, Prime Minister Sheikh Saad Al-Abdullah Al-Sabah, warned potentially hostile Shiites that grave consequences would accompany any attempt to 'undermine the stable conditions and security of the country' (ibid.). Additional political problems became prevalent as a nephew of the Ayatollah Khomeini, Ahmad al-Mahri, began using religious sermons to incite revolutionary fervor. Although Mahri was quickly expelled, Shiite clerics within Kuwait remained politically active. The real effects of Iranian propaganda campaigns were not felt until the early 1980s, when four terrorist attacks severely threatened Kuwaiti rulers' political legitimacy (Ramazani 1988, pp. 8, 44-46).

In short, by 1981 the conservative Sunni monarchies of the Gulf had ample reason to believe Iran was attempting to undermine their governments from within. Saudi Arabia had faced violent protest in its oil-rich Eastern region and an attempted coup at the Grand Mosque. Iran was training revolutionaries to overthrow the Bahraini regime. The Bahraini regime had survived demonstrations and revolutionary unrest that foreshadowed the coup attempt at the end of the year. Kuwait and the United Arab Emirates had been forced to crack down on Shiite religious leaders. And, while the U.A.E. and Oman also faced direct political-military pressure from Iran, all these regimes' internal vulnerabilities were potentially severe.

How the GCC Reduced Regime Vulnerability

The foreign ministers of the six Gulf states agreed to establish the Gulf Cooperation Council at a meeting in Riyadh in February 1981. The ministers argued that a regional grouping would bring 'stability to their peoples' (Ramazani, 1988, p. 12). In May they explained the basic rationale for the GCC:

> [I]nternational designs will not be able to find a foothold in a merged region which has one voice, opinion, and strength. However, they will be able to find a thousand footholds if this region, which is rich in oil and men, remains made up of small entities that can be easily victimized (Ibid., p. 29).

In essence, Gulf leaders hoped to build strength through unity. Without saying so directly, the phrase 'international designs' refers to Iranian clerics' desire to export their Islamic Revolution. Thus, the original, underlying purpose for creating the GCC was not economics or external security threats. Instead, the real catalyst for action was the common threat posed by Iran to domestic regime security.

The Gulf Cooperation Council responded to the domestic threat in three ways. First, it increased the monarchies' legitimacy by moving closer to the long-held goals of an Islamic community and an Arab community. Second, it facilitated cooperation by national intelligence services in combating domestic subversion. Third, it provided economic benefits that could be targeted to dissatisfied minorities.

Legitimacy

As Steven David emphasizes, regime legitimacy is usually a central concern for Third World governments (1991). And, since Islam is one of the most powerful legitimizing agents in the Middle East, coopting Islamic religious leaders has traditionally been crucial to the Gulf monarchies' survival. For the same reason, however, Islamic activism presents the greatest threat to the legitimacy of Gulf monarchies.

In order to counter the spread of Islamist beliefs since the Iranian revolution, Gulf rulers have emphasized a return to traditional Islamic principles, including stricter adherence to the *Qur'an*. For example, in Saudi Arabia the government drained swimming pools to prevent mixed-gender bathing and prohibited pictures of women in newspapers. In the United Arab Emirates, the government imposed strict new liquor laws. In Kuwait, the government adopted a more conservative school curriculum and used censorship to promote more Islamic values in television and publishing (*U.S. News and World Report,* 1984; Hindy, 1980; Doelling, 1979; Ghabra, 1997, pp. 60-61).

However, piecemeal attempts to enforce Islamic law were largely unspectacular and ineffective. As a result, legitimacy hungry Gulf monarchs developed a larger and more elaborate plan to quell domestic unrest: the formation of the Gulf Cooperation Council. By incorporating the traditional ideals of the Islamic community *(umma)*, and the Arab community *(qawmiyyah)*, the GCC was meant to simulate an Islamic Republic. Individually illegitimate in the eyes of many Islamists, the Gulf regimes gained collective legitimacy by partially undoing the division of the region by imperialist powers. Thus, the Gulf Cooperation Council helped pacify increasingly militant Shiite aspirations for an Islamic Republic (Whittingham, 1984, p. 8; Ramazani, 1988, pp. 13-14; Barnett and Gause, 1998).

Intelligence Sharing

Gulf states had strong reason to believe that subversive threats to their regimes might be transnational in origin. There are strong ethnic, religious, and economic ties between the people of each Gulf country, as well as a common external sponsor of subversive activity – Iran. For these reasons, national intelligence services were hampered in their ability to monitor unrest that might be emerging beyond their borders.

Intelligence cooperation then was a natural priority for the GCC. The first bilateral security treaty, focusing on internal security threats, was signed between Saudi Arabia and Bahrain only seven days after Bahrain's December 1981 coup attempt. A number of additional agreements were signed in early 1982. As Sterner notes, 'given the essentially domestic dimension of the Iranian threat,' intelligence sharing rather than military coordination has been the primary security endeavor of the GCC (Sterner 1985, pp. 17-18; Ramazani, 1988, pp. 206-7; Barnett and Gause, 1998, pp. 172-73).

Economic Benefits

At the same time, the Gulf Cooperation Council was formulated to allow Gulf regimes to provide economic benefits to some of their most restive populations, especially economically disadvantaged Shiite minorities. During the late 1970s and early 1980s, government welfare programs became the typical response to civil unrest. These social welfare programs targeted regions with high concentrations of Shiite Muslims, 'building new mosques, schools, houses, and other amenities and grooming Shiite mullahs.' The regimes also provided health clinics, low-cost housing, and easy credit in order to minimize civil unrest (Ramazani, 1986, p. 52; Doelling, 1979).

Although government works projects placated militant Shiites, these projects represented only a temporary solution. The 'constant flow of money and attention to the Shiites' was extremely difficult for the smaller Gulf monarchies to maintain (Goldberg, 1990, p. 166). After repeated incidents of civil unrest, Gulf monarchs met and agreed upon a long-term regional solution, which would provide employment to Shiite populations and bolster the smaller Gulf economies.

The most important result was the formation of the Gulf Investment Corporation. Hundreds of small projects developed, enlarging the GCC's bureaucracy and providing jobs for unemployed Shiite citizens. At the same time, reductions in trade barriers allowed Gulf companies to take advantage of regional economies of scale in production and marketing of their products and to pursue greater specialization. At a time when national leaders hoped to diversify their economic base beyond petroleum, regional trade liberalization was a useful way to reduce the disadvantages of small national markets. And with Shiite minorities over-represented among the unemployed, job growth in GCC countries would be expected to benefit Shiites disproportionately (El-Kuwaiz, 1987, p. 72; Cobban, 1981; Nakhleh, 1986, p. 24-25).

By providing 'freedom of movement, work and residence; right of ownership, inheritance and bequest; freedom to exercise economic activity; [and] free movement of capital,' the agreement established a system in which Shiite Muslims could move more freely and gain higher levels of employment (*Economist,* 1997). Better employment for Shiites was especially valuable in the United Arab Emirates where Shiite Muslims constituted a larger percentage of the total population and more viable commercial community. Additional employment opportunities for Gulf citizens were mandated by a government fiat requiring companies to hire citizens before cheaper expatriate laborers (Hiro, 1988; *Economist,* 1997).

In short, the Gulf Cooperation Council was designed to strengthen economic development across the Gulf states and could be used as an economic instrument for placating Shiite minorities. Liberalized labor mobility rules, common investment projects under the Gulf Investment Corporation, and job creating trade liberalization all increased economic opportunities for formerly disadvantaged Shiites.

Military Cooperation

By enhancing regime legitimacy, spurring intelligence cooperation, and creating new economic tools, the GCC improved these monarchies' political prospects by directly targeting their most substantial weakness: restive Shiite minorities inspired by the success of the Iranian revolution. It should also be pointed out that, looking at the internal security needs of Gulf monarchs, externally directed military cooperation served relatively little purpose. Therefore, it is not surprising that regional cooperation in this area has been sporadic.

But there is an additional reason for lack of substantial military cooperation, also the result of these regimes' concerns about domestic survival: Traditionally, GCC governments have feared strong militaries because of the possibility of coup or other military politicization (Quinlivan, 1999, pp. 141-44, 153-54; Dunn, 1993, p. 24). As a result of such fears, Oman's proposals for a 100,000-man regional military force have fallen on deaf ears in the Gulf (Dunn, 1993; Barnett and Gause, 1998, p. 182). Even though a joint force was seen as playing an important deterrent role against outside intervention in the region, it would have posed too great a threat to Gulf monarchies to be seriously considered.

Conclusion

This chapter has attempted to show that a realist explanation of the GCC fails to capture the mechanism for the creation of this regional organization. The six Gulf states were indeed threatened by Iran, but not in the manner balance-of-threat theory would predict. The primary Iranian threat was not to the Gulf states' territorial borders or political independence but to their internal stability. The example and ideology of revolutionary Iran stoked political opposition within the Gulf states, especially among dissatisfied Shiite minorities that constituted a potential Fifth Column. Without careful attention to domestic politics, we would miss the primary motivation for the GCC.

Once we understand the threat which the GCC was created to combat, we can better understand the nature and form of the institution. The Gulf Cooperation Council's primary objective was to reduce domestic threats to each government. Its significant economic cooperation was intended to create benefits that governments could target to disaffected domestic groups, especially minorities. Thus, regional trade ties benefited the Saudi government by increasing the economic development of the eastern province that was potentially most restive. Because intra-regional disunity could embolden opposition and diminish legitimacy, the GCC was used as a forum for regional foreign-policy consensus-building, and security cooperation emphasized domestic intelligence.

At the same time, we can understand why other kinds of regional cooperation have not emerged. Some analysts, for example, have proposed stronger regional military ties. But since the GCC is largely internally directed, security cooperation against external threats would be tangential to the core GCC project.

This chapter parallels earlier work on alliance and alignment patterns in the Third World which suggests that threats to domestic stability are a primary source of political alignments (Barnett and Levy 1991; David 1991). Our findings go beyond earlier arguments though in suggesting that a similar logic applies to many regional *economic* agreements. This study therefore suggests the value of further research on economic and security cooperation. Studies of states' regional alignment – whether military or economic – should pay special attention to each regime's domestic stability and the possibility that internal threats to the regime are the crucial determinants of regionalism.

References

Abir, Mordechai (1988), 'Saudi Arabia in the oil era. Part II: Potential sources of instability', *Middle East Executive Report*, Vol. 11 (November), pp. 19-21.

Ahady, A. (1994), Security in the Persian Gulf after Desert Storm, *International Journal*, Vol. 49 (Spring), pp. 219-40.

Al-Haj, Abdullah Juma (1996), 'The politics of participation in the Gulf Cooperation Council states: The Omani Consultative Council', *Middle East Journal*, Vol. 50 (Autumn), pp. 559-71.

Associated Press (1981), 16 December, PM cycle, Lexis-Nexis.

Bahry, Louay (1997), 'The opposition in Bahrain: A bellwether for the Gulf?' *Middle East Policy*, Vol. 5 (May), pp. 42-57.

Barnett, Michael, and Gause, F. Gregory III (1998), 'Caravans in opposite directions: Society, state, and the development of a community in the Gulf Cooperation Council', in Emanuel Adler and Michael Barnett (eds.), *Security communities*, Cambridge University Press, Cambridge, UK.

Barnett, Michael, and Levy, Jack S. (1991), 'Domestic sources of alliances and alignments: The case of Egypt, 1962-73', *International Organization* Vol. 45 (Summer), pp. 369-95.

Chawla, Kanhiya Lal (1991), *Economic cooperation among developing countries (with special reference to SAARC)*, RBSA Publishers, Jaipur, India.

Christie, John (1987), 'History and development of the Gulf Cooperation Council: A brief overview', in John A. Sandwick (ed.), *The Gulf Cooperation Council: Moderation and stability in an interdependent world*, Westview Press, Boulder, CO, pp. 1-20.

Chubin, Shahram (1990), 'Iran and the Persian Gulf states', in David Menashri (ed.), *The Iranian revolution and the Muslim world*, Westview, San Francisco, pp. 73-84.

Cobban, Helena (1981), 'Saudi Arabia: Ties with tribal regions may be fraying', *Christian Science Monitor*, 2 September, 7.

Cooper, Scott (1999), *Regional monetary cooperation beyond Western Europe*, Ph.D. diss., Duke University.

Cordesman, Anthony H. (1984), 'Gulf Cooperation Council: Security problems and prospects', in Shireen Hunter (ed.), *Gulf Cooperation Council: Problems and prospects*, Center for Strategic & International Studies, Georgetown University, Washington, DC, pp. 10-15.

Crone, Donald (1993), 'Does hegemony matter? The reorganization of the Pacific political economy', *World Politics* Vol. 45 (July), pp. 501-25.

David, Stephen (1991), 'Explaining Third World alignment', *World Politics* 43 (January), pp. 233-56.

Doelling, Otto C. (1979), Associated Press, 28 October, BC cycle.

Dunn, Michael Collins (1993), 'GCC again fails to act on serious joint security force', *Washington Report on Middle East Affairs*, Vol. 11 (February), pp. 24, 86.

Economist (1997), Gulf citizen, no qualifications, seeks well-paid job, 12 April, 41.

El-Kuwaiz, Abdullah Ibrahim (1987), 'Economic integration of the Cooperation Council of the Arab states of the Gulf: Challenges, achievements and future outlook', in John A. Sandwick (ed.), *The Gulf Cooperation Council: Moderation and stability in an interdependent world*, Westview, Boulder, CO, pp. 71-83.

Ghabra, Shafeeq N. (1997), 'Balancing state and society: The Islamic movement in Kuwait', *Middle East Policy*, Vol. 5 (May), pp. 58-72.

Goldberg, Jacob (1990), 'Saudi Arabia and the Iranian revolution: The religious dimension', in David Menashri (ed.), *The Iranian revolution and the Muslim world*, Westview, San Francisco, CA, pp. 155-70.

Gowa, Joanne S. (1994), *Allies, adversaries, and international trade*, Princeton University Press, Princeton, NJ.

Grieco, Joseph M. (1996), 'State interests and institutional rule trajectories: A neorealist interpretation of the Maastricht Treaty and European Economic and Monetary Union', *Security Studies*, Vol. 5 (Spring), pp. 261-306.

Grieco, Joseph M. (1997), 'Systemic sources of variation in regional institutionalization in Western Europe, East Asia, and the Americas', in Edward D. Mansfield and Helen V. Milner (eds.), *The political economy of regionalism*, Columbia University Press, New York, pp. 164-87.

Grieco, Joseph M. (1999), 'Realism and regionalism: American power and German and Japanese institutional strategies during and after the Cold War', in Ethan B. Kapstein and Michael Mastanduno (eds.), *Unipolar politics*, Columbia University Press, New York, pp. 319-53.

Gruber, Lloyd (2000), *Ruling the world: Power politics and the rise of supranational institutions*, Princeton, NJ: Princeton University Press.

Haas, Ernst B. (1958), *The uniting of Europe: Political, social, and economic forces, 1950-57*, Stanford University Press, Stanford, CA.

Haas, Ernst B. (1961), 'International integration: The European and the universal process', *International Organization*, Vol. 15 (Summer), pp. 366-92.

Haas, Ernst B. (1976), 'Turbulent fields and the theory of regional integration', *International Organization*, Vol. 30 (Spring), pp. 173-212.

Haas, Ernst B., and Schmitter, Philippe C. (1964), 'Economics and differential patterns of political integration', *International Organization*, Vol. 18 (Autumn), pp. 705-37.

Hindy, Steven K. (1980), Associated Press, 1 June, BC cycle.

Hiro, Dilip (1988), 'Iran's unlikely champions in the Gulf', *Wall Street Journal*, Vol. 26, January, 36.

International Monetary Fund (1997), *Direction of trade statistics yearbook*, International Monetary Fund, Washington, DC.

Ispahani, Mahnaz Zehra (1984), 'Alone together: Regional security arrangements in southern Africa and the Arabian Gulf', *International Security*, Vol. 8 (Spring), pp. 152-75.

Jaber, Mohamed (2000), 'GCC financial markets and the quest for development', *Middle East Policy*, Vol. 7 (February), pp. 20-46.

Jaber, N. (1992a), 'Qatar and Saudi Arabia: So much for "brotherhood"', *Middle East International*, n.s. 435 (9 October), pp. 5-6.

Jaber, N. (1992b), 'Strains on the Gulf Arabs' cohesion', *Middle East International*, n.s. 439 (4 December), p. 3.

Khashan, Hilal (1997), 'The new Arab Cold War', *World Affairs*, Vol. 159 (Spring), pp. 162-164.

Korany, Bahgat (1984), 'Defending the faith: The foreign policy of Saudi Arabia', in Bahgat Korany and Ali E. Hillal Dessouki (eds.), *The foreign policies of Arab states*, Westview, Boulder, CO., pp. 241-82.

Krasner, Stephen D. (1976), 'State power and the structure of international trade,' *World Politics*, Vol. 28 (April), pp. 317-47.

Lawrence, Robert Z. (1996), *Regionalism, multilateralism, and deeper integration*, The Brookings Institution, Washington, DC.

Lindberg, Leon N., and Scheingold, Stuart A. (eds.) (1971), *Regional integration: Theory and research*, Harvard University Press, Cambridge, MA.

Mainuddin, Rolin G., Aicher, Joseph R., Jr., and Elliot, Jeffrey M. (1996), 'From alliance to collective security: Rethinking the Gulf Cooperation Council', *Middle East Policy,* Vol. 4 (March), 39-49.

Mansfield, Edward D., and Milner, Helen V. (1999), 'The new wave of regionalism', *International Organization,* Vol. 53 (Summer), 589-627.

Mattli, Walter (1999), *The logic of regional integration: Europe and beyond*, Cambridge University Press, Cambridge, UK.

McNaugher, Thomas (1984), 'Principal components of the Gulf Cooperation Council security strategy', in Shireen Hunter (ed.), *Gulf Cooperation Council: Problems and prospects*, Center for Strategic & International Studies, Georgetown University, Washington, DC, pp. 6-9.

Nakhleh, Emile A. (1986), *The Gulf Cooperation Council: Policies, problems and prospects*, Praeger, New York.

Nye, Joseph S., Jr. (1968), *International regionalism,* Little, Brown, and Company, Boston.

Olson, Mancur, and Zeckhauser, Richard (1966), 'An economic theory of alliances', *Review of Economics and Statistics,* Vol. 48 (August), pp. 266-79.

Peterson, Erik R. (1988), *The Gulf Cooperation Council: Search for unity in a dynamic region,* Westview, Boulder, CO.

Priess, David (1996), 'Balance-of-threat theory and the genesis of the Gulf Cooperation Council: An interpretative case study', *Security Studies,* Vol. 5 (Summer), pp. 143-71.

Quinlivan, James T. (1999), 'Coup-proofing: Its practice and consequences in the Middle East', *International Security,* Vol. 24 (Fall), pp. 131-65.

Ramazani, Rouhollah K. (1986), *Revolutionary Iran: Challenge and response in the Middle East,* Johns Hopkins University Press, Baltimore, MD.

Ramazani, Rouhollah K. (1988), *The Gulf Cooperation Council: Record and analysis*, University Press of Virginia, Charlottesville, VA.

Rathmell, A. (1997), 'Qatar and Bahrain: Brothers at odds', *Middle East International,* 26 September, pp. 18-19.

Schmitter, Philippe C. (1969), 'Three neo-functional hypotheses about international integration', *International Organization* 23 (Winter), pp. 161-66.

Shah, Mowahid H. (1980), 'Modernity is not what Muslims resent', *Christian Science Monitor* 22, January, 23.

Sterner, Michael (1985), 'The Gulf Cooperation Council and Persian Gulf security', in Thomas Naff (ed.),*Gulf security and the Iran-Iraq war*, Washington, DC: National Defense University Press, pp. 1-23.

Taubman, Philip (1979), 'Mecca mosque seized by gunmen believed to be militants from Iran', *New York Times,* 21 November, A1, A5.

Tetreault, Mary Ann (1996), 'Gulf winds: Inclement political weather in the Arabian peninsula', *Current History* Vol. 95 (January), pp. 23-27.

Tripp, Charles, (1995), 'Regional organizations in the Arab Middle East', in Louise Fawcett and Andrew Hurrell (eds.), *Regionalism in world politics: Regional organization and international order*, Oxford University Press, Oxford, pp. 283-308.

Twinam, Joseph Wright (1987), 'Reflections on Gulf cooperation, with focus on Bahrain, Qatar, and Oman', in John A. Sandwick (ed.), *The Gulf Cooperation Council: Moderation and stability in an interdependent world,* Westview Press Boulder, CO, pp. 21-45.

Twinam, Joseph Wright (1992), *The Gulf, cooperation, and the Council: An American perspective,* Middle East Policy Council, Washington, DC.

UNCTAD (United Nations Conference on Trade and Development) (1996), *Handbook of economic integration and cooperation groupings of developing countries*. Vol. I, *Regional and subregional economic integration groupings,* United Nations, New York.

U.S. News and World Report (1984), 'Persian Gulf: Will the U.S. lose out there, too?' 9 April, 31.

Viner, Jacob (1929), 'International finance and balance of power diplomacy, 1880-1914', *Southwestern Political and Social Science Quarterly,* Vol. 9 (March), pp. 407-51.

Walt, Stephen (1987). *The origins of alliances,* Cornell University Press, Ithaca, NY.

Whittingham, Ken (1984), 'Arab investment dilemma: Where should the money go?' *Middle East Executive Report,* Vol. 7 (December), p. 8.

Zahlan, Rosemarie Said (1989), *The making of the modern Gulf states: Kuwait, Bahrain, Qatar, the United Arab Emirates and Oman,* Unwin Hyman, London.

Chapter 6

Two Funerals and a Wedding?
The Ups and Downs of Regionalism in East Asia and Asia Pacific after the Asian Crisis*

Douglas Webber

Introduction

Are the principal regional organizations in the East Asian and Asia Pacific regions moribund or verging on it? Any casual observer of the international relations of the two – overlapping – regions could be forgiven nowadays for so thinking. The majority of current commentaries on and analyses of ASEAN (Association of Southeast Asian Nations) and APEC (Asia-Pacific Economic Cooperation) seem to agree that both organizations are afflicted by a serious malaise. Even the organizations' champions are, for the most part, defensive in their analyses of the organizations' recent accomplishments and current health.

Only a few years ago, both ASEAN's and APEC's horizons looked a great deal rosier. At the beginning of the 1990s, ASEAN had earned a great deal of credit for the role it played in resolving the Cambodian conflict and securing Vietnam's withdrawal from the country. Drawing on this diplomatic success, ASEAN appeared to have been transformed or at least rejuvenated in the first half of the decade. The AFTA (ASEAN Free Trade Area) project was launched, the organization's secretariat was strengthened, the ARF (ASEAN Regional Forum) was created to discuss Asian security issues, also with the big powers present in the region, and the enlargement process to admit the mainly ex-Communist states of Indo-China was initiated. At roughly the same time, APEC too seemed to be prospering. The initiation of the annual leaders' meeting in 1993 gave the organization a new sense of dynamism, which was reflected the following year, at Bogor, in the adoption of a bold long-term programme for trade liberalization between member states. There were few signs, in the middle of the 1990s, that,

* Published in Pacific Review, 2001, pp. 339-372. Republished by permission.
http://www.tandf.co.uk.

within just a few years, the two organizations' fortunes would reach such a low ebb as seems to be the case today.

Paradoxically, at the same time as ASEAN and APEC both appear to have been waning, another, embryonic regional organization has been waxing. Whereas ASEAN organizes *South*east Asian states and APEC is a Pan-Pacific organization linking East Asian states (and Russia) with South and East Pacific states, the emergent organization – ASEAN Plus Three (APT) – organizes all but three of the states or quasi-states of East Asia.[1] Although the APT, like APEC, is not based on any treaty or formal, binding agreement between the participating states and although it has no central secretariat, the web of relations between the members has grown quickly since the first meeting of the heads of government in 1997. Not only heads of government, but also finance, economics and foreign ministers, central bank governors and senior government officials in some domains have meanwhile started meeting regularly. In 1998, the heads of government set up a 'vision group' to explore ways to 'expand cooperation in all sectors and at all levels among the countries of East Asia' (ASEAN Secretariat, 1999). At the APT summit in Manila in November 1999, the member governments' leaders agreed to cooperate more closely on a wide range of – monetary, economic, social, security and technological and cultural – issues and within international organizations such as the UN (United Nations) and the WTO (World Trade Organization). At Singapore in November 2000 they decided to explore the possibility of formalizing their ties and forming an East Asian free trade zone.

The first significant concrete 'product' of APT is an agreement, reached at Chiang Mai in Thailand in May 2000, to establish a regional currency-swap facility to enable the states to protect themselves better against any future financial crises of the kind that swept through much of the region, with such devastating economic and social consequences, in 1997-98. For two foreign observers, this agreement represents the 'beginning of a new era of regionalism' (Dieter and Higgott, 2000). For numerous political leaders and high-level officials in the region, the agreement constitutes no more than a first step towards closer regional monetary cooperation or integration. Some, beginning in 1999 with the chief executive of the Hong Kong Monetary Authority, have proposed the creation of a monetary union or common currency for East Asia. 'In little more than a year', according to one commentator, the idea of such a union or currency has gone from being a 'laughable concept to [a] possible policy goal', although 'substantial' challenges would have to be overcome for it to become a reality (Castellano, 2000, p. 9). The former Philippines president Estrada dreamed of the creation of an East Asian community with a common market and a common currency. Officials and Estrada himself acknowledged that such talk was 'only a vision of what might come in two or three decades' time' and Singaporean ministers dismissed the notion that APT could develop into an East Asian bloc comparable to the EU (European Union) or the NAFTA (North American Free Trade Agreement) (quotes from *Financial Times*, 1999 and *Straits Times*, 1999b). Nonetheless, the growing preparedness to discuss

---

[1]   The 'states' that do not belong to APT are Taiwan (Republic of China), Hong Kong and North Korea.

such projects in East Asia was, according to an ASEAN official, 'remarkable' (interview by the author). APT cooperation had indeed 'gained considerable momentum in a relatively short time' (Alatas, 2001, p. 2). The Malaysian government was especially pleased at the way the APT had developed. The Malaysian Prime Minister Mahathir had proposed the formation of an East Asian Economic Group already in 1990, only to encounter strong reservations among other ASEAN states and outright hostility from the US, so that, at that time, the project had in fact gone almost nowhere. According to a high-level Malaysian official, the APT process has meanwhile gone 'far beyond' what Mahathir originally proposed. Moreover, as globalization and growing economic interdependence were pushing the East Asian states towards ever closer cooperation, she said, 'time is on our side' (interview by the author).

What has precipitated the 'waning' of ASEAN and APEC and the simultaneous birth and 'waxing' of APT? Can the APT 'succeed' where ASEAN and APEC appear increasingly to be 'failing'? These are the two questions on which this chapter focuses. Drawing on some of the available literature on comparative regional integration, the chapter begins by trying to identify the pre-conditions of successful regional integration. Subsequently, it explores not only the immediate causes, but also the more structural, underlying roots of the current crises of ASEAN and APEC. It then describes the circumstances that have led to the emergence of APT and analyzes the probability of APT developing into a strong regional organization. By a 'strong regional organization' I mean one whose member states have adopted and implemented common or coordinated policies in a number of significant issue-areas and sustained them over a fairly long period of time. The argument made here is that the crises of ASEAN and APEC and the rise of APT have a common overriding immediate cause: the Asian financial crisis. The crisis has severely damaged the reputation of the former two bodies, while providing powerful momentum for the foundation of the latter. The crisis, however, has served only to expose the structural traits of ASEAN and APEC – especially the absence of a single, strong and uncontested hegemonic power or, alternatively, the lack of a sufficiently strong and cohesive 'duo' of hegemonic powers, together with high levels of political and economic diversity among member states – that likely preclude them from becoming powerful motors of successful inter-state cooperation or integration in, respectively, Southeast Asia and Asia-Pacific.

The crisis has, on the other hand, fostered *East Asian* cooperation because it has greatly strengthened not only perceptions of economic interdependence between South- and Northeast Asian states, but also, owing to the way in which it was managed by the IMF (International Monetary Fund), resentment against the United States and its (at least perceived) domination of international monetary and financial affairs. In as far as there is a much higher level of economic interdependence between its member states than ASEAN's, APT has greater integration 'potential' than ASEAN. To the extent that the divergence of preferences among APT members on trade and other economic policy issues is narrower than between those of APEC member states, it may also be more advantaged than APEC. However, APT also shares some of the traits, most notably the absence of strong and uncontested hegemonic power or of a strong and cohesive hegemonic 'duo', that militate against very close cooperation or integration among ASEAN and APEC member states. On balance, it therefore seems unlikely that APT will lead to the development of a very highly integrated East Asian, as opposed to Southeast Asian or Asia-Pacific, region. How much momentum the process of East Asian cooperation or integration develops will depend partly, however, on trends and processes that are external to the region, in particular the evolution of the multilateral trading system, regionalization processes elsewhere in the world, and the direction of US policy on international trade and towards Latin America and Asia. It is possible to envisage a scenario under which these external forces could accelerate moves towards closer East Asian cooperation and integration, but the historical record of such 'counter-integration' projects suggests that such cooperation or integration is unlikely to prove strong and durable.

Pre-conditions of Successful Regional Integration

Historically, there have been many attempts at voluntary regional integration, but far fewer successful ones, if success is defined as the achievement of 'stated integration goals' (Mattli, 1999a, p. 42). Why do comparatively few attempts at regional integration succeed? In one of the few comparative analyses of regional integration that draws on a large sample of cases, Mattli has identified two critical pre-conditions of successful integration. The first of these is 'strong market pressure for integration', which will arise where there is 'significant' potential for economic gains from market exchange in the region that is to be integrated. According to Mattli, 'if there is little potential for gain, perhaps because regional economies lack complementarity or because the small size of the regional market does not offer important economies of scale, the process of integration will quickly peter out' (Mattli, 1999a, p. 42). This is Mattli's *demand* condition of successful integration. The second – supply – condition of successful integration, for Mattli, is 'undisputed leadership' (Mattli, 1999a, p. 43). There must be a 'benevolent leading country' in the region, one that serves as a 'focal point in the coordination of rules, regulations, and policies' and may also 'help to ease tensions that arise from the inequitable distribution of gains from integration' (Mattli, 1999a, p. 42). To the above two 'strong' conditions for successful integration Mattli adds a third 'subsidiary (or weak)' condition: 'the provision by an integration treaty for the establishment of 'commitment institutions', such as centralized monitoring or third-party enforcement' that help to 'catalyze' the integration process (Mattli, 1999a, pp. 42-43). Further, 'economic difficulties' constitute an additional 'background condition' of integration. Valuing as they do political autonomy and power, political leaders sacrifice these goods only when economic difficulties convince them that they can survive in office only by promoting regional integration, which, he implies, is essential to improved national economic performance (Mattli, 1999a, p. 51). Regions with 'strong market pressure for integration and undisputed leadership' are most likely, according to Mattli, to experience successful integration, while regional groups that do not satisfy either of the two strong conditions are 'least likely to succeed' (Mattli, 1999a, p. 43). Of the world's current regional integration 'schemes', the two most 'successful' – the EU and the NAFTA – are the only ones that, in his view, combine the promise of significant market gains from integration with uncontested regional leadership, provided in the EU by Germany and in the NAFTA by the US (Mattli, 1999b, p. 17).[2]

Mattli's explanation of the differential outcomes of regional integration attempts is a hybrid. In emphasizing the centrality of the extent of potential market gains from integration in explaining integration outcomes, he is inspired by the literature on transaction costs and economic history: as the volume of cross-border exchange grows, the business interests engaged in this exchange apply mounting pressure on political authorities to promote integration to lower the costs of cross-border transactions. In this respect and to this extent, Mattli's argument is identical to that contained in transnational exchange explanations of European integration, which posit that 'as transnational exchanges rise, so does the societal demand for supranational rules and organizational capacity to regulate' (Stone Sweet and Sandholtz, 1998, p. 12). In simultaneously emphasizing the key role of undisputed leadership, Mattli takes his cue from Kindleberger's 'hegemonic stability' theory of the international economic system, underpinning his argument by reference to rational choice theory, specifically to the utility of a regional leader in resolving collective action problems that arise when no state in interaction with others can choose its policy without knowing what the other states intend to do, but there is no obvious point at which to coordinate (Kindleberger, 1973, pp. 291-308; Mattli, 1999a, pp. 55, 57).

Several objections or reservations may be lodged against Mattli's account of the differential success of efforts at regional integration. First, although this does not necessarily follow from his definition of the concept of integration, his focus is clearly on the integration of markets and the policies required to achieve this, whereas, in some regional integration schemes, the emphasis may be more strongly on the integration or coordination of other kinds of policies than on the creation of a free trade area or common market. Second, as he measures 'success' in terms of the accomplishment of 'stated goals', he provides no explanation of interregional variations in the scope of these goals. Why, for example, is the EU's integration agenda much bolder and more radical than NAFTA's? By any other definition of 'success' than Mattli's, could North American integration be viewed as equally successful as that in Western Europe? Third, is it correct to argue that Germany is the EU's 'undisputed leader'? While it is indeed undisputed that Germany has acted as the EU's 'paymaster', it is more controversial to regard it as the principal

---

[2]   In his analysis of integration in Asia, Mattli (1999a, p. 174) concludes that APEC and ASEAN 'may serve some useful ancillary political and security functions, but they do not appear to be viable vehicles of regional economic integration'. His explanation of the limits of these organizations emphasizes more strongly the impact of the lack of potential market gains from integration (in the case of ASEAN) and the lack of an undisputed leader (in both) than the one advanced in this chapter.

'focal point' of policy coordination. This contention is difficult to reconcile with the fact that no member state is outvoted as frequently in the EU Council as Germany (*European Voice*, p. 1998). A more plausible interpretation of the EU's history would be that leadership has been provided by a coalition of France and Germany, whose governments have developed a uniquely intensive bilateral relationship.[3] However, similar to Kindleberger, Mattli predicts that, when 'two or more potential leaders belong to the same group', 'coordination difficulties' will arise, although he does not argue that these difficulties will necessarily prove insurmountable (Mattli, 1999a, pp. 56-57).[4] Fourth, strong 'commitment institutions' – Mattli obviously has such EU organs as the European Commission and the European Court of Justice in mind – are arguably as much indicators or even the consequences as the pre-conditions of successful integration. Fifth, the notion that 'economic difficulties' are even a weak pre-condition of integration sits poorly with the fact that, in Western Europe, integration has tended to proceed most smoothly and rapidly in periods of higher rather than lower economic growth or recession. As we shall see below, the impact of the Asian financial crisis on regional integration has been extremely contradictory. While the crisis has fuelled the emergence of APT, it has gravely weakened both ASEAN and APEC. In any case, even if economic difficulties should have provided a motive for integration, it is hard to argue, and Mattli in fact does not seem to do so, that they have a strong influence on the success or failure (as opposed to launching) of attempts at regional integration. Sixth, Mattli provides no explanation of striking differences between (what would appear to be) potential and actual regional leadership. If, for example, when it accounts for 27 per cent of EU GDP (nine per cent more than the next biggest economy), Germany can 'lead' the EU, at least according to Mattli, why, when it accounts for 45 per cent of APEC GDP (17 per cent more than the next biggest economy), can or does the US not do the same for APEC? In terms of the proportion of material power resources (wealth, army, people) it controls in the 'region', Germany may be less well equipped to provide undisputed leadership in the EU than the US in either NAFTA or APEC. Such anomalies indicate that the provision (and perhaps also acceptance by other states) of regional leadership is not shaped exclusively by 'hard' variables, such as, for example, relative economic size, military capability and demographic weight, but may also be dependent on 'soft' variables, such as foreign policy strategies, history, perceptions of history, collective memories, and so on.

---

[3] See various contributions in Douglas Webber (ed.), *The Franco-German Relationship in the European Union* (London: Routledge, 1999). There is, of course, an on-going debate about the distribution of power between transnational (business) interests, supranational organs and national governments in the EU. For the present author, the empirical evidence on major EU decisions favours the 'intergovernmentalist' interpretation that stresses the centrality of the biggest member states, France and Germany in particular.

[4] For Kindleberger (1973, p. 308), a situation in which there are two potential 'hegemonic powers' appears to be the most unfavourable for the resolution of coordination problems.

Collectively, these objections and reservations suggest that some of Mattli's conditions of successful integration, namely the 'weaker' ones, 'economic difficulties' and 'commitment institutions', should be rejected and that one of the two 'strong conditions', the existence of 'undisputed leadership', should be modified to take account of the possibility that, as in the case of the Franco-German 'tandem' in the EU, a *coalition of leading states* may provide the requisite leadership for successful integration.

Other analyses of comparative regional integration, especially *monetary* integration, identify other variables that may shape regional integration outcomes.[5] In a comparative analysis of the survival of monetary unions, Cohen concludes that two conditions are critical to the durability of such unions: first, as Mattli argues, there must be a local hegemon or 'dominant state willing to keep such an arrangement functioning effectively on terms agreeable to all' and, second, there must be a 'broad constellation of related ties and commitments sufficient to make the loss of policy autonomy basically acceptable to each partner', the participating states must be linked by a 'well-developed set of institutional linkages' that reflects a 'genuine sense of solidarity – *of community*' (Cohen, 1998, p. 87) Both Cohen and Bordo and Jonung (1999) stress the overriding importance of the strength of the political commitment of members to the goal of monetary union for the union's robustness and survival. Cohen argues that the political will to integrate is critical if this is taken to mean 'the motivations of a local hegemon' or 'the value attached to a common endeavor' (Cohen, 1998, pp. 90-91). Similarly, Bordo and Jonung (1999) imply that, other things being equal, a monetary union will last as long as the participating states share 'common political goals' and a 'will to political unity'. In emphasizing the importance of the degree of political consensus around the goal of integration for the (in this case, monetary) project's success, Cohen and Bordo and Jonung connect up with an older strand of argument in comparative integration research that broadly identifies the degree of – cultural, social, political and economic – homogeneity (or strength of a common identity or 'sense of community') among member states as a critical determinant of the probability of regional integration.[6] One potential contributing factor to a sense of common identity is the actions and attitudes of states external to the region.[7]

---

[5] In as far as East Asian regionalism is more likely to be 'monetary' rather than trade-oriented, these analyses are especially relevant when it comes to assessing the prospective evolution of APT.

[6] For a brief overview of this literature, see Katzenstein, 1996, pp. 129-130. The objective of most of this literature, however, is to explain why regional integration is attempted rather than why it succeeds or fails. It should be noted, however, that there has been much less inter-state cooperation or integration in Northeast than in Southeast Asia, although the latter, on various dimensions, is more heterogeneous than the former. This contrast suggests differences of political system and ideology may be more important barriers to integration than ethnic, religious or cultural traits.

[7] Louis J. Cantori and Steven L. Spiegel, cited in Katzenstein, 1996, p. 129.

Finding the volume of cross-border exchange and capacities for hegemonic leadership unconvincing as explanations of cross-regional integration variations, Grieco has argued that the latter might be attributable in part to stability or shifts in relative disparities: 'When the relative disparities in capabilities [wealth – DW] are shifting over time, disadvantaged states will become less attracted' to integration, which is therefore 'less likely to occur' (Grieco, 1997, p. 176). In other words, if 'hegemonic powers' amass resources that strengthen their capabilities to exercise leadership, other states in the region will become increasingly reluctant to integrate more closely with it. It is difficult, however, to reconcile this argument with the facts that, since German unification, European integration has accelerated rather than receded, that the rise of China has made other East Asian states more rather than less willing to cooperate with it, that, since the Asian crisis, the harder-hit Southeast Asian states have displayed growing rather than declining interest in cooperating with the less hard-hit Northeast Asian states, and that most other East Asian states are displaying increasing preparedness to accept a Japanese leadership role in the region. Indeed, if anything, the empirical evidence seems to point, on balance, to the opposite of Grieco's thesis – to weaker states reacting to disadvantageous shifts in the distribution of power or at least power resources by trying to integrate increasingly powerful states in regional organizations so that these states' power will not be deployed against them.

All the above variables relate to the internal characteristics or traits of regions. Katzenstein, however, identifies an external variable that may be particularly relevant when it comes to explaining why hitherto there has not been more – and more successful – regional integration in Asia. For Katzenstein (1996, p. 141), a critical determinant of the relative strength of European, and relative weakness of Asian, regional integration lies in 'power and norms in the international system', specifically in the attitude taken towards integration in the region by the United States. Following the Second World War and during the Cold War, the US encouraged the growth of regional integration in Western Europe. This was not so, as Katzenstein points out (1996, pp. 141-143) in Asia: 'After 1945 the United States enshrined the principle of bilateralism in its dealings with Japan and other Asian states'.[8] As the US was more powerful vis-à-vis Asian states than in relation to West European states, it could block any initiatives to create strong Asian regional institutions, most of all those from which the US was to be excluded and which the US deemed detrimental to its interests, such as Mahathir's proposed East Asian Economic Group. To be sure, the US attitude to integration in a given region can only explain cross-regional variations in integration to the extent that the states in the region, especially those whose stance is critical for the 'success' of any attempted integration, are vulnerable to American influence, for example owing to their dependence on the US for the provision of their external security and/or as an

---

[8]   Grieco (1998, pp. 249-251) points out, however, that, after the Cold War broke out in Asia, the US initially favoured the creation of (non-Communist) regional economic institutions involving Japan, but other Asian states rejected such proposals because they feared falling (once again, shortly after the Second World War) under Japanese domination.

export market. Moreover, to the extent that the Cold War has ended, states in some regions may now be less dependent on the US for the provision of their security and consequently less susceptible to US influence.

The preceding review and analysis of the pre-conditions of successful regional integration suggests that the following variables could prove helpful in trying to explain the comparative weakness of integration hitherto in East Asia and the current crises of ASEAN and APEC as well as in analyzing the probability of APT developing into a strong regional organization. They are:

- The level of cross-border exchange, the most important dimension of which is generally taken to be trade, between regional states;
- The existence of a 'benevolent' leading or hegemonic state or coalition of such states with the capacity and will to pre-empt potential or mediate and resolve actual distributional conflicts in the region;
- The degree of economic and political homogeneity and corresponding strength of a sense of community or common identity among the region's states;
- For regions within the US's sphere of influence, the attitude of the US towards regional integration efforts.

The Crisis of ASEAN

The principal force that drove the formation and subsequent development of ASEAN in the first two decades of its existence was anti-Communism. ASEAN was designed, first and foremost, to ensure peaceful relations between its member states and to enable each of them, free of conflicts with non-Communist neighbours, to focus its resources on internal economic development and, through growing prosperity, to undercut the appeal of Communism. The organization was created at a time when the Vietnam War was intensifying (and the non-Communist Southeast Asian states were worried by the prospect of a decline in the Western military presence in Asia), it was strengthened when North Vietnam won the war with the South and Communist regimes came to power as well in Cambodia and Laos, and it appears to have achieved the pinnacle of its reputation in its common and ultimately successful struggle between the late 1970s and 1991 to reverse the Vietnamese invasion of Cambodia. Anti-Communism provided a sense of common identity to states that were otherwise so diverse that they were referred to collectively as the 'Balkans' of Asia. They joined forces primarily for 'political objectives, stability and security' (Lee Kuan Yew, 2000a, p. 370). Economic cooperation, not to mention integration, was of secondary importance and, up until the 1990s, actually very limited. The principal obstacle to closer economic cooperation or integration was the disparity in levels of economic development between the ASEAN states. Hence, Singapore, the richest member, long urged an increased emphasis to be put on economic cooperation, but was resisted by other member states, which feared that, as Singapore had a 'more advanced economy, open to the world and almost totally free of both tariff and non-tariff barriers', it would 'benefit disproportionately' from any liberalization of intra-ASEAN trade (Lee Kuan Yew, 2000a, p. 382). In addition, intra-ASEAN trade, at roughly one-fifth of the member states' total external trade, was so low that the prospective market gains from closer integration and, arguably, corresponding business pressure for a reduction of cross-border transaction costs were very limited.

The state that, more than any other, provided the impetus for closer cooperation in Southeast Asia was Indonesia. Suharto's replacement of Sukarno as Indonesian president and his ending of the policy of *konfrontasi* were decisive for ASEAN's foundation in the first place. Indonesia has been variously described as *primus inter pares, de facto* leader or the 'political centre of gravity' in ASEAN (Anwar, 1994, pp. 222-228, 318; Henderson, 1999, p. 445; Leifer, 1989, p. 154; Smith, 2000, p. 28). According to the long-time Singaporean Prime Minister, Lee Kuan Yew, Suharto's role was 'crucial for the success of ASEAN ... Under Suharto, Indonesia did not act like a hegemon. It did not insist on its point of view but took into consideration the policies and interests of the other members. This made it possible for the others to accept Indonesia as first among equals' (Lee Kuan Yew, 2000a, pp. 369-370). By the same token, however, the Indonesian government was co-responsible for the relative modesty of ASEAN's progress towards closer political and economic integration. The infrequency of ASEAN leaders' meetings up to the 1990s has been attributed by Lee Kuan Yew to Suharto's inability to speak English and consequent discomfort in multilateral settings (Lee Kuan Yew, 2000a, p. 371). Up until the late 1980s, Indonesia had the least open economy in ASEAN and was one of the member states most hostile to intra-ASEAN trade liberalization (Stubbs, 2000, p. 298). It was only after a precipitous fall in oil prices, a worsening balance of payments position and economic recession in the mid-1980s that Indonesia begins to shift towards a more liberal economic and trade policy stance, a shift that facilitated moves towards closer economic integration in ASEAN in the 1990s (Stubbs, 2000, p. 303).

Given the extent to which ASEAN depended on anti-Communism as a source of common identity and cohesion, the end of the Cold War could have precipitated a growth of centrifugal tendencies and, in a worst-case scenario, the disintegration of the organization. Indeed, once the Vietnamese had withdrawn from Cambodia, 'Asean solidarity weakened' (Lee Kuan Yew, 2000a, p. 381). In the event, however, far from disintegrating or threatening to do so, ASEAN at first seemed to gain a new lease of life with the launching of both the AFTA and ARF projects. The pre-condition of AFTA was the shift of power away from 'economic nationalists' to liberal reformers in numerous ASEAN member states, not only Indonesia, as a consequence of a recession in Southeast Asia in 1985-86 (Stubbs, 2000, p. 301). By itself, however, this shift of power does not explain the adoption – and subsequent acceleration of the implementation – of the AFTA project; it could have led equally to unilateral national trade liberalization or to an exclusive focus on global, as opposed to regional, trade liberalization. Apart from ASEAN leaders' search for an appropriate new *raison d'être* for the organization following the collapse of Communism, two factors appear to have supplied the momentum behind AFTA. First, since the Plaza Accord, which led to a massive appreciation of the Japanese yen in the middle of the 1980s, there had been a big increase in the volume of foreign, especially Japanese, direct investment.[9] The firms making these investments wanted to be able to move their products between ASEAN states 'without incurring too many costs in the form of tariffs or non-tariff barriers' (Stubbs, 2000, p. 308). They were backed by the Japanese government, which had begun to use the leverage it had over ASEAN governments, thanks to its development aid to them as well as Japanese firms' FDI (Stubbs, 2000, p. 308). The second factor was the economic rise of China, which was becoming an increasingly serious competitor for ASEAN states in low-cost manufactured goods and as a location for foreign direct investment (Stubbs, 2000, p. 309; Lee Kuan Yew, 2000a, p. 382). While, between 1991 and 1993, the volume of FDI in China rose from almost US$5 billion to US$26 billion, ASEAN's share of global FDI fell (Stubbs, 2000, p. 309). For the following decade, Chinese competition for FDI continued to be a major source of pressure on the ASEAN governments not to 'backslide' on their AFTA commitments.[10] Similarly, in combination with expectations that the end of the Cold War would provoke a reduction in the American military presence in Asia, the rise of China – especially concern over the security or strategic implications of its growing potential power in the Asian region – was the main driving force behind the creation of the ARF (Leifer, 1996, pp. 8, 18-19). Through the ARF, the ASEAN states hoped that they could exploit China's 'self-declared priority interest in economic development and cooperation and in a peaceful international environment' and curb any 'irredentist aspirations' it might entertain, for example in connection with the Spratly Islands (Leifer, 1996, p. 18).

The reversal of ASEAN's fortunes began in 1997, when it was hit almost simultaneously by the triple challenge of the Asian financial crisis, a coup in Cambodia shortly before it was due to accede to ASEAN, and the 'haze crisis' in maritime Southeast Asia emanating from huge forest fires in various regions of Indonesia.[11] ASEAN's failure or incapacity to respond very effectively to these issues dealt a severe blow to its image and credibility, a blow that was aggravated in 1999 by the East Timor crisis, the bloodshed caused by militias with the connivance of the Indonesian military following the East Timorese vote for independence. In as far as these crises were tackled, the principal actors involved were not ASEAN, but states or agencies external to the Southeast Asian region, in particular the IMF and the UN.

---

[9] For more comprehensive analyses of this process, see Pempel, 2000, pp. 62-68, Hatch and Yamamura, 1996 and Hughes, 1999.

[10] ASEAN economies are expected to receive 17 per cent of FDI flowing into developing countries in Asia in 2000, compared with 61 per cent in the early 1990s. China received 18 per cent of such FDI in the early 1990s, but will receive 61 per cent in 2000 (*Financial Times*, 2000d).

[11] The impact of the financial crisis on ASEAN is analysed in greater depth by Rüland, 2000, pp. 427-433. He concludes (p. 443) that the financial crisis has plunged Southeast Asian regionalism into a 'major crisis'.

The common denominator in most of these crises was Indonesia. By far the biggest ASEAN member state, it was also the one struck most severely by the economic crisis as well as the perpetrator of the haze and East Timor crises. Protests provoked by the economic crisis swept away the Suharto regime in May 1998 and heralded the arrival of a period of extreme political uncertainty and instability. This uncertainty and instability reduced the level of attention that the post-Suharto governments could give to regional affairs and thus undermined its capacity to fulfil its former leadership role in ASEAN, leaving the organization effectively leaderless. None of the most recent innovations – the approval of the concept of 'enhanced interaction' and the creation of a *troika* of the last, present and next ASEAN 'chair-states' – seems likely to greatly strengthen ASEAN's capacity to address or manage future crises more rapidly and effectively than it has done recent ones. Any significant improvement in ASEAN's crisis management capacity presupposes a preparedness among member states to pool their sovereignty in some regional institution and/or to acquiesce in a curtailment of the hitherto sacrosanct principle of mutual non-interference in member states' domestic affairs. The outcome of the conflict over a curtailment of the mutual non-interference principle in favour of 'flexible engagement' in 1998 sheds important light on the obstacles to closer integration within ASEAN. 'Flexible engagement' was promoted by one of ASEAN's most liberal governments, the Thai, and backed by another of the more liberal regimes, that of the Philippines (Haacke, 1999). Most other member states, however, opposed it. They regarded flexible engagement, according to Haacke, as 'possibly reviving dormant interstate conflicts, with incalculable consequences for national security', as challenging both ASEAN's identity as a regional grouping in which 'democratic and authoritarian states can more or less happily coexist' and the longstanding practice of 'excluding contentious bilateral issues from the agenda of the association', and as having – in the midst of the economic crisis – a possibly negative impact on members' 'pursuit of regime security', since flexible engagement was associated with 'political reform, open societies and the empowerment of civil society' (Haacke, 1999, p. 23). Notably, the governments of all the three new members of ASEAN at that time – Vietnam, Laos and Myanmar – opposed 'flexible engagement' because of worries that it would serve to undermine their authoritarian regimes (Haacke, 1999, pp. 31-33).[12] This shows that ASEAN's 'widening' in the second half of the 1990s has raised the obstacles to its 'deepening' and thus exacerbated its present difficulties.

The above analysis points to several factors as posing formidable obstacles to durable closer integration in Southeast Asia. First, although the growth of FDI in

---

[12]   Fears concerning the resuscitation of dormant inter-state conflicts related in particular to the ethnic and cultural diversity of most Southeast Asian states and the fact that some states' minorities are majorities in neighbouring states. Hence, the Singaporean foreign minister remarked that 'Most of us have diverse populations, with significant differences in race, religion and language, all of which are highly emotive issues. The surest and quickest way to ruin is for ASEAN countries to begin commenting on how each of us deals with these sensitive issues' (quoted in Haacke, 1999, p. 27).

the region since the middle of the 1980s has created a stronger lobby than previously in favour of a reduction of trade barriers between ASEAN members, the level of cross-border ASEAN trade is still much lower than in other major regional trading blocs, suggesting that the potential market gains from closer integration are more limited in Southeast Asia than elsewhere (see table 6.1 below).

Second, since Indonesia's descent into political instability and uncertainty, ASEAN no longer has an undisputed and effective leader – although Indonesia, given its relative poverty, had never been able to be the 'regional paymaster' that Germany has been in the EU. Third, ASEAN's capacity for collective action and crisis management is tightly circumscribed by the disparities among its member states in terms of their level of economic development (and economic policy philosophies) and the degree of openness of their economic systems. These traits or 'deficiencies' do not, of course, mean that ASEAN is destined to self-destruct or disintegrate. They do, however, create a high risk, perceived by ASEAN's own defenders and supporters, that, within and outside of Southeast Asia, the organization will come to be seen as increasingly irrelevant and will therefore increasingly be marginalized (Jayakumar, 2000). In any case, the obstacles to closer Southeast Asian integration are located predominantly within the region itself. ASEAN's anti-Communist *raison d'être* made the organization entirely congruent with and complementary to the US's military engagement in the region. The Johnson administration in the US approved its creation and even claimed to have played a 'critical role' in bringing it about.[13] During the Cold War, the non-Communist Southeast Asian states were 'in no position to move vigorously in a direction that Washington would discountenance' and the leaders of these states, moreover, had 'no inclination to do so' (Mahapatra, 1990, p. 36). The US's current attitude towards ASEAN may best be characterized as one of benign indifference. It is not hostile to Southeast Asian integration, but the region's strategic significance for the US has declined as a consequence of the end of the Cold War and as post-Cold War US foreign policy in general is increasingly subordinated to the primacy of domestic politics.

The Crisis of APEC

Overall, APEC should have been better equipped to bring about integration in the Asia-Pacific region than ASEAN in Southeast Asia. In contrast to Southeast Asia with its comparatively low level of cross-border exchange, as measured by trade interdependence, the APEC member states exhibit a higher level of cross-border exchange, so defined, than the members of any other regional organization, including even the EU (see table 6.1). According to the logic of transnational exchange theory, the potential market gains of integration are greater in APEC, and the pressure from business interests for a reduction of cross-border transaction costs should have been more intense, than in any other regional grouping world-wide.

---

[13] Official US government documents, cited in Mahapatra, 1990, p. 75.

Table 6.1 Regional organizations in comparison: Trade interdependence, capacities for hegemonic and bipolar leadership, economic and political diversity

Organization	Intra-Regional Trade	Hegemonic Leadership Capacity	Bipolar Leadership Capacity	Economic Development	Market Size	Economic Freedom	Political Freedom
	(Trade between member states as percentage of overall trade)	(Biggest economy's percentage of combined GDP of member states)	(Two biggest economies' percentage of combined GDP of member states)	(Ratio of p.c. income of richest to poorest member state)	(Ratio of GDP of largest to smallest economy)	(Ratio of economically 'most free' to 'least free' member state)[1]	(Ratio of politically 'most free' to 'least free' member state)[2]
EU[3]	62.9	27[4]	45[5]	1:3	1:36	1:1.5	1:2
NAFTA	45.8	89[6]	n.a.	1:8	1:22	1:1.7	1:3.5
APEC[7]	70.3	45[8]	73[9]	1:123	1:1853	1:3.3	1:7
ASEAN[7]	22.3	31[10]	n.a.	1:117	1:116	1:3	1:2.8
APT (ASEAN + 3)[7]	35.0[11]	68[12]	83[13]	1:136	1:2533	1:3	1:4.7

Sources: IMF (International Monetary Fund), *Direction of Trade Statistics*; WTO (World Trade Organization); The Economist, *Pocket World in Figures 2000*; Freedom House 1999; The Heritage Foundation 2000.

1. The index of economic freedom devised by The Heritage Foundation ranks countries on the basis of 10 indicators of how government intervention can restrict economic relations between individuals. The indicators relate to external trade, monetary policy, regulation, taxation, the banking system, property rights, government spending, the size of the 'black market' and the extent of wage controls.

2. The index of political freedom devised by Freedom House locates states on a scale from 1 (free) to 7 (not free), according to the degree to which they correspond to the ideals of freedom of expression, assembly and religion (civil liberties) and to the ideals of free and fair elections, having competitive political parties, having a strong opposition, protecting minority rights, absence of political violence, etc. See Freedom House, 1999, pp. 546-553.

3. Excluding Luxembourg in terms of population and market size.

4. Federal Republic of Germany.

5. Federal Republic of Germany and France.

6. USA.

7. Excluding Brunei in terms of population and market size.

8. USA.

9. USA and Japan.

10. Indonesia.

11. Total largely excludes trade involving Cambodia and Laos.

12. Japan.

13. Japan and China.

In addition, to the extent that the US accounts for a larger share of APEC members' combined GDP than Germany in the EU or Indonesia in ASEAN (see table 6.1), APEC had, in the US, a member state with a stronger capacity to provide benevolent leadership, also because of its relative wealth, than either of these two states in their respective organizations.

In the middle of the 1990s, APEC indeed looked as if it could develop into a vehicle for much closer trans-Pacific integration. Initiated by the Australian government, with Japanese government support, in the late 1980s, APEC had really been launched by the first leaders' meeting at Seattle in 1993.[14] The Seattle summit signified a strengthened American commitment to the organization's success and is said to have 'softened up' the EU and contributed to the successful conclusion of the GATT Uruguay Round in December the same year. At the following summit, at Bogor in Indonesia in 1994, the APEC leaders reached 'potentially the most far-reaching trade agreement in history' (US economist Fred Bergsten, quoted in Ravenhill, 2000, p. 320). APEC was poised to become, according to the same commentator, 'a driving force for worldwide trade liberalization' (Bergsten, 1994, p. 20). At the turn of the century, however, analyses of APEC's achievements and prognoses for its future were a great deal more sober. The same commentator again concluded that there was 'no evidence to date that any APEC country has taken additional liberalization steps solely due to APEC' (quoted in Ravenhill, 2000, p. 323). According to a recent analysis of APEC's first decade, the organization has so far 'failed to deliver' (Ravenhill, 2000, p. 320). APEC was 'adrift' or enveloped by a 'sense of crisis' that threatened to destroy the process of trans-Pacific economic cooperation and what it had so far managed to achieve (Ravenhill, 2000; Garnaut, 1999, p. 3).

Why is APEC threatening to derail? Two developments had dealt a strong blow to its credibility in the second half of the 1990s. The first of these was the incapacity of the member governments to agree on the implementation of the trade liberalization programme that they had adopted at Bogor. The Bogor programme was derailed, for the time being at least, by the collapse of the EVSL (Early Voluntary Sectoral Liberalization) scheme at the 1998 leaders' summit at Kuala Lumpur. The root cause of the failure of the EVSL scheme, which was intended to 'jump-start' the implementation of the Bogor programme, was irreconcilable conflicts over trade liberalization between the US, backed by the most developed, 'Anglo-Saxon' member states, on the one hand, and Japan, supported by most of the East Asian states, on the other. The second was the 1997-98 Asian financial crisis. Initially, the 'powerful influence' of the US in APEC had been underlined by the APEC finance ministers' affirmation that the IMF should continue to play the leading role in managing the Asian crisis. Asian member states' failure to back a Japanese proposal for an Asian bail-out fund was attributed to the US's ability, in contrast to that of Japan, to 'provide a growing market for Asian exports at a time when virtually all of the region's financially strapped economies are in desperate need of foreign exchange' (Altbach, 1997, p. 2). As the crisis hit home, however,

---

[14] For two analyses that argue that Japan's role in the birth of APEC was more central than normally acknowledged hitherto, see Terada, 1999, and Krauss, 2000.

other East Asian states came to evaluate the merits of an Asian monetary fund or functionally equivalent mechanism differently (see below). In as far as member governments felt constrained by APEC (rather than the IMF or WTO) undertakings to keep their markets open, APEC may have served as an important anti-protectionist 'bulwark' (interview with Australian APEC analyst; see also Harris 2000: 508). However, the fact that APEC itself did little to alleviate the crisis and that, in as far as it did anything, it backed the IMF's crisis-management prescription, severely damaged the organization's reputation and credibility in East Asia. As the New Zealand Prime Minister subsequently commented, trying to explain APEC's stagnation: 'There are terribly bitter feelings in Asia from the US response to the Asian economic crisis … What they saw was when Russia and Brazil had their crises, they [the Americans] rushed in, and they didn't do that for Asia, and yet these countries in Asia had been, they [the Asians] considered, very loyal friends' (Helen Clark, quoted in *Financial Times,* 2000a).

The intra-APEC conflicts over trade liberalization issues, manifested afresh in the organization's inability to agree on an agenda for a new round of world trade liberalization talks, and its impotence in the face of the Asian crisis have been the catalysts of the APEC's current malaise. The more 'structural' roots, as opposed to immediate causes, of this malaise lie, however, in the incapacity of the US to provide undisputed leadership of APEC, the incapacity of the US and Japan, in the absence of effective hegemonic leadership by the US, to provide stable bipolar leadership in the organization, and, combined with a weak or non-existent pan-Pacific sense of identity or community, the degree of disparity of levels of economic development of the APEC member states. First, American leadership of APEC has been contested by Japan, which, supported by most East Asian states, has opposed both the priority attached by the US to trade liberalization as opposed to APEC's other pillar, the promotion of economic and technical cooperation, and – successfully, as evidenced in the case of the failed EVSL – the US's preferred strategy of trade liberalization (see Ravenhill, 2000, pp. 321-326).[15] Second, the US's preparedness to provide leadership to APEC has receded since the early 1990s, when its strengthening served the useful purpose of expediting the conclusion of the Uruguay Round. This may reflect in part Washington's frustration at its inability to obtain acceptance of its trade liberalization agenda among other APEC member states, notably among the East Asian ones. However, it also reflects the rising domestic opposition to and eroding consensus over trade liberalization and globalization in the US itself, epitomized by the Clinton administration's failure to win Congressional approval for an extension of its fast-track authority for international trade agreements, and the US's *unwillingness* (as opposed to incapacity) to provide APEC with *benevolent* leadership (in the sense of Mattli and Cohen), which would have implied its lending stronger relative support to the economic and technical cooperation components of APEC's activities and displaying greater flexibility in the pursuit of its trade liberalization

---

[15] In his recent analysis of APEC (2000, pp. 488-489), Krauss also stresses the centrality of the US and Japan and their relationship to the organization.

goals and concerning the conditions for IMF financial aid to East Asian states stricken by the 1997-98 crisis. Underlying the conflicts between the US and most of the East Asian states over the pace and extent of regional trade liberalization was the East Asians' fear that their economies were too weak to cope with the competitive pressures to which they would be exposed if intra-APEC trade were to be liberalized at the rate demanded by the US. This fear explains in part the ASEAN states' resistance to a strong APEC in the first place.

The disparities in the level of economic development between the APEC members are even greater than those which divide the ASEAN states, although some of the poorest ASEAN members do not belong to APEC (see table 6.1). These disparities are arguably all the more important as sources of controversy over APEC's purposes and trade liberalization strategies as members are not linked by a strong sense of community or identity: 'There is no Pacific community in a linguistic, religious, cultural or ideological sense. Nor is [there] a history of regional consciousness or a framework of institutions comparable to those developed in Europe over the last thirty-five years' (Higgott, 1995, pp. 364-365). At the level of civil society, pan-Pacific linkages are also relatively weak.[16] As APEC itself has only engaged systematically with business interests and has a mainly adversarial relationship with other kinds of non-governmental organizations, it has ostensibly failed so far to contribute significantly to the development of a sense of pan-Pacific community or common identity that could form a bedrock for much closer cooperation or integration (Ravenhill, 2000, p. 327).

The Rise of ASEAN Plus Three

As noted above, the Malaysian Prime Minister Mahathir's proposal to found the EAEG had failed, in practice, to get off the ground in the early 1990s, owing to American opposition and the reluctance, at least partially attributable to the US hostility, of some key other East Asian governments, including the Japanese and the Indonesian. However, by the end of the decade, the APT, which is 'in effect' the EAEG,[17] had not only emerged, but had already 'gone far beyond' what Mahathir had originally proposed (see introduction). What had brought about this apparent transformation of the fortunes of attempts at closer East Asian cooperation or integration, at the same time as those of ASEAN and APEC, in contrast, were waning?

---

[16]   Grieco (1998, pp. 246-247) argues that 'Just as the absence of broader intergovernmental arrangements and networks creates an unfavorable context for the construction of an Asia-Pacific economic regime, so too the absence of a significant network of societal linkages spanning East Asia and the Americas makes the formation of such agreements more difficult and doubtful'.

[17]   Quote from Alatas, 2001, p. 8. For a similar observation, see also Garnaut, 1999, p. 28.

The first stimulus to closer East Asian cooperation came at least partially from outside the region. The first attempts at policy coordination between the APT states were made in preparation for the first ASEM (Asia-Europe Meeting) session staged in 1996.[18] The creation of ASEM had been the work in particular of Singapore, supported on the European side most strongly by France (Yeo Lay Hwee, 2000, p. 114). The East Asian states were interested especially in encouraging European FDI in Asia (Harris, 1999, p. 18). The EU states' primary interest had been in improving access to East Asian markets and securing a greater share of the benefits of the East Asian 'miracle'. But both sides of ASEM were interested in cooperating with each other to try to curb unilateralist propensities in the US (Yeo Lay Hwee, 2000, pp. 116-117). In as far as, in co-founding ASEM, the EU states fostered East Asian cooperation, this may have been a largely unintended consequence of the initiative. However, in co-launching and participating in the initiative, the EU states implicitly recognized East Asia as a 'distinct geographical and economic entity' (Leong, 1999, p. 19). They have explicitly encouraged closer East Asian monetary cooperation, while, on the East Asian side, 'these talks with Europe are helping us build up our own Asian identity' (Japanese finance minister Miyazawa, quoted in *Financial Times,* 2001b).

The second stimulus for the formation of APT stems from APEC's internal conflicts over trade liberalization and the relative priority assigned to trade liberalization and the promotion of economic and technical cooperation as goals of the organization. In most of the major APEC disputes, most of the East Asian member states have found themselves on one side, opposed to the US, supported by most of the other 'Anglo-Saxon' states, on the other. The US also stymied any APEC initiative to address the Asian financial crisis by any other means than the orthodox prescriptions of the IMF (Higgott, 1998). The perception of sharing a common opponent in APEC conflicts has fostered the growth of an at least limited sense of identity among East Asian states, while the incapacity of APEC, owing to these conflicts, to advance pan-Pacific trade liberalization has encouraged some of these states to search for other levels and frameworks at or within which closer economic cooperation may be explored (Bergsten, 2000b, p. 21).

The most powerful motor behind the rise of APT, however, has been the 1997-98 Asian financial crisis. Two repercussions of the crisis in particular have powered APT's take-off. The first is that the crisis, which exploded in Thailand and swept as far north as South Korea, has greatly strengthened perceptions of mutual economic interdependence and vulnerability between Southeast and Northeast Asia. APT leaders recognize, according to one of them, that 'you cannot talk about North-east Asia and South-east Asia. What happens in South-east Asia will have an impact on North-east Asia. The financial crisis which engulfed Asean's economies in 1997 later spread to South Korea, whose economic slowdown partly caused tourism receipts and investment flows into South-east Asia to contract. So now we are thinking in terms of evolving an East Asian community ...' (Goh Chok Tong, Singaporean Prime Minister, quoted in *Straits*

---

[18]   ASEAN consisted at this time of seven states, Myanmar, Cambodia and Laos all joined it later in the decade.

Times, 1999c).[19] At least some ASEAN leaders also see that the crisis has widened the economic gap between Northeast and Southeast Asia. Apart from trying to make the ASEAN states more attractive as locations of FDI through the AFTA and AIA (ASEAN Investment Area) projects, they are keen to hitch their bandwagon to the Northeast Asian economies in the expectation that this will be beneficial to economic development in Southeast Asia.[20] As the ASEAN states make up no more than about 1.5 per cent of the world economy, a proportion which pales in comparison with the collective share of Japan, China and South Korea, Southeast Asian leaders may also anticipate that, as part of a larger East Asian entity, they will be able to exercise a stronger influence than at present on the policies of major international organizations.

The second relevant repercussion of the crisis, as forecast by Higgott (1998), is that it has created a powerful backlash of resentment against the US and its dominant role in international economic and financial affairs. According to Bergsten (2000b, 22), 'most East Asians feel that they were 'both let down and put upon by the West' in the crisis.[21] They believe that the West, in particular the US, 'let down' Asia because Western financial institutions and other actors caused or exacerbated the crisis by withdrawing their money from the region and then refused, as did the US, for example, in respect of Thailand – to take part in rescue operations to manage it. They believe that East Asia has been 'put upon' by the West because of the way in which, through the IMF, the West dictated the international response to the crisis and because of the perceived consequences of the IMF's prescriptions, which were seen as having aggravated rather than alleviated the crisis (Bergsten, 2000b, p. 22). The perception that the crisis was exploited by the US for its own policy ends may have been strengthened by Malaysia's relative success at managing the crisis without having had recourse to IMF aid (Bergsten, 2000a, p. 3). In some circles and countries, the resentment may also have been fuelled by the US's greater indifference to the destabilization of

---

[19] For similar sentiments expressed by the South Korean president, Kim Dae Jung, see *Straits Times*, 1999a. See also Ito, 2000; Wanandi, 2000; and Alatas, 2001, pp. 1-2.

[20] For a description of the divergent economic trajectories of North- and Southeast Asia since the Asian crisis, see Lee Kuan Yew, 2000b, where he remarks that in view of higher growth rates in North- as compared with Southeast Asia, 'it is as well that Southeast Asia has established closer links with North-east Asia through the Asean + 3 annual meetings'. Among the Southeast Asian states, Singapore is especially worried about the growing economic divergence between North- and Southeast Asia (see *Financial Times*, 2001a).

[21] The Singaporean Prime Minister, Goh Chok Tong, has remarked similarly that anti-US rhetoric is 'striking a degree of resonance among some countries in the [Southeast Asian] region. The US has lost some goodwill ... since the Asian financial crisis .... Such resentment can be highly destructive. It will erode the goodwill that the US has built up in the region, and affect US and political interests' (*Straits Times*, 2000c).

authoritarian regimes which it supported when, during the Cold War, it was opportune for it to do so.[22] Mahathir continues to be the most vocal spokesperson for this sentiment in East Asia, but the extent to which his analysis of 'globalization' and the domination by the West/US of international economic organizations is shared in the region should not be under-estimated, as recent expressions and manifestations of anti-Western sentiment in some East Asian states, such as Indonesia, indicate. Democracy and democratization, in as far as it occurs, do not guarantee pro-Western or pro-American policies. Following the internecine trade policy conflicts in APEC and ASEM-motivated intra-regional consultations, the Asian crisis, through the heightened perceptions of economic interdependence between North- and Southeast Asia that it has generated and the way in which the crisis is perceived in the region to have been managed by the IMF, has given a further boost to the emergence of a sense of community or common identity in East Asia.

Since the Asian crisis, two other, related forces have served to propel the East Asian states towards closer cooperation. These are the stagnation of global trade liberalization, epitomized by the collapse of the 1999 Seattle talks intended to launch a new round of WTO trade negotiations, and the concomitant signs of increasing integration in other regions, of which the most striking manifestation is the launching of the common currency by 11 EU member states, also in 1999.[23] In East Asia, notably in Japan, there are fears that, combined and especially if the American economy should go into recession, these processes could lead to the unraveling of the multilateral trading system and the emergence of a system based largely on regional economic blocs in which Western (and Central) Europe and North (and perhaps South) America would constitute blocs, but East Asia, if it did nothing, would not (*Financial Times*, 2000c). Asian states, according to Lee Kuan Yew, must 'follow the global trend towards regionalisation ... because only then could Asia exercise its bargaining power against other regions' (quoted in *Straits Times*, 2001).

The rapid rise of APT, although triggered by the Asian crisis, has thus been fuelled mainly and unintentionally by the behaviour of external actors, first and foremost the IMF and the US, but also the EU. To these external sources of impetus towards closer East Asian cooperation or integration must be added one internal strategic motive: the objective of integrating an increasingly powerful China into its regional environment, parallel to the prospective integration of China

---

[22] Thus, the Indonesian ex-president Suharto, for example, allegedly blames his fall on the desire of 'the West' to have him out (Lee Kuan Yew, 2000a, p. 314). Conversely, of course, democratic reformers in Indonesia may appreciate the IMF for its having facilitated Suharto's downfall.

[23] These two factors are emphasized as engines of the 'new regionalism' in East Asia by Ito (2000). However, for Ito, the deputy vice-minister for international affairs in the Japanese finance ministry, the single most important factor is that 'Asians realise they have much in common. More than half the exports of Asian economies go to other Asian economies. Financial contagion is still present ...'.

into the multilateral trading system through its pending accession to the WTO. This has been identified as a critical function of APT in Japan (Owada, 2000, pp. 12-13). In Southeast Asia, too, APT is seen as a mechanism for coping with the rise of China as a 'great power', complementary in this purpose presumably to the more explicitly security-oriented ARF (Wanandi, 2000).[24]

The Prospects of ASEAN Plus Three

For a region that has long been distinguished by the relative poverty of its 'international society' (Segal, 1997, pp. 243-245), the momentum towards closer inter-state cooperation in East Asia that has developed within the last three years is indeed striking. As already noted, however, the APT's only concrete achievement hitherto is the Chiang Mai currency swap agreement. High-flying rhetoric aside, is there any reason to think that East Asian 'integration' will succeed where and when pan-Pacific integration is 'adrift' and when efforts to integrate the part of the region, the Southeast, which has the longest history of post-Second World War inter-state cooperation, have run into such grave difficulties?

There are a few such reasons. The first is that, with intra-regional trade accounting for a half of overall trade, the volume of cross-border exchange in East Asia, while it is considerably lower than that in the APEC and the EU, surpasses that in North America (NAFTA) and is more than twice as high as in ASEAN (*The Economist*, 2000).[25] To the extent that this creates corresponding potential market gains from integration and business pressure for regional integration, East Asia should have no less 'integration' potential than North America and a great deal more than the sub-region of Southeast Asia. The empirical question of whether such potential has indeed been translated into corresponding business pressure for greater integration and how 'successful' such pressure will prove is difficult to answer at the present time.[26] However, to the extent that East Asia recovers from the 1997-98 crisis and re-attains rates of economic growth higher than those elsewhere, the level of economic interdependence in the region is bound to increase in the same way that it did in the period prior to the Asian crisis, while the East

---

[24]   Wanandi identifies the rise of China along with the economic interdependence illustrated by the Asian crisis as the 'two main driving forces behind East Asian regionalism'.

[25]   Within the APT, which, of course, excludes the important regional economies of Hong Kong and Taiwan, internal trade accounts for 35 per cent of overall trade (see table 6.1).

[26]   An 'Asian executives poll', involving an undisclosed number of respondents, conducted in December 1999 found massive (77 per cent) support for the creation of an APT common market. A slight majority (50.6 per cent) of respondents rejected the idea of an Asian monetary union, but 43.3 per cent, including a majority of respondents in Japan, South Korea and the Philippines, supported it. Chinese executives were not surveyed (*Far Eastern Economic Review*, 1999/2000, p. 90).

Asian states' dependence on the American market, which is still strong, may decline.

The above analysis rests, in any case, on the assumption that the focus of East Asian regionalism will be primarily on (internal) trade liberalization. The distinguishing trait of the new East Asian regionalism, however, is that its initial focus has been less on trade than on money (Dieter and Higgott, 2000; Dieter, 2000a and 2000b). There may be two explanations for this phenomenon. First, following reductions in tariffs and non-tariff barriers through successive GATT /WTO trade liberalization agreements, the net benefits of regional free trade agreements are lower than they used to be. Second, as a consequence of the liberalization of capital movement worldwide, the potential benefits of monetary cooperation, coordination or integration, as the contrasting experiences of Asia and Europe in the last decade show, have grown (Dieter, 2000a; Bergsten, 2000a, pp. 3, 5-7). To the extent that cross-border capital flows continue to increase as a consequence of the globalization of financial markets, the incentives for closer regional monetary cooperation to combat currency instability are likely to rise – in East Asia as elsewhere. In this respect, globalization fosters regionalization. Not only has East Asia, in the wake of the 1997-98 crisis, a strong incentive to move towards closer monetary cooperation (which explains why the first concrete APT achievement has been a currency swap agreement), it also possesses the means, namely huge official monetary reserves (over $US 900 billion, far exceeding those of the EU states or the US in the year 2000), to protect itself against international monetary instability (Dieter, 2000a, p. 25; Bergsten, 2000a, p. 14). This is not simply an issue of mutual protection against the vagaries and instability of 'global capitalism'. Events such as the 1997-98 Asian crisis – witness Indonesia – may have profoundly destabilizing social and political consequences so that currency crises are not mere technical, economic or financial issues, but political issues relating to governmental or indeed regime survival. This may help to explain why, after first rejecting the Asian Monetary Fund proposed by Japan, China has meanwhile adopted a more positive stance on issues of Asian monetary cooperation.

Mattli's 'demand' condition for successful regional integration may and, to the extent that relatively rapid economic growth resumes, will probably increasingly be fulfilled in East Asia. In as far as business pressure to realize potential market gains through integration should be lacking, the goals of self-preservation and retaining political power may push incumbent political elites to forge ahead with plans for closer monetary cooperation or integration to strengthen their capacity to ward off currency crises. Whether the political or 'supply' conditions of successful integration will be met, however, is a great deal less certain.[27] The fulfilment of two such conditions is especially problematic. First, while East Asia has one state that may at present be a potential hegemonic power, namely Japan, it is not

---

[27] The present author thus concurs with Pempel (2000, pp. 58-59) and Zhu Zhiqun (2000, pp. 510, 512, 524), who both argue that the obstacles to closer regional integration in East Asia are more political than economic.

completely certain that it wishes to assert regional leadership and still less certain whether, should it unequivocally stake such a claim, this would be acceptable to other states in the region.

Of these potential obstacles to 'hegemonic leadership' in East Asia, the former is the less acute. Japan has, in one form or another, dispensed a vast sum of financial aid to other East Asian states, albeit the government's deepening fiscal crisis is bound to set increasing limits on its *financial* capacity to assert regional leadership and its still relatively closed economic system inhibits it from playing the role of 'consumer of last resort' for other East Asian states performed instead by the US (Lehmann, 2000).[28] Certainly, however, Japan is currently the only East Asian state that conceivably has the means to 'pre-empt potential or mediate and resolve actual distributional conflicts in the region' (see above). Despite being cast as a 'reactive state' (Calder, 1988), prevented by multiple constraints from playing a leadership role in international affairs, following the Second World War, Japan has in fact displayed a growing propensity to provide regional leadership since the Asian crisis, as testified by the tenacity with which it has tried to forge closer East Asian monetary cooperation (Hughes, 1999).[29] The growing paralysis of multilateral trade liberalization negotiations, coupled with the increasing vagaries of US trade policy and rising regionalism in other regions and continents, have all contributed to a reorientation in Japanese trade policy in favour of negotiating regional or bilateral agreements (Tett, 2000).

Even if Japan should be both able and willing to assume the leadership of an increasingly integrated East Asia, it is questionable whether such a leadership claim is or would be accepted by other states in the region. Other states' (variable) reluctance to accept a Japanese leadership role has been attributed to relative disparities of capabilities (Grieco, 1997, pp. 177-178 and 1998, pp. 250-251). More likely, however, it relates to a combination of perceptions and the reality of Japanese aggression in the Second World War and perceptions of how Japan has – or has not – come to terms with its war role during the last half century (see Phar Kim Beng, 2000). Many other East Asian states may nonetheless acquiesce in Japanese regional leadership as indispensable for closer regional cooperation or

---

[28]   According to Kojima (2000, p. 14), total Japanese financial aid to other East Asian states during the economic crisis amounted, up to the end of 1999, to $US 130 billion. Hughes (1999, p. 30) refers to a $US 42 billion Japanese contribution to the 'financial rescue effort in East Asia', at least up to mid-1998. In July 2000, the Japanese government unveiled a $US 15 billion five-year assistance plan to help East Asian states to develop their IT infrastructures and train workers (*Straits Times*, 2000b).

[29]   Other observers suggest that Japanese aspirations for regional leadership in Asia pre-date the recent crisis. Green (2000) argues that a 'broad consensus is emerging that Japan should assert its national interests more forcefully and be a more "normal" nation'. He attributes this development to generational change and to perceived threats to peace in Northeast Asia. See also Hatch and Yamamura, 1996, pp. 199-203.

integration.[30] It is unlikely, however, that the biggest of them, China, will do so. For reasons related to the past, present and the future, Sino-Japanese rivalry may prove to be the most intractable obstacle to closer East Asian integration. The *past* continues to bedevil the Sino-Japanese relationship, because, in China's view, Japan has not apologized for and adequately come to terms with the period of the Japanese invasion and occupation of China from 1937 to 1945 and arguably because the regime in Beijing manipulates anti-Japanese sentiments for domestic and external political gain. The *present* bedevils the relationship to the extent that there remains an element of systemic competition between a democratic Japan and a Communist China that is well on the way to becoming a market economy, but remains politically authoritarian. The *future* casts a shadow over the relationship because, if the present rates of economic growth (and the growth of military prowess) in China are projected into the future, it is not difficult to see the day when, in terms of the capacity for regional leadership in East Asia, China will eclipse Japan. This prospect makes Japan nervous (Zhang Xizhen, 2000). Very likely it also makes the Chinese leadership less willing to acquiesce in Japanese regional leadership than it would be otherwise.

The above considerations together account for the fact that, despite ever closer Sino-Japanese economic ties, 'enormous mutual suspicion' still characterizes the two states' relations (James Miles, quoted in Montagnon, 2000).[31] Unsurprisingly, since the Cold War divided China and Japan rather than forcing them together, Sino-Japanese relations have not been transformed in the way that Franco-German relations were transformed in Western Europe after the Second World War, resulting in the formation of a probably uniquely intense bilateral intergovernmental relationship (Webber, 1999, p. 2). Short of such a transformation or at least a substantial improvement in Sino-Japanese relations, neither of which seems imminent, APT is likely to be plagued by a similar constellation of 'dueling' would-be hegemons that has weakened APEC – only worse, to the extent that the dueling hegemons in APEC, the US and Japan, are at least linked in a tight bilateral security relationship, grounded partly in perceptions of a Chinese threat, while Japan and China still see themselves as potential military adversaries. Moreover, if a close bilateral Sino-Japanese relationship were to develop in regional affairs, it is not certain that this would be as acceptable to smaller East Asian states as has been Franco-German leadership to smaller member states in the EU, given the suspicions directed against Japan because of its Second World War role and against China because of its role as a vanguard of Communist revolution from 1949 to the middle of the 1970s, its rapidly growing economic power and its territorial disputes with a number of other states in the region.

---

[30]   The most 'Japanophile' Asian leader, Malaysian Prime Minister Mahathir, has actually chastised Japan for not displaying stronger regional leadership (*Financial Times,* 2001c).

[31]   The Chinese scholar, Zhang Xizhen (2000) argues that the evolution of Sino-Japanese relations during last decade has become 'increasingly worrying'. *The Economist* too (2001) describes the bilateral relationship as 'bad and getting worse'.

Are there, in East Asia, any conceivable surrogates for a legitimate regional hegemon or close Sino-Japanese cooperation? In the past, ASEAN itself has played a key role as a 'catalyser' of dialogue between the big powers of the region, including the US, as manifested not only by its instigation of the APT, but also by its creation and management of the ARF and the role it played in trying to resolve the Cambodian crisis in the 1980s. Could it, for example through creative mediation between Japan and China, transform the embryonic APT into a strong East Asian regional organization? The hitherto at best marginal and at worst non-existent role of the ARF in the management of the major regional security issues (East Timor, North Korea, cross-strait relations, etc.) gives little cause for optimism that ASEAN could provide a surrogate to Japanese or Sino-Japanese regional leadership. The resolution of the Cambodian crisis, on the other hand, had more to do with the progressive harmonization of the big powers' interests and positions on the issue than ASEAN diplomacy (Alagappa, 1993). Together these cases suggest that ASEAN is unlikely to be able to serve as a powerful motor of East Asian integration where Japan and China do not judge closer regional cooperation in any case to be in their own respective interests. In other words, ASEAN may be able to lead Japan and China to the water, but is unlikely to be able to force them to drink. Such a scenario is all the more unlikely as long as ASEAN itself is weakened by economic weakness and political uncertainty or instability in many of its own member states. Any expectation that ASEAN, directly or indirectly, could serve as the motor of much closer integration between the APT states must rest on the hope that conflicts of interests between big powers on economic issues prove much more susceptible to mediation and reconciliation than on security or strategic issues.

Apart from the likely absence of an *undisputed* leading state or stable and accepted joint Sino-Japanese leadership and the incapacity of ASEAN to provide the leadership which therefore will be lacking, APT is also burdened by a level of internal political and economic diversity that naturally exceeds ASEAN's and is comparable with that of APEC (see table 6.1).[32] It is not so relevant that, whereas, if one takes Huntington's controversial classification of 'civilizations' (Huntington: 1996) as a guide, all the 15 current EU member states except for Greece belong to the same (Western) civilization, APT members embrace four distinctive (Sinic, Japanese, Islamic and Buddhist) civilizations. Cultural-religious heterogeneity in Southeast Asia did not prevent the creation and survival of ASEAN, whereas, in culturally less heterogeneous Northeast Asia, no inter-state integration took place at all. Patterns of subregional integration in East Asia after the Second World War had less to do with culture and religion than with political ideology and the competition of Communism and (partly democratic and partly authoritarian) capitalism. In a more subdued form than during the Cold War, this cleavage, to which the tensions on the Korean peninsula and in 'cross-strait' relations bear

---

[32] Zhu (2000, p. 525) argues that 'the diverse levels of economic and political developments' constitute the primary barrier to the 'formation of economic and political union in Pacific Asia'. In the present author's view, however, his analysis overlooks the countervailing forces militating in favour of closer East Asian integration.

witness, continues to form a powerful obstacle to closer inter-state cooperation in East Asia. It is complemented and, to the extent that the still or former Communist regimes belong simultaneously to the poorest in East Asia, reinforced by vast disparities in levels of economic development which are likely to translate into divergent preferences on issues of trade liberalization in the region.

The driving force behind the formation and development of ASEAN up until the end of the Cold War, despite its culturally, economically and politically diverse make-up, was anti-Communism. Internal divergences were put aside in the face of a (perceived) common external threat or challenge. In part, the historical origins of the EU too underline the utility of such a threat or challenge for the formation of a sense of 'common identity' or 'community'. The 'other' that helped to mould a common European identity was the Soviet Union or Russia (Neumann 1996). The perceived common external threat or spectre that has so far driven the process of inter-state cooperation in East Asia is that of Western or, in particular, American domination, generated by the 1997-98 Asian crisis – the new, *East Asian* integration is taking place in effect in opposition to the West in general and the US in particular.

How will the US react to an East Asian integration process from which it is excluded, but which it has inadvertently fostered? Will it acquiesce in it or oppose it and if it does oppose it, will it succeed in blocking it, as Mahathir evidently fears?[33] In contrast to the preceding Republican administration, which railed against 'lines being drawn down the Pacific' (former Secretary of State James Baker), the Clinton administration displayed a more relaxed attitude to East Asian regional cooperation.[34] It tempered the longstanding US preference for bilateralism in its security relationships with Asia by, for example, proposing the formation of multilateral 'security communities' involving erstwhile adversaries such as China (*Straits Times*, 2000a). If George W. Bush's administration should prove as hostile to East Asian integration as his father's was, the US's allies in the region would come under strong pressure to put a brake on this process. However, the inhibiting impact of such a stance on East Asian integration may be outweighed by the catalyzing impact of other policies emanating or not emanating from Washington. Although the administration itself may be strongly in favour of free trade, the extremely even balance of power between Republicans and Democrats in the Congress is likely to pre-empt any strong new American initiatives for world trade liberalization. At the same time, the new president (and ex-governor of Texas) has indicated that in terms of foreign economic relations he will give priority to the deepening of ties with Mexico and the rest of the Americas, thus promoting closer integration between North and South America (US Trade Representative Robert Zoellick, quoted in *Financial Times*, 2001d). Especially if accompanied by a general re-assertion of unilateralism in US foreign security policy (cf. Higgott,

---

[33] See the article based on an interview with Mahathir in *Financial Times*, 2000b.

[34] See Leong 1999, pp. 14, 21-22 and remarks attributed to the US State Department East Asian specialist in the Clinton administration, Stanley Roth, in *Asiaweek*, 2000, pp. 45-46.

2000, pp. 14-18), such a combination of stagnation in world trade liberalization and growing North/South American integration would give strong additional encouragement to states in East Asia to forge closer ties with each other. The net combined (and unintended) effect of Bush's policies and the balance of power both between the administration and the Congress and within the Congress may thus be to accelerate moves towards closer East Asian integration.

Conclusions

Contrary to occasional reports, ASEAN and APEC are certainly not on the verge of 'dying'. But, while there will be no 'funeral' for ASEAN or APEC, there is a high risk that the two organizations will remain to a greater or lesser extent incapacitated. The Asian crisis has exposed their underlying structural weaknesses. The ASEAN member states may be insufficiently economically interdependent and economically and politically too diverse, and the absence, since the demise of Suharto's Indonesia, of an undisputed and effective 'leader' or coalition of leading states may be too debilitating, for Southeast Asian integration to proceed much further than it already has. For its part, APEC is enfeebled by an even higher level of economic and political diversity among its member states than in ASEAN, by the unwillingness of the US to play the role of a benevolent Asia-Pacific hegemon, and, in the absence of benevolent US leadership, the incapacity of US and Japan to align their positions on key issues confronting the organization.

Will the East Asian states 'wed' instead in the APT, which has started to fill the vacuum left by ASEAN and APEC? East Asia is already a feasible 'monetary' region and as to the extent that it recovers from the 1997-98 crisis it may also increasingly constitute a feasible 'trading' region. Whether, to adopt the phraseology of Karl Marx, it will develop from being a 'region-in-itself' into being a 'region-for-itself' will depend predominantly on political variables. At present, the vast intra-regional political-systemic disparities pose an extremely high obstacle to the development of much closer inter-state cooperation, although these disparities could gradually be reduced to the extent that the democratization process advances in the region and that overt military conflict can be averted in the region's major (Northeast Asian) flashpoints. Neither of these scenarios, however, can be taken for granted. APT's prospects also hinge heavily on the willingness and capacity of either Japan to provide undisputed and effective regional leadership or, failing this, on the capacity of Japan and China to provide the nascent organization with such leadership in tandem. Japan might be willing and capable of providing leadership to APT, but Japanese leadership is likely to be contested, if not by other states then at least by China. Joint Sino-Japanese leadership is improbable, given the tensions that still plague relations between the two states, and it might be contested by the region's smaller states even if it were to be on offer. External forces, in particular the direction of the US's foreign and external trade policies under the new administration of George W. Bush, could, in the short term, boost moves towards closer East Asian integration. In the longer term, however, it is unlikely that external forces could supply the cohesion required for successful regional integration where the internal pre-conditions are absent or too weak. As Mattli observes (1999a, pp. 63-64), the 'overwhelming majority' of 'counter-integration' projects, those stimulated by the launching of integration projects in other regions, has failed. Overall, therefore, the odds are against APT developing into a strong regional organization. That the emergence of regional economic blocs may not be the most likely alternative to a global multilateral trading system is shown by the current explosion of interest in bilateral free trade agreements between states of mostly similar levels of economic development, often located in different geographic regions. If this scenario materializes, it would not be the EU, but rather Singapore and New Zealand, signatories of such an agreement in the year 2000, that would show East Asia its future.

Acknowledgements

This chapter is a revised version of a paper presented to the 17th conference of the Euro-Asia Management Studies Association (EAMSA) at INSEAD's Campus in Asia, Singapore, 23-25 November 2000. The author would like to thank officials of the ASEAN Secretariat in Jakarta and the Indonesian, Malaysian and Australian foreign ministries and APEC and ASEAN scholars at the Institute for Strategic and International Studies, Kuala Lumpur and the Australian National University, Canberra for their agreement to be interviewed on the issues with which this chapter deals. To preserve their anonymity, they are not identified by name where quoted in the chapter. The author would also like to thank Melina Nathan, Tommy Koh, Stuart Macmillan, Anthony Smith and an anonymous referee for their comments on earlier versions of the paper. As always, the author, of course, bears sole responsibility for the chapter's contents. INSEAD too is thanked for the financial support which enabled the research on which this chapter is based to be conducted.

References

Alagappa, Muthiah (1993), 'Regionalism and the Quest for Security: ASEAN and the Cambodian Conflict', *Journal of International Affairs,* Vol. 46(2) (Winter).
Alatas, Ali (2001), *'ASEAN Plus Three' Equals Peace Plus Prosperity,* Institute of Southeast Asian Studies, Singapore (Working Paper No. 2, January).
Altbach, Eric (1997), 'News from South Korea, Japan casts cloud over APEC summit', *JEI Report,* No. 45, 5 December, 3 pp.
Anwar, Dewi Fortuna (1994), *Indonesia in ASEAN: Foreign Policy and Regionalism,* Institute of Southeast Asian Studies, Singapore.
ASEAN Secretariat (1999), *ASEAN Annual Report 1998-1999* (www.aseansec.org).
Asiaweek (2000), 'Southeast Asia adrift', 1 September, pp. 45-46.
Bergsten, Fred (1994), 'APEC and World Trade: A Force for Worldwide Liberalization', *Foreign Affairs,* Vol. 73(3), pp. 20-26.
Bergsten, Fred (2000a), *The New Asian Challenge,* Institute for International Economics, Washington, DC (Working Paper 00/4).

Bergsten, Fred (2000b), 'Towards a tripartite world', *The Economist*, 15 July, pp. 20-22.

Bordo, Michael D. and Jonung, Lars (1999), *The Future of EMU*, unpublished paper.

Calder, Kent (1988), 'Japanese Foreign Economic Policy Formation: Explaining the Reactive State', *World Politics*, Vol. 60(4), pp. 517-541.

Castellano, Mark (2000), 'East Asian Monetary Union: More than just talk?', *JEI Report*, no. 12A, 24 March, 9 pp.

Cohen, Benjamin (1998), *The Geography of Money*, Cornell University Press, Ithaca/London.

Dieter, Heribert (2000a), *Monetary Regionalism: Regional Integration without Financial Crises*, Centre for the Study of Globalisation and Regionalisation, University of Warwick, Coventry, (CSGR Working Paper No. 52/00).

Dieter, Heribert (2000b), 'Ostasien nach der Krise: Interne Reformen, neue Finanzarchitektur und monetärer Regionalismus', *Aus Politik und Zeitgeschichte*, B 37-38/2000, pp. 21-28.

Dieter, Heribert and Higgott, Richard (2000), 'East Asia looks to its own resources', *Financial Times*, 16 May.

The Economist (2000), 'Happy neighbours', 26 August, p. 71.

The Economist (2001), 'Japan starts picking on China', 10 February, pp. 31-32.

European Voice (1998), 'Bonn exposed as EU's loudest dissenting voice', 15-21 October.

Far Eastern Economic Review (1999/2000), 'Asian Executives Poll', 30 December/6 January, p. 90.

Financial Times (1999), 'East Asian nations vow to forge closer ties', 29 November.

Financial Times (2000a), 'APEC has run out of steam, says New Zealand', 30 June.

Financial Times (2000b), 'Mahathir's last stand', 6 October.

Financial Times (2000c), 'New balance in Asia', 11 October.

Financial Times (2000d), 'Foreign investors desert south-east Asia for China', 13 October.

Financial Times (2000e), 'Japan's first bilateral trade deal shifts policy', 23 October.

Financial Times (2001a), 'Singapore seeks strength via Asian model of regionalism', 11 January.

Financial Times (2001b), 'Japanese and French bridle at dominion of the dollar', 16 January.

Financial Times (2001c), 'Mahathir blames Japanese woes on copying the West', 19 January.

Financial Times (2001d), 'Zoellick warns on world trade talks', 31 January.

Freedom House (1999), *Freedom in the World: The Annual Survey of Political Rights and Civil Liberties 1998-1999*, Freedom House, New York.

Garnaut, Ross (1999), *APEC Ideas and Reality: History and Prospects* (unpublished paper presented to the 25th Pacific Trade and Development Conference, Osaka, 16-18 July).

Green, Michael (2000), 'The Forgotten Player', *The National Interest*, No. 60, Summer.

Grieco, Joseph (1997), 'Systemic Sources of Variation in Regional Institutionalization in Western Europe, East Asia, and the Americas', in Edward D. Mansfield and Helen V. Milner (eds), *The Political Economy of Regionalism*, Columbia University Press, New York, pp. 164-187.

Grieco, Joseph (1998), 'Political-Military Dynamics and the Nesting of Regimes: An Analysis of APEC, the WTO, and Prospects for Cooperation in the Asia-Pacific', in Vinod K. Aggarwal and Charles E. Morrison (eds), *Asia-Pacific Crossroads: Regime Creation and the Future of APEC*, St. Martin's Press, New York, pp. 235-256.

Haacke, Jürgen (1999), *'Flexible Engagement': On the Significance, Origins and Prospects of a Spurned Policy Proposal*, Institute of Southeast Asian Studies Singapore (International Politics and Security Issues No. 3).

Harris, Stuart (1999), *The Asian regional response to its economic crisis and the global implications*, Department of International Relations, Research School of Pacific and Asian Studies, Australian National University, Canberra (working paper No. 1999/4).

Harris, Stuart (2000), 'Asian multilateral institutions and their response to the Asian economic crisis: the regional and global implications', *The Pacific Review*, Vol. 13(3), pp. 495-516.

Hatch, Walter and Yamamura, Kozo (1996), *Asia in Japan's Embrace: Building a Regional Production Alliance*, Cambridge University Press, Cambridge/New York/Melbourne.

Henderson, Jeannie (1999), *Reassessing ASEAN*, Oxford University Press for the International Institute of Strategic Studies, Oxford/London (Adelphi Paper 328).

The Heritage Foundation (2000), *2000 Index of Economic Freedom* (www.heritage.org/index).

Higgott, Richard (1995), 'Economic co-operation in the Asia Pacific: a theoretical comparison with the European Union', *Journal of European Public Policy*, Vol. 2(3), pp. 361-383.

Higgott, Richard (1998), 'The Asian economic crisis: A study in the politics of resentment', *New Political Economy*, Vol. 3(3), pp. 333-356.

Higgott, Richard (2000), *US Foreign Policy After the Election: Will it Make a Difference Who Wins?*, Centre for the Study of Globalisation and Regionalisation, University of Warwick, Coventry (CSGR Working Paper No. 50/00).

Hughes, Christopher W. (1999), *Japanese Policy and the East Asian Currency Crisis: Defeat or Quiet Victory?*, Centre for the Study of Globalisation and Regionalisation, University of Warwick, Coventry (CSGR Working Paper No. 24/99).

Huntington, Samuel (1996), *The Clash of Civilizations and the Remaking of the World Order*, Simon and Schuster, New York.

Ito, Takatoshi (2000), 'Asian countries must stand together', *Financial Times*, 21 November.

Jayakumar, S. (2000), 'Regaining ASEAN's lost ground', *Straits Times*, 25 July.

Katzenstein, Peter J. (1996), 'Regionalism in Comparative Perspective', *Cooperation and Conflict*, Vol. 31(2), pp. 123-159.

Kindleberger, Charles (1973), *The World in Depression 1929-1939*, University of California Press, Berkeley and Los Angeles.

Kojima, Tomoyuki (2000), 'The Sino-Japanese Relationships: From a Neighbouring Friendship to a Partnership for Cooperation', *China Perspectives*, No. 30, July-August: 4-16.

Krauss, Ellis S. (2000), 'Japan, the US, and the emergence of multilateralism in Asia', *The Pacific Review*, Vol. 13(3), pp. 473-494.

Lee Kuan Yew (2000a), *From Third World to First. The Singapore Story: 1965-2000*, Singapore Press Holdings/Times Editions, Singapore.

Lee Kuan Yew (2000b), 'A more self-assured East Asia in the making', *Straits Times*, 17 August.

Lehmann, Jean-Pierre (2000), 'Why Asia needs a Japanese engine', *Financial Times*, 8 March.

Leifer, Michael (1989), *ASEAN and the Security of South-East Asia*, Routledge, London/New York.

Leifer, Michael (1996), *The ASEAN Regional Forum*, Oxford University Press for the International Institute of Strategic Studies, Oxford/London (Adelphi Paper 302).

Leong, Stephen (1999), 'The East Asian Economic Caucus (EAEC): "Formalised" Regionalism Being Denied', in Bjorn Hettne, Andras Inotai and Osvaldo Sunke (eds), *National Perspectives on the New Regionalism in the South*, Macmillan/St. Martin's Press, London/New York.

Mahapatra, Chintamani (1990), *American Role in the Origin and Growth of ASEAN*, ABC Publishing House, New Delhi.

Mattli, Walter (1999a), *The Logic of Regional Integration: Europe and Beyond*, Cambridge University Press, Cambridge/New York/Melbourne.

Mattli, Walter (1999b), 'Explaining Regional Integration Outcomes', *Journal of European Public Policy*, Vol. 6(1), pp. 1-27.

Montagnon, Peter (2000), 'Disillusion leads to growing spirit of co-operation among Asian nations', *Financial Times*, 21 July.

Neumann, Iver B. (1996), *Russia as Europe's Other*, European University Institute, Florence (RSC Working Paper).

Owada, Hisashi (2000), *Japan-ASEAN Relations in East Asia* (text of speech delivered to a conference of the Singapore Institute of International Affairs and the Embassy of Japan, Singapore, 16 October).

Pempel, T.J. (2000), 'International finance and Asian regionalism', *The Pacific Review*, Vol. 13(1), pp. 57-72.

Phar Kim Beng (2000), 'Sorry seems to be the hardest word for Japan', *Straits Times*, 12 October.

Ravenhill, John (2000), 'APEC adrift: implications for economic regionalism in Asia and the Pacific', *The Pacific Review*, Vol. 13(2), pp. 319-333.

Rüland, Jürgen (2000), 'ASEAN and the Asian crisis: theoretical implications and practical consequences for Southeast Asian regionalism', *The Pacific Review*, Vol. 13(3), pp. 421-451.

Segal, Gerald (1997), 'How insecure is Pacific Asia?', *International Affairs*, Vol. 73(2), pp. 235-249.

Smith, Anthony (2000a), *Strategic Centrality: Indonesia's Changing Role in ASEAN*, Institute of Southeast Asian Studies, Singapore.

Stone Sweet, Alec and Sandholtz, Wayne (1998), 'Integration, Supranational Governance, and the Institutionalization of the European Polity', in Sandholtz and Sweet (eds), *European Integration and Supranational Governance*, Oxford University Press, Oxford, pp. 1-26.

Straits Times (1999a), 'Kim calls for forum to encompass all East Asia', 23 November.

Straits Times (1999b), 'ASEAN is perceived as a successful grouping', 27 November.

Straits Times (1999c), 'Asean to push free-trade plan as part of recovery', 29 November.

Straits Times (2000a), 'Security communities for a secure Asia', 1 April.

Straits Times (2000b), '"ASEAN Plus Three" move closer', 27 July.

Straits Times (2000c), 'PM warns against taking US-Asean ties for granted', 8 September.

Straits Times (2001), 'US presence in E. Asia will become more vital, says SM', 23 January.

Stubbs, Richard (2000), 'Signing on to liberalization: AFTA and the politics of regional economic cooperation', *The Pacific Review*, Vol. 13(2), pp. 297-318.

Terada, Takashi (1999), *The Genesis of APEC: Australian-Japan Political Initiatives*, Australia-Japan Research Centre, Australian National University, Canberra (Pacific Economic Papers, No. 298).

Tett, Gillian (2000), 'Japan strays from the true path of multilateral trade', *Financial Times*, 17 May.

Wanandi, Jusuf (2000), 'East Asian regionalism - the way ahead', *Straits Times*, 4 December.

Yeo Lay Hwee (2000), 'ASEM: Looking Back, Looking Forward', *Contemporary Southeast Asia*, Vol. 22(1), pp. 113-144.

Zhang Xizhen (2000), 'Tokyo in the throes of China syndrome', *Straits Times*, 26 November.

Zhu Zhiqun (2000), 'Prospect for Integration in Pacific Asia', *Asian Profile*, Vol. 28(6), pp. 509-526.

PART IV
Constructivist Perspectives

Chapter 7

Rethinking the Mediterranean: Reality and Re-Presentation in the Creation of a 'Region'

Michelle Pace

Introduction

Inasmuch as the sustained political relevance of regions depends on people considering them to be relevant to their activities, the study of regions must in some way include the study of meaning and identity. The main objective of this chapter is to analyse the relevance of 'regions' in general and more specifically the case of the Mediterranean 'region'.

Critical/constructivist approaches to region building and discourse analysis highlight the social/political creation of spaces and specifically of regions through discursive practices. In seeking to problematise conventional conceptions of regionality and to specifically re-think the Mediterranean 'region' in an open, relational, political context, this chapter opts for a 'discursive-constructivist' approach as the way forward to the study of regions. This involves both agency and structure in its focus on the *processual* aspects of region making. Hence, it follows that regions are determined by discourses. A concept such as that of 'region' is always in the making and, thus, requires flexible analysis. Therefore, rather than presenting the Mediterranean as a unified, fixed concept, this chapter chooses a critical and flexible framework for the analysis of regional studies and for the understanding of this area. An examination of European Union (EU) discourses on the Mediterranean – in particular its Euro-Mediterranean Partnership (EMP) – reveals practices that give this area a fixed meaning. The resulting Mediterranean is just one of the many 'others' in Europe's self-identification process.

In line with the social constructivist approach adopted in this chapter, section one will present the background for an understanding of regions as socially constructed phenomena, with a specific focus on the Mediterranean area. The next section will present the theoretical framework that influenced this thinking. The third section is devoted to an application of this theoretical approach to the Mediterranean. The next section presents the background of EU-Mediterranean relations since the 1960s up to the most recent initiative, the EMP. The following section offers a critical, analytical review of EU discourses on the Mediterranean inherent in the latter policy. The final section draws some conclusions from these arguments.

Background

The geographical term 'region' usually refers to a homogenous area of the earth's surface with characteristics that make it distinct from the areas that surround it. Moreover, a geographical area is generally specified as a 'region' when there is a certain pattern of regular relations and interactions among the countries in that area. The distinction between areas may be based on natural or man-made characteristics or a combination of both. Scale distinctions are made between large-scale regions of continental proportions (*macro regions*) down to very small structures (*micro regions*).[1]

In the case of the Mediterranean, the classification of this '(macro) region' is a rather contentious one.[2] In fact, there are two different representations of the Mediterranean commonly found in the literature: the Mediterranean as a 'region' (with sub-regions) or the Mediterranean as an interface between coherent regions. In the case of the former, the Mediterranean is said to embody many 'sub-regions' (geographically speaking).[3] These can broadly be said to be southern Europe, which includes southern European Union (EU) member states as well as Malta, Cyprus and (at least parts of) Turkey; North Africa which consists of Algeria, Libya, Mauritania,[4] Morocco, and Tunisia; and the Levant which comprises Egypt,[5] Israel, the Palestinian Territories, Jordan, Lebanon and Syria.[6] Once again, these classifications are debatable: Some would further differentiate between

---

[1]   Moreover, regions with common region-wide characteristics (*uniform regions*) are distinguished from those in which the characteristics are most strongly discernible at or near the centre of the region and least strongly at the boundaries (*focal regions*).

[2]   It is important to note that this chapter aims to investigate the study of macro – that is, transnational regions rather than micro or sub-national – regions.

[3]   It is essential to clarify at this point that there is no incompatibility between regarding the Mediterranean as a region and then saying that it is composed of sub-regions – the two views are compatible.

[4]   Mauritania is often considered a marginal state although it has been mentioned as a potential future partner in the Euro-Mediterranean Partnership (EMP) (EuroMed Report, 2001).

[5]   In many ways, it may be argued that it makes sense to include Egypt under the Levant sub-region, even if it also features as part of North Africa.

[6]   There is a reluctance to include the Balkans (as a Mediterranean sub-region), which instead is seen as a separate region ('Balkans' or 'South East Europe').

southern Europe (four EU states) and south-eastern Europe. Moreover, many would call southern Europe and North Africa regions (or something other than sub-regions). One may argue that these can be both regions and sub-regions, namely that for example North Africa can be classified as a region, but also as a sub-region of the Middle East.

Despite these controversies, there is a growing inclination to consider the Mediterranean in a holistic fashion in all Western institutions, as a geopolitical unit that ties the nations around its rim with common 'concerns' and shared 'interests'. Various academic studies, especially those within the field of international relations (IR), also treat the Mediterranean as a 'region' due to the interdependent nature of the political, economic and social issues affecting the area as a whole.[7] Before presenting the theoretical framework of this chapter, there is a question which needs to be dealt with: One may ask, but why the Mediterranean? The Mediterranean is an area that involves the leading states and international organisations across the world. Also it is often conceived of as a meeting point of the 'North' and 'South' and of different cultures in the area: as an interface between three continents, North Africa, Europe and Asia: as a 'region' with diversity and as a complex case which presents challenges – perhaps more than other areas. It is also a reasonably contemporary theme to test the condition of regionality. Moreover, there seems to be a gap in the available material with a critical approach to the study of the Mediterranean area.

As its title suggests, this chapter seeks to problematise conventional conceptions of regionality and to specifically re-think the Mediterranean 'region' in an open, relational political context. It also aims to suggest a re-imagining of this 'region' politically, geographically, socially and culturally. In an era of globalisation, boundaries are constantly shifting and changing. The major objective of this chapter is to *conceptualise* the social construction of this area (as a holistic 'region') and the underlying assumptions of such imaginings, and in so doing to reveal how regions, in particular the Mediterranean region, are produced and reproduced over space and time. Despite the several references to the Mediterranean as a taken-for-granted concept, there does not seem to be one common understanding of this area. The biggest problem I wrestled with was 'What is the Mediterranean?' The issue I struggled with (considering my critical approach to the study) was that, on the one hand, any attempt to map the (social) relations of the Mediterranean and their overlapping points runs the risk of misinterpretation. On the other hand, there is an obvious need (especially for an academic investigation like this one) to ensure that the Mediterranean is recognizable as an object of study and that all those interested in this area are in fact talking about the same 'thing'. The boundary lines that govern the physical and political relationships of the Mediterranean 'region' may provide such a common understanding. However, to draw such precise boundaries is bound to lead to misunderstanding and misinterpretation. Once such lines are drawn, they give the impression that all relations pertaining to this 'region' fall neatly within

---

[7]   Most of these studies focus on security issues in the Mediterranean. (Aliboni, 1992; Kinacioglu, 2000; Latter, 1992).

these boundaries. The result in effect is to fix the Mediterranean's changing geography and to leave the 'region' without meaning. Therefore, whether one takes the view of the Mediterranean as a 'region' or as a meeting place between regions, one runs into this problem, so neither is satisfactory. But one can ask does this mean that we stop talking about 'regions'? This chapter has started by criticising the notion of the Mediterranean as a 'region' sufficiently strongly to put the term *region* in inverted commas. The next question that follows from such a stance is then whether there is any justification for continuing to refer to the 'region' (even in inverted commas) or whether one should advocate a policy of referring to the Mediterranean as 'the Mediterranean area', thereby adopting a more neutral term. The latter option is the one chosen for this chapter. This rethinking of the Mediterranean has been encouraged by the fact that this area is a complex space in the making and involves overlapping and intersecting relationships. It also involves some concept of evolution, of dynamics. Since it does not seem justifiable to talk about the Mediterranean region, the latter will be treated as an area to which theories of regionalism have been (controversially) applied.

Regionalism is often said to result from increasing interdependence between states. For instance, after the Arab-Israeli war of 1973, the Euro-Arab Dialogue was created as a means of regularizing, controlling and manipulating the emerging system of Euro-Arab interdependence. The then European Community (EC) member states attempted to influence the economic policies of oil-rich Arab states through economic aid to resource-poor Arab countries (what one author calls 'the evolving substance of associative diplomacy' (Al-Manì, 1983, p. 36)). The Euro-Arab Dialogue was rather unsuccessful because European policy remained politically motivated.[8] During the early 1970s, the EC also looked at the Mediterranean and perceived this area's potential as an interface between the two regions of Europe and Africa. In seeking to establish relations with its southern neighbours, the EC launched its (so-called) Global Mediterranean Policy (GMP). Following the end of the 'Cold War' and the collapse of the bi-polar international system, regionalism once again appeared as a natural phenomenon in the new international order. The EC saw the transition to a new European order as a positive opportunity to develop its external role. (The Maastricht Treaty of December 1991 adopted a Common Foreign and Security Policy [CFSP]). Euro-Mediterranean relations were enhanced through the New Mediterranean Policy (NMP, also known as the Renewed or Redirected Mediterranean Policy or RMP) that was introduced in December 1990. EC-Mediterranean initiatives however failed to adopt the necessary long-term policies required to tackle the increasing disparities between the two sides of the Mediterranean. In an effort to revive the

---

8   Europeans advised Arab states to avoid capital-intensive industries and to concentrate on labour-intensive industries geared for Arab markets rather than for export. Thus, the Europeans anticipated the potential danger of competition resulting from a possible future Arab industrial surplus and thereby sought to protect European markets (Al-Manì, 1983, p. 61). It should come as no surprise that the Euro-Arab dialogue did not succeed since any EC/EU political policy is usually clothed in trade clothes, for most European attempts at political/regional unification have functional goals.

potential of the Mediterranean (to become a region), the EU launched the EMP in November 1995. To date, this policy is believed to be the most successful of all EU Mediterranean initiatives since it addresses political, economic and cultural relations between European and Mediterranean partners. But have EU member states reflected on what constitutes this Mediterranean area? And if so, what type of Mediterranean are they dealing with? Is the Mediterranean just an 'other' in Europe's self-identification process? This chapter holds that EU identity is forged partly through the effect of a security threat it feels from the Mediterranean area. Before going any further, it is worth introducing the theoretical framework that has informed the approach adopted here.

Theoretical Framework[9]

The questions of 'place', boundaries, borders and space have raised issues of theoretical approaches to the study of 'regions' and even of the nature of theory itself; of the conceptualisation of regions and their practical definitions and of the criteria that make regions, or what should be studied 'within' them. These questions have recently found themselves on the agenda of IR.[10] The following brief outline relates to conventional theories that mostly focus on regional arrangements based on security co-operation issues. These will lead us on to the more critical theoretical approaches to the study of regions that look into the processes of region making through the practice of foreign policy and identity politics.

In the edited book of Lake and Morgan, Pervin claims that:

> (T)he transformations generated by the end of the Cold War and the demise of the Soviet Union as a superpower create an opportunity to re-evaluate the interrelation between regional subsystems and the global system, and to distinguish the autonomous dynamics of the region from the impact of external influences (Pervin, 1997, p. 272).

The historical development of the past twelve years together with advances in IR theory, have led to a renewed interest in explaining the origins and the management of conflict at the regional level. The authors' theoretical framework is based on the basic unit of analysis being the regional security complex (or RSC, a term introduced by Barry Buzan, see below) that is defined as 'a set of states continually affected by one or more [positive or negative] security externalities that

---

[9]   Although the theory reviewed may initially seem odd – since most of it does not address regionalism explicitly – I draw upon these works and connect them with the analysis of regions through the common underlying theme in these works, that is, identity politics.

[10]   See for example Buzan (1991) on regional security complex theory or one of the standard textbooks in the area, Lake (1997).

emanate from a distinct geographic area' (Pervin, 1997, p. 12). Membership in an RSC includes great powers whose actions generate externalities in the region or who are affected by the externalities produced there.[11] Morgan proposes a 'ladder' of regional order ideal types where successive rungs on the ladder represent greater levels of interstate cooperation with the final stage being integration (Lake and Morgan, 1997). The very fluidity of one of the empirical cases cited in this book – that of Pervin on the Arab-Israeli conflict – reflects the complexity of the concept of regional order and the need for additional theoretical work. As Lake points out, 'negative security externalities will always be greater, and positive security externalities smaller, than the states of a regional security system desire' (Lake and Morgan, 1997, p. 59).

In his 1991 book, Buzan claims that 'In security terms, "region" means that a distinct and significant subsystem of security relations exists among a set of states whose fate is that they have been locked into geographical proximity with each other' (Buzan, 1991, p. 188). He also introduced the notion of a *security community* and a security complex theory. For Buzan '(A) security complex is … a group of states whose primary security concerns link together sufficiently closely that their national securities cannot realistically be considered apart from one another' (p. 190). A security community is one of the extreme relational possibilities along the spectrum of a given complex that defines security interdependence. In a security community 'disputes among all the members are resolved to such an extent that none fears … either political assault or military attack by any of the others' (p. 218). Moreover, for Buzan, a mature anarchy is a position on his continuum of regional security configurations, related to the idea of a 'security community'.[12]

Following Buzan's work, there has been further exploration of such a security 'problem' at the Centre for Peace and Conflict Research in Copenhagen. This 'Copenhagen school' of security studies – which includes Buzan – took a new turn and refined the concept of security. The new focus and emphasis shifted from the primacy Buzan originally gave to the state, to society and identity. It was recognised that societal identity is a core value vulnerable to threats and in need of security. As examples, the authors state that identity has been a source of resistance to integration in the EU and the major cause of upheaval in central and eastern Europe. In this revised work, Wæver et al. (1993) gave an old idea a new angle in *discourse* on international affairs. Identity was no longer consigned to the neorealist category of soft security concepts. The analysis of collective identity

---

[11] A similar work is that of Cantori and Spiegel (1970).

[12] For Buzan the movement on a spectrum of weak to strong states directs attention to the domestic level, and the corresponding movement from immature to mature anarchy (or in regional terms from security complex to security community) introduces the possibility and need for change at the international level. However, this advance depends on maintaining the realist doctrine on state primacy. The agency of change in the domestic as in the international sphere cannot be attributed to sub-state or supra-state actors.

started to be approached from a deconstructionist, sociological angle, focusing on the practices and processes by which people and groups construct their self-image. However, the work of Wæver et al. (as a continuity with the seminal work of Buzan) appears to have remained somewhat realistic. Their term 'society' is not meant to connote a process of negotiation, affirmation and reproduction, or even to embrace the 'system of interrelationships which connects the individuals who share a common culture', as in Giddens's (1989, p. 32) more traditional sociological formula. Wæver et al. prefer a less fluid reality. Their work remains at a level of reification that excludes discussion of questions of process. If these authors were really concerned with the process of social construction, they would not regard society as 'a social agent that has an independent reality' (Wæver et al. 1993, p. 26) and they would have to conduct an analysis at the sub-social level.

Wæver et al. briefly acknowledge that economic threats to particular groups within a society can affect the security of society as a whole. But this passing interest in the multi-dimensionality of threats is not sustained. They therefore approach the apparent fact of societal identity as a taken-for-granted reality that defines the security problem. However, identity is not a fact of society; it is a process of negotiation among people and interest groups. Being Maltese, Greek, Danish, Belgian or Moroccan is a consequence of a political process, and it is that process of identity formation, not the label symbolizing it, which constitutes the reality that needs explication (McSweeney, 1996). Moreover, where identity is relevant, it is just as likely to be the *effect* of a security problem rather than its cause. This may be analysed by deconstructing the process of identity formation at the sub-societal level. Identity is often constructed and articulated as a result of a labelling process that mirrors a conflict of interest at the political level.[13]

The perennial struggle between different discourses about the definition of the categories and phenomena that make up our world is the agenda of the work of critical theorists. By following Foucault's studies, critical/constructivist approaches point to the need for pluralist methods in an analysis of discourses. These works offer tools that can be applied to regionalism and region-building and which can then highlight the social/political creation of spaces and specifically of regions. Boundaries have a crucial role in the construction of regional consciousness. Therefore, this process of region-construction is linked to the politics of identity since regions can be formed in response to discursive formations of an 'other'.

Neumann (1996) is one such scholar who works within the field of regional and identity studies. Within this strand of constructivists in IR, Wendt (1999) holds that the structures of human association are determined primarily by shared ideas rather than material forces. Hence, it follows that regions are determined by discourses. He further argues that identities and interests of purposive actors, including states, are constructed by these shared ideas rather than given by nature. Wendt criticizes neo-realists (like Buzan) and neo-liberals, who see the structure of the international system as a distribution of material capabilities, with the neo-liberals adding institutions to the material base. He maintains that it is ideas and culture that

---

[13]   For instance, because the EU feels a security threat from the Mediterranean, its identity is, as an effect, threatened.

constitute the meaning and content of material factors. He further states that ideas shape the identities and interests of actors. Wendt develops a complex theory of structure, agency and process based on three distinctions: macro and micro levels; causal and constitutive effects; and effects on behaviour and on identities and interests. Since Wendt argues that social structures (such as regions) may constitute agents (states), 'the nature of states might be bound up conceptually with the structure of the state system', and that 'the ideas held by individual states are given content and meaning by the ideas which they share with other states'.[14] In contrast to Waltz (1979), Wendt demonstrates that many of the states' essential qualities (including identities) are contingent and socially constructed. Whereas neo-realists explain structural change in terms of the distribution of capabilities, Wendt sees it in terms of the evolution of identities through natural and cultural selection. He also discusses how interdependence, common fate, homogenisation and self-restraint may be responsible for collective identity formation (that is, including regional identity).[15]

Wendt's work brings us back to the discussion of regions and how it is approached in this chapter. In fact, this research has been influenced by works of the same vein as Wendt's. Rather than applying conventional, static theoretical approaches which reify a social configuration of region as an entity that exists, there is a need to shift from these approaches into a process based framework (such as that of Wendt) where the project of region-making is analysed as an ongoing process and not as a fixed concept; and, moreover, as a process through which collective identities are negotiated and continuously in the making. This approach does not imply discarding conventional theoretical frameworks. Rather, in order to have a more informed view of 'reality', we need to work with theories in parallel, that is, to take a multi-disciplinary approach to the study of regions.

Foucault claims that 'discourse in general and scientific discourse in particular, is so complex a reality that we not only can but should approach it at different levels and with different methods' (Foucault, 1973, p. xiv). In his approach, fragmentation becomes both politically and theoretically explicit. Foucault concentrates on representations of an external world as an 'extra-discursive' order – the institutional structure out of which discourses develop and that embodies discourse. He therefore takes discourses or discursive practices as his units of analysis. It is important here to broaden out what is considered to be 'discursive'. Foucault (1972; 1977) has a broad conception of discourse. Discourse could be said to be the production of meaningful ensembles. This includes the manner in which 'objects' become objects in particular meaningful ensembles (we should recognize that 'object' is merely another meaningful category). For example, in his *History of Sexuality*, Foucault (1979-1986) argues that the idea of sexuality as something meaningful, with some social significance, became possible when people started 'talking' about something called 'sexuality' in the Victorian era.

---

[14]   For example, what makes 'us' European?

[15]   In effect, this is what the EU does with the 'regions' it co-operates with: it homogenises them in order to develop a European (EU) collective identity.

Foucault is here actually talking about discourse and the construction of social reality. He argues that it is only when a society points out 'something', talks about it, attempts to classify it, categorize it, regulate it and administer it that this something becomes 'real', that is, socially relevant and meaningful. When these practices are repeated thereafter in a regular fashion and in a similar manner over long periods of time, they then acquire a sense of durability and stability. It thereby follows that for Foucault (1972), discourse is always a kind of 'event', in the sense that it is always in the making. In this manner, he analyses the whole context in which things are uttered and therefore points to the varied nature of the social world. Accordingly, the world is a product of our ideas; we are left only with general meanings.

Following Foucault, we can then analyse social actions as part of a wider process of the social construction of 'reality'. In the case of region building, we can see this in terms of an attempt by international organizations to define and extend their power over wider geographical spaces. It is as if region-formation constitutes a realm of an area's reality that in turn defines the reality of those empowered to carve this area out. The process of region building can also be seen as part of a wider process of political control – a sort of 'political engineering' by means of which a politically, economically or socially desirable area is constituted. Such control implies that there is somebody who does the controlling but in terms of Foucauldian thought, regionalism can be seen as one of the multitude of power centres which might, often in contradictory ways, be involved in the constitution of political, economic and social control. Discourse analysis can thereby be used as a method to analyse the social world, specifically those statements which point to the varied nature of this world. Foucault's methodological works can therefore be seen as tools for studying the world in the light of statements that constitute our social world.

Arguing in the same direction as Wendt's critical thinking, the work produced by political geographers with an IR interest has also influenced the approach followed in this chapter. The work of Gearóid Ó Tuathail (1996) in particular shows how the end of the Cold War brought about the need to understand a vast and differentiated world that can no longer be reduced to a set of overriding categories – such as East versus West – that drove conventional perspectives on world affairs for so long. Ó Tuathail argues that geopolitical claims are implicit in the practices of foreign policy and can be deconstructed from the texts and speeches of political leaders and the various 'intellectuals of state-craft', from scholars to popular commentators and television 'experts'. Such works are concerned with how 'hidden' or implicit geographical assumptions about state territories and global geopolitics affect both political theory and practice.

The edited collection by Herb and Kaplan (1999) also provides a good discussion on the possibilities and limitations of a regional identity, making the point that, for example, a European identity is not akin to a national identity writ large. Rather, a whole array of events/discourses and activities is producing a sense of European identity as an addition to existing national and local ones. These events range from the EU passport and rights of residence in other member countries to trade disputes with the United States, common attitudes to foodstuffs, and collaboration (or 'twinning') with regions and localities in other countries. These works adopt an approach which defines geopolitics as a type of 'governmentality' – a term coined by Foucault to refer to a means of organizing population, security and territory. Therefore, it follows that, in this perspective, geopolitics is how global politics is made visible and meaningful to both political leaders and national populations. Critical geopolitics problematises this linkage by questioning the essential identities upon which geopolitics relies, its strategies of mapping the world, and its interpretations of the maps so constructed. These approaches also explore the techniques of 'seeing' that make global political mapping possible. Rather than functioning as mirrors of nature, maps select and order information according to authoritative sources as sites of global power. Thus, attention focuses on the institutions and people producing geopolitical knowledge[16] and the corresponding types of knowledge produced.[17] For Foucault (1972, p. 32), 'the unity of a discourse is based not so much on the permanence and uniqueness of an object (but) on the space in which various objects emerge and are continuously transformed'. He also talks about institutions and how they are 'fixed' by the power relations inherent in them. For him, knowledge is power to define others. Any order that exists is seen as coming from a 'process of signification' or the drawing of differences within the chaos. According to Foucault, we bring a momentary order to the world when we make a statement. As mentioned earlier, he refers to a collection of related statements or events as 'discourse'. Therefore, through the production of statements in discourses, 'subjects' are created or 'constituted' by 'signifying practices'. Discourses must therefore be treated as and when they occur. Following Foucault, it can be asserted that foreign policy makers occupy a set of sites or places which are constructed to fit into global schemas of security interests and commitments that inform day-to-day global 'problem solving'.[18]

In line with the deconstructivists' work on these topics, this chapter holds that collective identity is a matter of discursive practices, inasmuch as security and insecurity depend on discourses of vulnerability and threat. Thus, EU discourses of the Mediterranean reflect upon EU identity, and it is usually the *kind* of Mediterranean that the EU constructs (mostly through its foreign/Mediterranean

---

[16] Michel Foucault equates such a production of knowledge to the attainment of power (1972).

[17] See Mignolo (1995) where the author states that roughly during the thirteenth century, 'the centre of the world ... was not Jerusalem, but the Mediterranean, a geopolitical centre around which the main places of the Arab world are located (p. 237)'.

[18] One can also mention the disciplinary (that is, geography) site, or the particular ways of seeing the world that have been sponsored by academic geography. These privileged eyewitness and travel accounts, as well as cartographic portrayals that survey and monitor the place characteristics of the world. Another site complex is that of popular culture wherein films, magazines, and video games, for example, produce and reproduce colonial, ideological and other geopolitical images. This chapter mainly deals with the foreign policymakers' site.

policy) which reveals a lot about the security/insecurity felt in Brussels. It is therefore important to take discourses seriously and to have some criteria for assessing them and where possible to correct them. It is often left to the anarchic struggle of the most powerful interests to judge what counts as the parameters of collective identity. The collective question 'Who are we?' implicitly makes the point that collective identity is a choice made by people (through processes of negotiations), not a property of society which transcends their agency. The question is how (that is, what is the process whereby) these diverse individual choices come together in a clear or vague collective image, and how disputes about identity, with security implications, are settled. Collective identity is not just 'out there', waiting to be discovered. What is 'out there' is an identity discourse on the part of political leaders, intellectuals and many others, who engage in the process of constructing, negotiating and affirming a response to the demand for a collective image (this demand is at times urgent, especially in times of crisis). However, even in times of crisis this is never more than a provisional and fluid image of ourselves as we want to be. This argument clearly has relevance to the concept of societal security and the main interest of this chapter: namely, the processes of the social construction of the Mediterranean by EU actors as a response to the need of forging an EU collective identity.

In Berger and Luckmann's (1966) sense of the social construction of reality, such a focus views 'society' and 'state' and (by extension) 'region' as an 'objectification' of social interaction – that is, they are a particular class of dependent, not independent, variables. Thus, a region is constructed through a process, or through processes of 'action'. What is therefore required in terms of methodology for an inquiry into the construction of a 'society' or 'region' is what is here being termed 'a *processual* level of analysis' that is constituted by social practices. In terms of societal identity, this approach points to process and negotiation, that is, we are who we want to be, subject to constraints of history that set limits to the boundaries of possibility. Within such constraints, disagreements about identity can and do flourish and they give rise to conflict and have security implications – yet they can be settled, but only through value judgements informed by factual observation. In such a case one needs to investigate which interests are at stake and who are the interested parties pursuing them. Therefore, one needs to interpret identity claims, rather than assume their validity and coherence. Such critical works have been seminal in guiding the approach adopted here about the social construction of the Mediterranean as a holistic area in EU policy. In fact, the Mediterranean is a good example of the manipulation of identity by political elites. The following section applies this social constructivist framework to the case of the Mediterranean.

Theoretical Application: The Study of the Mediterranean 'Region'

Background to EU-Mediterranean Relations

From its conception, the European integration process included the Mediterranean element within its framework. The Rome Treaty, which established the European Economic Community (EEC), left its doors open to other 'European' countries that wished to become members (Art. 237).[19] Greece and Spain did so (in 1981 and 1986 respectively).[20] Malta, Cyprus and Turkey[21] are hoping to become members in the near future. The Treaty also contains a section (Art. 131–136) which pertains to the association of 'non-European countries and territories which have special relations' with the founding members.[22] Article 237 however leaves no possibility of these or any other countries from the Maghreb or the Mashrek becoming full members, as Morocco found out.

Prior to 1989, the EC addressed the Mediterranean only in the context of bilateral agreements (Commission of the European Communities, 1993). Throughout the 1960s, the EC signed trade agreements with various Mediterranean countries granting their manufactured products free or preferential access to the EEC, and a limited access for some specified agricultural products. In the mid-1970s, the EC adopted its GMP and proceeded to sign cooperation and association agreements with various MNCs (Mediterranean non-member countries): Algeria, Morocco and Tunisia in 1976 and Egypt, Jordan, Lebanon and Syria in 1977. It is important to note that during the GMP period, the EC tended to regard Morocco, Tunisia and Algeria (the 'Maghreb')[23] as a grouping, differentiated from eastern Mediterranean countries such as Jordan. In addition to traditional trade provisions, the new agreements included a financial component in the form of five-year protocols designed to support the process of economic development in the recipient countries. From the mid-1980s onwards, the development of several important

---

[19]   On the other hand, there is some vagueness here. Non-European countries (whatever these may be!) are not specifically excluded. The phrase in Art. 237 is: 'any European nation can apply' (Croft et al., 1999, p. 61).

[20]   Spain and Portugal signed up in June 1985, but only became members from 1 January 1986.

[21]   At the December, 1999 Helsinki summit, EU leaders decided to treat Turkey as a full candidate for Union membership (and to commit themselves to resolving the outstanding issues concerning Cyprus). See Sofos (2001).

[22]   The concept of 'association' with the EEC refers to a set of initiatives taken towards a multilateral dialogue and cooperation between European and southern Mediterranean countries.

[23]   This is not to imply that the EU established the dichotomy of Maghreb-Mashreq. This distinction emanates from Arab culture (the 'labels' are of Arab origin).

events had a direct or indirect impact on Euro-Mediterranean relations; Spain and Portugal became members of the European club, the Communist bloc disintegrated and the Berlin Wall fell. There was also a rise of social, political, and economic crises in several countries of the southern Mediterranean; as in the case of Algeria where increased activism by fundamentalist movements led to an overturning of the election results in January 1992[24] with the resulting outbreak of a civil war and the outbreak of the Gulf war.

In response to some of these events, the EC felt the need to revise its policy towards the Mediterranean and eventually adopted its RMP.[25] In addition to the traditional financial protocols, a new facility was introduced to promote regional and decentralized cooperation through projects that involved two or more MNCs; several programmes were then set up to that effect including Med-Invest, Med-Campus and Med-Urbs.[26] Under the RMP there was an initial attempt to add a trans-regional approach to certain questions/issues,[27] but this initiative was badly underfunded. It took six years (from the date of the RMP, that is 1989) to commit the EU to a reinforced Mediterranean policy.

During 1992 and 1993 the Commission proposed that future relations with MNCs should go beyond the financial sector and economic sphere to include a political dialogue between the parties, the creation of a Euro-Mediterranean free-trade area and social, economic and cultural cooperation. These recommendations, initially looking just to a Euro-Maghrebi partnership, were approved at the Lisbon summit in June 1992 and confirmed at the Corfu summit in June 1994 (these summits are in fact European Council meetings). In the meantime, negotiations got underway with Tunisia, Morocco and Israel on the basis of mandates specifying these four basic elements. Moreover, during the Essen summit of December 1994 a declaration was made of the EU's support for Spain's intention to convene a Euro-Mediterranean conference in the second half of 1995[28] to carry out an in-depth appraisal of all major political, economic, social and cultural issues of mutual interest and to work out a general framework for permanent and regular dialogue and cooperation in these areas. The Council adopted a document (Commission of

---

[24] The first round of elections was held and gave a plurality to the FIS (Front Islamique du Salut), although only about one quarter of the electorate voted FIS.

[25] It is important to clarify that the RMP was approved in principle in 1989, but was not immediately implemented. Morocco rejected its funding at first owing to the EP (European Parliament) and French criticisms of Moroccan policies towards human rights and on the issue of the Western Sahara. (That is, Morocco 'rejected' assistance under the RMP, but only because the EP had already vetoed such aid to Morocco, pending improvements in respect for human rights, etc.)

[26] Since suspended, although some programmes may be resuming. See Giammusso (1999).

[27] See for example Commission of the European Communities (1991 and 1994a).

[28] That is, during the Spanish presidency of the EU.

the European Communities, 1994b) which defined the EU's position and which was to be presented at the Cannes summit in June 1995.[29]

The Euro-Mediterranean Partnership

In order to achieve its stated objectives of immigration management, trade, prosperity and peace, the EU has adopted a strategy that it termed a 'Partnership' with the MNCs. According to its formulators, this approach seeks to provide a framework where the MNCs and the EU can work as full and equal partners towards achieving mutually beneficial goals. This partnership was defined and adopted by the Euro-Mediterranean Conference in Barcelona in November 1995.[30] The EMP was introduced to complement and not replace existing or forthcoming bilateral agreements linking the EU to individual MNCs. For the purpose of this chapter, only the major points of the Barcelona declaration will be highlighted. The EMP includes three main areas:

Political and security area: The Mediterranean countries committed themselves to setting up a regular political dialogue in order to promote peace, stability and security in the area. The dialogue was to be based on the respect of certain principles such as non-interference in internal affairs, the use of peaceful means for the settlement of disputes, and the adoption of confidence-building measures for the consolidation of peace and stability. It would further seek to achieve specific objectives such as fighting organised crime, drug trafficking and terrorism.

Economic and financial area: The Partnership would promote sustainable and balanced economic and social development with view to building an area of shared prosperity. To this end a Mediterranean free trade area would be set up by the year 2010.[31] In addition, cooperation and consultations would be undertaken in various fields such as investment, environmental protection, water conservation, energy,

---

[29] It is important to note here that the Mediterranean countries, (the other party to the supposed dialogue), were not invited to submit a document of their own defining their position on what was to be discussed (although there were a few bilateral consultations). It may be argued that the Mediterranean countries did not have an organisation capable of articulating a common position (certainly not in the case of Israel and Syria, for example). However, for the sake of the EU's democratic structure, one would have at least expected the partners to be invited to give their views.

[30] The participants in this conference – the 15 member states of the EU and the 12 Mediterranean partners were: EU: Belgium, Denmark, Germany, Greece, Spain, France, Ireland, Italy, Luxembourg, the Netherlands, Austria, Portugal, Finland, Sweden and the United Kingdom: Mediterranean partners: Algeria, Cyprus, Egypt, Israel, Jordan, Lebanon, Malta, Morocco, Syria, Tunisia, Turkey, Palestinian Authority.

[31] This has been revised. For example, the date envisaged in the latest association agreement with Morocco is 2012.

rural development and infrastructure. Finally, the EU would supply financial aid to assist the implementation of the above objectives.[32]

Social, cultural and human areas: The general aim here would be to develop human resources, increase knowledge of cultures, and encourage exchanges between civil societies. To this end, efforts would be made to improve educational and training systems, control demographic growth, reduce migratory pressures and fight racism, xenophobia and intolerance.

The Mediterranean in EU Discourses

The construction of the Mediterranean, which has been constituted so far in the EU's policies towards the area, reads in terms of security discourses, discourses of social stability, strategic discourses and economic discourses.[33] There is a cultural discourse too but this is rather romantic and flimsy. From various Commission documents it is possible to identify these various discourses:

Security discourses: discourses on the threat of 'immigrant flow from the south into the European borders' – the EU's objective is to manage this flow and at the same time to check the 'drug traffic'.[34] The current debate centres on what kind of immigration is essential for the EU (King and Black, 1997).[35] Other such discourses include those on 'fundamentalism'. Here, the EU seeks to prevent Muslim fundamentalists from gaining power in a Mediterranean country and setting up regimes that would be hostile to Western interests. During my interview with Michael A. Köhler at the European Commission (Pace, 2001), Köhler quoted the then President-designate of the Commission Romano Prodi who, in front of the EP on 13 April 1999, said that in his view the future relations of the EU with the

---

[32] Obviously, the EU alone lacks the resources to underwrite all these objectives!

[33] This is especially the case in the EMP which policy (as a discursive practice) constructs priority areas for the partner countries.

[34] This chapter is based on my Ph.D.-dissertation (Pace, 2001). For this purpose interviews were carried out in Brussels at the European Commission. When questioned about what the EMP is trying to achieve, one of my interview subjects, Michael A. Köhler, (Administrator, European Commission, Directorate-General IB – External Relations: Southern Mediterranean, Middle and Near East, Latin America, South and South-East Asia and North-South Co-operation: interview carried out on 18 May 1999) referred to the question of migration under the third pillar of the 'coming together of people'. There therefore seems to be a more positive EU sub-discourse on migration (in Pace, 2001).

[35] In the Tampere conclusions it was noted that halting immigration could be disastrous for the EU, especially for Italy and Spain. Available at:
http://europa.eu.int/council/off/conclu/oct99/oct99_en.htm

Islamic countries are a question of life and death for the EU – which according to Köhler may seem a little exaggerated but it does indicate that 'we have to do with vital interests and not only with, let's say, marginal economic or trade or whatever interests' (Ibid.).

The debate about the 'Mediterranean' is primarily focused on a security appeal by Western Europe on behalf of an imagined community. The discourse of the Mediterranean does not carry the negative loading a discourse of Arab does in European eyes.[36] Therefore, this is the case of how specific carriers / speaking subjects of discourses – statesmen / policy officials / diplomats for one group, are able to change the framing of one particular discourse in what they consider to be an advantageous direction.

Economic and trade discourses: EU member states aim to secure oil and gas supplies on which Europe is dependent. Moreover, in the long term, the MNCs are a large potential market for European goods. The EU has committed itself:

> to the creation of the Euro-Mediterranean economic area, namely the establishment of free trade, reforms for economic transition and promotion of private investment [thus aiming at] creating a Euro-Mediterranean economic area of shared prosperity .... (Commission of the European Communities, 1999, p. 1).

In the area of investments, the *Financial Times* in March 2000 announced that the countries of the southern and eastern Mediterranean face growing marginalisation from the global economy with a share of global foreign direct investment (FDI) of just above 1 per cent, despite attempts over the past decade (including those of the EMP) to increase FDI through investor protection and privatisation, which have so far failed (Huband, 2000). Furthermore, it is interesting to note that the MENA (Middle East and North Africa) area 'risks becoming increasingly specialised in energy exports and in labour intensive, low-skilled manufactures' which seems to confirm where EU member states' interests lie. What is still missing is a 'regional' regulatory and rules structure despite the existence of 140 bilateral trade agreements between Arab countries and the existing agreements between the EU and most of the EMP Mediterranean partners. Moreover, as Professor Mohamed Lahouel of Tunis University claimed, 'Competition laws are necessary to achieve trade liberalisation. What is needed in the MENA region is a multilateral competition framework containing a minimum set of rules and principles' (Huband, 2000). Clearly, the voices of the Mediterranean partners need to be heard, especially in this respect, within the EMP. What could emerge from the rustrations of many of the Mediterranean partners is the creation of an (in)formal

---

[36] Some may wish to argue that EU policy practitioners may well be more enlightened than Europeans in general, in terms of seeing benefits to be derived from allocating resources to a Mediterranean policy. Moreover, they are aware that such a policy is more easily 'sold' to tax payers / voters if presented as a Mediterranean policy, as opposed to an Arab, Jewish / Israeli or Middle East policy.

contact group to co-ordinate their trade issues. However, some of the administrators at the Commission may disagree with such a proposal as they would deem it more important to set up some kind of Mediterranean group on political issues. If the internal governance of the EU retains exclusionary features as it does in the area of Common Agricultural Policy (CAP), the Mediterranean partners will soon be pushed to address these issues.

Prosperity discourse: the EU seeks to improve standards of living in Mediterranean countries so as to ensure social and political stability in the area and indirectly in Europe. According to Köhler, the most important role of the EU in this process is perhaps not the one of providing finance to the Partnership, but rather to act as a catalyst to bring these Mediterranean partners closer together. The Barcelona declaration has made it easier for these partners to cooperate amongst themselves due to the fact that it enshrines some basic principles including economic principles, principles of respect for human rights and democracy – which all these countries have agreed to adhere to (in principle at least). This does not mean that they implement them but at least there is a kind of consensus on basic principles (Pace, 2001). The Commission emphasises the need for 'promoting understanding between *them* and improving *their* perception of each other'[37] but does not deal directly with the European side in this respect within the Partnership.

Peace discourses: the EU aims to prevent internal and interregional conflicts that may make European intervention necessary.[38] According to Köhler, the Kosovo crisis definitely had an impact on what the EU has been doing with the Mediterranean and resulted in a further encouragement to look into the region and to try economically, politically and also if possible through cultural means to develop links through dialogue and to stabilize the region.

All these discourses are somewhat interrelated. The EMP encourages economic development, promotes the rule of law, seeks the protection of human rights and supports the growth of democratic institutions – all of which objectives are here being recognized as discursive practices (security policies) of the EU. This can be seen, for example, in the following quote from a Commission document of 1995 where it is stated that:

> The Community and its partners in the Mediterranean are interdependent in many respects. Europe's interests in the region are many and varied, including as they do the environment, energy supplies, migration, trade and investment. The drug problem ... is one which all the countries involved will have to tackle together. Instability in the region cannot fail to have negative consequences for all the

---

[37] My emphasis: Commission of the European Communities (1995a).

[38] It is important to note the EU's growing capacity to intervene as a result of the EU-WEU merger and the decision to create a rapid deployment force (Norton-Taylor, 2000).

countries of the European Community (Commission of the European Communities, 1995b, p. 2).

One surely cannot challenge the EU for defending its interests – yet, one can and should evaluate the approach used to define those interests and the methods applied to achieve them (Chourou, 1999).

The term European-Mediterranean Partnership has several problematic connotations one of which is the concept of 'European' – this prefix extends to encompassing in this new millennium an enlarging Union to the East as well as to the North and South – the latter of which could be countries designated in the 'Mediterranean' part of the term (like Malta). The latter thus involves the EU in further line drawing exercises over time.

European line drawing still defines the primary borders of its identity. On the other hand, the persistence of national discourses on Europe may well prevent the construction of a European collective political identity (as does EU enlargement) that is necessary for an effective European foreign policy (White, 1999). However, it may be argued that national discourses can exist as long as they are subsumed under the heading of a common threat. On the other hand, the EU has its own dynamics. This echoes Foucault's thinking in that he claims that discourses are marked by contradictions. Perhaps, in this case, this is why a European foreign policy is important which implies that this is also why boundaries and distinctions become important. EU discourse and national discourses can exist together and what is important is the manner in which they are articulated. The EU claims to be developing a Common Foreign Policy and a Common Security Policy – the CFSP[39] – two discourses subsumed under a threat. Thus, while some analysts (White, 1999) see national discourses as contradictory, it may be argued that these may well possibly be complementary. The manner in which the Mediterranean is conceived of within national discourses as well as at the EU level implies that the EU can claim to have both a Mediterranean (that is Foreign) Policy as well as a Security Policy. This process of articulation shows that there is nothing that can be neutralized in discourse. The articulation of a discourse makes it a discourse.

Therefore, the nature of the foreign policy process is an important consideration in itself. The understanding of the ways in which policy is formulated is crucial, in particular the relationship between knowledge and ideas, and the process whereby ideas are translated into policy proposals and move onto the policy agenda. Thus, in line with the discourse analysis methodology adopted in this chapter, policy implementation can be assessed through this process. In this context, the manner in which the idea of the Mediterranean found its way into the various EU Mediterranean initiatives, in particular into the EMP, is important. An assumption about the relationship between ideas, interest formation and agenda setting is crucial to the formulation of policy and ultimately to policy outcomes/

---

[39] CFSP is an outgrowth of other forms of European integration (Eliassen, 1998), the EU also includes its Common European Security Defence Policy (CESDP). This is interesting considering the lack of a military threat to the EU.

implementation. Both interests and identities are essentially constructed by, or are endogenous to, processes of social interaction.[40] In sum, what is necessary is a more effective linkage between foreign policy analysis and other approaches to the study of policy-making at the domestic and international levels.

In its various initiatives, the EU has vacillated in its conceptualisation of Mediterranean 'otherness', exposing the limits of its representation: ideas of a European missionary purpose to civilize and democratise the (Arab) world is one example. While understandings of the Mediterranean shifted and European imaginings of the 'foreign' grew to include many other countries,[41] one thing does not change: the Mediterranean (I would say Arab as a thematic object of the EU discourse on the Mediterranean) alterity remains the continuous object of European foreign policy. It is here important to stress that as Borneman states 'a conceptual framework or model is a perceptual orientation for political action; it is intellectual labour and distinct from the labours of (those) who themselves (work) as administrators in the carrying out of foreign ... policy' (1995, p. 667).

The EU's notion of the Mediterranean consists of individual member states' discursive practices. These range from Spain's and France's discourse as being primarily a fixation on the Maghreb to Italy's (and Greece's) focus on the Balkans (and Eastern Europe). The Balkans is not, however, included in the EU discourse on the Mediterranean (as a whole group). What unites these discursive practices on the Mediterranean is the common discursive practice about the Mediterranean as a security threat – which the individual member states cannot attend to alone and this explains their interest in drawing the attention of the EU to the Mediterranean. This is how the attempts of Spain, Italy, France, Portugal (and Greece, albeit to a very limited extent) to avoid the exclusion of the Mediterranean from the EU foreign policy agenda should be analysed. One may speculate that, perhaps, the lack of a coherent EU discourse on the Mediterranean explains why, even in an area where its members have particular interests and potential influence, the EU (as a whole) resorts to a continuous self-assessment as the basis of enhancing the development of its Mediterranean initiatives such as the EMP.

The EMP still suffers from a clear definition of the *type* of Mediterranean the EU is trying to deal with (in effect a lack of defining the aims and instruments that need to be utilized to achieve security in the Mediterranean and thereby security in Europe). EU member states still regard the defence of their interests as requiring the identification of an 'adversary', an 'other', who could endanger them (and the drawing up of a defensive strategy). With its phobia about security in the Mediterranean, the EU has failed to mobilize sufficient resources within its EMP to

---

[40] Obviously, interests are also created by resource considerations.

[41] For example, Libya has recently been considered as a potential partner in the EMP – albeit for a very short time. Libya may join the EMP group in the medium term if it manages to consolidate the *rapprochement* with the EU following the lifting of UN sanctions in 1999.

fulfil its policy aims.[42] Nor does the EU's security discourse on the Mediterranean justify the predominance of its members' commercial and corporate interests, whose discourse is echoed by senior officials responsible for these areas, together with entrepreneurs and agricultural and fishing interests. The interests of EU member states are represented by those who argue for the development of the non-EU Mediterranean countries, but action is lacking in this direction so far. Among other things, the EU needs to contribute decisively to the development of the productive sectors of the Mediterranean partners that are labour intensive (such as agriculture, tourism and textiles), act to reduce the burden of their foreign debt (60 per cent of which is owed to EU countries), apply a free trade regime to Mediterranean agricultural exports and establish a less restrictive immigration policy (Núñez Villaverde, 2000, pp. 144-145).

As Borneman points out:

> The foreign is not something that has meaning in and of itself, nor is it territorially fixed. It is an unstable counter concept, opposed to the native and constitutive of the human. Our task is to situate ourselves more clearly in relation to the foreign and to justify our positions more rigorously. Such positions ... provide the grounds on which foreign policy is made and on which distinctions between us and them are drawn (1995, p. 669).

Therefore, it follows that the division between Europe and the Mediterranean is not necessary but contingent. The EU's Mediterranean area is just one among many possible readings of the EU system of governing the Mediterranean. It is such EU constructions that the practices discussed above are about: that is, the Mediterranean is not a neutral reality but a 'contested concept', the meaning of which is not fixed but fluid. There are numerous ways to construct such an area (in content, nature and scope). In the case of the EU's Mediterranean, it is discursive practices about security, stability, prosperity, etc., which make this area 'real' – discourses which attempt to organise the area, to classify it, to manage it and to govern it. Obviously enough there could be no Mediterranean area without on the one hand, actors acting on behalf of an object they perceive as the Mediterranean and on the other hand, without these actors having the necessary structures to act within them over long periods of time in similar and repeated fashions.

Concluding Remarks

The alternative approach to the study of regions offered in this chapter is not meant as an attempt to replace any other approaches discussed here. What is being suggested is an opening up of the debate on regions that takes as its guiding question the manner in which regions are socially constructed and imagined.

---

[42] One suspects that if the phobia did not exist, even less resources might be mobilized!

In the specific case of the Mediterranean what is being suggested is that we need to examine the processes through which geopolitical and other imaginings of the Mediterranean 'region' sustain this concept. This framework for analysing the social construction of regions insists on a refusal of traditional approaches to the study of regions that take these concepts for granted. The Mediterranean is a social construction as its existence depends on the acceptance of all the actors concerned that there is some meaning in the term. From a theoretical point of view, the study of the Mediterranean requires an eclectic approach to theory: in practical terms, the Mediterranean mosaic must be analysed in terms of the processes that lead to its shared meaning – these can then enable analysts to cope with the multi-dimensionality of the area.

There are, however, discourses and practices that have existed and have been reproduced and repeated over long periods and have therefore become institutionalised. These might have been embedded in the imaginaries of Mediterranean societies and other actors and might be more influential in contrast to more recent discourses, or might be more difficult to challenge and dislodge.

A constructivist analysis to the study of regions therefore does not ask 'what is a region' but 'how and why is a region defined in such and such a manner?' By so doing, such an approach highlights how the principal actors, in the process of the construction of such an entity, construct a multiple definition of an area that changes over time and by issue. This is a very important consideration to take on board in our theoretical understanding of how regional identities are constructed. The reality of regions and region-formations is complex and our theoretical frameworks that study these entities and processes must be likewise.

The Mediterranean as a (free-floating) political phenomenon is constituted in and by discourse and therefore needs a descriptive theory of the interplay of general meanings of this area. The meaning of the Mediterranean can therefore be analysed through processes or modes of discourse. Looking into the production of knowledge on regions can considerably sharpen our insights into what makes a region, how this knowledge is produced, by whom and in what settings. It is hoped that the arguments presented in this chapter can point us towards useful directions for further investigations into the study of regions.

References

Al-Manì, Saleh A. (1983), *The Euro-Arab Dialogue. A Study in Associative Diplomacy*, Frances Pinter (Publishers), London.

Aliboni, Roberto (ed.) (1992), *Southern European Security in the 1990s*, Pinter Publishers, London.

Berger, Peter L. and Luckmann, Thomas (1966), *The Social Construction of Reality: A Treatise in the Sociology of Knowledge*, Penguin Books, New York.

Borneman, John, (1995), 'American Anthropology as Foreign Policy,' *American Anthropologist*, Vol. 97(4), December, pp. 663-672.

Buzan, Barry (1991), *People, States and Fear: An Agenda for International Security Studies in the Post-Cold War Era*, 2nd ed., Harvester, Hemel Hempstead.

Cantori, Louis J. and Spiegel, Steven L. (1970), *The International Politics of Regions. A Comparative Approach*, Englewood Cliffs, NJ.

Chourou, Béchir (1999), *A Challenge For EU Mediterranean Policy: Upgrading Democracy From Threat to Risk*, Paper presented at the international workshop on The Human Dimension of Security and the EMP, Malta, 14-15 May.

Commission of the European Communities (1991), Communication from the Commission to the Council on *The Implementation Of Trade Arrangements Under The New Mediterranean Policy*. COM(91)179 final, 22 May.

Commission of the European Communities (1993), *EEC Mediterranean Agreements*, Bureau D'Informations Europeennes S.P.R.L., Brussels.

Commission of the European Communities (1994a), Report from the Commission to the Council and the European Parliament on *The implementation of financial and technical cooperation with Mediterranean non-Member countries and on financial cooperation with those countries as a group*, COM(94)384 final, 18 November 1994.

Commission of the European Communities (1994b), *A Strategy for Euro-Mediterranean Partnership*, IP/94/1156, 06/12/94, Essen.

Commission of the European Communities (1995a), *Barcelona Euro-Mediterranean Conference (27-28 November 1995) – Declaration and Work Programme*, DOC/95/7, 04/12/95.

Commission of the European Communities (1995b), *Strengthening The Mediterranean Policy of the European Union: Proposals for Implementing A EMP*, COM(95)72 final, 08/03/1995.

Commission of the European Communities (1999), *Survey On Free Trade And Economic Transition In The Mediterranean*, DG1B/A/4, April, 1999.

Croft, Stuart et al. (1999), *The Enlargement of Europe*, Manchester University Press, Manchester.

Eliassen, K.A. (ed.) (1998), *Foreign and Security Policy in the EU*, Sage, London.

EuroMed Report (2001), *Final Declaration of the Second Session of the Euro-Mediterranean Parliamentary Forum*, Issue 25, 9 February, European Commission, Brussels.

Foucault, Michel (1972), *The Archaeology of Knowledge*, Tavistock, London.

Foucault, Michel (1973), *The Order of Things*, p. xiv, Pantheon, NY.

Foucault, Michel (1977), *Discipline and Punish*, Allen Lane, London.

Foucault, Michel (1979-1986), *The History of Sexuality*, (3 volumes), Allen Lane, London.

Giammusso, Maurizio (1999), 'Civil Society Initiatives and Prospects of Economic Development: The Euro-Mediterranean Decentralized Co-Operation Net-works,' *Mediterranean Politics*, Vol. 4(1), Spring, pp. 25-52.

Giddens, Anthony (1989), *Sociology*, Polity Press, Cambridge.

Herb, Guntram H and Kaplan, David H. (eds.) (1999), *Nested Identities: Nationalism, Territory, and Scale*, Rowman and Littlefield, Lanham, MD.

Huband, Mark, (2000), 'World News: Trade: Mediterranean region facing marginalisation,' *Financial Times*, 9 March, p. 16.

Kinacioglu, Muge (2000), 'From East-West Rivalry to North-South Division: Redefining the Mediterranean Security Agenda,' *IR*, Vol. 15(2), August.

King, Russell and Black, Richard (1997), *Southern Europe and the New Immigrations*, Sussex Academic Press, Brighton.

Lake, David A. and Morgan, Patrick M. (eds.) (1997), *Regional Orders: Building Security in a New World*, Pennsylvania State University Press, Pennsylvania UP, University Park.

Latter, Richard (1992), *Mediterranean Security*, HMSO, Wilton Park papers, London.

McSweeney, Bill (1996), 'Identity and security: Buzan and the Copenhagen School,' *Review of International Studies*, Vol. 22(1), November, 81-93.

Mignolo, Walter, D. (1995), *The Darker Side of the Renaissance. Literacy, Territoriality, And Colonization*, The University of Michigan Press, Ann Arbor.

Neumann, Iver B. (1996), *European Identity, EU Expansion and the Integration/Exclusion Nexus*, Paper presented at the conference: Defining and Projecting Europe's Identity: Issues and Trade-Offs, Institut Universaire de Hautes Etudes Internationales, Geneva, 21-22 March.

Norton-Taylor, Richard (2000), 'Comment and Analysis: Analysis: Intelligence test. Features', *The Guardian*, 20 December, p. 17.

Núñez Villaverde, Jesús, A. (2000), 'The Mediterranean: A Firm Priority of Spanish Foreign Policy?', *Mediterranean Politics*, Vol. 5(2), Summer, pp. 129-147.

Ó Tuathail, Gearóid (1996), *Critical Geopolitics: The Politics of Writing Global Space*, University of Minnesota Press, Borderlines Series, 6, Minneapolis.

Pace, Michelle (2001), *Rethinking the Mediterranean. Reality and Re-Presentation In the Creation of a 'Region'* (unpublished doctoral dissertation, University of Portsmouth).

Pervin, David J. (1997), in David A. Lake and Patrick M. Morgan (eds.), *Regional Orders: Building Security in a New World*, Pennsylvania State University Press, Pennsylvania UP, University Park.

Sofos, Spyros (2001), 'Reluctant Europeans? European Integration and the Transformation of Turkish Politics', *Southern European Societies and Politics*, Vol. 5(2), (forthcoming).

Waltz, Kenneth, N. (1979), *Theory of International Politics*, Addison-Wesley, Reading, MA.

Wendt, Alexander (1999), *Social Theory of International Politics*, Cambridge University Press, Cambridge.

White, Brian (1999), 'The European Challenge to Foreign Policy Analysis', *European Journal of International Relations*, Vol. 5(1), pp. 37-66.

Wæver, Ole et al. (1993), *Identity, Migration and the New Security Agenda in Europe*, Pinter, London.

Chapter 8

Two Sides of the Same Coin: Mutual Perceptions and Security Community in the Case of Argentina and Brazil

Andrea Oelsner

Introduction

In 1957 Karl Deutsch coined the concept 'pluralistic security community' (Deutsch, 1957), reintroducing the old debate of realism and idealism in International Relations (IR). This time, however, it was no longer about whether independent states could coexist peacefully, but, instead, under which circumstances they could do so. That is, under which conditions a group of sovereign states could exist as a community in an international, anarchic scenario. Deutsch's security community is characterised by the assurance that its members would not resort to violent means to resolve their disputes, but would settle them peacefully. The concept challenged mainstream International Relations theory of nearly fifty years, bringing sociology and IR closer. Traditional IR thinking has been intellectually grounded on a Hobbesian approach, which regards the international system as an anarchic, self-help scenario, where nation-states struggle for power and survival. Deutsch, conversely, applied a typically sociological concept ('community') to the international arena (Adler and Barnett, 1998). Contrary to what realism traditionally suggested, he argued that there can exist a community not only within the boundaries of a state, but also across states, and that peace and peaceful change can be expected within such international communities.

Constellations of states in 'no-war' or even in stable peace situations have in fact been much more frequently the case than those in war. Since the 1990s, and possibly reflecting on some new post-cold war realities, many authors have employed the term 'security community' drawing on Deutsch to describe the highest stage on gradations of regional peace and security (among others, see Morgan, 1997; Holsti, 1996; Kacowicz, 1998; Buzan, 1991; Hurrell, 1998). In their works, security communities represent the most advanced and stable international stage of peace before proceeding to a situation of integration, where there exists a centralised authority capable of (coercively) preventing violence.

There is, though, a subtle difference between a 'zone of peace' and a 'security community.' According to Holsti, in a zone of peace capabilities are not targeted toward fellow members of the zone and operational war plans do not include conflict hypotheses against them. Militarised disputes may break out from time to time (e.g., the Anglo-Iceland cod wars in 1972 and 1975), but war has literally become unthinkable in mutual relations. Similarly, Kacowicz asserts that a zone of stable peace precludes the expectation of violence among states. A pluralistic security community, on the other hand, 'rests on the social foundations of community between individuals and societies' (Holsti, 1996, p. 148) that 'share common norms, values, and political institutions, sustain an identifiable common identity and are deeply interdependent' (Kacowicz, 1998, p. 11). Thus, while all security communities are in a situation of stable peace, not all stable peace situations necessarily make up a security community (Kacowicz et al., 2000). It is fair to say, for instance, that Canada and the United States constitute a security community, as well as countries in Western Europe do.

Further, security communities do not necessarily entail formal agreements or instrumental arrangements. States in a community may not have actively sought its formation or their participation in it, and may yet be engaged in one. A pluralistic security community can exist even when its members do not give it a name or recognise it as such. It is rather a socially constructed regime that rests upon mutual trust to account for the expectation of peaceful change. It does not preclude the emergence of disputes. Rather, it implies the confidence that their resolution will not involve the use or threat of military violence. In sum, there is no preparation to resort to force against other members.

The process of emergence of a security community involves social learning, trust building, and changes in the mutual and self perceptions. In addition, some element of calculation and self-interest must also be present in order to allow this process to develop. This is especially the case of former adversaries, like Argentina and Brazil. If they perceive one another as potential enemies, none of the conditions toward a security community will arise. When instead they perceive other threats to their development and survival as greater,[1] and eventually view co-operation as a plausible (and needed) tool to confront those threats, then *rapprochement* may begin to unfold. In other words, when they perceive that, say, their economic development and survival may be at stake by not following a co-operative strategy with their neighbours, military *détente* becomes a necessary step. For this to happen, the image of the neighbour as an adversary needs to change too, of course. It needs to become, instead, a legitimate player in a potentially co-operative enterprise, a partner; not least because, as Hurrell argues, some material incentives are expected (Hurrell, 1998). In this process of cognitive change the self-perception is certainly altered as well.

This chapter deals with the changes in the Argentine-Brazilian relationship since the late 1970s. The focus is principally on the dramatic transformation in this relationship, which, after many decades of rivalry and hostility, resulted in the

---

[1]   The definitions of threat and security used here are broad ones, including not only military threats. According to Buzan, threats may be perceived in five different security areas: military, economic, political, societal, and environmental. See Buzan, 1991.

emergence of a security community and in parallel changes in their mutual perceptions.

Argentina and Brazil are seen here as the key actors of a Regional Security Complex (RSC) that involves the Southern Cone of South America.[2] According to this definition, an RSC exists when the security concerns of a group of states, and their processes of securitization and desecuritization are so relevant to each other that they cannot be realistically examined apart (Buzan, 1991; Buzan et al., 1998).[3] Because of their historical ties and geographic position, Argentina's and Brazil's national security and concerns – whether they be in tense relations or in interdependent integration – cannot realistically be considered independently of one another.

But if security concerns are interdependent, domestic instability—both political and economic – is also seen with preoccupation by neighbours in the Southern Cone RSC. Indeed, domestic stability across the region has become a shared goal in the last two decades or so. The present analysis will focus on the Argentine-Brazilian core, however, as it has been this particular relationship which has changed more remarkably.

This chapter argues that the Southern Cone is becoming a security community as a result of the *rapprochement* between Argentina and Brazil, and the subsequent creation of Mercosur. The next section offers a historical background to the Argentine-Brazilian *rapprochement* process, beginning with their historic rivalry and continuing with their domestic situations between the 1970s and 1990s. The following section discusses the foundation of Mercosur as an Argentine-Brazilian product, its economic and political aspects, and the gradual emergence of a shared identification between Argentina and Brazil as well as among their peoples. In particular, the emergence of such mutual image changes, it is argued, has played an important role in the transformation of the Southern Cone from a 'zone of peace' into an incipient security community. The final section draws some conclusions from the arguments.

---

[2] The Southern Cone of South America includes Argentina, Bolivia, Brazil, Chile, Paraguay and Uruguay. However, it is not a unified criterion, provided that some authors exclude Brazil and/or Bolivia from their accounts. It is defined in geographic rather than political terms, and it does not constitute any kind of formal arrangement.

[3] In Buzan et al. 1998, the authors refer to 'a set of units' rather than to 'a set of states.' Without ignoring the relevance for IR theory of the debate about units in the international system, I leave this aside, as my analysis concentrates on two states, Argentina and Brazil.

Background to the *Rapprochement*

Historical Rivalry

Authors dealing with Argentine-Brazilian relations date back the origin of the rivalry to the seventeenth and eighteenth century, when their fatherlands, the Spanish and Portuguese empires, would compete to assert their control of the River Plate. Since Portugal founded the city of Colonia del Sacramento in 1680 in an effort to establish itself on the east bank of the River Plate, it was constantly faced with Spanish opposition. The Spaniards, in turn, tried to assert their dominance on both banks of the river, and the later foundation of Montevideo (1729) was part of this campaign (Olmos, 1986, pp. 71-72).

This competition continued after independence, and eventually in 1825 war broke out between the Argentine Confederation and the Brazilian Empire. After long negotiations and the intervention of a British mediator, the peace treaty of 1828 created the Oriental Republic of Uruguay as an independent (buffer) state. That war was, as a matter of fact, the only one that Argentina and Brazil fought against one another. Four decades later, they engaged in war again. This time, however, they formed a coalition together with Uruguay to fight the bloody War of the Triple Alliance against Paraguay (1865-1870), a terrible conflict above all for the Paraguayans, who lost territory, saw their industrial infrastructure destroyed, had to face formidable post-conflict debts, and suffered the loss of between 60 and 80 per cent of their population (Cisneros and Escudé, 2000).[4]

By the end of the nineteenth century, it was clear that Argentina and Brazil were engaging in different strategies to pursue their development. Argentina, on the one hand, sought its economic consolidation and growth in close association with Great Britain. Between 1860 and 1930 it had achieved such a rapid modernisation that it was considered 'a small Europe' in the Americas (Olmos, 1986, p. 73). Brazil, on the other hand, under the Baron of Rio Branco (the very influential minister of Foreign Affairs between 1902-1912) prioritised relations with the United States, anticipating surely the weight that this country would have on the hemisphere's affairs. After the First World War, and more strikingly so after the Second, Great Britain and Europe started to withdraw their influence from the new continent while the alliance Brazil-U.S. grew stronger.

At the beginning of the twentieth century, '[i]ncreasingly, each country viewed the other as a competitor, as an opponent in many areas, and even as a possible enemy (de la Fuente, 1997, p. 37). The different paths taken by Argentina and Brazil reinforced a relationship characterised by a mutual suspicion of expansionist and hegemonic attitudes. As most authors acknowledge, 'the relative absence of war did not amount to a peaceful, cooperative region' (Solingen, 1998, p. 132).

The Argentine-Brazilian rivalry was mainly driven by threat perceptions rather than by concrete disputes. Argentina would see in Itamaraty (Brazil's Ministry of

---

[4] For the electronic version, see http://www.argentina-rree.com/6/6-055.htm. On a good account of the War of the Triple Alliance allowing for different historiographic approaches, see also Chapters 29, 30 and 31 of the same work.

Foreign Affairs) the source of Brazil's imperial ambitions to pursue 'the expansion and westward movement (*la marcha hacia el oeste*) of the Portuguese-speaking world,' while Brazilian geopoliticians would express concern 'over the Argentine dream of restoring the viceroyalty of the Rio de la Plata [River Plate], a restoration that would be partially at Brazil's expense and would tend to polarize the South Cone' (Child, 1985, pp. 98-99). Indeed, Hilton claims that the 'enduring image of Argentina as an aggressive, expansionist state lies at the core of the sense of threat that has pervaded Brazilian strategic circles for generations' (Hilton, 1985, p. 28).

The perception of irreconcilable and competing destinies would only intensify throughout the twentieth century, fostered by divergent foreign policies that led them, for instance, to maintain different positions during the First World War, when Brazil joined the Allies while Argentina remained neutral; to support opposing sides during the bloody Chaco War (1932-1935) that erupted between Paraguay and Bolivia, where Argentina backed Paraguay, and Brazil and Chile supported Bolivia; and again during the Second World War, when Argentina took a neutralist and ultimately pro-Axis path throughout the conflict, declaring war on the Axis only in the last minute, whereas Brazil had a committed participation in the Allied cause. According to Cisneros and Escudé, during the Second World War the Brazilian foreign minister declared that he was more concerned about a potential Argentine attack on its Southern border than about a Nazi threat to the Northeast. They go on to suggest that the regime established in Argentina after the 1943 *coup* only helped to increase those suspicions, as it campaigned openly for the establishment of a "bloc of nations with similar ideas to isolate Brazil and combat the influence of the United States" (Cisneros and Escudé, 2000, Volume XIII, Chapter 60).[5]

The victory of Perón in the Argentine elections of 1946 did little to pacify Brazilian fears, nor did Perón's overthrow in 1955. The Peronist administration was a populist nationalist regime that maintained an unusually high level of expenditures on the armed forces, promoting at the same time closer commercial, financial, and cultural ties with its Spanish-speaking neighbours. But even in the post-Perón era Brazilians remained extremely distrustful, and Argentina did not cease to be at the core of their national defence strategy (see, for instance, Hilton, 1985, pp. 31-35).

At the same time, Argentina saw with great concern the U.S.-Brazilian special relationship; a concern that would be but exacerbated by Brazil's ostentation of this partnership, and more seriously aggravated 'by the large amounts of U.S. economic and military aid that flowed to Brazil during World War II and shortly thereafter' (Child, 1985, p. 101). Another factor that constantly worried Argentines since the early 1920s was the emphasis of Brazilian geopolitical thinking on its 'inevitable path to *grandeza*' (greatness); 'the code word for the moment when (and never if) Brazil will become the first superpower to emerge from the Southern Hemisphere' with U.S. support (Child, 1985, p. 34).

The United States played indeed a role in the relationship between Argentina and Brazil. Except for short periods, since the beginning of the twentieth century

---

[5] For the electronic version, see http://www.argentina-rree.com/13/13-007.htm.

and until the mid-1970s Brazil saw the U.S. as its major ally with whom to align its foreign policy, expecting in return support for subregional leadership. Argentina, instead, systematically opposed the United States at almost every opportunity since 1889, when the First Pan-American Conference took place in Washington. Regardless of the ideological orientation of the government – whether it be conservative of the late nineteenth and early twentieth century; democratic, as the governments of Irigoyen and Alvear; the military that assumed power in 1930; or again conservative and authoritarian that alternatively took office until the rise of Perón – none of them were enthusiastic about American hegemony, and all looked with distrust and even disdain at Brazil's alignment (Gaveglio, 1992, p. 83).

The rivalry had important reverberations, too, for the domestic and international politics of the region, as it constantly involved the 'buffer states' of Uruguay, Bolivia, and Paraguay (Kacowicz, 1999). Both Brazil and Argentina would hurry to increase their influence on these states by signing agreements with them to complete rail links uniting their major cities with Argentine or Brazilian ports – especially in the case of the landlocked Bolivia and Paraguay – to open banks, build bridges and highways, co-operate in communications and trade, and to undertake joint developments of oil fields (Hilton, 1985, pp. 44-48).

Child also points to the competition for the buffer states' arms market, as both Brazil and Argentina possessed developed arms industries, and for providing military advisors and awarding scholarships to cadets from those states to attend military academies in Argentina and Brazil (Child, 1985, pp. 99-100 and 106). Finally, the ultimate examples of this rivalry were the competition for natural resources, such as Paraguayan hydroelectric energy, and the competition in the nuclear field. All this drove them not only to draw up contingency war plans against one another, but also to an expensive arms race in the 1960s and 1970s.

The competition over the exploitation of the River Plate basin, in particular the hydroelectric power and water resources of the River Paraná, took an unprecedented dimension in the 1970s. The River Paraná has its source in Brazilian territory, marks then the border between Brazil and Paraguay and later between Paraguay and Argentina, its final stretch being exclusively Argentine. Both Brazil and Argentina were planning the construction of dams in association with Paraguay in Itaipú and in Corpus, respectively. Argentine geopoliticians agued that the Brazilian project at Itaipú on the upper Paraná River – which would be the world's largest hydroelectric plant – would considerably endanger the viability of downstream Argentine ventures. The issue became a major diplomatic dispute, taking the form of both bitter bilateral and multilateral negotiations, and a wide range of strategies and recommended military actions to be taken by both sides.

The nuclear competition was subtler, but by no means less entrenched. Already in 1950, Perón was determined to drive Argentina through the path of nuclear grandeur to the forefront of industrial-technological development. For that purpose, the newly founded National Commission of Atomic Energy hired the best technicians and was placed under the strong influence of the Navy to centralise and promote scientific and technological nuclear research. Argentina achieved important developments in the nuclear field during the 1970s, finally accomplishing in 1983 the long-pursued goal: mastery of the complete nuclear fuel cycle.

As in Argentina, nuclear research in Brazil was motivated by the vast potentialities offered by nuclear energy. From the foundation of the National Commission of Nuclear Energy (CNEN) in 1956 until 1975 progress was very modest. But that year Brazil closed a deal with West Germany for an extensive transfer of sensitive technologies. It was a wide-ranging agreement, by which Germany committed itself to provide Brazil with technology covering all aspects of the nuclear fuel cycle, from uranium exploration to nuclear waste storage. It represented 'the largest transfer of nuclear technology to a developing country' (Reiss, 1995, p. 49).

Needless to say, this German-Brazilian agreement aroused the deepest fears of Argentine strategists and geopoliticians, as the deal was closed in the midst of the Itaipú dispute and when Brazil was still enjoying the prosperity of its 'economic miracle.' The fiercest opposition to the agreement, though, came from the United States, whose active non-proliferation campaign had just been challenged by the Indian nuclear explosion of 1974. In addition, Brazil's and Argentina's nuclear developments, and their refusal to adhere to the Treaty for the Prohibition of Nuclear Weapons in Latin America, and the Caribbean (Treaty of Tlatelolco) and the Nuclear Non-Proliferation Treaty (NPT) hardened even further the U.S. position regarding technology transfer and safeguards.

Ironically, U.S. obstructionism to the deal of Brazil and West Germany provoked an Argentine public manifestation in support of Brazil. Clearly, Argentina's support was not entirely disinterested. Buenos Aires could foresee the same future conflicts with Canada, its principal nuclear supplier at that time, if that country backed the U.S. non-proliferation policy. Nonetheless, the fact is that the dispute with the U.S. helped to grow a feeling of solidarity to resist international pressure on nuclear issues in general, a pressure that for a long time actually backfired. Ferreira states:

> were it not for the insistence of the U.S. government that Buenos Aires and Brasilia sign the Nuclear Non-Proliferation Treaty (NPT), both countries would not have felt the need to coordinate policies in the face of pressures that affect them equally (Ferreira, 1992, pp. 64-65).

However, as long as the Itaipú-Corpus dispute was not entirely resolved, the bilateral relationship was rather marked by tension and discord; a fact that is further reflected on in the literature (in addition to the already cited, see also Moniz Bandeira, 1998, especially pp. 296-314; Herrera Vega, September 1995; Scenna, 1975; Guglielmelli, 1974; Rosenbaum, 1973; Correa, 1973), and is constantly brought up in interviews with relevant actors.[6]

---

[6] In April 2001 interviews were conducted with two former Foreign Ministers of Brazil, Ambassadors Mario Gibson Barboza and Ramiro Elysio Saraiva Guerreiro; and with the following Brazilian diplomats, who served periods in Buenos Aires holding different positions: Ambassadors João Hermes Pereira de Araújo, Marcos Henrique C. Côrtes, and

Eventually, on 19 October 1979, Argentina, Brazil and Paraguay signed the Tripartite Agreement on Itaipú-Corpus that brought the dispute to an end. It did not totally satisfy anyone, but it marked a watershed after which the two countries were able to find a different way to relate to one another. Immediately following the resolution of the hydroelectric dispute, 1980 stands out as a key year, marking the turning point on which all later changes in the Argentine-Brazilian relationship rested. In May that year, the two military presidents General Figueiredo of Brazil and General Videla of Argentina signed an agreement for nuclear fuel cycle co-operation, which – despite failing to achieve any impressive results – represented the end of competition and the beginning of collaboration on nuclear matters. It signalled, too, the possibility of economic and political co-operation in the years to come, as the nuclear agreement was accompanied by many others, such as shared water resources, electric interconnection, and the establishment of a consultation mechanism on issues of common interest.

Indeed, both countries had more to win from the easing of tension and loosening of military doctrines than otherwise. For the first time, they were able to shift away from their zero sum perspectives. Argentina's explicit siding with Brazil in the issue of technology transfer was paid back by Brasilia during the Falklands/Malvinas war. Brazil voted in support of Argentina's position in key votes in the Organisation of American States and even supplied Argentina with two reconnaissance aircraft. Thus, starting in 1979 under military governments, Argentina and Brazil managed to carry out a *rapprochement* process that bore concrete fruits within six years, changed mutual perceptions, and finally set up a durable, 'strategic alliance': Mercosur.

There are at least three milestones in the development of the relationship. The first one is the 1979 Itaipú-Corpus Treaty. The satisfactory negotiation of this treaty left a door open for the signature of several co-operation agreements on development and application of nuclear energy for peaceful uses, the first of which was signed in 1980. It is from here that the beginning of *rapprochement* should be seen. The second milestone is the 1985 Declaration of Iguazú, which was signed once democracy had been restored in both countries. The Declaration of Iguazú was followed by a myriad of bilateral declarations and accords that help build up confidence and trust. Finally, the signing of the Treaty of Asunción in 1991, by which Mercosur was created, constitutes the third milestone.

This was undoubtedly a successful *détente*. Nonetheless, however effective such a process may be, there is a wide gap between the mere easing of tension and full-scale co-operation; a gap that Argentina and Brazil managed to bridge quite rapidly. As will be discussed below, Mercosur was envisaged as more than just a trade agreement. It was, rather, a *political alliance* aimed at strengthening democracy, increasing international leverage, and overcoming common political

---

Eduardo dos Santos. In March and April 2001 interviews were also conducted with former Argentine Ambassadors to Brazil and former Foreign Ministers Carlos Manuel Muñiz and Oscar Camilión, and with Horacio Jaunarena, Minister of Defence between 1986 and 1989 and again since March 2001. In both countries, distinguished members of the academic community were also interviewed.

and economic problems. Mercosur was only possible because there was a security community under construction, which underpinned the alliance.

This marks a striking difference with the way in which the European Community evolved, where the agreement was established with the aim of overcoming the rivalry between France and Germany. After the Second World War, it was rightly thought that an economic agreement could function as a tool to bring the two countries closer and help them develop stronger ties, which was the ultimate goal in mind.

In contrast, the only time war broke out between Argentina and Brazil was in 1825. Nevertheless, most of the twentieth century progressed tensely, constituting Argentina and Brazil, at best as a mere no-war zone. In the late 1970s, finally, this relationship began to change, moving away from a no-war zone to going even beyond a zone of peace. The need for co-ordinated political and economic action was felt, as it will be described below. For that to happen, however, old rivalries had to be overcome. This permitted, first, the hope for economic co-operation, and, later, the foundation of Mercosur. Hence, *rapprochement* was the tool – not the end – that would facilitate the achievement of the goal: an economic and political co-operation agreement. At present, the bilateral relation constitutes an emerging security community in that the use of force between Argentina and Brazil has become absolutely unthinkable, and individuals and societies are acquiring a sense of commonality of destiny, perceiving their present and future welfare and security as inescapably intertwined.

The Domestic Framework: the Governments of Argentina and Brazil

To better understand the context of the *rapprochement*, let us turn for a moment to the domestic level. Argentine and Brazilian domestic politics have been characterised in the past by feeble attempts at democracy, some strongly populist experiments and numerous military interventions that led to repressive authoritarian governments, which resulted in 'bureaucratic-authoritarian regimes' (O'Donnell, 1973). Only in 1983 in Argentina and 1985 in Brazil was democracy finally restored.

The last successful military *coup d'état* in Argentina (1976) overthrew the government of María Estela Martínez de Perón, who had assumed power after her husband's death in 1974. By that time, the country was plagued by violent guerrilla attacks, state terrorism, and general chaos. After the *coup* a repressive military government was established, which declared its aim of eradicating the 'international Marxist subversion' and bringing back economic order through pragmatic, liberal economic policies. Those years saw also both the peak and later the slow end of competition with Brazil.

It was only after seven years that democracy was finally restored in Argentina, following great discredit and failure of the military on almost every front.[7]

---

[7] The economy was in fact left in a more lamentable state than before the *coup*, with a hugely augmented foreign debt, deficit, and increase of poverty. Although the military leaders managed to defeat terrorism, they did so at the very high price of the state itself

Alfonsín's administration (1983-1989) put great emphasis on the strengthening and consolidation of democratic institutions, but had serious difficulty in responding to socio-economic demands. Despite having implemented several stabilisation plans, inflation could not be controlled except for short periods. The foreign policy of the government of President Alfonsín was centred on three main criteria. First, attachment to Western culture and opposition to the mere strategic components of the East-West conflict. Second, reaffirmation of commitment to the Non-Aligned Movement provided that it returned to its founding principles. And third, selective support for different co-operation and integration schemes with countries from the developing world, especially in Latin America, and particularly with Brazil (Hirst and Russell, 1987). Integration with Brazil became a key political and economic strategy, as will be discussed in the next section.

In 1989, and again in 1995, Carlos Menem was elected president. Menem's two administrations (1989-1999) were centred on the implementation of a neoliberal economic programme, which included privatisation, currency convertibility, economic stability, rationalisation, and restructuring of industry. Foreign policy was characterised by 'automatic alignment' with the United States, active participation in United Nation's peacekeeping operations, and strong support for Mercosur. Thus, despite all the changes his administration carried out, economic integration with Brazil remained one of the key points, thus becoming a State policy, rather than just the policy of a government.

Although more durable, the Brazilian military regime (1964-1985) was more benign and certainly more successful than its Argentine counterpart. In Stepan's words, '[t]he Brazilian military as an institution had taken some pride in the fact that they had been less violent and more economically successful than their colleagues in Uruguay, Argentina, and Chile' (Stepan, 1988, p. 65). As a consequence, the military in Brazil retained some prestige, and were able to engage in a very long, negotiated, and gradual transition toward democracy. The *abertura* process – process of gradual political liberalisation that would lead to the democratic transition – was initiated under the Geisel administration (1974-1979) and completed by João Figueiredo (1979-1985).

President Sarney's civilian government (1985-1990) was confronted by a serious economic and social crisis that could not be solved. The next two governments of Fernando Collor de Mello (1990-1992) and Itamar Franco (1992-1995) managed only partially to stabilise the economy and reduce inflation. Stability was eventually achieved with Cardoso's neoliberal *Real* Plan (1994), which helped him to move from the finance ministry to the national presidency (1995 to date).

Brazil's foreign office, Itamaraty, has historically enjoyed a high level of autonomy. Thus, foreign policy priorities have not changed significantly with the changes of government. During the 1970s and 1980s it was centred on three basic principles. First, a break in the policy of 'automatic alignment' with the United

---

using terrorist methods, and gross violations of human rights. In addition, the performance of the armed forces in the Falkland/Malvinas war proved that their professional skills were also very poor.

States; second, ideological neutrality; and third, *rapprochement* with the Third World, particularly with Sub-Saharan Africa, the Middle East, and above all with the rest of Latin America. It was only during the 1990s that foreign policy shifted strikingly towards improved relations with the U.S. and a strong (re)assertion of Brazil's 'Western' character.

The fact that there was a certain similarity in the general political and economic orientation of the different governments in Argentina and Brazil – broadly speaking, opposition to the U.S. non-proliferation policy in the 1970s, democratic transition and heterodox economic plans in the 1980s, and institutional consolidation and economic liberalisation in the 1990s – certainly contributed to feel some sense of complicity.

Mercosur

Given Latin America's past (failed) attempts at integration – Latin American Free Trade Agreement (LAFTA-1960) and Latin American Integration Association (LAIA-1980) – and the rivalry that had characterised relations between Argentina and Brazil until the late 1970s, it was not surprising that Mercosur's launch did not give rise to very promising forecasts. Nevertheless, there is now a shared consensus among academics, business leaders and policy-makers that since its beginnings, Mercosur has constituted a fairly successful enterprise. Between 1991 and 1997, intra-Mercosur exports rose at a rate that trebled the growth of exports from the Mercosur countries to the rest of the world, accompanied by greater co-operation among firms in the establishment of subsidiaries and joint ventures, as well as by a stepped-up purchase of equity shares within the region. The actual goal of implementing the common market is, however, still to be achieved (Bouzas, 1999; Valls Pereira, 1999).

This section on Mercosur offers an overview of the treaties leading to its foundation, and analyses advantages and expectations, both economic and political, of this integration agreement. Next, it analyses the impact of Mercosur on the mutual and self-perception of Argentina and Brazil as part of the process of transformation of the region into a security community.

History of the Treaties

Mercosur was born out of an initiative by Argentina and Brazil. Although it was created by the Treaty of Asunción in 1991, the 1985 Declaration of Iguazú constitutes its direct precedent. Thereby, the democratically elected Argentine and Brazilian presidents, Raúl Alfonsín and José Sarney, created a High Level Joint Commission to advance a bilateral integration process. Economic integration was a top priority of their agendas.

Many bilateral and regional declarations, agreements and accords followed,[8] most of which were economic. However, the economic integration process was only possible in the context of the political *rapprochement* between Argentina and Brazil, a *rapprochement* that had begun some six years before the 1985 Declaration. Two factors played a major role. First, the termination both of concrete controversies – such as the River Paraná dispute that came to an end with the Itaipú-Corpus Treaty (1979) – and of a more subtle rivalry for regional prestige, such as the covert competition that was overcome by the nuclear agreements signed during the 1980s.

The second important factor on the road towards bilateral co-operation was a change at the level of public discourse and attitudes. This shift was symbolised by a myriad of joint declaration on peaceful intentions that came out after 1979, and more numerously in 1985. This was accompanied by gestures of goodwill even before democratisation. For instance, after the signature of the Tripartite Treaty, two presidential summits between Videla and Figueiredo took place in Buenos Aires and Brasilia in May and October 1980 respectively. These constituted visits of diplomatic importance, since they lasted several days and the presidents were accompanied by a delegation of ministers and government secretaries. According to Pastor, Argentine Foreign Minister at that time, the increasingly stronger personal ties between the presidents developed into an authentic mutual understanding, which in turn was reflected in the signing of 22 documents. They put in motion joint infrastructure enterprises – as the bridge over the River Iguazú – and nuclear and hydroelectric co-operation agreements (Camilión, 1999, p. 221; Pastor, 1996, pp. 286-289). A further example of this attitude of goodwill is illustrated by the mutual visits to sensitive facilities carried out for the first time ever in Argentine-Brazilian relations by Presidents Alfonsín and Sarney in 1987 and 1988.

Some argue that these declarations and gestures did not go far beyond rhetoric and failed to constitute any concrete co-operation scheme (Solingen, 1998, p. 141). While it is true that the *rapprochement* of the early 1980s did not lead to an immediate programme of action, this 'mere rhetoric' should be given greater credit: the easing of tension at the discursive level was a crucial step for improvements on the bilateral relationship. After four decades of nuclear and regional competition for hegemony between Argentina and Brazil, the importance of this shift in the 'discursive mood' should not be underestimated, as they were crucial signs that the governments were sending to each other and to the general public.

Grand gestures backed by determined political decisions were essential to overcome mutual distrust and to convince public opinion in both countries that the other state did not constitute a realistic threat any longer. These two factors – signature of treaties and agreements, on the one hand, and rhetoric as the manifestation of political will, on the other – were the necessary steps to help build

---

[8] For an exhaustive chronology of agreements on Latin American integration, see de Alemida, 1993.

up trust, confidence and co-operation between these states, and develop these into viable policies backed by the public.

After the 1985 Declaration of Iguazú, a rapid political and economic process unfolded. That declaration was followed in 1986 by the Accord on Brazilian-Argentine Integration, which established a gradual and flexible Programme for Integration and Economic Co-operation (PICE). In 1988 a further Treaty on Integration, Co-operation and Development was signed. The aim this time was the consolidation of the bilateral integration process, and the establishment of a first period of ten years to build up a common economic area by gradually dismantling reciprocal trade barriers. There would be a second stage, when all other policies would be gradually harmonised to form a common market. In July 1990, however, the newly elected presidents Carlos Menem and Fernando Collor de Mello signed the Buenos Aires Act accelerating the timetable for the establishment of the bilateral common market by the end of 1994 and instituting automatic tariff reductions and elimination of non-tariff barriers across the board, although these initiatives have not been completely achieved yet.

Soon thereafter, on 26 March 1991, Argentina, Brazil, Paraguay and Uruguay signed the Treaty of Asunción, finally creating Mercosur. In this treaty the constitution of a regional common market by 31 December 1994 was provided for, by stipulating the free circulation of goods and services, automatic schedule for tariff reductions, a common external tariff, harmonisation of laws and regulations concerning rules of origin and dispute settlement, and co-ordination of macroeconomic policies.

When Collor and Menem established unilateral trade liberalisation programmes in their countries in the early 1990s, and gave a more decisive push to the integration process as part of a fundamental component of their domestic economies' restructuring, a new impetus was felt. The 1990s promised a period of major regional change with regard to economic plans and economic co-operation.

Economic and Political Aspects of Integration

Mercosur was clearly conceived as a strategy with multiple purposes, both economic and political, as well as domestic, regional, and international. Regional trade blocs were consolidating in the world, and Mercosur sought to serve as a tool for the competitive inclusion of Argentina, Brazil, Paraguay and Uruguay into the global economy. It sought to improve its members' productivity by taking advantage of economies of scale, and to become a more attractive region for international trade and investment. In this sense, it does not sound radically different from past endeavours.

However, beyond its present economic focus, the PICE spirit of 1986 – when it was only a rising co-operation project between Argentina and Brazil – was overtly marked by politics. At that time, Latin America was still in the midst of its 'lost decade,' and democracy was expanding only gradually and uncertainly throughout the region. Moreover, neither new government in Argentina and Brazil was convinced of the exhaustion of the import substitution model. Integration efforts were carried out at the same time as domestic heterodox economic policies tried to stop inflation, control fluctuations in exchange rates, and pursue macroeconomic equilibrium.

Sarney and Alfonsín saw in co-operation the potential for economic viability and growth, thus avoiding the plight of failed states that some African countries had become. While economic viability was naturally a major concern – above all for Argentina – the political flank appeared to be critical, too. The context for co-operation was the consolidation of the recently re-established democracies, the building up of confidence and trust not only between their militaries but also between their societies, and the strengthening of their bargaining capacity in international forums. It was a process driven by the governments, rather than by industrial and agricultural groups, or by the private sector in general. An extensive debate about integration only started after, and not before, the 1986 agreement, as its signature took many by surprise (Cason, 2000).

The fact that integration was not the natural outcome of intensive commercial exchange becomes yet more apparent when one looks at trade figures. Even when Mercosur was formally founded in 1991, the level of interdependence among member countries was remarkably low, and pre-eminence was given to domestic programmes of stabilisation and reform. To be sure, integration was first and foremost dependent on the political will of the governments.

Although trade has always been central to Mercosur's rationale, it was rather the political and strategic dimensions of the bilateral relation that gave Mercosur substantive character and made it such a challenging enterprise. The earlier bilateral co-operation scheme between Argentina and Brazil and the later foundation of Mercosur rested upon three main and immediate purposes besides the commercial advantages of the preferential trade agreement. First, it aimed at the consolidation of democracy throughout the region. Second, it sought to strengthen the members' political leverage and economic inclusion in the world. And third, it hoped to help the states to overcome serious domestic economic difficulties, by offering a more stable context to their unstable situations. With respect to all three matters, there was a shared sense that a co-operation agreement in the Southern Cone would constitute the right strategy. However, it would be a challenging task too, as co-operation was to take place among states that showed a low level of interdependence, and that for most of the century had looked at each other as potential enemies, rather than as potential partners.

Despite this background, between 1990 and 1993, there was an impressive increase in intra-Mercosur trade flows and investment, and economic interests began to consolidate. These were, undoubtedly, some of the goals of Mercosur since its early days, and since the mid-1990s the genuine dynamics of interdependence between the economies of the area have been evident. Whereas in 1990 Mercosur accounted for 4.2 per cent of Brazilian exports and for 11.2 per cent of its imports, by 1996 these figures had increased to 15.5 and 15.6 per cent respectively. If this is true for Brazil – Mercosur's largest and strongest partner[9] – the other three member countries have become even more dependent on access to their partners' markets, especially Brazil's.

---

[9] In 1995 Brazil accounted for approximately 70 per cent of Mercosur's total GDP.

The consolidation of the association was to work also as an 'image improver,' and this was a major consideration on the part of the members. It was expected that the arrangement would strengthen the idea of bloc and of a 'regional habitat,' (Peña, 1999, p. 54) and, if this proved successful, it would then maximise the political weight of Mercosur members in international negotiations, whether conducted individually or as a bloc, enhancing in turn their image.

And this did indeed happen. In 1995, for instance, Mercosur and the European Union signed an agreement creating an institutional mechanism to carry forward a regular policy dialogue between the two regions, and to pursue co-operation regarding entrepreneurial matters and economic and social reforms. This was possible because the EU has seen in Mercosur a trade and investment partner; an image of partnership that the EU would not have had of the region before. Another example illustrates how Mercosur has helped maximise the political leverage of the region. In December 1994, during the negotiation on the Free Trade Agreement of the Americas (FTAA), it was finally agreed that negotiations towards this agreement would be carried out by the already existing subregional blocs, as Brazil claimed, rather than by the individual states, as advocated by the United States. Brazil, backed by Mercosur, managed to maximise its bargaining power and prevail over the U.S. position.

A shared perception of vulnerability also helped reinforce the integration process and identify its benefits. After the 1994 Mexican *Peso* crisis, there was a growing consciousness among political leaders in the Southern Cone that their own countries were equally vulnerable to erratic global financial movements. This realisation led them to start thinking in terms of 'mutualism', as Mônica Hirst puts it. This growing sense of mutualism in the Argentine-Brazilian relationship at the core of Mercosur 'is one of many examples of the recent world-wide trend toward intergovernmental co-operation based on the identification of common interests and values' (Hirst, 1999, p. 39).

A further aspect of this convergent perception of vulnerability and mutualism had to do with the need for democratic consolidation and economic stability. Therefore, although these goals go far beyond the purposes of a preferential trade agreement, they did play a role in the rationale behind Mercosur's creation and consolidation. Liberal democracy and an open economy were at the centre of the region's new political identity, and these ideals were reflected in the agreement. Once democracy had become the political system in place across the Southern Cone, it developed into an explicit *sine qua non* to promote further integration and a written condition for membership to Mercosur.

As Andrew Hurrell highlights, leading actors from all Mercosur member states have constantly placed particular emphasis on democracy. They have stressed the role that democracy has played in redefining the interests of the Southern Cone states and in reshaping their identities and sense of common purpose. This can be identified in both the language and symbols consciously chosen to talk a community of shared identity into existence (Hurrell, 1995).

The Two Sides of the Coin

If the integration process has been a state-led development, the same is true for the gradual emergence of a common identification.[10] It has been very much a state-led, politically engineered development rather than a spontaneous mutual identification of the populations involved. Yet this is not a completely new experience in the Western Hemisphere. Nation-states in both North and South America were the result of conscious nation-building enterprises in the years of colonial dependency, and independence and civil wars (see 'Creole Pioneers' in Anderson, 1991). In the case of the Southern Cone, the advance of Mercosur started to timidly arouse some sort of shared identification among the populations, mainly those of Argentina and Brazil. This only happened after the project of integration was set in motion. However, it must be said too, public opinion backed the process.

The shift from opponent to partner in the perception of each other has been a parallel and concomitant outcome – not a by-product – of the transformation of the Southern Cone into a zone of peace. The further emergence of common identification and of security community are two sides of the same coin, in so far as they are mutually reinforcing parts of a single process.

The present section discusses how Mercosur contributed to forging a common, distinct identification between Argentina and Brazil. The recent history of similar political experiences certainly contributed to their consideration of convergent solutions. Not only had both undergone fierce dictatorships during the 1970s, but they had also experienced economic instability, the debt crisis of the 1980s, underdevelopment, and hyperinflationary peaks. Their authoritarian governments, too, were marked by similarities. They were all military, conservative, and exclusionary regimes in nature, and repressive and violent in form. Moreover, as Remmer rightly observes, even though proximity punctuated their relationships with military tensions and rivalries, shared frontiers, riverine systems, and transportation linkages created an extended history of subregional links and co-operation (Remmer, 1998, p. 32).

In recent years there has been a rather active, although not explicit, policy to promote a common identification. This enterprise has been carried out through, at

---

[10] The term 'identification' ('common or shared identification') is preferred here over that of 'identity,' as the former suggests a looser conceptual understanding, implying a common perception of potential shared benefits and costs; mutual sympathies; recognition of areas of common interests that promote co-operation and coordination in different fields, both at the public and private levels; growing curiosity and knowledge about the other's politics, culture, society, etc., that is in fact reflection of a growing interest in the other as such; and, in general, a positive image of the other that tends to advance co-operation rather than competition, and that does not see a negative impact on one's own state in the other state's gain, but appreciates that it can instead redound to one's own benefit. In other words, I am not arguing that what has emerged between Argentina and Brazil is a common identity similar to the European one that, many say, is shared by most citizens in the European Union, but a much looser concept of positive perception of commonalities.

least, three areas, of which trade and economic integration constitutes the first and most apparent one. The second area lies in the realm of politics, while the third is constituted by culture. Further, it is argued here that the conditions listed by Karl Deutsch as contributing to developing a security community – and hence to a common identification – are present in the Brazilian-Argentine case.[11]

The increasing level of trade and economic exchange is in evidence in a growing interdependence, which, in turn, has facilitated the uncovering of important grounds for joint profits, as well as for joint losses. Once this happens, Deutsch's condition of *mutual responsiveness* tends to grow between the countries. And this has been the case time and again: At governmental level, economic concerns about, say, trade imbalances are taken seriously and eventually resolved co-operatively, most often, however, at the level of the Executives, as Andrés Malamud's chapter 3 shows. An example of this occurred as early as in 1986 and 1987, when Brazil, in response to an Argentine request, agreed to correct trade imbalances that could have weakened the economic integration process, and to establish a mechanism of workshops and meetings aimed at improving communication and overcoming potential obstacles.

Furthermore, increased exchange and interdependence have naturally brought closer the business communities of both countries, which in turn resulted in increased communication and co-operative interaction amongst them. Once the business circles realise that they have more to win together than otherwise, it becomes easier for them to develop some kind of identification related to their shared interests. In this way, a clear perception has grown in Argentina that economic growth in Brazil cannot harm Argentina but only redound to its benefit. The growth of the Brazilian economy easily translates into higher imports from Argentina, as some sectors of the Brazilian industry soon reach the limit of their production capacity, thus generating demand from foreign suppliers. When this happens, Argentina is in a privileged position to cover that need.

There is yet another positive impact on the Argentine economy. When the Brazilian domestic demand grows, Brazilian industries find themselves compelled to satisfy the needs of their domestic market, reducing thus their export capacity and leaving their foreign markets open to Argentina. Similarly, when Brazil experiences a break or a fall in its growth, this is immediately felt in Argentina, which sends 30 per cent of its exports to Brazil (Gosman, 2000). Although to a lesser degree, Brazil, too, is affected by Argentine economic performance. While in 1990 Argentina ranked 10th on the list of Brazil's most important markets, accounting for just two per cent of its total exports, in 1994 Argentina had become

---

[11] Deutsch identifies three essential conditions for the formation of a security community, and eleven conditions that are helpful but not essential. The essential ones are mutual compatibility of major values, mutual responsiveness, and mutual predictability of behaviour. The inessential ones are distinctive way of life, superior economic growth, expectation of joint economic reward, wide range of mutual transactions, broadening of elites, links of social communication, greater mobility of persons, reluctance to wage 'fratricidal' war, free of military threats, strong economic ties, and ethnic and linguistic assimilation (Deutsch, 1957).

Brazil's second largest trading partner, taking up half of Brazil's trade with South America, and making up 10 per cent of its exports. On a more negative note, with the latest financial crisis of Argentina (2001), the Brazilian *Real* lost 20 per cent of its value in less than a year. The cause lay probably more on concerns about Argentina's debt spreading to Brazil than on inherent problems with the Brazilian economy.

Somewhere between the first area – trade and economy – and the second – politics, including foreign policy – a co-operative foreign economic policy can be spotted. A first example of this was the joint position of the Mercosur countries in the FTAA negotiations. Here, Mercosur appeared as a united bloc with a shared perception of interests in international trade. Thus, Cason asserts, 'the partners have begun to forge a Mercosur "identity" with respect to the rest of the Americas, and the bloc appears quite strong as it faces the possibility of a hemisphere-wide free-trade area' (Cason, 2000, p. 24).

Further, Mercosur common foreign policy is yet to evolve, although it has not been in evidence so far. Argentine and Brazilian foreign policies have proved too divergent in the years of Menem and Cardoso. Even in the height of the co-operation wave, the two countries have consistently followed different foreign policy lines. Hence, as Argentina upgraded 'automatic alignment' with the United States to the status of foreign policy *principle* and later became an extra-NATO ally, Brazil maintained a greater distance from the U.S. and looked at the whole picture with suspicion, at the same time as it claimed a permanent chair in the Security Council of the United Nations without Argentine support. But even these prickly situations were eventually resolved satisfactorily with the intervention of the Executives, a fact that still does not undermine the reality of the different foreign policy orientations.

To account for the political aspect of the construction of a common identification, some examples from another of Deutsch's essential conditions for a security community – *mutual compatibility of major values* – can be drawn. Democratisation and democracy have undoubtedly strengthened the presence of this factor between Argentina and Brazil. The fact that democracy has become a *sine qua non* for membership to Mercosur only reinforces this point. Grabendorff goes even further to assert that values such as human rights, the rule of law, market economy, and the social responsibility of the state constitute core values that can already be taken for granted. This should be understood, Grabendorff goes on to suggest, in the context of Mercosur's willingness to join 'the Western Club' and play by its rules, a fact, at least partially, due to historical and cultural links between the Southern Cone and Europe (Grabendorff, 1999, p. 97).

Again symbol of *mutual responsiveness* (political, this time) has been Brazil's official support in several international forums to Argentine claims regarding sovereignty over the Malvinas/Falklands. Indeed, Argentina and Brazil have worked extensively from the realm of politics on the construction of a common identification. An illustrative example, briefly mentioned earlier, is given by the official visits of Presidents Alfonsín and Sarney in 1987 and 1988 to an Argentine gas diffusion enrichment plant, and a Brazilian hitherto officially unacknowledged ultra-centrifuge enrichment plant. These visits demonstrated the shift away from tension, distrust, competition, and a search for nuclear autonomy, to an era of peaceful commitment. They explicitly aimed at building confidence and predictable behaviour.

Finally, another sign of Argentina and Brazil working together for a security community is the Brazilian-Argentine Agency for Accounting and Control of Nuclear Materials (ABACC). It was set up under an agreement signed between Argentina and Brazil for the Exclusively Peaceful Use of Nuclear Energy in 1991. The ABACC is responsible for the administration and application of the Common System of Accounting and Control (SCCC), which is a comprehensive safeguards system that applies to all nuclear materials and all nuclear activities in both countries. The ABACC was the result of six joint declarations and agreements between 1980 and 1990 on the peaceful uses of nuclear energy. This example supports the third of Deutsch's essential conditions for a security community, *mutual predictability of behaviour.*

The third area, culture, from which this shared identification has been forged, is the one that has a more immediate impact on the identity of the population. The shared experience of a similar, recent history, as already mentioned earlier, as well as common experiences of democratic transition, recovery of civil and political rights, slow economic stabilisation and growth, and adoption of neo-liberal economic policies and its drawbacks, have created a kind of commonality of interests and attitudes among populations that goes deeper than economic and political agreements. Certainly, an important part of this process was led by political and economic elites through formal *rapprochement* and official integration. In any case, the result is a partial but growing identification in terms of self-image and interests, mutual sympathy and loyalties, of an increasing sense of 'we-feeling.'

Intensified links of social communication also add up to shaping some sort of shared culture. And here, too, an active policy is under way. For instance, at the Argentine National Institute of Foreign Service, under the Ministry of Foreign Affairs, Portuguese has become a mandatory language. At its Brazilian counterpart, candidates get Spanish classes besides English and French. Recently, an Argentine newspaper reported that the multiplication of Argentineans studying Portuguese led to the need to open an institute to train local teachers, as Brazilian teachers alone would not cover the demand for language courses (Lanusse, 2001).

A further example is the emergence of topics such as 'Brazil,' 'Mercosur' and 'Regional Integration' as sub-disciplines at Argentine and Brazilian universities and research centres. The University of Buenos Aires created in 1996 a Masters programme in Regional Integration with emphasis on Mercosur, while the University of Brasilia has a Centre of Mercosul (Portuguese for Mercosur) Studies. This has taken place in response to academic, political, and private enterprises' demands for specialists able to efficiently understand, advise and predict the effects of the integration process.

Final Remarks: A Worthy Coin

Argentine-Brazilian bilateral relations shifted in much less than a decade from open hostility and mutual jealousy under the authoritarian governments through *rapprochement* to co-operation under civilian rule. Though the re-adoption of the democratic system partly explains the goodwill between the two countries, the first signs of a *détente* occurred as early as 1979 with the Itaipú-Corpus Treaty, and in 1980, when they signed a co-operation agreement for the development and application of nuclear energy for peaceful uses.

After the critical decade of the 1970s, the 1980s were characterised by a search for alternatives. Provided the relative unviability of their independent projects, both Argentina and Brazil finally envisaged co-operation, rather than competition, as a better strategy for survival, institutional consolidation, economic development, and inclusion into the global economy. It would enable them, it was then thought, to achieve economic benefits, strengthen their political systems, and increase their international political capacities. We see, there was indeed an element of calculation in the *rapprochement*.

What has developed parallel with this, and as a part of the same process, is a deeper common identification of risks and opportunities. The bilateral *rapprochement* was both reflected on and reinforced by the creation of Mercosur, and resulted in the transformation of the region into a zone of peace, and the slow emergence of a security community between Argentina and Brazil. Not only is war between Argentina and Brazil unthinkable, but there is also a growing sense of common identification, shared destinies, and 'mutualism.' Mutual images and perceptions have changed, and in so doing, they have affected self-perceptions. The transformation in terms of the quality of peace achieved is strikingly positive. The impact of this process, in turn, stretches beyond the two countries, permitting the move of the Southern Cone as a whole away from the mere 'no-war zone' that it used to be until the late 1970s to an incipient pluralistic security community.

References

Adler, Emanuel and Barnett, Michael N. (1998), 'Security communities in theoretical perspective' in E. Adler and M.N. Barnett (eds.), *Security Communities,* Cambridge University Press, Cambridge.
Anderson, Benedict (1991), *Imagined Communities: Reflections on the Origin and Spread of Nationalism,* Verso, London.
Bouzas, Roberto (1999), *A Mercosur-European Union Free Trade Agreement. Issues and Prospects,* FLACSO, Buenos Aires.
Buzan, Barry (1991), *People, State and Fear: An agenda for International Security Studies in the Post-Cold War Era,* Lynne Rienner, Boulder, CO.
Buzan, Barry, Wæver, Ole and Wilde, Jaap de (1998), *Security: A New Framework for Analysis,* Lynne Rienner, Boulder, CO.
Camilión, Oscar (1999), *Memorias Políticas: De Frondizi a Menem (1956-1996),* Planeta-Todo es Historia, Buenos Aires.

Cason, Jeffrey (2000), 'On the road to Southern Cone economic integration', *Journal of Interamerican Studies and World Affairs*, Vol. 42, pp. 23-42.

Child, Jack (1985), *Geopolitics and Conflict in South America: Quarrels among Neighbors,* Praeger Publishers, New York.

Cisneros, Andrés and Escudé, Carlos (2000), *Historia General de las Relaciones Exteriores de la República Argentina,* Grupo Editor Latinoamericano, Buenos Aires.

Correa, Benavides (1973), *Habrá guerra próximamente en el cono sur?,* Siglo Veintiuno, Mexico.

de Almeida, Paulo Roberto (1993), *O MERCOSUL no Contexto Regional e Internacional,* Edicoes Aduaneiras Ltda., São Paulo, Brazil.

de la Fuente, Pedro Luis (1997), 'Confidence-Building Measures in the Southern Cone: A model for regional stability', *Naval College War Review,* Winter, pp. 36-65.

Deutsch, Karl (1957), *Political Community and the North Atlantic Area: International organization in the light of historical experience,* Princeton University Press, Princeton.

Ferreira, Oliveiros S. (1992), 'Goals of Argentine-Brazilian Nuclear Cooperation, in P. L. Leventhal and S. Tanzer (eds.), *Averting a Latin American Nuclear Arms Race: New Prospects and Challenges for Argentine-Brazilian Nuclear Cooperation,* Macmillan, London.

Gaveglio, Silvia (1992), 'Estados Unidos en la relación Argentina-Brasil', in I.M. Laredo (ed.), *La Integración Latinoamericana en el Actual Escenario Mundial: de la ALALC-ALADI al Mercosur,* UNR Editora, Rosario, Argentina.

Gosman, Eleonora (2000), 'Un salto del 6% en la economía,' *Clarín Digital,* 6 July, http://www.clarin.com.ar/diario/2000-07-06/e-01901.htm

Grabendorff, Wolf (1999) 'Mercosur and the European Union: From cooperation to alliance?' in R. Roett (ed.), *Mercosur: Regional Integration, World Markets,* Lynne Rienner Publishers, Boulder, CO and London.

Guglielmelli, Juan E. (1974), 'Argentina, Brasil y la bomba atómica', *Estrategia,* September-October, pp. 1-15.

Herrera Vega, Jorge Hugo (September 1995), *Las Políticas Exteriores de la Argentina y del Brasil,* ISEN, Buenos Aires.

Hirst, Mônica (1999), 'Mercosur's complex political agenda', in R. Roett (ed.), *Mercosur: Regional Integration, World Markets,* Lynne Rienner Publishers, Boulder, CO and London.

Hirst, Mônica and Russell, Roberto (1987), *Democracia y Política Exterior: los casos de Argentina y Brasil,* FLACSO, Buenos Aires.

Holsti, Kalevi (1996), *The State, War, and the State of War,* Cambridge University Press, Cambridge.

Hurrell, Andrew (1995), 'Regionalism in the Americas', in L. Fawcett and A. Hurrell (eds.), *Regionalism in World Politics. Regional Organization and International Order,* Oxford University Press, Oxford.

Hurrell, Andrew (1998), 'An emerging security community in South America?' in E. Adler and M. Barnett (eds.), *Security Communities,* Cambridge University Press, Cambridge.

Kacowicz, Arie M. (1998), *Zones of Peace in the Third World: South America and West Africa in Comparative Perspective,* State University of New York Press, Albany, NY.

Kacowicz, Arie M. (1999), 'Stable Peace in South America: The ABC Triangle, 1979-1999', *CISS/ISA,* Paris.

Kacowicz, Arie M., Bar-Siman-Tov, Yaacov, Elgström, Ole and Jerneck, Magnus (Eds.) (2000), *Stable Peace Among Nations,* Rowman & Littlefield Publishers, Lanham.

Lanusse, Agustina (2001), 'Cada vez más argentinos quieren hablar portugués' in *La Nación Line,* 5 November, www.lanacion.com.ar/01/11/05/dq_348822.asp.

Moniz Bandeira, L.A. (1998), 'As relações regionais no Cone Sul: iniciativas de integracão' in A.L. Cervo and M. Rapoport (eds.), *História do Cone Sul,* Revan and Editora Universidade de Brasília, Rio de Janeiro and Brasília.

Morgan, Patrick M. (1997), 'Regional Security Complexes and regional orders', in D.A. Lake, and P.M. Morgan (eds.), *Regional Orders: Building Security in a New World,* Pennsylvania State University, Pennsylvania.

O'Donnell, Guillermo (1973). *Modernization and Bureaucratic Authoritarianism: Studies in South American Politics,* Institute of International Studies, University of California, Berkeley.

Olmos, Mario (1986), *La Cooperación Argentina-Brasil: Núcleo Impulsor de la Integración Latinoamericana,* Instituto de Publicaciones Navales, Buenos Aires.

Pastor, Carlos Washington (1996), 'Chile: La guerra o la paz. 1978-1981', in S.R. Jalabe (ed.), *La Política Exterior Argentina y sus Protagonistas. 1880-1995,* CARI-Grupo Editor Latinoamericano, Buenos Aires.

Peña, Félix (1999), 'Broadening and deepening: Striking the right balance', in R. Roett (ed.), *Mercosur: Regional Integration, World Markets,* Lynne Rienner Publishers, Boulder, CO and London.

Reiss, Mitchell (1995), *Bridled Ambitions: Why countries constrain their nuclear capabilities,* Woodrow Wilson Center Press, Washington, D.C.

Remmer, Karen L. (1998), 'Does democracy promote interstate cooperation? Lessons from the Mercosur region' *International Studies Quarterly,* Vol. 42, pp. 25-52.

Rosenbaum, H. Jon (1973), 'Argentina-Brazilian Relations: A Critical Juncture', *World Today,* Vol. 29, pp. 537-546.

Scenna, Miguel A. (1975), *Argentina-Brasil: Cuatro Siglos de Rivalidad,* Ediciones La Bastilla, Buenos Aires.

Solingen, Etel (1998), *Regional Orders at Century's Dawn: Global and Domestic Influences on Grand Strategy,* Princeton University Press, Princeton.

Stepan, Alfred (1988), 'Las prerrogativas de los militares en los nuevos regímenes democráticos', *Desarrollo Económico,* Vol. 27, pp. 479-504.

Valls Pereira, Lia (1999), 'Toward the common market of the South: Mercosur's Origins, Evolution, and Challenges' in R. Roett (ed.), *Mercosur: Regional Integration, World Markets,* Lynne Rienner Publishers, Boulder, CO and London.

Chapter 9

Integration in Times of Instability: Exchange Rate and Monetary Cooperation in Mercosur and the EU

Susana Borrás and Michael Kluth

Introduction

The process of regional integration is essentially a process of institutionalising a new political and economic order. Both in the strong political variant of the EU's and in the 'common market' version of Mercosur, regional agreements entail a partial restructuring of previously existing frameworks of socio-economic policy action. Firstly, the decision to move a specific issue from a national to an international level means a partial reshuffling of authority by moving up the locus of decision-making, and a partial re-consideration of the nature of the state, as the sole regulator of socio-economic life. Secondly, this entails a political re-negotiation of how civil society, the economy and the relevant (new) level of public authority have to be organised, thus opening the door for political struggles among ideological/ideational alternatives. This is what has fascinated social scientists who try to explain the phenomenon of regional integration. Why and how do states agree to undertake such challenging political tasks? And what are the factors that drive the integration process?

The extensive literature dealing with these issues, mostly dealing with the EU, has somehow tended to disregard the question of what explains continuity in times of instability. Why do states have a tendency to continue sticking to a co-operation agreement when the economic and political contexts have changed, and the conditions for the initial agreement might be different than they were at the onset? Once the decisions have been made at regional level, what makes them persist? As several authors have pointed out, the political decisions enshrined in a treaty or formal agreement are not the end of story, but the beginning of it, as there is no guarantee that the arrangements will wither away by inaction. This is to say that the 'substance' and reality of a regional integration project come with the almost daily political decisions made by each partner to comply with their agreements.

All this might be strongly challenged by considerable instability in the wider context in which the regional arrangement took place. If the instability generates a high degree of uncertainty in the form of high risk, and if the results of these

207

uncertainties are asymmetrically distributed among partners, instability might put substantial pressure on the constituted order. Given this situation, the actors have, essentially, two possibilities, namely they can either disrupt the established order by searching for new political arrangements (collectively or individually, defecting or making a new arrangement lowering the previous level of mutual commitment) or they can stick to the existing order by reinforcing the initial view that this is the best of all possible solutions. Tilting in favour of one or the other is essentially a political choice where material interests, societal demands, cognitive parameters and world-views all have a role to play. Hence, our research question here is not what factors drive the integration process in the direction of more integration, but rather what makes it hold in stormy and unstable times.

Instability and continuity in regional integration agreements deserve careful comparative analysis. For this purpose, we have chosen two recent events in Mercosur and the European Union. The recent macro-economic crises in Brazil and Argentina have put considerable pressure on Mercosur's integration. While somewhat less dramatically, the EU also experienced an unexpected situation. The newly launched single European currency, the Euro, suffered a constant loss of value against the US Dollar. In connection with this, some voices questioned how far the European Central Bank (ECB) had to strictly pursue its institutionalised objective of fighting against inflation. To different extents, both events have put pressure on the institutionalised order of the regional arrangements. This chapter will proceed as follows. First, it will elaborate a succinct theoretical framework based on recent developments in institutionalism and social-constructivism, which tries to accommodate a perspective on ideational/cognitive factors without undermining the explanatory value of interests. After that, we will examine the institutionalisation process and the nature of macro-economic co-operation in Mercosur and the EU. This will allow us to investigate the recent instability, its causes and its scale, and most importantly, the responses to it. The concluding remarks of the chapter will again bring to the fore the question of instability in different integration processes.

Regional Integration and Ideals: Theorising Continuity in Unstable Times

We mentioned above that regional integration is an institutionalised political order. This focus helps us understand the elements at play in the integration process and the continuity of its arrangements. As Mansfield and Milner have put it:

> (I)nternational institutions create incentives for states to cooperate by reducing collective action problems; by lengthening the 'shadow of the future', thereby enhancing the prospects for states to engage in strategies of reciprocity; and by increasing the ability to link various issues, thereby increasing the costs for states of failing to comply with established rules and norms (Mansfield and Milner, 1997, p. 6).

This quotation contains two of the most important factors explaining continuity, namely, reciprocity and issue-linking, both of which raise the costs of non-compliance.

Institutionalist perspectives on regional integration have recently gained ground. The overall success of neo-institutionalism stems from its willingness to strike a balance between the structuralist and the methodological individualist traditions. Institutions are supposed to constrain individual actor's behaviour but in such a way that social action is not reduced to the mere expression of the given political-economic-social structures. However, not all institutionalists hold the same position. The relatively crowded institutionalism reflects, though, important differences in conceptual and theoretical understandings of what institutions are.

The liberal institutionalist tradition, to which Mansfield belongs, holds a rather strict definition of institution, as the negotiated order resulting from the specific national interests and preferences, and the strategic choices of the bargaining procedure (Moravcsik, 1995). Historical institutionalism by contrast emphasises the processes through which actors over time are subjected to value alignment mechanisms leading to institutionalisation as certain conventions and political goals become 'habits of thought', as paraphrased by Thorstein Veblen. Within the regional integration field, historical institutionalism has recently been viewed as an intellectual cousin to the neo-functional school of thought. Neo-functional statements and references are thus found in the works of historical institutionalists such as Simon Bulmer (1994), Wayne Sandholtz and John Zysman (1994), and Pierson (1998). Considerable attention has been paid to institutionalist approaches in political science up through the nineties. Johan P. Olsen and James March (1989 and 1995) have captured the centre-stage with their crusade against rational choice institutionalism. Their endeavours can be seen as a delayed extension of similar research agendas within sociology. Yet their work also explicitly draws a line back to early political science and economics which had previously embodied institutional thinking as represented by e.g. Thorstein Veblen.

While the institutionalism of March & Olsen does pose a challenge to the behaviourist paradigm once dominant in political science, they represent a middle-of-the-road position when measured up against the more radical rejection of behavioural social science found among certain sociologists.

Radical social constructivism can arguably be grouped as a brand of institutionalism rejecting the existence of material/objective interests (Torfing 2001). Insisting upon the primacy of verbal struggles over the content and meaning of lingual codes, they affiliate themselves with an anti-essentialist and anti-realist stance at odds with the epistemological and ontological views of the other institutionalists.

Given the large differences about the conceptual breath of institution, any scholar is compelled to choose among them. Historical institutionalism seems to be a balanced starting point for a pragmatic inquiry. Its appeal lies in the fact that the applied definition of institution has neat borders leaving room for the role that interests (national and private) play in the integration process. But for historical institutionalists institutions are not subordinated to interests.

Both radical and more conventional advocates of 'bringing institutions back in', have been instrumental in bringing back to the fore a number of issues which occupied leading scholars in the hey-days of neo-functionalism. The process of socialisation, as highlighted by e.g. Ernst B. Haas, bears some resemblance to the notion of 'discourse formation' advanced by social constructivists and 'logic's of appropriateness' associated with James March and Johan Olsen (Haas, 1992).

The latter's approach implies a broad interpretation of institutions, as a set of assumed norms and patterns of behaviour in the 'logic of appropriateness' that most actors choose instead of the 'logic of consequentiality'(March and Olsen, 1989; March and Olsen, 1998). As a result, institutions are everywhere and are essentially constraining social devices to which individual actors adapt through behaving 'appropriately'.

Radical constructivist approaches can contribute to integration studies with their appreciation of the enabling capability of institutions. Given a set of norms, verbalised meanings and conventions have been institutionalised in a particular setting, paths of action 'invisible' or 'unthinkable' to players attached to other institutional settings, may become both viable and obvious.

In other words, interests do not explain everything. At least not why the different examples of regional integration have very different contents and patterns, nor why regional arrangements tend to persist even in adverse conditions, when reciprocity is not straightforward and when issues might be de-coupled in order to keep the whole boat from sinking.

Historical institutionalism couples politics and political processes within a historically given context. The norms, rules and patterns of social conventions that inform, constrain, and enable single actor's actions have been established long beforehand. This is where the notion of 'path dependency' comes in, stressing the tendency that political actors generally stick to partly known patterns of action when confronted with a new situation. This means that change and transformation is normally a gradual (and even parsimonious) process. Radical change exists, but it is an anomaly in political life.

However, historical institutionalism needs further development to explain how ideational cognitive parameters form part of this historically built, path-defined forms of states' political action in an international arena (Borrás, 1999), aligning it to the social-constructivist approach (Christensen, et al., 2001) and the focus on identity formation (Higgott, 1998).

Unlike institutions, ideas are intellectual constructs facilitating only reflected action – as opposed to unreflected social praxis. Ideas are often defined in opposition to other ideas or even ideational proxies. They are consciously normative and typically prescribe solutions to wrong-doings of the established ways. If ideas impose some sort of intellectual hegemony, they become institutionalised and thus are often confronted with new ideas.

Ideas have an enabling role. Ideas are sources of change in highly institutionalised orders. Ideas define political problems and have an interpreting ability, giving meaning to the situation. This is what we can call '*the ideational basis of problem-identification*'.

Secondly, ideas articulate political solutions. This is related to the ability of ideas to appeal to some commonly shared assumptions, and to suggest new courses of action on this basis. This is what we can call *'the ideational basis of political action'*. Ideas might not be sharply defined, or even uniformly interpreted by the different actors, in order to provide for change. This goes equally for the ideational basis of problem identification and of political action. The important thing is that *ideas are generally accepted as meaningful and suggestive*. Ideas have to be also commonly regarded as viable. Hence, ideas need a certain degree of relevance for the actors.

And here the notion 'state ideals' seems particularly well suited. By state ideals we understand those fundamental values and preferential biases regarding public authority, modes of governance and public approaches to economic growth and distribution, which are dominant among national elites. State ideals are the fruits of history, and have an important enabling dimension as they operate as the 'ideational basis of problem-identification' and of 'political action' within the state context.

State ideals constitute the basis for the formation and articulation of 'regional ideals', that is, the patterns of perspectives and visions about regional integration. And there might be contending regional ideals. This contention is essentially an ideational-cognitive one, between alternative ideals, and is typically resolved within the borders of political space. This means that we can consider the EU and Mercosur as two cases of regional integration stemming from two different regional ideals, which have been developed on the basis of the historically constructed state ideals.

Hence, we predict that the institutional ensemble of a consolidated case of regional integration like the EU and Mercosur is subject to further continuity and stability than that assumed by 'liberal institutionalists'. And this is so because stability cannot just be understood in terms of national interests' 'reciprocity' and 'issue-linkage', but also to in-depth cognitive parameters among national elites. These cognitive parameters are regional ideals. Hence, national elites believe that regional arrangements are the best possible political solution to a given context of the world economy and politics, and these beliefs make them stick to the arrangements even in unstable times. But how unstable can these be? How resilient are these institutional arrangements which bind states' interests and ideals into a collective action in the event of unexpected political-economic turmoil?

Instability is really the testing time for regional integration. Continuity will depend on:

• How ideational battles have been articulated and what regional ideal has emerged from them. How all-embracing the regional ideal might be, how it might appeal and be accepted at national level.
• Also the structure of the elite: how corporate-political-administrative circles are articulated, and how autonomous they are from specific demands.

The next sections examine these issues in the context of exchange rate co-operation in the EU and Mercosur.

One Single Currency in Europe

Creating the EMU

The creation of the European Economic and Monetary Union (EMU) is an unparalleled event in contemporary history. Certainly there have been previous examples of monetary unions, but never in the current conditions of advanced capitalist economies. No wonder, then, that most scholars have been fascinated by the political boldness shown by European leaders all through the complex exercise of setting up the EMU. Even if some commentators have pointed out that the relative success of the EMS (European Monetary System) was a 'de facto' union, the further steps of creating a single currency and of establishing an ensemble of new institutions to command it, are still rather stunning, especially when considering their effect upon national sovereignty. Hence, the EMU is an extraordinary event in the European integration process.

The idea of a single currency for Europe is an old aspiration of Europeanists since the inception of the European Communities in the 1950s, and was never fully abandoned throughout the more than forty years of European integration. Despite failed attempts, in the late 1960s, to launch an Economic and Monetary Union, the ideas of the Werner report survived several decades. The rather successful European Monetary System, which had a very stable exchange rate system for more than fifteen years, provided a good basis for moving ahead with the EMU project in the late 1980s. The Maastricht Treaty, ratified in 1993, created a three-phased process for achieving EMU, the last of which was accomplished in January 1999. The European Central Bank (ECB) works as the linchpin of this monetary integration, holding exclusive powers in monetary policy. The birth of the EMU means that we can no longer talk about European co-operation, but of a single European exchange rate policy designed and implemented by the ECB. However, the EMU has still a rather decentralised structure, since member states retain full powers over fiscal policy. In order to avoid distortions, national policies are guided by the principles of the 'stability and growth pact' and those of the economic guidelines.

A great deal of literature in the field of political science has addressed the question about what conditions and factors made the EMU possible. The rich and diverse scholarly interpretations are based on alternative, theoretical explanatory frameworks. Neo-neofunctionalists and transactionalists argue that the EMU is the political response to the growing interdependency of the European economies (indicated by rising levels of intra-EU trade). After three decades of political discussions, EMU has finally addressed this essentially economic imperative, responding to the tensions generated by the distinct, national exchange-rate policies in this heavily interdependent economic scenario. In other words, EMU is the necessary and unequivocally sole political move able to address the given economic reality (Cameron, 1998). Intergovernmentalists partly share this argument. While recognising the growing economic interdependency among EU members, they subsume however political decisions concerning EMU to the hegemonic position of Germany in the political and economic concerted scenario of the early 1990s (Moravcsik, 1998).

Last, social-constructivists and cognitive institutionalists have stated that these two reasonings tend to have deterministic undertones. For, independently of how integrated the economy really was, or of the hegemonic position of Germany, the main underlying element in the course of the events leading to EMU was the advancement of specific macro-economic policy ideas among political and economic elites. McNamara has stressed the rising neoliberal policy consensus across European countries in relation to a widespread belief that the previous Keynesian approach failed to generate stable growth (McNamara, 1999); Verdun has pointed out the pivotal role of the Delors Committee, through which experts worked as a powerful epistemic community in a transnational context (Verdun, 1999); and Macussen has referred to the cyclical evolution of ideas related to the EMU (Marcussen, 2000). Consequently, the ideational background of elites is the clue to understanding the complex move towards EMU in the late 1980s, and as Dyson and Featherstone have remarked, cognitive and strategic elements were both present in the long negotiations during and after the Maastricht Treaty (Dyson and Featherstone, 1999). Furthermore, Risse et al. link these policy-ideas with identity patterns of national political elites. National identities are specially well-endowed to explain variation among national preferences regarding the single currency, most notably among the three countries that decided not to join the EMU (Risse, et al., 1999). This chapter follows this latter strand of thinking, assuming the centrality of the cognitive dimension in the process of regional integration (both as a set of policy ideas, and as national identity constructions), while recognising that material interests (given by economic asymmetric interdependency) and strategic bargaining (present in the negotiation dynamics) also play an important role.

The Debates About EMU Sustainability

The national elites' debate about whether the EMU is a sustainable economic exercise and whether it has positive consequences, has been rather lively. On the one hand, supporters of the Euro have pointed to three possible economic benefits, namely, its ability to reduce transaction costs, increase price transparency, and growth generation through stability. The Euro, it is said, will unleash market forces within Euroland, working as the natural complement of the single market in the EU post-national order. Furthermore, the size of the new currency will invariably generate a new international monetary system, characterised by the bipolarity of the US dollar and the Euro.

Sceptical national elites and economists point to different factors that might challenge the EMU's existence and future functioning. One of the most recurrent arguments is that the EMU is ill-fitted to cope with asymmetric shocks which are bound to happen given the largely diverse economic structures in Europe. Thus, the 'one size fits all' monetary policy of the ECB would invariably put different pressures on the 11 members (Feldstein, 2000). A second argument is that the actual challenge for the EMU lies at a medium-term perspective, in the fiscal burden coming with population ageing. The fiscal problems caused by generous social security and pension systems will need to be solved by either raising taxes, reducing expenditures or printing money. All of them likely to generate intra-Euroland tensions with centrifugal effects upon EMU (Ferguson, 2000). This is a structural fiscal problem that will need a new policy mix for structural reform, mainly through tight fiscal and structural policy co-ordination (Dornbusch, 2000). A third argument about the challenges for the Euro has to do with its expected international role. Agnostic views about the likelihood and optimality of the Euro becoming a central currency in a bipolar monetary system, counterbalancing the US dollar, have been raised. The Euro ought instead to focus on generating prosperity within Euroland and cast aside its international ambitions (Bismut, 1999).

Counterarguments to the above sceptical views are as follows: disparities in the Eurozone, even if not inconsiderable, are not much greater than those already present in large economies like the US. This means that given the high level of economic integration, asymmetric shocks will not be disproportionate, at least not more than what is already the case in the US. Likewise, the fiscal structural problem related to ageing populations is very much the case for all 11, and the instruments for economic policy co-ordination are already well defined in the EMU (Trichet, 2001). Last, the international role of the Euro will evolve piecemeal, as only occasionally has the international monetary system suddenly been completely remodelled (Eichengreen, 2000). Despite this contrast between the sceptic's and optimist's views, the plans for the Euro have evolved on schedule, with an overwhelming back-up from most political and corporate elites in its 11 members. There is no doubt that at the elite level, the ideational battle was won by Euro-supporters.

What has happened in the first two years of the Euro's existence? Have the sceptics or orthodox forecasting been confirmed? How stable has the launch of the Euro proved to be? The launch of the Euro in 1999 has been an undeniable success.[1] The well functioning of the ECB, and the growth of the European economy in the period seem to validate that fact. Nevertheless, amid the élan of its materialisation, the EMU faced a completely unexpected loss of value against the US dollar. This is an interesting topic. Neither sceptics nor orthodox economists ever imagined such a situation. Quite the contrary, in the late 1990s concerns were of a rapidly overvalued Euro in the aftermath of its launch. The outstanding depreciation of the Euro has been the sole staggering feature of its birth, but a rather bewildering one. The next section examines the economic consequences and political reaction that this situation generated.

---

[1]   The launch of notes and coins at the beginning of 2002 can also be seen as a success, since it has taken place without apparent difficulties.

The First Two Years of the Euro

In its first one and a half years of life, the Euro lost 25% of its value against the US dollar. Economists have devoted a significant amount of effort in trying to identify the factors that might explain this. But still, it seems to be rather complex. The conventional wisdom that it simply reflected the differential in the US and European economic performance seems puzzling, since the latter was giving strong indications of a rapid recovery and relative improved performance (growth rates were increasing faster in the Eurozone than in the US, the same was true for industrial production rates, and unemployment was decreasing faster). If the European economic 'fundamentals' were in order, the decline of the Euro is explained by the considerable uncertainty about the true equilibrium value of the Euro-Dollar exchange rate (De Grauwe, 2000), and the uncertainties about the pace of two economies dealing simultaneously with the unknown effects of technical change and unprecedented monetary reform (Corsetti, 2000).

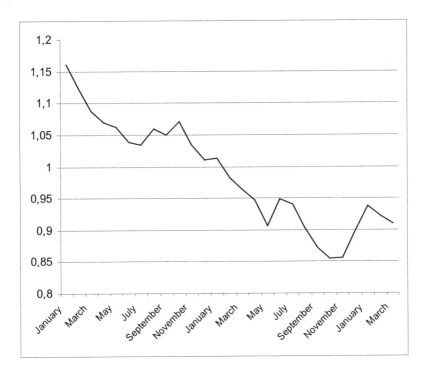

Figure 9.1 Euro-Dollar exchange rate, January 1999-March 2001

Source: ECB monthly data.

For some other authors, the explanation has to be found in a host of other factors: '(...) a high initial exchange rate, an unexpectedly strong US economy, a reviving yen, careless comments from policy-makers, and disappointment over the pace of European structural reform' (Cottrell, 2000, p. 78). The conjunction of these events triggered uncertainty in euro-investors, who disregarded the signs of recovery, and focused on the relative outperformance of the US economy from a static point of view. In June 2000, the Euro bounced, as signs of a deteriorating US economy became very visible with the burst of the technology stock market bubble.

Common to all these explanations is the understanding that the Euro's loss of value represents the cautious reaction of the international financial forces to the new currency, in a context of unstable global economic outlook. Several political and economic consequences can be pointed out. Firstly, it gave a bad public image of the EMU. The more the Euro was falling, the more it spread the notion among investors of a relatively wrecked European economy. For the general public, a falling Euro contrasted sharply with the fanfare at its onset. And it certainly did not help to get a Danish 'yes' in the national referendum in September 2000. Secondly, the weak Euro doomed to futility the prospects of a prompt emergence of a bipolar international monetary system. Thirdly, and most importantly, there was a general feeling of uncertainty among economic actors.

Regional Ideals and Uncertainty

Instability might not be the right word to describe the two first years of the single European currency. However, the unexpected situation of fast and insurmountable loss of value generated a high degree of uncertainty among economic operators and political elites as to the position of the Euro in the international financial markets, and the EU performance in international trade.

The interesting point is that one might have expected that this uncertainty could have unleashed distinct national political pressures for tackling the situation. All this emphasises the distinct traditions of national macro-economic policies and central banking that have developed in the 11 Euro states since the post-war period. In other words, the uncertainty of the first two years of Euro could have stressed the different state ideals as to macro-economic policy. For example, the Germans were not happy with a weak currency because their model of macro-economic management was based on a combination of stable currency and inflation control, while the Euro has been rather unstable as a currency. On the other hand, the French could equally have put pressure to make the ECB more politically accountable, and tackle more directly the loss of value as a question of prestige. The uncertain Euro smashed the French expectations of creating a bipolar international financial system of Euro and US dollar, and more clear-cut pressures from the French government to the ECB to intervene more strongly and being willing to redress the situation could have been expected on this basis.

However, nothing like this happened: Euroland members had kept their heads all through the turmoil, and no real cross country alternative visions were really put forward. How can we understand this situation? How can we understand the lack of political debate about how to tackle or whether to tackle the situation, and the apparent apathy of national elites in this regard? Our suggestion is that this sort of 'consensuated non-politicisation' is because the Euro represents a very strong regional ideal. A regional ideal that has existed all through the forty years of European Communities/Union, and that has slowly but invariably permeated into most of the different national elite's world view. In the 1990s, when the monetarist paradigm gained a firm foothold among central bankers and ministries of economic affairs, the regional ideal of a single currency becomes strongly coupled to the German model of the Deutsche Bank and the success of its macro-economic policy driven by stability and inflation-fighting strategies. This means that the cognitive-ideational strength of the Euro and the overall EMU project is such that the uncertainty generated by its deceiving performance vis-à-vis the US dollar in its first two years, is not perceived as politically problematic by the different national elites, but rather as a temporary situation.

Two further phenomena support this argument. One is that the adaptation of national institutions took place over a relatively long period of time, aligning them with the dominant monetarist paradigm in national macro-economic circles. So, institutional adaptation goes relatively smoothly and in a rather extended period of time, and in most cases this time has helped avoiding the political backlash of some elites. The second one is the long and stable story of the EMS experience, which has provided national elites with a clear historical anchor about the positive effects that macro-economic co-operation is able to bring. Also this successfully prevented a political backlash against further macro-economic integration.

Exchange Rate Re-alignment and Mercosur Integration

Mercosur's launch was intrinsically linked to the successful monetary stabilisation in the two dominant economies of Argentina and Brazil. The Treaty of Asuncion signed in March 1991, only came into force after Brazil had instigated its 'plan Real' in 1994. Even if Mercosur has no stated common monetary policy, macro-economic co-operation in terms of exchange rate stability has always lain at the heart of this model of regional integration.

In both countries, monetary stabilisation involved a peg mechanism vis-à-vis the US Dollar. In itself, this did not represent a break with past policy trajectories. Yet in the light of previous instability and the grotesque inflation rates characteristic of the eighties, the new 'hard-peg' monetary regimes installed were novel in their severity and the consequent restraints they posed on economic policy choices.

Southern Cone Currencies and Trade Policy

Since the turn of the last Century, currency pegs have been the monetary policy choice of Southern Cone countries subjected to the reign of 'liberal' export-oriented elite's. Hence Brazil maintained a fixed exchange rate until the 1929 Wall Street crash provoked a major political-economic re-configuration under Getúlio Vargas. Although Argentina was not as severely affected by world recession of the nineteen thirties as other Southern Cone Countries, it also suffered a retreat from previous policy principles. A move towards monetary realignment was made under the first wave of regional integration in the post war period (Dugini, 1997).

On 26 March 1991, the treaty of Asuncion establishing the Mercosur was signed in Paraguay by the heads of States and Governments of the four founding members: Argentina, Brazil, Paraguay and Uruguay. Coming into operation on 31 December, 1994, Mercosur comprises a vast array of legal provisions and joint policy making bodies designed to bring about economic – and political – integration of South America's largest and most advanced economies (Barraza and Jardel, 1998; Bizzozero, 1993; Campbell, Rozenberg et al., 1999).

With the debt crises looming, the question of monetary stability and convertibility was not seriously addressed by the governments of Argentina and Brazil before power had been handed over to civilian administrations. Austral (1985) and Cruzado (1986) were 'heterodox' schemes launched by the transitory administrations of respectively Alfonsín of Argentina (1984-89) and Sarney of Brazil (1986-90). The latter was modelled after the former and ultimately shared its fate!

Alfonsin's radical party government had opted for a heterodox set of measures to counter inflation. These included a price and wage freeze accompanied by the introduction of a new currency: the Austral. After some initial success, the situation deteriorated rapidly as inflation by 1987 once again was running into four digit figures. Argentine monetary stability was sought and achieved in a highly volatile macro-economic environment. De-regulation of the banking industry, initiated during military rule and further enhanced by the Alfonsin administration, left the economy exposed to the global financial markets. This proved incompatible with heterodox stabilisation programmes neglecting deep-rooted problems in the fiscal realm. Government budgets thus witnessed no real improvements before the Menem administration under the direction of economy minister Cavallo's first term introduced an orthodox convertibility plan in – March/April – 1991, including austerity measures and privatisation aiming to balance public sector budgets. A new currency, pegged to the dollar on a one-to-one basis by law, was introduced fully backed by central bank dollar reserves.

This plan proved successful in blessing Argentina with monetary stability until Christmas 2001. In the period between the plans introduction in 1991 and the Mexican Peso-crises, Argentina also enjoyed enviable growth rates. The Mexican crash severely challenged the system which was amended in a number of ways. Changes related to the role of the central bank vis-à-vis the domestic financial system and the composition, on various types of financial instruments, of commercial bank reserve requirements. Yet convertibility and the peso value was maintained both domestically and internationally.

Brazil's Crusado plan was undermined by a similar lack of commitment to addressing the havoc in the fiscal realm as suffered by the Austral plan. Unlike Argentina, Brazil's financial system was largely sheltered from global markets and the government exercised rigorous capital control. The Brazilian growth regime relied less on the influx of foreign capital than Argentina did. Nonetheless, the country managed to accumulate the largest foreign debt in the third world

(Falaiche, 1992).

Although the Cruzado plan quickly proved incapable of keeping inflation in check, it was not replaced by effective stabilisation measures until June 1994. Failed attempts in 1987 and 1988/89 to rejuvenate the heterodox scheme did not prevent high inflationary pressures. By autumn 1991 the rate of inflation had steadily climbed to around 40 per cent. This eventually prompted the minister of finance, Fernando Henrique Cardoso, to launch his plan Real in July 1994. Its success carried him all the way to the top-job, which he still holds.

Under the Real regime Brazil has maintained capital control and a sheltered banking industry. The currency is pegged to the dollar within a self-imposed band. Austerity measures, including improved tax collection and privatisation, have made public finances historically sound.

At the Mercosur level, the adoption of the Real plan fuelled the expectation that 'spontaneous' convergence would pre-empt the need for excessive joint institutionalisation of the integration process (Arnaudo and Alejandro, 1997). This explains why progress in the realm of financial integration has been so modest. Beside loose frameworks of macro-economic co-ordination and informal consultation, financial market initiatives have so far been limited to the adoption of a common framework for investments in the stock market, the agreement on eventually applying the Basle rules for financial institutions, and a joint investment protection agreement (Gabriel Porcile, 1995) (de Paira Abreu, 1997).

Yet the depth of the current crises, sadly demonstrated by the Argentine default of January 2002, counter-veils the perception of the Southern Cone that national developments are in tune to an extent that renders thorough joint regulation unnecessary.

The Asymmetries of the Brazilian and the Argentine Crises

Argentina's convertibility plan involved the setting-up of a currency board monitoring that peso circulation was backed by dollar reserves. In effect, the dollar was accepted as tender in nearly all commercial transactions in Argentina, and Argentine residents and companies could have dollar accounts until the melt-down in December 2001.

This hard peg approach quickly reduced inflation and commercial interest rates in Argentina were close to OECD levels throughout most of the life-span of the convertibility plan. This occasionally produced credit and liquidity squeezes in the Argentine economy, particularly in the provinces. But the orthodoxy of the plans ensured a rapid reduction of inflation and interest rates.

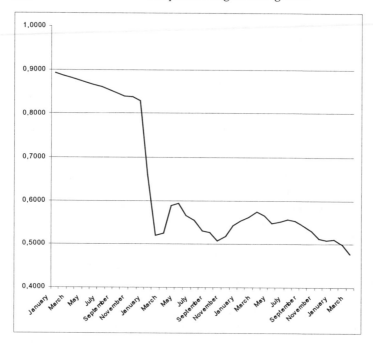

**Figure 9.2 Dollar-Real exchange rates. Monthly averages, January 1998-
          March 2001**

Source: Federal Reserve Statistical Release.

By contrast, Brazil's Real Plan combined orthodox and heterodox measures leaving a much wider span of discretion and autonomy for monetary policy makers. This was achieved, however, at the expense of a much higher interest rate. More importantly, the rate of inflation was reduced over a long time period and has consistently been higher than in Argentina and the United States of America.

This caused Brazilian goods to become more expensive on export markets as inflation was not adjusted via currency rate alignment. Thus, Brazil accumulated a trade deficit which was inconsistent with its enormous debt burden. In spite of heavy central bank lending with a view to amassing sufficient reserves to withstand runs on the Real, Brazil had to succumb and loosen the ties between the overvalued Real and the Dollar. This produced in the first months of 1999 a 40 per cent devaluation largely as a one-off effect.

As a result of Mercosur integration, Argentina has grown increasingly dependent on the Brazilian market. As Argentina had opted for a hard-peg, devaluing the Peso was inconsistent with the established monetary regime. Moreover, the economic fundamentals did not dictate such a step since inflation had been kept in check and interest rates were competitive.

The Brazilian devaluation left the Argentine elite shocked and locked up with no immediate possibilities of adjusting to the radical deterioration of its competitive position on the Brazilian market. The country had barely recovered from the Mexican and later the Asian crises and the Russian default as it slipped into a prolonged recession with soaring unemployment and depressed property markets.

Argentina is, in many ways, a fairly prosperous country and as such able to sustain slumps in demands for it exports over fairly long periods. The factor which made the Argentine crises so dramatic is the manner in which it has financed its sizeable foreign debt.

Unlike most non-OECD countries, Argentina issues foreign currency bonds on the international markets and expresses no preferences as to whether they are bought by international or national investors. This is done to avoid crowding out local markets and to reap the benefits of the efficiency of international capital markets. Still, it has been estimated that half of the bonds issued in 2000 were purchased by domestic investors (Financial Times, 19 March 2001). Argentine debts accounted for between 1/4 and 1/5 of all tradable emerging markets' debts (Financial Times, 19 November 2000).

So market reactions to changing fortunes were prompted by the transparency of the financing scheme. In good times this secures Argentina, which has an annually financing requirement of 26.6 billion USD, cheaper finance than Brazil which has an annually financing requirement of 159.4 billion USD (Figures for 2000, source Financial Times, 19 March 2001).

In view of the international financial community, the Brazilian crisis compounded the ill effects Argentina had suffered from the Mexican, Asian and Russian crises. Still, in July 2000 prospects seemed relatively bright for getting Argentina out of the prolonged recession as tax collection contributed to a significant improvement of public finances. Yet a sentiment of crisis was accelerated by political instability in Argentina. Hence the resignation of vice-president Carlos Alvarez nearly brought down the Radical Party and the left-wing Frepaso coalition which were behind President Rúa. As a result, interest rates on bonds rose leading to the near default in December 2000 as the country was about to reschedule debts worth 19.5 billion USD.

A rescue package and a change in government with important policy implications have been the immediate effects of the December 2000 crisis. The IMF with USA assistance rallied support among creditors for a package containing the rescheduling of 40 billion USDs' worth of debt. In early 2001, following the bail-out, a number of swift tenures paved the way for a return of Domingo Cavallo as Minister of Economic Affairs.

Cavallo's return was preceded by the brief but controversial spell of Ricardo López Murphy's term as Minister of Economic Affairs. The latter's austerity programme prompted the resignation of six cabinet ministers and fierce opposition from students, teachers and unions. Murphy's plan called for spending cuts of 2 billion USD. Cavallo initially planned to increase that from 2 to 3 billion USD stating that additional cuts were to affect bureaucracy only.

Soon Cavallo redirected the main thrust of his rescue efforts as he introduced tariff cuts for capital goods and tariff increases for consumer goods. This was directly at odds with Mercosur policy which, on Brazilian insistence, included fairly high tariffs for capital goods in order to protect the Brazilian engineering industry.

Brazil was consulted by Cavallo on the matter and, surprisingly, accepted this deviation on what had hitherto been declared a strategic element of the Mercosur venture – that is ensuring trade liberalisation and exposure to globalisation in a manner not jeopardising the development of a diverse Brazilian industrial base.

Yet Mercosur was without doubt thrown into a crisis which effectively retrenched previous integration advances. Argentine-Brazilian trade thus declined as Argentine exports were no longer competitive in the only market where their price/quality ratio appeared equitable. As the Argentine furthermore deepened, Brazilian exports also dwindled.

More seriously, in Domingo Cavallo, the Mercosur arrangement had one of its most outspoken opponents. Cavallo argued that Argentine exports suffered from poor competitiveness as the Mercosur imposed high tariffs on extra-Mercosur capital goods imports. In addition, Brazil constituted a too sheltered market place for Argentine exports to experience the competitive pressure of the wider world market.

Although Cavallo was fairly isolated on these accounts in the Radical administration, his role as 'saviour' and 'miracle man' made his voicing of such views send shivers down the spines of Argentine and Brazilian policy makers and business leaders.

Following the resignation of the Radical administration, the Duhalde government has explicitly denounced any talk of defecting Mercosur (Financial Times, January 9, 2002). On the contrary, Mercosur integration has been declared a corner stone in the post-meltdown Argentine strategy (Financial Times, January 21, 2002).

State Ideals, Regional Ideals and the Viability of Mercosur Integration

Currency pegs in the Southern Cone have historically been associated with liberal export-oriented political-economic regimes. These regimes were challenged domestically in the wake of the 1929 crash in both Argentina and Brazil. Proponents rallied around what was to be termed the 'developmental state ideal'. The developmental state ideal had both democratic and authoritarian elements. Most notably the authoritarian elements are associated with people such as Juan Peron of Argentina and Getúlio Vargas of Brazil.

In Argentina the developmental state ideal only gained prominence for a limited period and faced stiff opposition from proponents of more liberal ideals. In Brazil the developmental ideal has been absorbed in the overall state ideal.

Argentina's currency policy and the accompanying measures accordingly reflect this more thorough adherence to liberal ideals in all its gung-ho orthodoxy. Likewise the more moderate Brazilian regime combines orthodox and heterodox measures leaving more room for policy discretion and ultimately contributing to the devaluation of the Real.

In short, underneath the surface of the remarkable level of policy co-ordination in the realm of currency stabilisation fuelling the creation of Mercosur, partly divergent state ideals were rooted.

Yet the Mercosur project draws on preconceived ideas nurtured simultaneously among Argentine and Brazilian elites. Furthermore, the process has in itself further strengthened a shared understanding among elites on the desirability, aim and overall direction of the Mercosur venture. As such we may speak of a regional ideal which reinforces integrative efforts, even when particular events would seem to make it advantageous for member states to defect at least in part.

The regional ideal linking partly divergent state ideals across Argentine and Brazilian elites has three dimensions. One is economic. In spite of developmental tendencies among Brazilian policy, administrative and corporate elites, there is a strong belief in monetary stability, sound public finances and free product markets.

The other dimension is of a political nature. Mercosur aims to consolidate the principle of democratic government. A case can certainly be made for the importance of civilian rule as countries join forces to the extent witnessed in Mercosur. Hence the formation of Mercosur was a state-led process. It was national executives rather then legislators, government rather than business and national elites rather than the populace who provided the initial impetus for the integration process. Consequently, Mercosur serves to underpin a liberal state ideal at the expense of an authoritarian-bureaucratic developmental state.

Finally, Mercosur also provides a globalisation safeguard. Rather then seeking immediate integration with world markets the regional initiative is designed to shelter the Southern Cone states from the onslaught of liberalisation – ideally enabling them to follow re-structuring at their own pace, and devising a societal model in tune with their cultural, institutional and political preferences.

These shared ideals constitute an important element in explaining the willingness of Argentina to remain within the Mercosur framework in spite of the high costs imposed upon her by Brazil's devaluation. Likewise Brazil's willingness to accept Argentina's unilateral abolition of the capital goods duty which is a strategic element of the Mercosur construct viewed from Brasilia, must be seen in light of the overall importance attached to the integrative venture at the ideational level. Further evidence of that is found in Brazil's tolerance of nationalist and populist rhetorics following the political crisis in wake of the default.

Concluding Remarks: Bringing in the Cognitive Dimension

The continuity of regional arrangements in times of instability is a phenomenon that deserves careful analysis. Our study is a preliminary attempt to address such an issue, and in some cases it raises more questions than it is in a position to answer. Nothing daunted, though, the two cases have provided a concrete starting point for such a line of analysis. The most significant conclusion arrived at is that we need to bring in the cognitive-ideational dimension. This perspective has already been extensively used when addressing the historical process for the set up of new regional arrangements, but has not been very much used for understanding the persistence of these institutions. Regional institutions resiliency might be related to the relatively high costs of defection, as liberal institutionalists suggest. Yet states might be willing to pay these costs if there is a generalised conviction among national elites that the initial institution no longer serves national interests. Worse, rather than paying the costs, regional arrangements might instead wither away by states' inaction or apathy in a unilateral or collective way.

Continuity is not a futile matter in regional integration, especially in times of instability. Here the conditions for reciprocity and issue linkage might have changed in a way that co-operation seems difficult. This was what happened in the EMU and exchange-rates' crisis of Mercosur. As we have discussed in detail in this chapter, the considerable loss of value of the Euro in its first two years does not constitute a truly institutional instability of the overall EMU project, but it has certainly introduced an important element of uncertainty that should not be disregarded. The 'heavily institutionalised' EMU has never been under inter-state attack, and the degree of reciprocity and commitment is extremely high. In any case, EMU has closely followed the German model, where there is a strong detachment between monetary policy and other macro- and micro-economic policies. Hence, continuity cannot be strictly related to the 'issue-linkage' of other policy areas. What is surprising in the Euro case is that the uncertainty generated by its depreciation vis-à-vis the US Dollar has not triggered political tensions between the different state ideals about monetary policy, most particularly between Germany and France. This lack of political discussion might, perhaps, be explained as the policy rationale of EMU has now permeated so deeply in the political-economic elites that previous state ideals have been significantly transformed. This might be particularly true of those states with the strongest 'Keynesian' tradition. Hence, cognitive battles and cognitive transformation have effectively de-politicised the weak Euro.

The crisis of the exchange rates in Brazil and Argentina is another more dramatic story. The situation was rather asymmetric, Argentina suffering an important loss of economic growth and industrial output and, it would seem, full scale economic collapse. This relates to a partial but important lack of reciprocity, especially considering that Brazil has repeatedly devaluated thereby smashing any attempt of the Argentinean government to redress the deteriorating situation while still pegged to the US Dollar. Even if the overall Mercosur initiative was strongly linked to exchange rate stability projects in both economies, it did not prevent reciprocity from being put under pressure. There are two striking things. One is that Argentina did not devalue until a full scale default was a reality. And the other one is that Mercosur has survived the turmoil, as it is still a relevant point of reference for the four member states, and keeps on constituting so far the most successful case of regional integration in Latin America. This, we argue, has to do with the way in which the cognitive parameters of both countries' elites have been put together. Even if state ideals continue to show differences, which are constrained and defined historically, the regional ideals emerging in both the EU and Mercosur are strongly embedded in national elites' consciousness and world views. And this is what explains the elasticity of regional agreements, even when reciprocity and issue-linkage are not perfect nor neatly defined.

References

Arnaudo, A.A.J., Alejandro, D. (1997), 'Macroeconomic Homogeneity within MERCOSUR: An Overview', *Estudios Economicos,* Vol. 12(1), pp. 37-51.

Barraza, A. and Jardel, S.L. (1998), *Mercosur: aspectos jurídicos y económicos,* Ediciones Ciudad Argentina, Buenos Aires.

Bismut, C.J.P. (1999), 'The Euro and the Dollar. An Agnostic View', *Tokyo Club Papers,* Vol. 19, pp. 75-97.

Bizzozero, L. (1993), *Los inicios del Mercosur y el ingreso de Uruguay,* Facultad de Ciencias Sociales, Unidad Multidisciplinaria, Montevideo.

Borrás, S. (1999), 'The Cognitive Turn(s) in EU Studies', RUC.

Bulmer, S. (1994), 'The Governance of the European Union: A New Institutionalist Approach', *Journal of Public Policy,* Vol. 13(4), pp. 351-380.

Cameron (1998) 'Creating Supranational Authority in Monetary and Exchange-Rate Policy: The Sources and Effects of EMU, in W. Sandholtz and A. Sweet Stone (eds.), *European Integration and Supranational Governance,* Oxford University Press, Oxford, pp. 188-216.

Campbell, J., Rozemberg, R. et al. (1999), *Mercosur: entre la realidad y la utopia,* Grupo Editor Latinoamericano: Centro de Economia Internacional, Buenos Aires, Argentina.

Christensen, T., Jørgensen, K. E. and Wiener, A. (eds.) (2001), *The Social Construction of Europe,* SAGE London.

Corsetti, G. (2000), 'A perspective on the euro', *CESifo Forum, Summer 2000,* pp. 3-7.

Cottrell, A. (2000), 'Softer Euro, Stronger Europe', *Journal of Common Market Studies,* Vol. 38(3), pp. 77-80.

De Grauwe, P. (2000), 'The Euro-Dollar Exchange Rate: In Search of fundamentals', University of Leuven and CEPR, June (preliminary draft).

de Paiva Abreu, M. (1997), 'Financial Integration in MERCOSUR Countries,' *Integration and Trade,* Vol. 1(1), pp. 79-94.

Dornbusch, R.J.P. (2000), 'Making EMU a success', *International Affairs,* Vol. 76(1), pp. 89-110.

Dugini de, I. (1997), *Argentina, Chile, Mercosur: cambios y continuidades,* Ediciones Ciudad Argentina, Buenos Aires.

Dyson, K. and Featherstone, K. (1999), *The Road to Maastricht. Negotiating Economic and Monetary Union,* Oxford University Press, Oxford.

Eichengreen, B. (2000). 'The Euro One Year On', *Journal of Policy Modeling,* Vol. 22(3), pp. 355-368.

Feldstein, M. (2000). 'The European Central Bank and the Euro: The first year', *Journal of Policy Modeling,* Vol. 22(3), pp. 345-354.

Ferguson, N.K., L.J. (2000), 'The Degeneration of the EMU', *Foreign Affairs,* vol. 79, no. 2, pp. 110-21.

Haas, Peter M. (1992), 'Introduction: epistemic communities and international policy coordination', *International Organization,* Vol. 46, no. 1, pp. 1-35.

Higgott, R. (1998), 'The international Political Economy of Regionalism', in W.D. Coleman and G.R.D. Underhill (eds.), *Regionalism and Global Economic Integration,* Routledge, London, pp. 42-67.

Mansfield, E.D. and Milner, H.V. (1997), 'The Political Economy of Regionalism: An Overview', in E.D. Mansfield and H.V. Milner (eds.), *The Political Economy of Regionalism*, Columbia University Press, New York, pp. 1-19.

March, J. G. and Olsen, J. P. (1989), *Rediscovering institutions: the organizational basis of politics*, Free Press, New York.

March, J.G. and Olsen, J.P. (1998), 'The Institutional Dynamics of International Political Orders', *International Organisation,* Vol. 52(4), pp. 943-969.

Marcussen, M. (2000), *Ideas and Elites: The social construction of Economic and Monetary Union*. Ålborg University Press, Ålborg.

McNamara, K.R. (1999), 'Consensus and constraint: Ideas and Capital Mobility in European Monetary Integration', *Journal of Common Market Studies,* Vol. 37(3), pp. 455-476.

Moravcsik, A. (1995), 'Liberal Intergovernmentalism and Integration: A Rejoinder', *Journal of Common Market Studies,* Vol. 33(4), 611-628.

Moravcsik, A. (1998), *The Choice for Europe*, UCL, London.

Pierson, P. (1998), 'The Path to European Integration: A Historical-Institutionalist Analysis', in A. Stone Sweet and W. Sandholtz (eds.), *European Integration and Supranational Governance,* Oxford University Press, Oxford, pp. 27-58.

Risse, T., Engelmann-Martin, D., Knopf, H.-J. and Roscher, K. (1999), 'To Euro or not to Euro? The EMU and identity politics in the European Union', *European Journal of International Relations,* Vol. 5(2), pp. 147-187.

Torfing, J (2001), 'Path dependent Danish Welfare Reforms: The Contribution of the New Institutionalisms to Understanding Evolutionary Change', *Scandinavian Political Studies,* Vol. 24(4), pp. 277-310.

Trichet, J. C. (2001), 'The Euro after Two Years', *Journal of Common Market Studies,* Vol. 39(1), pp. 1-13.

Verdun, A. (1999) 'The role of the Delors Committee in the Creation of EMU: An Epistemic Community', *European Journal of Public Policy,* Vol. 6(2), pp. 308-328.

PART V
Neofunctionalist and Historical Institutionalist Perspectives

Chapter 10

The ECOWAS: From Regional Economic Organization to Regional Peacekeeper

Peter M. Dennis and M. Leann Brown

Since its inception in 1975, the Economic Community of West African States (ECOWAS) has struggled along as a fairly unsuccessful regional economic organization. Its original goal, creating a regional trading bloc to compete with more developed economies, was all but abandoned, and the very future of the organization was often in question. Then in 1990, the organization took on the extremely difficult task of peacekeeping in the Liberian civil war. What prompted an already weak organization take on this challenge? Scholars have offered several potential explanations for this very complex empirical puzzle. Some contend that persuasion and encouragement from multilateral organizations and powerful states convinced ECOWAS leaders that the regional organization possessed advantages in the situation that would make it the most effective guarantor of regional stability. Others believe that Nigeria seized upon the Liberian crisis as an opportunity to further solidify itself as the regional hegemon, to enhance its status in international and regional affairs. A third possible explanation is suggested by the work of Ernst Haas and others,[1] which articulates a neofunctionalist (proto)theory focusing on various process mechanisms including spontaneous and/or cultivated spillover to explain the expanding activities of regional organizations. While most neofunctionalist analyses have focused on processes in the European Union, these hypotheses may bring insights to ECOWAS behavior in this case.

The data from this qualitative case study suggest that the international discourse in the post-Cold War era about the possible advantages of employing regional organizations as an extension of United Nations peacekeeping may well have served to legitimize the role assumed by the West African organization, and to salve the conscience of the international community which refused to assume responsibility in the face of the mounting disorder in Liberia. Further, Nigeria

---

[1] See e.g. Haas, 1958, 1961, 1964, 1968, and 1971; Lindberg, 1963 and 1965, Haas and Schmitter, 1964; and Nye, 1971.

certainly had aspirations to maintain and augment its power and leadership in the region, and to enhance its reputation internationally and regionally. Nigeria's interests in regional order and economic cooperation coincided with ECOWAS' goals, and its interests, leadership and resources were a necessary but not sufficient explanation for ECOWAS behavior in the sub-region during the decade of the 1990s. Focusing on the ECOWAS itself as the primary unit of analysis leads us to conclude that the ECOWAS' embracing peacekeeping functions was a consequence of spontaneous spillover in the long-term. The next segment provides context by providing a cursory history of the ECOWAS and the ECOWAS Cease-Fire Monitoring Group (ECOMOG).

The History of ECOWAS and ECOMOG

On May 28, 1975, representatives of fifteen West African states met in Lagos to create what would come to be known as the Economic Community of West African States.[2] ECOWAS' founding members recognized the need to coordinate and accelerate economic development and agreed to pursue policies of regional self-reliance.

The ECOWAS' stated objectives were comprehensive and far-reaching, including: (a) cooperate to enhance and liberalize trade; (b) free movement of goods, persons and capital; (c) improve transportation; (d) coordinate telecommunications; (e) promote industrial and agricultural growth; (f) raise citizens' standard of living; and, (g) increase and maintain economic stability (Kacowicz, 1997, p. 378).

The economic rationale for creating ECOWAS was persuasive. Multiple obstacles deterred free movement of people, goods and capital. An example: West Africans were often forced to make connecting flights in Western Europe to travel to neighboring countries. A more serious problem, national policies deterred the migration of skilled workers, distorting labor markets and impeding economic development. Would-be investors were discouraged from buying stocks and securities; sometimes countries refused to divulge the prices and status of stocks to foreign persons and companies. West African countries dumped goods on markets at prices designed to destroy neighbors' production of the same commodity (Lay, 1982, p. 11).

From the outset, ECOWAS was little more than a loose confederation plagued with problems. These "growing pains' derive from a cluster of historical, social, political, and economic factors. Most ECOWAS members are former British and French colonies. The Francophone states are Benin, Burkina Faso, *Cote d'Ivoire*, Guinea, Mali, Mauritania, Niger, Senegal, and Togo, and the Anglophone states include The Gambia, Ghana, Liberia, Nigeria, and Sierra Leone. (The remaining two members, Cape Verde and Guinea-Bissau, are Lusophone.) The political obstacles to ECOWAS achieving its goals are formidable, including frequent

---

[2]   See Ojo (1980), pp. 571-604, for a discussion of Nigeria's role in the founding of the ECOWAS.

political upheaval and changes in Member State leadership and a lack of democratic governance. Economic obstacles include the diversity of currencies and complex exchange controls, low levels of intra-regional trade and communications, the competitiveness rather than complementarity of the national economies, and disparities among its members in terms of size, population, and level of economic development. Many regarded the ECOWAS a failure, because most members put national interests above those of the region (Howe, 1996, p. 150). Despite the fact that ECOWAS' economic integration goals remain unfulfilled, the organization's existence reduced regional conflict. While the countries in West Africa have experienced significant domestic instability, they have been able to maintain relative interstate stability, aside from minor frontier disputes (Kacowicz, 1997, pp. 378-389).

The Liberian Civil War began on December 24, 1989, when Charles Taylor and a group of 'dissidents' who came to be known as the National Patriotic Front of Liberia (NPFL), launched a small-scale attack on security personnel on the Liberian-*Cote d'Ivoire* border. Joined by politically disillusioned members of the Mano and Gio ethnic groups, the NPFL quickly grew in numbers and advanced toward Monrovia, Liberia's capital, with the goal of overthrowing the autocratic regime of President Samuel K. Doe. By May 1990, the NPFL controlled more than 90 per cent of the country.[3]

That month, the ECOWAS convened a summit in Banjul at the suggestion of Nigeria's President Ibrahim Babanghida to consider the escalating violence in Liberia. At this meeting the alliance created a Standing Mediation Committee (SMC) to foster a peaceful settlement of the conflict that would lead to general elections. It is important to note that the most powerful Anglophone states (The Gambia, Ghana, and Nigeria) constituted the SMC, whereas participating Francophone members, Mali and Togo, were not among the most powerful, i.e. Burkina Faso, *Côte d'Ivoire*, and Senegal.

For three weeks in July, the SMC and representatives from all warring Liberian factions tried in vain to reach a peace settlement. By August, with no peace in sight, the SMC decided to create the ECOWAS Cease-Fire Monitoring Group (ECOMOG). The Committee continued to hope for a political solution to the conflict, and called for creation of a broadly-based, interim government to rule Liberia until internationally-supervised elections could be held (Howe, 1996, p. 151). Several ECOWAS states expressed concern about the safety of their nationals and Liberian civilians trapped in Monrovia seemingly facing a bloodbath (Vogt, 1996, p. 166). This seemed particularly true of Nigeria, which decided to go ahead with the deployment of ECOMOG without securing full regional political support. Initially, troop contributions came only from Anglophone states; Francophone members of the SMC, Mali and Togo, declined to send troops. *Cote*

---

[3] At one point, Taylor was Director-General of the General Services Agency under the Doe regime. He was charged with embezzlement, fled to the United States, and was arrested in Massachusetts. He escaped from jail while awaiting extradition to Liberia (Levitt, 1999, p. 9).

d'Ivoire and Senegal expressed reservations about the ECOMOG operation, and the President of Burkina Faso, Blaise Compaoré, openly condemned it (Mortimer, 1996, p. 152).

ECOMOG was perceived by its critics as a move by ECOWAS to prevent the toppling of Liberian leader Samuel Doe, who had murdered former president William Tolbert, *Cote d'Ivoire* President Felix Houphouet-Boigny's son-in-law. Blaise Campaore was now married to Houphouet-Boigny's daughter (the wife of the late William Tolbert) and therefore was son-in-law to Houphouet-Boigny (Adibe, 1994, p. 198). A West African journalist describes this somewhat confusing situation in this way:

> Everyone is aware that Blaise Campaore of Burkina Faso is son-in-law to ... (Houphouet-Boigny of Cote d'Ivoire). The Ivorian President sponsored the NPFL [Charles Taylor's National Patriotic Front of Liberia] in its war against late Samuel Doe. Doe killed William Tolbert, former Liberian President and in-law of Boigny. Boigny rarely forgives or forgets a slight. He was enraged that Doe killed Tolbert despite his pleas.[4]

Burkina Faso and *Cote d'Ivoire* served as training grounds and launching areas for Charles Taylor, and well into the ECOMOG operation, continued to support Taylor. This explains why Burkina Faso and *Cote d'Ivoire* opposed ECOWAS intervention in the Liberian conflict.

As was noted, three explanations have been advanced as to why the ECOWAS embraced regional peacekeeping. Few dispute that outside intervention in the Liberian civil war at some point became a necessity, but even before that time the international community had discussed the means whereby intrastate conflicts which had proliferated in the wake of the Cold-War might be addressed. Many, including then-United Nations (UN) Secretary General Boutros Boutros-Ghali, thought that regional peacekeeping efforts might prove more effective than those of the larger organization, and, following this logic, some believed that the ECOWAS was the logical choice to undertake conflict management in Liberia. A second explanation for the ECOWAS taking on Liberian peacekeeping is that the ECOWAS serves as an instrument of Nigeria's hegemonic aspirations in West Africa. ECOWAS' undertaking peacekeeping efforts in Liberia under Nigerian instigation and financial backing would reinforce that country's leadership at home

---

[4]   The source is an unnamed diplomat (Offor, 1992). It might be reiterated that ECOWAS heads of state have unique histories and relationships. During the 1967-70 Nigerian Civil War, President Houphouet-Boigny of *Cote d'Ivoire* committed some of his personal fortune to support the secessionists. A former president of Nigeria expressed Nigerian resentment for this act and toward some Francophone countries when he pointed out that "This was a bid to reduce Nigeria to the status of just another country.' (Inegbedion, 1994, p. 221). Nigerian leaders supported the creation of ECOWAS in part because some of its neighbors' role in the Civil War demonstrated the ineffectiveness of previous Nigerian regional diplomatic efforts. They came to view economic integration as a means of increasing control over regional political affairs (Brown, 1994, p. 79).

and abroad, limit outside powers' (such as France and Libya) influence in the region, and help deflect attention from Nigeria's chronic internal governing problems. A third possible explanation derives from neo-functionalist analysis which posits that process mechanisms, such as spontaneous and/or cultivated spillover, may result in a regional economic organization taking on additional tasks for self-preservation and enhancement. The following sections will explore these three hypotheses with special consideration as to their strengths and shortcomings in relation to ECOWAS peacekeeping.

Did the ECOWAS Take on Peacekeeping Because it Possessed Advantages Relative to Global Intergovernmental Organizations?[5]

Several often-cited, interrelated theoretical advantages of regional peacekeeping over that of larger multilateral organizations include: a) regional actors are more effective peacekeepers because of their in-depth understanding of the conflict; b) a shared history, cultural heritage and regional identity convey to regional peacekeepers greater acceptance and legitimacy in the eyes of combatants and civilians in the country of conflict; c) regional peacekeepers have strong incentives to foster long-term stability because of geographical proximity and economic interdependence; d) a greater consensus for action may be obtained among members of regional organizations than in organizations like the United Nations (UN) with its large and diverse membership; and, e) regional peacekeepers possess more suitable equipment and personnel for battlefield conditions.

Referring specifically to the ECOWAS intervention, Herbert Howe writes:

> Such a force could enjoy greater political acceptance among combatants, display more knowledge about the contested country's political issues and physical geography, and maintain a greater commitment to ending a nearby struggle whose suffering could affect neighboring states. Additionally it could employ more suitable military capabilities (Howe, 1996, p. 160).

Two important empirical questions suggested by these theoretical assertions are whether the ECOWAS indeed enjoyed practical and logistical advantages in

---

[5] The recent record of regional peacekeeping operations may incline one to wonder why they are hailed as a viable solution in the developing world. For example, in 1965, the Organization of American States launched peacekeeping operations in the Dominican Republic. While it restored peace, in the aftermath many states in the hemisphere questioned the United States' dominant role and the neutrality of the operation. The League of Arab States authorized a peacekeeping force in Lebanon in 1976, whose neutrality was called into questioned under allegations that it used excessive force in some situations. The Organization for African Unity undertook what is widely considered a failed peacekeeping attempt in Chad in 1981. In this instance, the peacekeepers were unable to stop the fighting and they themselves became the target of military offensives.

Liberian peacekeeping, and secondly, whether these arguments and/or potential advantages were the basis for the ECOWAS decision.

Conditions of interstate conflict requiring traditional peacekeeping are very complex, however, in the post-Cold War context, many situations requiring peace-keepers are intrastate in nature and frequently ethnicity-influenced. The larger international community may have difficulty identifying and understanding the motives of the combatants. Some analysts suggest that because of its proximity to the conflict and longer history with the conflict and actors involved, a regional organization may have superior understanding of those actors and issues, and, therefore, undertake the operation in a more effective and timely manner.

However, in actual practice, regional peacekeepers' proximity and in-depth understanding of the conflict may actually represent a disadvantage. Neutrality is generally assumed to be a prerequisite for effective peacekeeping, and regional organizations' associations and intimate knowledge of the conflict may preclude their actual and/or perceived neutrality in the conflict. Spear and Keller assert: 'Existing regional organizations tend to be perceived as partial to one side or another in many regional conflicts' (Spear and Keller, 1996, p. 120). From the beginning, one of the major problems of ECOMOG was that it was regarded by some, including some ECOWAS Member States, as a means whereby Nigerian President Ibrahim Babanghida could rescue his Liberian counterpart and friend Samuel Doe and enhance Nigeria's regional influence. Certainly ECOWAS possessed superior understanding of the situation relative to the UN or Organization of African Unity, but some argue that its associations corrupted the neutrality of the operation. Had the Nigerian-led ECOMOG troops remained bastions of neutrality, there remained perceptions of connections between Babanghida and Doe. Neutral peacekeepers are essential to guarantee combatants' willingness to cooperate (Diehl, 1993, p. 124).

The second argument supporting regional peacekeepers also relates to effectiveness and legitimacy issues. Some posit that combatants and the public may find it easier to accept external intervention if peacekeepers hail from the regional. Paul Diehl (1993, p. 125) writes: 'People in governments and regions have a natural affinity with those in that geographic area and an inherent suspicion of what they perceive as outside intervention.' It is paramount that all involved parties trust and accept the peacekeepers, otherwise they can easily become another participant among warring factions. However, greater legitimacy deriving from a shared history and culture among regional actors is not applicable in this case of mixed colonial heritages. As has been noted, ECOWAS members possess diverse histories and cultures owing to their colonial pasts, precluding its peacekeepers' deriving legitimacy and solidarity from common history and culture.

A third rationale for regional actors to undertake the role of peacekeeper is their strong economic and political interests in establishing and maintaining regional stability and peace (Howe, 1996, p. 151; Adeleke, 1995, pp. 569-593; Diehl, 1993, p. 124). In many cases, states contributing to peacekeeping are physically and economically connected with the country in conflict. War threatens their nationals, the spillover of refugees, political destabilization and conflict, and further disruption of their economies. For these reasons, it is in the interests of regional states to intervene and find lasting solutions to the conflict. Regional peacekeeping forces cannot just go into a warring country, remain a discrete period of time, and return to their home, never to be confronted with the issue again. Regional peacekeepers have powerful incentives to ensure that the solution they broker promotes long-term stability. These incentives may facilitate the regional organization's ability to achieve a consensus to act, compared to larger multilateral organizations such as the UN and Organization of African States, with their larger and more diverse memberships.

Regional actors' incentives for brokering a long-term peace, however, may be intertwined and/or confused with hegemonic regional interests, as is apparent with the ECOMOG case. The peacekeeping force's effectiveness was hampered by suspicions that ECOMOG was a Nigerian scheme to promote itself as the regional hegemon. Many feared that the ECOMOG force was not necessarily seeking the most effective peaceful solution, but instead an outcome that would allow Nigeria to reap the most benefits. In theory, a hegemon may have little incentive to end the conflict because a weakened, dependent neighbor may serve its interests rather than conflict resolution. This reasoning shaped the perspective of some Francophone countries toward the ECOMOG operation.

A fourth rationale for employing regional peacekeepers relating to equipment suitability is particularly relevant for much of the less developed world. In many cases, international forces may be unable to use certain equipment such as tanks or armored vehicles because humidity or rough terrain may cause machinery malfunctions. Regional peacekeeping operations do not have to address the issue of equipment appropriateness and/or transport equipment over long distances, saving valuable time. However in practice, most regional organizations lack the equipment and resources to be effective. In some cases, regional forces are equipped with Cold War-era technology from the United States and former Soviet Union. Even in cases where the countries have environment-appropriate technology, it is almost always not as technologically advanced as that of multilateral organizations with First World backing. In the case of ECOMOG, at one point the entire operation had only one helicopter. In most cases, less developed countries do not manufacture their own weaponry; instead it is procured from the First World. Therefore, the equipment employed by regional forces is roughly the same equipment available to international peacekeeper, only in most cases in poorer condition. Since many developing countries lack the resources available to an international force, they may be forced to restrict use of certain equipment due to cost of maintenance or fuel.

While regional peacekeepers may be more familiar with the terrain and regional climate, this is not necessarily the case. Africa possesses stark climatic and geographical differences, and ECOMOG was constituted at certain points by peacekeepers from as far away as Tanzania, Uganda and Zimbabwe. If one considers the geographical contrasts between Liberia and Uganda, it is difficult to believe that a Ugandan would possess better understanding of the Liberian climate and terrain than an international peacekeeper. Thus, while in theory a regional peacekeeper may be better equipped to undertake operations in specific regions, in practice this is often not the case.

Regional organizations may also suffer additional disadvantages with regard to peacekeeping operations, including lacking the institutional capacity to undertake peacekeeping functions. In most cases, they are relatively young, primarily economic organizations, without previous experience in this area or the proper infrastructure to support military operations. For example, some opine that the larger Organization of African Unity lacks the experience and institutional foundations for organizing and directing such operations. Regional organizations also often lack the resources necessary to sustain large-scale peacekeeping operations.

While some of these theoretical assertions may have been useful to encourage and/or justify the ECOWAS intervention in Liberia, a more important question is whether or to what degree these arguments influenced the organization's behavior. It must be concluded that they did not. Faced with mounting disorder in Liberia, most West African states desired and preferred outside intervention by the United Nations, OAU, or international powers such as the United States. This assistance was not forthcoming, however. Whether the ECOWAS was the most effective and/or legitimate actor to undertake the task was academic; the only actors with the interests and wherewithal to undertake the mission were Nigeria and a Nigeria-led ECOWAS.

Was ECOMOG an Expression of Nigeria's Hegemonic Aspirations?

A second possible explanation for the creation of ECOMOG is that it essentially served as an instrument of Nigerian hegemonic influence in West Africa. Nigeria played a primary role in the founding of the ECOWAS, over the years has provided approximately 30 per cent of its budget, and hosts the community's headquarters (Falola and Ihonvbere, 1985, p. 191). Integration, regime and hegemonic stability theories postulate that a hegemon may be essential to states' ability to overcome collective action and coordination problems. Over time, particularly in the context of less developed states, the paucity of resources and concerns about equitable distribution of the benefits of integration may plague regional organizations. A benevolent hegemon may facilitate policy coordination and contribute 'side payments' to reduce incentives to free ride and allay distributional equity concerns. In most regional organizations, a single state (or in the case of the European Union two powerful states) serves as a focal point for negotiating treaties, institution building and policy initiatives (Mattli, 1999, pp. 55-56).

The Liberian civil war affected Nigerian national and regional concerns in four ways: 1) it threatened to topple a government traditionally friendly to Nigeria; 2) it threatened Nigerian economic interests; 3) a Charles Taylor government could 'unleash dissidents in his army to overthrow governments friendly to Nigeria in Gambia, Guinea and Sierra Leone;' and, 4) ongoing civil war could encourage intervention and/or increase the influence of extra-regional states like France and Libya (Mays, 1998, p. 111). Concerns about external intervention were not exclusive to Nigeria, but were shared by several ECOWAS Member States and extra-regional actors including the OAU, UN, and the United States.

Nigerian and West African analysts debated how the war would affect Nigeria, and many opined at the outset that the ECOWAS intervention would enhance Nigerian influence. However, as is common with hegemons, Nigerian leaders largely regard national and regional security interests as one and the same. Margaret Vogt, Senior Research Fellow at the government-sponsored Nigerian Institute for International Affairs, explains Nigeria's policy toward West Africa and the continent:

> Nigeria cannot take on itself the responsibility of guaranteeing African Security without first ensuring its own territorial boundaries, of the states contiguous to it, of the West African sub region, and then one can operate with confidence at the regional (African continent) level (Vogt, 1990, p. 94).

At the outset of the ECOWAS mission, Nigerian President Babangida stated:

> Nigeria's participation in ECOMOG fell in line with Nigerian foreign policy over the past three decades.... There is therefore no gain in saying that when certain events occur in the sub region depending upon their intensity and magnitude, which are bound to affect Nigeria's politico-military and socio-economic environment, we should not stand by as helpless and hapless spectators (Lardner, 1990, p. 51).

And, after a decade of peacekeeping in the region, Nigerian President Olusegun Obasanjo stated:

> Nigeria has over the years played a very active role in the ECOMOG for the restoration of peace in Liberia and Sierra Leone. Our national interest requires the establishment and maintenance of peace and stability in the West African Sub-region (*Nigerian Guardian*, 6 July 2000, p. 24).

Political instability in the area negatively impacted economic and political cooperation in the region, and 'The Nigerian general consensus included the point that ECOWAS cannot achieve its ultimate objective of economic integration and cooperation unless the sub region was considerably free of political tension and conflict' (Lardner, 1990, p. 51).

Nigeria's concerns coincided with those of its ECOWAS partners, and the ECOMOG was a community-wide effort. It was clear to political and economic leaders across the region that achieving economic integration and growth was contingent on military security in the region. And, as was noted previously, all acknowledged that the Liberia situation represented a genuine security and humanitarian crisis. Abbas Bundu, former ECOWAS Executive Director, explained in July 1991:

> You cannot talk meaningfully about economic integration by itself without also relating [it] to the underpinning political instability within the sub-region. The two are inseparable and therefore have to be discussed *inter alia....* Regional solidarity and

commitment to integration will be considerably enhanced where political stability becomes a common identity and is also perceived as a shared responsibility (West Africa, 1-7 July 1991, p. 1085 quoted in Aning, 1999, p. 25).

ECOWAS decisions are commonly made by consensus, and the Standing Mediating Committee which decided to intervene in Liberia was comprised of Anglophone and Francophone countries. As illustrated in the table below, Nigeria contributed the largest number of troops and nearly 80 per cent of the funding, although not entirely by choice. These disproportionate contributions derived in part from the suspicious and uncooperative attitude of the Francophone Member States. Burkina Faso, *Cote d'Ivoire* and Senegal either refused to contribute, or did so only on a limited, short-term basis.[6] Nigeria exerted significant efforts to include several ECOWAS Member States within the ECOMOG to reinforce the impression that it was a regional undertaking.

Table 10.1 Participation in ECOMOG by country

Country	Troops in ECOMOG
Gambia	150
Ghana	1,500
Guinea	600
Mali	6
Nigeria	9,000
Sierra Leone	700
Senegal	1,600

Source: Inegbedion, 1994, p. 231.

Although Mali's troop contribution was a token, it should be noted that Mali and Togo were active in ECOMOG through their role on the SMC and continuing support for the operation. Toward the end of the operation in 1997, the 11,000 ECOMOG troops included representatives from ten of the sixteen ECOWAS Member States, only 6,000 of whom were Nigerian.

   The commitment to incorporate representatives from all ECOWAS countries actually deterred the operation's success. The command structure included the Force Commander from Ghana, the Chief of Personnel from Gambia, and the Chief of Operations from Sierra Leone (Iweze, 1993, p. 218). Care was taken to balance the smaller members' role with that of Nigeria. This is evident in the operational logistics; for example, combined Ghanaian and Nigerian forces were charged with securing Liberia's chief port before ECOWAS forces disembarked. Then, 'Guinea battalion was to advance toward the center and secure the bridge at

---

[6]   Senegal received US$10 million from the United States and contributed 1,600 troops for two years of the ECOWAS operation.

Stockton Creek and capture Garnersville, while the Sierra Leone battalion was to hold the breakwaters as from the outer perimeter of defense …' (Iweze, 1993, p. 223).

The ECOWAS undertaking this mission under Nigerian leadership is congruent with the broader post-Cold War trend of global (as in the case of the United States in the Gulf War and the Balkans) and regional hegemons providing leadership to ameliorate conflict within the context of multilateral coordination and legitimization. However, Nigerian hegemonic interests were perhaps a necessary but not sufficient explanation for the ECOWAS involving itself in West African peacekeeping. Employing institutionalist discourse, while some may consider Nigeria the principle and ECOWAS the agent, the ECOWAS possessed institutional autonomy and reputation interests independent of Nigerian interests, and its role was not exclusively one of agent. The purpose of this chapter is to explain ECOWAS' taking on peacekeeping rather than Nigeria's role in Liberia. Haas reminds us that…

> The study of federalism, national unification, nation and empire building is necessarily replete with attention to the use of force by the federalizer or the catalytic agent – external colonizing elite, military conqueror, or hegemony seeking state. Our task is to explain integration among nations without recourse to these historical agents. Not because they are not important, but because they make the explanation too simple and too time-bound (Haas, 1971, p. 4).

Does Spontaneous Spillover Explain ECOWAS Peacekeeping?

Theoretical interest in the causes and processes whereby a regional economic organization might take on additional roles is hardly new; in the 1950s and 1960s, Ernst Haas and Joseph Nye analyzed several intergovernmental organizations that had broadened their mandates over time. The European Community began as a steel and coal community, but now as the European Union (EU) concerns itself with a wide range of economic, political, social and security issues. All acknowledge that the economic development of its Member States fosters complexity and provides the EU with more resources than its counterparts in less developed regions, but the relationships between level of economic development and the institutional development of regional economic organizations are not straightforward ones.

Joseph Nye discusses seven process mechanisms associated with increased integration: a) the inherent functional linkage of tasks (natural, pure or spontaneous spillover); b) deliberate linkages and coalitions (cultivated spillover); c) elite socialization; d) regional ideology and intensification of regional identity; e) external actor involvement; f) increasing flows and transactions; g) and regional group formation (Nye, 1971a, pp. 199-208). Haas conceptualizes spontaneous spillover in this way:

[T]he accretion of new powers and tasks to a central institutional structure, based on changing demands and expectations on the part of such political actors as interest groups, political parties, and bureaucracies. It refers to the specific process which originates in one functional context, initially separate from other political concerns, and then expands into related activities as it becomes clear to the chief political actors that the achievement of the initial aims cannot take place without such expansion (Haas, 1968, p. 523).

Because complex linkages characterize modern society and issues, regional economic organizations find they are unable to perform at the highest capacity unless they engage multiple economic, social and political sectors (Caporaso, 1972, p. 32). A 1967 European Community document describes the impetus in this way: 'The material logic of the facts of integration urges us relentlessly on from one step to the next, from one field to another' (Hallstein, 1967, p. 11). And, Haas concurs that 'Sector integration…begets its own impetus toward extension to the entire economy even in the absence of specific group demands' (1958, p. 297).

Processes of 'cultivated spillover' yield consequences similar to that of spontaneous spillover, i.e. the regional economic organization broadens its agenda to include tasks not originally part of its mandate, but these new tasks are not inherently and substantively connected to earlier functions. Cultivated spillover is more a consequence of deliberate choice by policy-makers. Nye explains:

In contrast to pure spillover in which the main force comes from a common perception of the degree to which the problems are inextricably intertwined in a modern economy, problems are deliberately linked together into packaged deals not on the basis of technological necessity but on the basis of political and ideological projections and political possibilities (Nye, 1971, p. 202).

Philippe C. Schmitter further contributes to the analysis of the spillover effect by identifying three additional possible spillover mechanisms: reward-generalization, imitation, and frustration. ECOWAS was not a successful trade organization. Its decision to enter into the peacekeeping operation did not derive from its status as a fully functioning and integrated economic organization ready to expand to other sectors. Many ECOWAS Member States had seen their economies crippled by structural adjustment programs, and Nigeria's once robust oil revenues had declined. Worldwide exports from the region were minuscule; the majority of intra-regional trade was restricted to the four largest countries. The average number of intra-regional trading partners for any member state was six (Adibe, 1994, pp. 190-195). Nor was the involvement of the organization in the peacekeeping an effort to duplicate similar efforts in other sectors or by external actors. However, the third mechanism, frustration, at first blush may seem to have relevance for the ECOWAS case. Schmitter describes frustration-generated spillover as:

The process whereby members of an integration scheme – agreed on some collective goals for a variety of motives but unequally satisfied with their attainment of these goals – attempt to resolve their dissatisfaction either by resorting to collaboration in another, related sector (expanding the scope of mutual commitment) or by intensifying their commitments to the original sector (increasing the level of mutual commitment), or both (Schmitter, 1964, p. 19).

As has been noted, ECOWAS had failed to achieve the original objectives set out 15 years earlier in Article 2(1) of the ECOWAS treaty:

> It shall be the aim of the Community to promote co-operation and development in all fields of economic activity particularly in the fields of industry, transport, telecommunications, energy, agriculture, natural resources, commerce, monetary and financial questions and in social and cultural matters for the purpose of raising the standard of living for its peoples, of increasing and maintaining economic stability, of fostering closer relations among its members and of contributing to the progress and development of the African continent (quoted in Adibe, 1994, pp. 187-188).

In 1986, just over a decade after the creation of ECOWAS, Nigerian President Babangida said, 'The hallmark of integration has been inaction and cosmetic commitment' (*Africa Research Bulletin*, 1986, p. 8264). In 1990, many doubted that ECOWAS would survive into the new decade. That year, Phoebe Kornfeld wrote, 'If ECOWAS is not to be doomed to failure, national-interest must be replaced by regional priorities' (Kornfeld, 1990, p. 109). There seems little doubt that the most committed among ECOWAS leaders were frustrated by the organization's continued embryonic state. However, it must be noted that the organization had been ineffective since inception. Regional economic organizations among less developed countries are prone to languish due to a lack of resources and commitment and political instability within member states, etc. It is unlikely that the ECOWAS decision to take on peacekeeping in 1990 derived from some sudden burst or accumulated frustration. The security threat posed by the Liberian conflict represents a more credible explanation for ECOWAS behavior.

To what extent was ECOMOG a consequence of concern that the Liberian conflict threatened the organization's overall economic objectives? Most agree that 'Planning [within regional organizations] in particular becomes problematic because political fluidity detracts from long-term stability desired for the success of these development schemes' (Okola and Wright, 1990, p. 4). In order to pursue economic integration, the primary goal of the organization, ECOWAS leaders had to expand cooperation to protect political and social sectors as well.

Earlier ECOWAS actions had recognized the importance of political stability to achieving the organization's objectives. In 1975, a border dispute between Benin and Togo was settled amicably due to ECOWAS efforts. In 1978, the Authority adopted a Protocol on Non-Aggression to create a 'friendly atmosphere, free of any fear of attack or aggression of one state by another' (Okolo, 1984). Members agreed to refrain from attacking one another and recognized their borders as inviolable.[7] This pact had not been tested, however, and did not enjoy the support

---

[7]   As with the previously described conflicts in the region, relations among ECOWAS member states immediately after the founding of the organization were turbulent. In January 1977, President Kerekou of Benin accused several states, including *Cote*

of all ECOWAS member states. Senegal was among its main opponents, and at the 1979 Dakak Summit, proposed its own version of a mutual defense plan. In 1981, the Non-Aggression Pact and Senegal's mutual defense plan were merged in the ECOWAS Protocol for Mutual Assistance in Matters of Defense (Shaw and Okolo, 1994, p. 222). It provided ECOWAS the right to intervene in "internal armed conflict within any member state engineered and supported actively from the outside, [which was] likely to endanger the security and peace in the entire region' (Iweze, 1993, pp. 218-223). This protocol was signed by all member states save Cape Verde, Guinea-Bissau, and Mali, but did not became part of the ECOWAS treaty until 1986. The Liberian civil war was the first test of the Defense Protocol (*Africa Research Bulletin*, 15 July 1981, p. 6072). A declaration of political principles by the Authority of Heads of State and Government of ECOWAS in Abuja in 1991 stated that it was not only through coordinated economic strategies and policies that regional cooperation and integration can contribute to a better life for all, but also through sub-regional peace, political stability, and shared political beliefs (Quashigah, 1997).

There is academic support for this spontaneous spillover argument. Earl Conteh-Morgan writes:

> The response of ECOWAS as a community to the dynamics of change, increased domestic demands, and the growing challenges from abroad, is to invoke its adaptive reflex – that is, to put into operation its cooperative norms and new practices that are essential to sustaining the entire ECOWAS system (Conteh-Morgan, 1998).

For ECOWAS, the Liberian civil war was a novel challenge that 'constituted the greatest threat to the stability of the sub-region' (Mays, 1996, p. 135). ECOWAS had to find a peaceful solution to the conflict, because the war in the region would destroy the already precarious balance within the organization and any hopes of economic integration.

For ECOWAS' behavior to fulfil the definitional requirements of 'spontaneous' rather than 'cultivated' spillover, it must be demonstrated that the new role was

---

d'Ivoire, Senegal, and Togo, of involvement in a mercenary attack on his capital. The Benin-Togo border was closed, reopened, and re-closed, deterring movement of goods and people. Sekou Toure of Guinea, allying with Kerekou, accused Senegal and Cote d'Ivoire of providing a 'spring-board for anti-Guinea activities.' In September 1976, he had accused Guinea-Bissau of similar activities, which resulted in the close of Guinea-Bissau's embassy. Political difficulties also arose between Nigeria and Togo when the latter offered asylum to General Yakubu Gowan when he fled Nigeria in the wake of the February 1975 coup.

Border disputes characterized relations between several ECOWAS members. In 1974-1975, lives were lost in disputes between Mali and Upper Volta (now Burkina Faso). In January 1977, Ghana warned Togo that military action might result from the latter's providing support to the secessionist movement in Ghana's Volta region. Near the end of 1978, disagreements arose between Senegal and Guinea-Bissau over maritime frontiers believed to contain oil resources. (See Davies, 1983, pp. 170-176, Gambari, 1971, p. 36; Brown, 1994, pp. 77, 96.)

undertaken as a natural, spontaneous choice, as a necessary part of its economic integration mission. 'The political economy of development is thus intimately bound up with security... How prevalent is security as a policy concern to ECOWAS states and others? Several contributors argue that it is central.' (King, 1996, p. 26). When viewed over the long-term, the case may be made that this behavior was indeed a natural part of ECOWAS' development. However, an equally strong case may be made that, in the short-term, the decision to establish the ECOMOG was based upon immediate, security needs, independent of long-term considerations of economic integration.

Is ECOMOG a Consequence of Cultivated Spillover?

Cultivated spillover, i.e. deliberate linkages, provides an alternative potential explanation for the ECOWAS peacekeeping operation. As noted earlier, this is the process in which a regional organization consciously takes on new roles not inherently connected to its original mission of economic integration. There is persuasive evidence that deliberate linkages were involved in the creation of ECOMOG. A consensus existed in West Africa and the wider international community that the escalating violence and humanitarian crisis in Liberia necessitated intervention. Since assistance from the United Nations, Organization of African Unity and Western states was not forthcoming, it fell to the ECOWAS and Nigeria to act. Aside from unilateral Nigerian action, the regional organization was, as it were, 'the only game in town.' Sufficient evidence to support this short-term explanation of cultivated spillover relies on demonstrating that ECOWAS leaders believed that the Liberian conflict posed an immediate threat of spreading to neighboring countries, were concerned about its humanitarian consequences, and, although they preferred intervention from global powers and/or the United Nations, that they were resigned to the reality that help was not forthcoming from other sources.

From the beginning, ECOWAS leaders explained and justified the intervention on humanitarian grounds. King explains that ECOWAS leaders regarded the Liberian people as fellow-West Africans, and that:

> The wanton destruction of lives and property; the displacement of people and the incidence of starvation were too much to bear for the members to sit idly by and watch (King, 1996, p. 216).

A leading ECOWAS official stated that ECOMOG was established, 'as a result of the seeming concern for the loss of lives and property of fellow Africans. This to my mind remains so. Fellow Africans albeit at a sub regional level, will continue to feel for their brothers in dire straits like the Liberian debacle' (King, 1996, p. 238). Nigerian President Babanghida (1992, pp. ix-x) echoed this sentiment in 1992: 'Nigeria's role is basically informed by our traditional sense of responsibility to our African brothers and sisters. It would have been indefensible if we had turned a blind eye to the carnage in Liberia.' When hosting a workshop on the Liberian crisis in 1991, Abbas Bundu, the Executive Secretary of ECOWAS, spoke of the Liberian war as a tragedy for Liberia and for the whole of Africa. He referred to the Liberian citizens as 'hopeless people,' and called upon ECOWAS Member States to learn from this experience: 'My fervent hope is that out of the Liberian crisis will emerge an ECOWAS more determined more purposeful and more resilient, indeed a beacon that would eliminate Africa's latent capacity to solve its own problems in the furtherance of African Unity and aspirations' (ECOWAS, 1991).

A final factor that clearly went into the short-term security calculations surrounding the necessity of ECOWAS taking on the peacekeeping role relates to the ante- and post-intervention responses of external actors. The ECOWAS under Nigerian leadership was quite simply the only actor with the interest and wherewithal to take on the task because the international community refused to do so. There was insufficient interest in the United Nations Security Council and among the major powers, such as the United States, in putting an end to the growing disaster in the country. As was noted, the United Nations supported the resolution for action presented to the Security Council, and later encouraged ECOWAS involvement in expanded regional peacekeeping operations. In 1995, former Secretary General Boutros Boutros-Ghali suggested more involvement of regional organizations in peacekeeping and other activities in the groundbreaking document *Agenda for Peace* (Boutros-Ghali, 1995, pp. 62-65).

Unsurprisingly, given its perceived lack of 'vital national interests' in West Africa, the United States remained at arms-length from the conflict. It October 1991, it provided Senegal US$10 million to encourage its joining the peacekeeping effort in Liberia, after which Senegal sent 1,600 troops (da Costa, 1993, p. 23). The United States also financially subsidized Nigeria's involvement for many years (although these subventions would later be reduced in the face of governance concerns). Serious talks on ECOMOG began only after it became clear that US Marines landing in Liberia were solely to evacuate American nationals and would take no part in bringing order to that country (Inegbedion, 1994). This lack of initiative by the United Nations and United States sent a clear signal to ECOWAS leaders that if anything was to be done it would be through them.[8]

---

[8]   Aning (1999, p. 26) contrasts United States' interest in Liberia during and after the Cold War. Between 1980 and 1988, the US viewed Liberia as a 'key ally in Africa' (among others such as Kenya, Somalia, Sudan and Zaire). It was the highest per capita recipient of US aid in Africa, between US$70-80 million per year. He quotes a US Institute for National Strategic Studies report that said: 'The United States has essentially no serious military/geostrategic interests in Africa any more, other than the inescapable fact that its vastness poses an obstacle to deployment in the Middle East and South Asia.... The disorder in Liberia did not represent post-Cold War incentives for extra-regional intervention.'

Conclusions

The civil war in Liberia was an extremely difficult situation from every prospective. The combatants demonstrated time after time that they had little respect for citizens' survival, human rights or property. It was this situation that the ECOWAS leaders confronted when the decision was made to send troops into Monrovia in 1990. What motivated ECOWAS to take this action? This paper has explored three possible explanations.

The international community and scholars heralded regional peacekeeping as a way to address post-Cold War intrastate conflicts. There certainly may be theoretical advantages to regional peacekeeping over United Nations or Organization of Africa Unity peacekeeping, however, in the case of ECOWAS these advantages were non-existent. ECOWAS was struggling in every sense – the idea that it possessed any advantage quickly disappears as one considers the reality of the situation. ECOMOG was a conglomeration of at best second-rate militaries. All but Nigeria provided their troops with minimal support, and many voiced concern that ECOWAS states would withdraw from the operation after suffering their first substantial loss. With poor technology, training, will, support, and in some cases a lack of neutrality, ECOWAS had few advantages to offer over *any* other organization, except its willingness to intervene.

Nigeria committed more troops and more money than any other country in ECOWAS to the operation. In a country where many struggle to meet basic human needs, it is reasonable to ask why it took up this challenge. Nigeria is the regional hegemon of West Africa and many saw this as another tactic to increase its already dominant presence. The evidence provided here that Nigeria was not motivated exclusively by hegemonic aspirations may be problematic for some, because it relies in large part on the speeches and rhetoric of seasoned politicians. We are all well aware of the difficulties in distinguishing between indicators of causation and the rhetoric used to build political support for and justify political action. Had Nigerian foreign policy rather than the ECOWAS been the primary unit of analysis, the ECOWAS may have been conceptualized as an instrument of Nigerian foreign policy. There is, however, no evidence that Nigeria ever wished ECOMOG to be a unilateral operation. Public statements made by Nigerian officials during and since this operation always stressed the need for regional solidarity. Most expressions of concern about Nigerian hegemony came from Francophone states that refused from the outset to play a substantial role in the operation.

Nigeria certainly was not blameless for a good deal of this criticism. From the beginning, neither Nigeria nor the ECOMOG were perceived as neutral in the conflict. If increased regional influence had been Nigeria's primary objective, this might have been pursued in more effective ways. For example, Nigeria might have entered into Liberia unilaterally, which would have proved less difficult and possibly less expensive then the multinational ECOMOG. Current President of Nigeria Olusegun Obasanjo said of ECOWAS:

Personally, since my modest contribution to the birth of ECOWAS, I have firmly believed in cooperation with our immediate neighbours as a major plank and a starting point of Nigeria's foreign policy. Our Administration fully accepts the challenge of making ECOWAS a viable regional organization that will also serve as major building block for the continental integration of Africa as a whole (*Nigerian Guardian,* 29 May 1999, p. 2).

While some analyses tend to vilify or glorify various actors, neo-functionalist assumptions allows one to examine the situation in a more theoretically useful way. What began as cultivated spillover to address short-term security concerns may in the long-term translate into spontaneous spillover that enhances institutionalization. The imperative and opportunity to create ECOMOG may very well have been the most propitious event since the ECOWAS was founded in 1975. ECOWAS Member States are now more inclined to attend the meetings and meet their financial obligations than before. And, ECOWAS' intra- and extra-regional reputation as a force in West Africa has been significantly reinforced.

The issue of whether and how regional economic organizations can and should expand their agendas to take on additional roles including those associated with security has import for most regional cooperative entities. For examples, the *Mercado Comun del Sur* (Mercosur) has facilitated resolution of border disputes among member and associated states, as has the Association of Southeast Asian Nations. And, the Southern African Development Coordination Conference has involved itself in conflict resolution in the Congo and other disputes. Although the European Union has debated establishment of a common foreign and defense policy for decades, recent moves within the organization to add a second pillar to the treaty structure and to create a 60,000-person rapid deployment force may be traced to needs arising out of and accentuated by consecutive crises in the former Yugoslavia. In general, regional economic organizations do not bestir themselves to take on security functions unless a pressing need presents itself. With regard to the ECOWAS, this ineffective, and by some standards moribund, intergovernmental organization would not have acted to take on this new challenge without a powerful catalyst, in this case the threat of regional chaos. Only the future will reveal the ultimate impact of the Liberian experience on the ECOWAS and whether this spontaneous and/or cultivated spillover in security functions will translate into a more viable regional economic cooperation. More than a decade of unspeakable war across the region can deepen existing cleavages as well as provide increased incentives for economic cooperation and development.

References

Adeleke, Ademola (1995), 'The Politics and Diplomacy of Peacekeeping in West Africa: The Ecowas Operation in Liberia', *The Journal of Modern African Studies,* Vol. 33(4), pp. 569-593.
Adibe, Clement Emenike (1994), 'ECOWAS in a Comparative Perspective', in Emeka Okolo and Timothy Shaw (eds.), *The Political Economy of Foreign Policy in ECOWAS,* St. Martin's Press, New York, NY, pp. 187-217.

Africa Research Bulletin, Economic, 15 July 1981, p. 6072; 31 July 1986, p. 8264.

Aning, Emmanuel Kwesi (1999), *Security in the West Afrcan Subregion: An Analysis of ECOWAS' Policies in Liberia*, Institut for Statskundskab, Københavns Universitet, Copenhagen.

Babanghida, I.B. (1992), 'Foreword', in Nkem Agetua's, *Operation Liberty: The Story of Major General Joshua Nimyel Dogonyaro*, Hona Communications, Ltd., Lagos, pp. ix-x.

Boutros-Ghali, Boutros (1995), *Agenda for Peace*, United Nations, New York, NY.

Brown, M. Leann (1994), *Developing Countries and Regional Economic Cooperation*, Praeger, Westport, CT.

Caporaso, James A. (1972), *Functionalism and Regional Integration: A Logical and Empirical Assessment*, Sage Publications, Beverly Hills, CA.

Conteh-Morgan, Earl (1998), 'Adapting Peace-Making Mechanisms in an Era of Global Change', in Earl Conteh-Morgan and Karl Magyar (eds.), *Peacekeeping in Africa, ECOMOG in Liberia*, St. Martin's Press, Inc., New York, NY.

da Costa, Peter (1993), 'Talking Tough to Taylor', *Africa Report,* January-February, pp. 18-21.

Davies, Arthur (1983), 'Cost-Benefit Analysis with ECOWAS', *The World Today*, Vol. 39(5) (May), pp. 170-176.

Diehl, Paul E. (1993), *International Peacekeeping*, The Johns Hopkins University Press, Baltimore, MD.

ECOWAS (1991), Third Meeting of the Committee of Five on the Liberian Crisis held in Yamoussoukro, 29-30 October, Final Communique.

Falola, Toyin and Julius Ihonvbere (1985), *The Rise and Fall of Nigeria's Second Republic, 1979-1984*, Zed Books, London.

Foreign Broadcast Information Service (1990), 'Lukman Welcomes Foreign Support in Liberia', *Daily Report on Africa*, 10 August.

Gambari, Ibrahim A. (1971), *Political and Comparative Dimensions of Regional Integration: The Case of ECOWAS*, Humanities Press International, Inc., Atlantic Highlands, NJ.

Haas, Ernst B. (1958), *The Uniting of Europe: Political, Economic and Social Forces, 1950-57*, Stanford University Press, Stanford, CA.

Haas, Ernst B. (1961), 'International Organization: The European and the Universal Process', *International Organization*, Vol. 15(3), pp. 366-392.

Haas, Ernst B. (1964), *Beyond the Nation-State*, Stanford University Press, Stanford, CA.

Haas, Ernst B. (1968), 'Regional Integration', in D.L. Sills (ed.), *International Encyclopedia of Social Sciences*, Macmillan and Free Press, New York. NY, p. 523.

Haas, Ernst B. (1971), 'The Study of Regional Integration: Reflections on the Joy and Anguish of Pretheorizing', in Leon N. Lindberg and Stuart A. Scheingold (eds.), *Regional Integration: Theory and Research*, Harvard University Press, Cambridge, MA, pp. 3-42.

Haas, Ernst B. and Schmitter, Philippe (1964), 'Economic and Differential Patterns of Political Integration: Projects about Unity in Latin America', *International Organization*, Vol. 18 (4), pp. 705-737.

Hallstein, Walter (1967), 'The Dynamics of the European Community', *European Community*, June, No. 103, pp. 10-12.

Howe, Herbert (1996), 'Lessons of Liberia: ECOMOG and Regional Peacekeeping', *International Security*, Vol. 21(3), pp. 145-176.

Inegbedion, John E. (1994), 'ECOMOG in a Comparative Perspective', in Okolo and Timothy Shaw (eds.), *The Political Economy of Foreign Policy in ECOWAS*, Emeka St. Martin's Press, New York, pp. 218-236.

Iweze, C.Y. (1993), 'Nigeria in Liberia:The Military Operations of ECOMOG', in M.A. Vogt and A.E. Ekoko (eds.), *Nigeria in International Peacekeeping 1960-1992*, Malthouse Publishing Ltd., Oxford, pp. 218-223.

Kacowicz, Arie M. (1997), '"Negative" International Peace and Domestic Conflicts, West Africa, 1957-96', *The Journal of Modern African Studies*, Vol. 35(3), pp. 367-386.

King, Mae C. (1996), *Basic Currents of Nigerian Foreign Policy*, Howard University Press, Washington, DC.

Kornfeld, Phoebe (1990), 'ECOWAS, the First Decade: Toward Collective Self-Reliance, or Maintainance of the Status Quo?', in Julius Okolo, Julius Emeka and Stephen Wright (eds.), *West African Regional Cooperation and Integration*, Westview Press, Boulder, CO, pp. 87-113.

Lardner, Tunji, Jr. (1990), 'The Babanghida Blues', *Africa Report*, Vol. 35(3) (July-August), p. 51.

Lay, Benjamin (1982), 'West Africa's Economic Realities', *Defense & Foreign Affairs*, (September), Feature Reports, pp. 11-12.

Levitt, Jeremy (1999), 'Pre-Intervention Trust-Building, African States and Enforcing the Peace: The Case of ECOWAS in Liberia and Sierra Leone', *Liberian Studies Journal*, Vol. 24(1), pp. 1-26.

Lindberg, Leon N. (1963), *The Political Dynamics of European Economic Integration*, Stanford University Press, Stanford, CA.

Lindberg, Leon N. (1965), 'Decisionmaking and Integration in the European Community', *International Organization*, Vol. 19, pp. 56-80.

Mattli, Walter (1999), *The Logic of Regional Integration, Europe and Beyond*, Cambridge University Press, Cambridge.

May, Roy; Cleaver Gerry (1997), 'African Peacekeeping, Still Dependent?', *International Peacekeeping*, Vol. 4(2), pp. 1-21.

Mays, Terry (1998), 'Nigerian Foreign Policy,' in Earl Conteh-Morgan and Karl Magyar (eds.), *Peacekeeping in Africa*, St. Martin's Press, Inc., New York, NY.

Mortimer, Robert A. (1996), 'ECOMOG, Liberia and Regional Security in West Africa', in Edmond J. Keller and Donald Rothchild (eds.), *Africa in the New International Order: Rethinking State Sovereignty and Regional Security*, Lynne Rienner Publishers, Inc., Boulder, CO, pp. 149-164.

Nigerian Guardian, 6 July 2000, p. 24; 29 May 1999, p. 2.

Nye, Joseph S. (1971a), 'Comparing Common Markets: A Revised Neo-Functionalist Model', in Leon N. Lindberg and Stuart A. Scheingold (eds.), *Regional Integration*, Harvard University Press Cambridge, MA, pp. 192-231.

Nye, Joseph S. (1971b), *Peace in Parts: Integration and Conflict in Regional Organizations*, Little, Brown, Boston, MA.

Obasanjo, Olusegun (1999), 'The Summit of the Southern African Development Community', (SADC), *Nigerian Federal Government report*, 17 August, Maputo, Mozambique.

Offor, Chinedu (19929, 'Liberia: The Quagmire Widens', *The African Guardian*, Vol. 23(27), November.

Ojo, Olantunde J.B. (1980), 'Nigeria and the Formation of ECOWAS', *International Organization* (Autumn), pp. 571-604.

Okolo, Julius Emeka (1984), *West African Regional Integration: ECOWAS*, Paper presented at the 25th Annual Meeting of the International Studies Association, Atlanta, GA, USA, 27 March -April 1.

Okolo, Julius Emeka and Stephen Wright (1990), *West African Regional Development*, Westview Press, Boulder, CO.

Oyewumi, Adremi (2001), 'Nigerian Foreign Policy: 40 years On', *Nigerian Guardian*, 8 March, p. 7.

Quashigah, E.K. (1997), 'Human Rights and Integration,' in Real Lavergne (ed.), *Regional Integration and Cooperation in West Africa*, Africa World Press, Inc., Trenton, NJ, pp. 259-278.

Schmitter, Philippe C. (1964), *The Process of Central American Integration: Spillover or Spill-around?*, Institute of International Studies, Series 5, University of California, Berkeley.

Shaw, Timothy M. and Julius Emeka Okolo (1994), *The Political Economy of Foreign Policy in ECOWAS*, St. Martin's Press, New York.

Spear, Mary and John Keller (1996), 'Conflict Resolution in Africa: Insights from UN Representatives and U.S. Government Officials', *Africa Today*, Vol. 43(2), p. 120.

Vogt, Margaret Aderinsola (1990), 'Nigeria's Defense Policy: An Overview', in Ekoko and M.A. Vogt (eds.), *Nigerian Defense Policy*, Malthouse Press, Ltd., Lagos, pp. 92-110.

Vogt, Margaret Aderinsola (1996), 'The Involvement of ECOWAS in Liberia's Peacekeeping', in Edmond J. Keller and Donald Rothchild (eds), *Africa in the New International Order: Rethinking State Sovereignty and Regional Security*, Lynne Rienner Publishers, Inc., Boulder, CO., pp. 165-183.

Chapter 11

Path Dependence and External Shocks: The Dynamics of the EU Enlargement Eastwards

Svetlozar A. Andreev

Not so long after the sudden collapse of state socialism in Central and Eastern Europe, the Eastern Enlargement project of the European Union was initiated with the declared ambition to assist the countries of the region with the difficult transformations they were undergoing, to promote peace, democracy and prosperity in the eastern part of the continent and to advance the European integration process further. Despite considerable enthusiasm about the successful realization of these goals and the assertion made by some Western politicians and Brussels officials that new member states from Eastern Europe would be admitted in the EU with a minimal possible delay, the initially optimistic scenario of this initiative has not seemed to be realized so far. A large number of political, social and economic factors as well as some other permanent constraints of a purely technical character, have prevented the EU and its institutions from acting more decisively on this score and, as a result, the promotion of the Union's policies eastwards has been significantly slowed down.

Nowadays, after approximately a decade of intensive EU institutions and member states' activity in Eastern Europe, the outcomes of such a well-intentioned initiative do not appear to be so straightforward or consistent with the original mission of this project. Unfortunately, the bulk of academic research, dedicated to studying and conceptualizing normatively the effects and concomitants of the process of European integration in its eastern dimension, has not been able to achieve any major theoretical breakthrough or produce any practical insight that could explain the nature of Eastern Enlargement to a sufficient extent. Some authors, even those who have written extensively about enlargement, have not been able to predict the probable agenda and final objectives of the recent fifth wave of enlargement. Most studies have often been overburdened with the tedious citation of official documents and the enumeration of well-known facts about the procedural aspects of the contractual relations between the EU and its Eastern

European partners (Van den Bempt and Theelen, 1996; Preston, 1997; Avery and Cameron, 1998).[1]

This chapter takes a different perspective from the predominant trend of treating the subject of the Eastern Enlargement of the EU descriptively and proposes an alternative approach of understanding some key aspects of its development. This new way of analyzing the present EU drive to enlarge itself eastwards uses a path dependence method, already known from other social science disciplines such as history and economics (North, 1990, Brian Arthur, 1994, Goodstein, 1995). This research should be considered as a first attempt to investigate some of the recent tendencies characterizing EU–Eastern European relations in a way that is more innovative, but consistent from a methodological point of view. The Eastern Enlargement of the EU is conceptualized not as a linear process, with clearly defined beginning and end points, but, rather, as a randomly developing and difficult-to-predict venture, which can be described by means of a path dependence theory. Therefore, it is assumed that a certain set of initial conditions was very important during the early period of EU-Eastern European relations immediately after 1989, when there was a general lack of information about the countries on the Eastern side of the former Iron Curtain and the real intentions and interests of the major actors participating in the process of European integration were very hard to predict. Later on, however, the signing of important bilateral treaties between the EC/EU and the Eastern European countries (the Europe Agreements) and the adoption of a set of criteria for enlargement (the 'Copenhagen' criteria) put this process firmly on track and greatly reduced uncertainty. Parallel to this, it is hypothesized that the occurrence of several major political crises in the broader environment external to the EU, such as the collapse of the Soviet Union and the outbreak of ethnic and civil-military conflicts in the territory of the former Federal Republic of Yugoslavia, had a considerable impact on the evolution of the EC/EU relations with Eastern Europe as well as the pattern of development of its foreign policy towards the region, especially as with regard to a prospective enlargement eastwards. Finally, this chapter brings all of the above elements together in order to build a somewhat coherent picture of how EU enlargement policies have developed so far, and to determine whether significant changes could be expected in this respect in the future.

Negotiating the EU Enlargement Eastwards and Accompanying Problems

Currently there are ten Eastern European countries that are official candidates to become members of the European Union.[2] These are Bulgaria, the Czech Republic,

---

[1]   For some good attempts to analyse this fifth round of enlargement normatively see H. Wallace, 1997, Mayhew, 1998, Friis and Murphy 1999, 2000.

[2]   The Essen Summit in December 1994 selected those Eastern European countries that might be considered as candidates for membership in the EU. All of them had previously concluded Europe Agreements with the EU/EC. One year later, however, the

Estonia, Hungary, Latvia, Lithuania, Poland, Romania, Slovakia and Slovenia. In addition, Cyprus, Malta and Turkey are also applying as candidates from the South and the Mediterranean basin. In July 1997, the European Commission presented its opinion on the applications for membership and in its official communication, *Agenda 2000*, it recommended that negotiations begin with the Czech Republic, Estonia, Hungary, Poland and Slovenia (EU Commission 1997). This position was re-confirmed at the December 1997 European Council in Luxembourg, where it was decided to begin accession negotiations with these five countries and with Cyprus.

Only two years later, however, the humanitarian and military crisis in the former Yugoslav province of Kosovo took place. Having in mind the possible considerable political and geo-strategic complications that might have resulted both for the EU and its member states been directly involved in the region, it became gradually clear that most of the traditional diplomatic interventions and economic measures employed by the Western governments and international organizations towards the Milosevic regime in Yugoslavia, the Balkans and Eastern Europe, would need some kind of re-adjustment and re-formulation. In the context of prevailing instability and threat posed by the conflicts in South Eastern Europe for the entire European security environment, following the end of the military hostilities and return of refugees in Kosovo in the summer of 1999, a number of important developments occurred in the realm of EU foreign policy, which suggested that a more comprehensive Eastern Enlargement with all ten candidate countries participating simultaneously might well take place (EU Commission 1999a).[3] Indeed, what had seemed to be a distant possibility several months before that became a real argument at the European Council meeting in Helsinki in December 1999, when the date for beginning negotiations with the remaining five candidate countries, Bulgaria, Latvia, Lithuania, Romania and Slovakia, plus Malta, was moved ahead in schedule and was fixed for the second half of February 2000.[4]

---

group of official applicants increased after the joining in of the three Baltic states and Slovenia. Thus, its number reached thirteen, including not only Eastern Europeans but also candidates from the Mediterranean 'wave of enlargement' such as Cyprus, Malta and, most recently, Turkey.

[3] In October 1999, the European Commission released its annual Progress Reports on the current state of affairs of the individual applicant states, where it praised the developments in several countries from the so-called 'second wave' of enlargement, among which, Bulgaria and Romania, had supported the military operation of NATO in Kosovo earlier that same year; EU Commission (1999); 'Regular Report from the Commission on Progress towards Accession by each of the Candidate Countries', 13 October 1999, IP/99/751.

[4] It should be recognised, however, that Latvia, Lithuania, Malta and Slovakia had already achieved a substantial economic and political progress which would probably have permitted them to join the 'first-wave' applicant group; the problem obviously remained only for Bulgaria and Romania, which were threatened with relegation in a reduced in

Not surprisingly, some countries that were more advanced in their preparations for entry in the EU East-Central European countries expressed their preoccupation about the likelihood that the enlargement process might get 'diluted' and that no objective criteria would be applied by the European decision-making bodies as to whether the applicant countries would truly be ready to assume the responsibilities for membership. Since the beginning of 2000, the governments of the formerly-known as 'first-wave' applicant states have also been concerned by the fact that, by taking six new countries on board and by giving Turkey a clearer perspective of becoming a member of the EU one day, might lead to a stalemate in the work of the European institutions and provoke the 'sudden death' of the Eastern Enlargement process in the incipient stages of its evolution.[5] Parallel to that, pressure has been mounting on the individual candidates, regardless of their position in the long list of countries negotiating an accession, following the decision of the EU General Affairs Council from the 31st of May 1999 to give the opportunity, albeit a distant one, to a number of other Eastern European countries to apply for membership of the Union (Commission, 1999). During the current round of negotiations, however, it turned out rather obvious that the EU would not be prepared to accept more than a handful of new member states (most certainly, not even all of the best-prepared applicant countries). Moreover, the potential candidates for associate membership, such as Croatia, Albania, Bosnia and Herzegovina, and the FYR of Macedonia, would probably not be able to fulfil a sufficient part of the 'Copenhagen criteria' (European Council, June 1993)[6] in the near future, bearing in mind their present substantial political and economic difficulties.

In the ongoing discussion about the intrinsic characteristics and probable timetable of Eastern Enlargement, it has been increasingly uncertain, however,

---

numbers 'second wave'. The possibility of starting immediately negotiations for enlargement with Turkey was less certain, so, this country was given a longer period of time to comply with some of the basic membership requirements of the EU, namely the political and economic ones.

[5]   In its official communication COM (99) 235 of 26 May 1999 to the Council and Parliament, the Commission proposed the start of a Stabilisation and Association process to the countries of Southeastern Europe. The General Affairs Council (GAC) of 31 May 1999 concluded on 4 June that EU reaffirms *'the readiness of the European Union to draw the countries of [South-eastern Europe] closer to the prospect of full integration into its structures'*.

[6]   The 1993 European Council in Copenhagen decided that the Eastern European applicants should meet three essential criteria for membership: 1) stable institutions guaranteeing democracy, rule of law, human rights and the protection of minorities, 2) the existence of a functional market economy as well as the capacity to cope with competitive pressures and market forces within the Union, and 3) the ability to take on the obligations of membership including adherence to the aims of political, economic and monetary union. European Council, Copenhagen, 21-22 June 1993, Conclusions of the Presidency, SN 180/93, p. 13.

whether the EU, in its present format and under its current system of rules, would be able to follow its domestic and foreign policy agendas simultaneously. For instance, much has been said and written about the presumably contradictory nature of the *deepening* and *widening* of the Union,[7] whatever normative value these two terms could have for the proper conceptualization of EU integration, which in itself is an indication of the political confusion and tensions prevailing at the core of the official European institutions regarding this process. These problems have been vividly debated at the recent IGC meeting in Nice, but, unfortunately, they have not received a satisfactory solution even after the voting system in the Council of Ministers had been substantially modified to accommodate new members in the near future. Beside the frequent and often just criticism directed at the Eastern European applicant states about various aspects of their preparedness to join the EU, it has been suggested with equal poignancy by those working for the EU and by some others analyzing the performance of its structures, that the majority of complications with the Eastern Enlargement might actually stem 'from the inherent ambiguity of the European Union's integration project itself' (Zielonka, 1997, p. 8), while the candidate states from Eastern Europe are mere policy-takers and 'affected party' of the decisions adopted in Brussels.[8]

Although it is a well-recognized reality that the goals and identity of the EU have been undergoing constant evolution since its creation as the EEC/ECSC in the mid-1950s, it must also be acknowledged, that realization of this 'flexible indefiniteness' has created a lot of confusion and general suspicion about the Union's proclaimed objectives, particularly in the field of foreign policy. Moreover, it has been repeatedly stated that a reform of the structural policies and the common agricultural policy (CAP), as well as a radical revision of the EU budget, are indispensable pre-conditions for enlargement (Baldwin, 1994; Hyde-Price, 1996; Schimmelfennig, 1999). Virtually ten years after the signing of the first series of association agreements with the countries of East-Central Europe, agriculture is still a major impediment for the accession of new member states to the EU, and no serious discussion of reform of the CAP has been conducted at the level of the European institutions and among the actual fifteen member states. Hence, it is possible to conclude that Eastern Enlargement has consistently been held hostage to the internal problems of the current member states and the EU

---

[7] See for example EU Commission (2000); '*Agenda 2000*: For a stronger and wider Union', COM(97) 2000, 16 July 1997.

[8] In an article in *The Financial Times*, the Enlargement Commissioner Günther Verheugen expressed serious concern about the slow and painful reforms that the EU had to conduct internally. (*The Financial Times*, 2000). One year later, France opened a new debate in the EU about the Union's enlargement strategy when the French Foreign Minister Hubert Vedrine suggested that 12 candidates should join at the same time. Mr Vedrine surprised his fellow foreign ministers at the General Affairs Council meeting in Brussels by suggesting that Bulgaria and Romania should also be included in the first wave of enlargement in 2004 (Lungescu, 2001).

itself, and it has never managed to influence substantially the integration and transformation processes developing within the Union.

There is a popular misapprehension among Eastern European government officials and various media sources occupied with monitoring the advancement of enlargement that the European Commission and representatives of individual member states at the different levels of administration in Brussels play a central role in the organization and promotion of enlargement. It is believed that no progress could be made in any policy area without the latters' necessary commitment and direct involvement. However, in reality, it is the Council of Ministers together with the European Parliament that take the most important decisions about enlargement. Not all the people dealing with enlargement issues, least of all those politicians and individuals who defend parallel national, sectorial and social group interests within the EU, are equally committed to the cause of spreading European integration eastwards. The reasons for this attitude are many, but they are basically rooted in the well-calculated reluctance of the individual member states to release control over certain EU policy areas, over which they have a vested interest to maintain control. This reluctance is also partly the result of the substantial pressure exerted by different national and supra-national interest groups and social movements on the Union's institutions during the enlargement negotiations.

Tracking Down the EU Enlargement Policies Eastwards

This chapter attempts to examine the record and make sense out of the sometimes controversial developments in the sphere of the European enlargement policies eastwards. If one assumes that the Eastern Enlargement project is driven by two major sets of actors, the EU and its member states on the one hand and the applicant states on the other, then some important points of mutual interdependence appear in a number of policy areas.

Primarily, it is asserted that, after the downfall of communism and the resumption of EU-Eastern European relations, the historical memories and emerging contacts between the Western states and their Eastern European counterparts have influenced the EU to relate towards some applicant countries more favourably than others on the basis of certain 'initial conditions'. With the passage of time and the increase in the number of applicant states, however, new challenges have emerged both for the EU and Eastern European countries. These came as a result not only of a strong desire on the part of some former communist countries to be perceived once again as European in cultural and political terms and to join the group of socially prosperous Western European states, but also because of the abrupt dissolution of the former Soviet Union and the Federal Republic of Yugoslavia and the violent inter-ethnic conflicts that were associated with this. The initial response of the EU towards this type of crisis, which happened to take place in its immediate environment, was sluggish and misleading both for the conflicting parties and for the members of the international community involved in the resolution of those regional problems. Nevertheless, until the mid-

1990s, the EU's enlargement initiatives were developing reasonably well in other former Communist-Bloc countries and the EU was also playing a relatively major social and economic role in the region. It was both the biggest capital and know-how investor in Eastern Europe and, following the collapse of the CMEA, it was the principal market for the industrial goods and other kinds of produce from those states. Hence, the EU seized the historical opportunity to assert its political role at three levels by using enlargement as the most appropriate policy instrument: (1) domestically, by promoting to most members of Western societies the vision of a 'united' European continent after centuries of authoritarian systems dominating some part of its territory (it might be argued, that the re-unification of Germany was presented as the first important act contributing to the realization of this ideal at the national level); (2), by providing its near-abroad countries, and East-Central Europe in particular, with the opportunity to join the EU one day (this meant that the former had to open up their markets almost overnight and start adopting the *acquis communautaire* as the main legal and administrative basis for the organization of their respective states); and (3) internationally, by relying on the reality that enlargement will inevitably affect the strategic interests of some of its neighbors further East and South as well as those of its Trans-Atlantic partners (this vision is given added salience by the EU's intention to extend its borders towards new social and political milieus, and an intriguing parallel could be drawn here between the competing and sometimes complementary policies of NATO and the EU to enlarge eastwards).

Of course, not everything has gone smoothly for the EU and its member states especially in the latter respect. Nevertheless, the European institutions have gradually tried to streamline the normative provisions of the Union as regards enlargement and to transform their policies towards the Eastern European and other candidate states into a far better structured and more predictable process. The various EU initiatives in Eastern Europe have been conditioned by two major factors: the desire of the EU to enlarge itself eastwards and the strong impact of domestic actors. The latter refers not only to the member states but also to a large number of societal and other pressure groups, whose behavior has been conditioned by their perception of the above process more as an opportunity than a danger to the already established economic and political *status quo* in Europe.

Before beginning an analysis of the events that have shaped EU policies on eastward enlargement and before applying any normative conceptualization, two obvious but necessary assumptions must be made. The *first* is that the EU preserves a dominant role and has important leverage *vis-à-vis* the Eastern European applicant states in most fields of European integration. *Secondly*, the EU, under its current institutionalized practice of allocation of tasks and responsibilities between the Union and its member states, cannot be conceived as having a single decision-making center in dealing with the problems of Eastern Enlargement.

As far as the first statement is concerned, almost a decade after the crumbling of the authoritarian regimes in Eastern Europe, it is quite certain that the EU has played and continues to play a key role by providing a model and setting up the conditions for membership of the new applicant states from the region (Krenzler, 1997; Grabbe and Hughes, 1997). The Union has also extended various forms of assistance to those countries during their painful transition towards modern political democracy and a liberal-market economy. From the perspective of the Eastern Europeans, the state of their bilateral relations with the Union seems somewhat different but nevertheless the overall perception remains that the EU and its member states have been *the* leading actors during this period of time.

Many reasons have been cited in relation to the growing export of institutions to Eastern European candidate states and the conditionality imposed on them (Grabbe, 1999). One possible explanation focuses on the behavior of the various elites in Eastern Europe, who have happened to be mostly policy-takers in their multiple interactions with EU actors. The initial phase of the implementation of the Eastern Enlargement policies has demonstrated that in their integration endeavours Eastern European leaders have been led by a mixture of practical considerations and a dose of political idealism. These motivations have ranged from economic and political ones to security to national-identity ones and have acted as incentives for them to perform certain functions and respond to particular EU policies proposed by different Western experts (Balász, 1997). One could even speculate that a number of policies have been directly aimed at solving broader systemic problems of those elites' respective states: i.e., completing the modernization of their economies after decades of socialist inefficiency, rendering the political changes in their countries irreversible, building democratic regimes, and asserting their nations' European identity after a prolonged period of foreign communist rule.

The second assumption, relating to the absence of a single EU decision-making centre able to deal with enlargement, has so far been more difficult to prove empirically, because of the 'obscure nature' of the decision-making process in the EU (Zielonka, 1998). This has been especially true of those foreign policy decisions, in which the competing interests of the individual member states have come at odds both with each other and with those of the Union (Sbragia, 1992; Scharpf, 1996). Whether a given issue relating to EU foreign policy in Eastern Europe and enlargement in particular obtains the consensus of the various member states, or is rejected outright, depends on the issue at stake and, as a result, it might obtain the approval of the relevant decision-making bodies and institutions. For example, there have been several critical situations in the European close international environment, like those in Bosnia and Herzegovina and in Kosovo, where these problems could no longer remain solely the competence of the EU as a supranational organisation. They have instead required the collective effort of the majority of EU member states and of the international community too. A significantly higher level of diplomatic, political, financial and even military support from a larger number of European countries, and even from international bodies and organisations external to the EU, has been necessary for resolving these types of conflict. Eastern Enlargement is no exception to the above trend, simply because the majority of problems associated with enlargement are mainly perceived as foreign policy and not partly internal to the EU ones. Although they have not evoked so strong emotions on the part of Western societies and political class as the military conflicts in former Yugoslavia, issues of immigration, reform of the common agricultural policy (CAP), and the free movement of labour between Eastern and Western countries have provoked acrimonious comments and strong debate in European media and among national politicians.

Path Dependence and the Eastern Enlargement

An examination of the EU foreign activities, and a detailed analysis of the factors which have influenced the decisions of the Union and its member states to integrate a large number of countries from Eastern Europe, may create the impression that the present enlargement consists of a difficult to predict and, at times, random process. Solutions to different types of problems and criteria for enlargement have not been identical under the same circumstances and at various points of time. Both the EU and the Eastern European candidate states have increasingly been learning about each other's characteristic features and behavior, and their activities have mostly been *anticipatory* of the expectations and needs of the other side. Consequently, the spread of European integration to the eastern part of the continent should not be depicted as a static, pre-determined process, but rather as a dynamic, non-linear one. Using a similar line of reasoning, W. Brian Arthur, the 'father' of the 'positive feedback method' in economics, has examined uncertain situations of this type in the life of different complex social entities and organizations. He asserts that:

> [S]ometimes one solution would emerge, sometimes (under identical conditions) another. It would be impossible to know in advance which of the multiple solutions would emerge in any given run, but it would be possible to record the particular set of random events leading to each solution and to study the probability that a particular solution will emerge under a certain set of initial conditions (Brian Arthur, 1990, pp. 96-97).

It would not be too far-fetched to conclude that, during past decade, the Enlargement policies of the EU in Eastern Europe have followed such a 'winding path'. It would therefore be useful to trace back the sequence of random events which have prompted one of the sides in the process (be it the EU or the Eastern European states) to choose a given policy and initiate it. Such a policy decision could also have a direct impact on the other side if it decides to follow track. It might be equally important to determine the set of factors which may have induced a particular party to abandon the previously-established conditions of leading the enlargement game and look for a new equilibrium under a different set of rules. This might in fact present a case of what has been named a 'path dependence' method of analysing large-scale social events.

The notion of path dependence looks for the existence of a few key determinants, such as the presence or absence of *initial conditions* and *points of equilibrium*, while the participants in such a process try to secure competitive advantages for themselves. In social science literature, path dependence is also used to support several important assumptions: (a) the timing and sequence of the process matter; (b) considerable consequences may result from relatively small and contingent events; and (c) a wide range of social outcomes is often possible, however insignificant a factor may initially appear to be. In political science, Paul Pierson is probably the one who has contributed the most to clarifying the theoretical meaning of this concept and the one who has begun studying it in relation to European integration (Pierson, 1996, 1997). Unfortunately, the practical understanding of the events characterizing the current EU enlargement eastwards is still rather poor and its normative conceptualization – mostly atheoretical. Enlargement and its related policies, however, seem to bear features similar to the ones outlined above and hence this method opens new avenues for researching different aspects of regional integration.

If there is still agreement about the validity of the two assumptions presented at the beginning of the previous section (i.e. that the EU has an important leverage over the Eastern European candidate states in most policy areas of European integration, and that the Union does not have a single decision-making center to deal with its Eastern Enlargement), then it becomes somewhat easier to determine the general trajectory of the EU Eastern Enlargement process. This is accomplished by solving the much simpler problem of finding a set of possible cases, in which the EU is perceived as the *dominant* actor *vis-à-vis* Eastern European applicants, but which also plays the role of an *unpredictable* actor because of the 'skewed' nature of the decision-making process within the Union and among its member states. The next important step of this analytical exercise would be to determine the type of political, economic, cultural and historical factors or even random events that have brought about instability to the relations between the EU and the Eastern European countries which had already been established under the influence of initial conditions. Those could include social and political factors, which may have induced one of the sides to withdraw partially or completely from the enlargement project.

Finally, it would be interesting to try to falsify our initial hypothesis concerning the Eastern Enlargement process by noting that, in the case of the EU as a supranational organization of states, it has *the* major center(s) of European integration situated on its territory. This could either be the European capital, Brussels, or any of the other capitals and big cities in the rest of the EU. In this way, the EU might be in a position to modify the rules of the game and enjoy the advantages of its favourable geo-political position. It might even be possible for it to postpone the effects of some of the policies that had previously been agreed upon between itself and the associate countries of Eastern Europe until a more suitable period of time arrives. In the event of such an occurrence, it would be interesting to analyze the reaction of the Eastern European states, namely, whether they have any substantial powers to modify or influence any of the decisions already taken by the Union.

Temporal Dimensions of the Accession Process

The Point of Departure

Determining the point of departure is an important act in the whole method of conceptualizing Eastern Enlargement of the EU as a non-linear and randomly-developing process. It fixes the periods 'before' and 'after' a certain initial moment and, parallel to this, permits one to concentrate on the most important information from the beginning phase of such a process. This phase is characterized either by a breakthrough or gradual evolution, and it is presumed that certain events might potentially be repeated in subsequent periods of time.

It is very complex to determine precisely what consists of a *point of departure* for the Eastern Enlargement process. Is it the moment of the collapse of state socialism in the different countries of the region? Is it the decision of the EU member states to conclude a new generation of Europe Agreements with the applicant countries? Is it the outcome of the 1994 European Council at Essen after which a clearer perspective was offered to a number of Eastern European states to become members of the EU? Or is it the proposal of the Commission from June 1997 to name in an official document of its own (*Agenda 2000*) the countries that can begin pre-accession negotiations for joining the Union? The problem here is to provide a specific date after which the policies of the EU regarding its enlargement eastwards were put firmly on track and became virtually irreversible. It is, in other words, a moment when the EU and its member states and the Eastern European countries establish contractual relations and from which it is very difficult for one of the parties to retreat from leading negotiations for enlargement.

Undoubtedly, one of the most crucial things since the establishment of bilateral relations between the EU and the Eastern European candidate states has been the disclosure of the criteria for a future enlargement of the Union by the Copenhagen European Council (21-22 June 1993). The essential requirements for membership laid down in the so-called 'Copenhagen Criteria' represent the main legal framework and, even, some might say, an initial version of a 'written constitution' of the European enlargement process. They have been evoked on various occasions since being made explicit and have also been used as the most important argument in the hands of the EU official representatives to allow or to deny the beginning of accession negotiations with a given country. Most recently, as was the case with the renewed Turkish application for joining the Union, the overall political and economic situation of the country was scrutinized to ascertain whether it conformed with the 'Copenhagen Criteria'. These criteria have served as the main basis for evaluation of individual applicant states from Eastern Europe in the annual Progress Reports produced by the Commission. Furthermore, during the last couple of years, the 'Copenhagen Criteria' have been used increasingly as a set of relevant provisos invented by the EU for comparison both among the new associate countries and between the EU as a regional initiative and other countries and regions in the world where the model of European integration has been analyzed and occasionally replicated.

Ultimately, if there is a normative consensus about the fact that in the case of Eastern Enlargement of the EU the spelling out of the 'Copenhagen Criteria' presents a *point of departure* for this process indeed, then, one might be able to describe the factors and establish analytically the record of the EU enlargement policies in Eastern Europe during the period between the collapse of communism in the region (1989-91) and the recent war in Kosovo (1998-99). This historical period consists of ten years and the introduction of the 'Copenhagen Criteria' in June 1993 stands out as an approximate mid-point of this time span.

The Point of Arrival

The point of arrival should ideally indicate the moment at which the negotiations for membership are finalized and the enlargement of the Union is sanctioned by the European Council and the European Parliament as well as by the national governments and parliaments of the member states. The Eastern Enlargement negotiations have shown that the EU officials, unlike some Western politicians defending concrete national interests, have been extremely reluctant to fix precise deadlines for admitting a particular country or group of countries so far. The temporal dimension of the Enlargement process has thus remained largely unspecified and this has become one of the main reasons why Eastern Enlargement has not been able to transform itself from a mere 'project' of the European elites into a reality, which benefits the majority of people living on both sides of the former Cold-war divide. One can even speculate that until the first Eastern European countries enter the EU, Eastern Enlargement might represent anything one would like it to be, i.e., a political concept, historical ideal or social reality, but still *not* a hard fact that would confirm the completion of an important stage of the European integration process. And this means that the *point of arrival* of the EU eastward enlargement has not been reached yet.

Evidence of Path Dependence Before and During Enlargement

The Importance of 'Initial Conditions' (1989-93)

In the theory of multiple-equilibria it is stated that the initial conditions play a central role. A correct understanding of these conditions may provide a prime explanation for the occurrence and sequence of certain events after the beginning of the process. In the case of the EU-Eastern European relations before the summer of 1993, such events could have been of a historical, economic, political, social, ethno-cultural or other nature. It is very difficult to establish which set of factors has contributed most to decision-making as regards enlargement in the EU and its Eastern European partners after the adoption of the 'Copenhagen Criteria'. Bearing in mind that in the first couple of years after the collapse of the communist system, some of the most urgent priorities of the political elites in Eastern Europe were connected with abolishing the former authoritarian regime structures, with completing successful transitions to democracy and with rebuilding their respective

Table 11.1 Initial conditions in Eastern Europe (1989-1993)

	Roman-Catholic/ Protestant Region	Previous Experience with Democracy	Previously Organised anti-Communist Resistance	Political Reforms before 1989-91	Economic Reforms before 1989-91	Anti-Communist Political Opposition Movement	Visible Opposition Leaders During Former Regime	Negotiated Transition (Round-Table Talks)	Free and Fair Elections	Non-Communist Come to Power After First Elections
Bulgaria	-	-	-	-	-	-	+	+	+	-
Czech Republic	+	+	+	-	-	+	+	+	+	+
Estonia	+	+	-	-	-	-	+	-	+	+
Hungary	+	-	+	+	+	+	+	+	+	+
Latvia	+	+	-	-	-	-	+	-	+	+
Lithuania	+	+	-	-	-	-	+	-	+	+
Poland	+	-	+	+	-	+	+	+	+	+
Romania	-	-	-	-	-	-	-	-	+	-
Slovakia	+	-	-	-	-	+	+	+	+	+
Slovenia	+	-	-	-	+	-	+	-	+	+

Results:

Hungary - 9/10   Group I
Czech Republic - 8/10
Poland - 8/10
Slovakia - 6/10   Group II
Estonia - 5/10
Latvia - 5/10
Lithuania - 5/10
Slovenia - 5/10   Group III
Bulgaria - 3/10
Romania - 1/10

economies. The EU and its member states kept track of these changes and became almost immediately and decisively involved in all of these domains of activity. Certainly, the precise list of priorities of the West European decision-makers in Eastern Europe cannot be re-established with one-hundred percent confidence, but the official discourse and concrete actions of these people have prompted the majority of researchers to look at the combination of broadly-defined legacies shown in Table 11.1 as the principal one (Stark and Bruszt, 1998; Ekiert, 1999).

Table 11.1 presents a set of ten factors, described as initial conditions, which may provide a possible explanation for the attitude of the major EU actors towards the Eastern European applicant states according to the presence or absence of some of these factors in a given country or group of countries. Summing these factor variables makes the overall ranking of the Eastern European states. The variables are intended to coincide with the above-mentioned three basic areas of EU intervention in Eastern Europe, namely, abolishing the remnants of the communist ideology and conducting political and economic transformation. The results from this survey clearly demonstrate that Catholic/Protestant countries, countries with some previous experience with democratisation, countries which had begun earlier their political and economic reforms and countries in which people who had not been officially connected with the former communist/socialist regime came into power after elections in the period 1989-91 have been viewed much more favourably by both the EU decision-makers and Western public opinion as a whole. The Eastern European countries are tentatively divided into three groups according to their level of overall performance, as indicated by the aggregate sum of positive answers obtained in each of the above ten categories. The polities from group I and some from group II have been those which have received the largest share of EU and member states' attention and assistance with regard to enlargement initiatives and different bilateral and multilateral types of contacts. The states from group III and some from II have been mostly disregarded in one or more of these respects and, as a consequence, have been considered unlikely candidates for early membership together with other Eastern European potential applicants.

As a rival hypothesis, it could also be proposed that some regions and groups of countries amass historical chance simply because of a more favourable geographical position. The holding of close and special relations with a neighboring country, which may happen to be a key player in the EU 'bargaining game', may give somebody the reason to believe that certain countries are in a better situation to integrate themselves in the EU than others which cannot enjoy such a proximity to the European core where some of the most important decisions about the future of the continent are being taken. This statement may well hold true for a number of cases, but it cannot explain everything and enter deep enough into all the aspects of the Eastern Enlargement policies of the EU. A geographical closeness to the main centers of European integration and, conversely, a greater distance from the centers of the previous authoritarian system, has benefited one group of countries during the initial period of transition from communism. It has helped those countries that had formerly been part of major Western and Central European empires to sustain more easily their claim of a historically based European identity. But proximity has also meant unresolved territorial problems

Table 11.2   EU reaction to Eastern European transformation and European integration efforts (1989-1999)

	Trade and Cooperation Agreement Signed	Europe Agreement Signed	Europe Agreement Comes into Force	Extension of the PHARE Program to the Partner Countries	Visa-Free Travel to at least one EU/EFTA Member State	EU Member States' Financial Assistance* (Billion ECU)	EU Overall Assistance* (Billion ECU)	G-24 Grants* (Billion ECU)	Inflow of FDIs** (US$ Million)	Share of EU Imports from Eastern Europe***
Bulgaria	May 1990	March 1993	Feb. 1995	1990	No	0.7	1.8	2.6	157	4.2
Czech Republic	May 1990 †	Dec. 1991 † (Oct. 1993)	Feb. 1995	1990 † (1993)	1991	3.0	4.15	5.2	2,735	18.8
Estonia	May 1992	June 1995	Feb. 1998	1992	1995	0.3	0.5	0.7	248	1.0
Hungary	Sept. 1988	Dec. 1991	Feb. 1994	1989	1991	4.2	6.6	8.7	5,291	15.6
Latvia	May 1992	June 1995	Feb. 1998	1992	1991	0.3	0.5	0.7	34	2.1
Lithuania	May 1992	June 1995	Feb. 1998	1992	1991	0.4	0.7	0.9	22	2.1
Poland	Sept. 1989	Dec. 1991	Feb. 1994	1989	1991	13.7	16.1	23.3	2,784	26.6
Romania	Oct. 1990	Feb. 1993	Feb. 1995	1991	No	2.6	4.3	5.2	211	7.8
Slovakia	May 1990 †	Dec. 1991† (Oct. 1993)	Feb. 1995	1990 † (1993)	1991	2.1	2.75	3.8	1,531	6.3
Slovenia	April 1993	June 1996	Feb. 1999	1992	Before 1989	0.4	0.6	0.7	223	9.1

*   *Source*: G-24 Scoreboard of Assistance Commitments to the CEEC 1990-95, 1996.
**   *Source*: UN World Investment Report, 1994. Period: 1989-93.
*** *Source*: Eurostat, 1995, 1996.
†   Trade and co-operation agreement, Europe Agreement and PHARE program have been signed with the then-existing Czechoslovakia.

with one's neighbours and increased criticism in case of non-fulfilment of the previously highly set expectations for a speedy enlargement. Even more importantly, the conceptual method of explaining facts solely in terms of one's geographical position overlooks the influence of individual actors. For example, dissidents and immigrants from the East, as well as a large number of political actors in the West, have contributed significantly both by hastening the collapse of communist rule and by helping establish an entire set of official and unofficial conacts between the EU and the governments of Eastern Europe and thereby assisting the enlargement process and European integration.

The EU Responses in Eastern Europe (1989-2000)

Table 11.2 (above) lays down some basic facts from the field of politics, economics and finance, as well as the responses that the EU and its member states have given to the Eastern European countries in view of the latters' aspiration to join the EU and become further integrated into its structures.

When one analyses the above data, two major trends can be discerned in connection with the reaction of the major West European actors to the attempts of the Eastern European countries to become part of a more general process of integration. The *first* refers to the institutionalized reaction of the EU as a supranational regional organization, while the *second* relates to the answers provided by the individual member states of the Union to the same type of problem.

Regarding the signing of Trade and Co-operation Agreements between the EU and the former Communist Bloc countries, this process was initiated relatively early and was completed in April 1993 with the adherence of Slovenia to it. Meanwhile, the Europe Agreements, which were created with a view to integrating Eastern European candidate states, began to be implemented by the Commission on schedule. However, the EU member states have been relatively slow and inefficient concerning their prompt sanctioning and, as a consequence, the official ratification of the Europe Agreements with Slovenia and the three Baltic States has been considerably delayed. Although they have entered into force in February 1998, still, in late 1999, the Europe Agreements with the three Baltic States have not been ratified by the parliaments of all the EU member states yet.

As a whole, the official institutions and administrators within the EU have treated the Eastern European applicants on an equal footing. After Poland and Hungary, the PHARE program was quickly extended to the other Eastern European states, while the financial assistance provided by the EU through its various funds has benefited the associate countries in accordance with the approximate size of their population and level of economic development. As regards the financial help given to the Eastern Europeans by the EU member states' governments directly or through alternative channels, such as the G-24, it becomes clear that the reaction here was less unbiased and selfless towards each and every country of the region. Conversely, certain preferences have been evident in those actors' relation with particular East-Central European and Baltic states. Concerning the introduction of laws allowing the free movement of persons in the territory of EU/EFTA member states, only the very recent inclusion of Bulgaria and Romania (as of April 2001 and January 2002, respectively) in the group of countries benefiting from such a privilege suggests that the criteria from Table 11.1, which divide Eastern European countries according to their historical, social and cultural and political background, has not yet been completely overcome either at the level of the EU institutions or at the level of the member states.

The flow of foreign direct investments (FDIs) towards and the import of goods from the Eastern European countries into the Union present a more balanced picture, especially when one takes into consideration the fact that both of these processes require the active participation and creation of the necessary political, economic and legal conditions by the authorities of those former communist states internally. Nevertheless, the role of the EU and the direct support of individual member states on behalf of their Eastern European partners should not be underestimated: all the above-mentioned factors tend to contribute to a generally more stable social and political environment for a few selected Eastern European countries. They also provide foreign investors with some important indications of how the economies of those countries would develop in the future or whether the EU would 'open' itself earlier towards some them in order to accelerate their full integration in the European institutions and structures.

Major 'External Shocks' Influencing the EU Eastern Enlargement

Looking back at the history of EU-Eastern European relations over the last ten years, one can see that there are *two* major international political events which have substantially changed the attitude and behavior of EU actors towards the region and launched the current enlargement eastwards. The *first* is the downfall of communism (1988-89 in Central and Eastern Europe, and 1990-91 in the former Soviet Union and the Federal Republic of Yugoslavia). The *second* is the recent war in Kosovo (1998-99). While the former represents a beginning of EU-Eastern European bilateral relations, the latter is a major military and humanitarian crisis, in which a number of EU member states as well as almost all of the associate states from Eastern Europe have been directly involved – some as NATO members, others as candidate-members. During no other period, including the conflict in Bosnia, have similar situations as the collapse of communism and the Kosovo crisis been perceived as truly European and have become the preoccupation of both Western and Eastern European governments to the extent that they would be ready to resolve them in common and intervene with military force. On these two occasions, a consensus was reached both at all-Union level and at the member state level that it was necessary to act and provide an adequate response to the challenges that arose.

The objectives of the policies proposed on each occasion coincided with and served the interests of both the EU and those of the majority of its member states. For the applicant countries, the downfall of communism and the pacification of South Eastern Europe have been of critical importance. Those were issues of strategic importance for the governments of the region and Eastern European public opinion was generally in favour of the co-operation with and intervention of

Western European countries and EU in particular in their countries' internal affairs. Another important factor, which is certainly related to the current discussion of enlargement, is that the EU elite and that of its member states have ultimately figured out that enlargement itself or, to an extent, even the promise of enlargement can serve as important foreign policy instruments. Thus, member states are able to force the prospective applicant countries to resolve their internal and regional problems peacefully and in a less costly way for the EU.

Conclusion

In this chapter, it is demonstrated that the policies connected with the Eastern Enlargement project have unraveled rather unevenly and not always in unison with the integration endeavours of the majority of European states. Although the reasons for this are multiple, certain factors can be identified and clustered together in two relatively concentrated periods of time: during the early and late 1990s. The first period spans the moment of the collapse of communist rule in Eastern Europe (1989-91) with the adoption of the so-called 'Copenhagen Criteria' (1993), while the second – the Kosovo conflict (1998-99) with the developments of nowadays.

Until the adoption of the 'Copenhagen Criteria' (June 1993) as the main political document regulating the admission of and monitoring the progress accomplished by the Eastern European candidates towards joining the EU, a limited set of 'initial conditions' influenced the EU, and especially EU member states, to establish closer relations with and assist certain Eastern European countries more than others. Gradually, the EU official institutions and the Commission in particular have responded to most of the individual and collective problems of the applicant states with greater professionalism and in a more balanced manner from a local and regional point of view. Still, there remain policy areas, which are traditionally at the discretion of the national authorities of the fifteen member states, including the free movement of persons and labor force as well as the extension of various forms of financial assistance to neighbouring countries. These policy fields have been characteristic of the growing structural and political inequalities between the various regions, sub-regions and states not only within the EU itself, but also among the Eastern European applicants.

Finally, it is hypothesized that European integration and enlargement have been particularly strongly influenced by two important exogenous factors (or 'shocks'): the end of communist rule in Eastern Europe and the recent Kosovo crisis. These landmark events managed to consolidate European public opinion towards being in favour of the Western governments' more decisive involvement in the problems of Eastern Europe and they gave a strong boost to the ongoing integration process on the continent as well. Furthermore, whilst the collapse of communism created an opportunity for the start of the Eastern Enlargement process as such, the war in the former Yugoslavia probably demonstrated some of the shortcomings of the initial plan (or absence of plan) of the EU to deal with the emerging problems linked with enlargement in the post-authoritarian environment of Eastern Europe. Of course, comparable events of major international political and social significance may not completely be ruled out from happening in the future, but present experience with enlargement policies in the region has shown that (a) the more the EU and the Eastern European countries have learned about each other, (b) the more 'institutionalized' that process has become, and (c) the more the European integration has advanced qualitatively and quantitatively among the EU member states, the smaller the probability that such an important project as the eastward enlargement of the EU would fail.

References

Avery, Graham and Cameron, Fraser (1998), *The Enlargement of the European Union*, Sheffield Academic Press, Sheffield.

Balász, Peter (1997), 'The EU's Collective Regional Approach to its Eastern Enlargement: Consequences and Risks', *CORE Working Papers*, No. 1, Copenhagen Research Project on European Integration, Copenhagen, pp. 2-9.

Baldwin, Richard (1994), *Towards an Integrated Europe*, CEPR, London, pp. 161-179.

Bempt van den, Paul and Theelen, Greet (1996), *From European Agreements to Accession. The Integration of the Central and Eastern European Countries into the European Union*, European Interuniversity Press, Brussels.

Brian Arthur, William (1990) 'Positive Feedbacks in the Economy', *Scientific American*, No. 262, February, pp. 96-97.

Brian Arthur, William (1994), *Increasing Returns and Path Dependence in the Economy*, University of Michigan Press, Ann Arbor.

Ekiert, Grzegorz (1999), 'Do Legacies Matter? Patterns of Postcommunist Transitions in Eastern Europe', *Occasional Paper*, No. 53, Woodrow Wilson Center, East European Studies Program, pp. 11-24.

EU Commission (1997), *Agenda 2000*, 15 July, Supplement to the Bulletin of the European Union 5/97.

EU Commission (1999), 'Regular Report from the Commission on Progress towards Accession by each of the Candidate Countries', October 13, 1999, IP/99/751.

EU Commission (2000), '*Agenda 2000*: For a stronger and wider Union', COM(97) 2000, 16 July 1997.

European Council (June 1993), Copenhagen 21-22 June, 1993, Conclusions of the Presidency, SN 180/93, p. 13.

The Financial Times (2000), September 6, 2000; 'EU's Challenge'.

Friis, Lykke and Murphy, Anna (1999), 'The European Union and Central and Eastern Europe: Governance and Boundaries', *Journal of European Public Policy*, Vol. 37(2), pp. 211-32.

Friis, Lykke and Murphy, Anna (2000), *The Enlargement of Europe: Theory, Practice and the Boundaries of Governance*, SAGE, London.

Goodstein, Eban (1995), 'The Economic Roots of Environmental Decline: Property Rights or Path Dependence?', *Journal of Economic Issues*, Vol. 29(4), December, pp. 1029-1043.

Grabbe, Heather (1999), 'A Partnership for Accession?: The Implications of EU Conditionality for the Central and East European Applicants', *EUI working papers of the Robert Schuman Center*, RSC 99/12, European University Institute, Florence.

Grabbe, Heather and Hughes, Kirsty (1997), *Eastward Enlargement of the European Union*, The Royal Institute of International Affairs, February, pp. 14-23.

Hyde-Price, Adrian (1996), *The International Politics of Eastern Europe*, Manchester University Press, Manchester, p. 203.

Krenzler, Horst-Guenter (1997), 'The EU and Central-East Europe: The Implication of Enlargement in Stages', *European University Institute policy paper*, RSC No. 97/2, p. 3.

Lungescu, Oana (2001), 'France Proposes Fast EU Enlargement', *BBC News*, November 20, 2001, Brussels.

Mayhew, Allan (1998), *Recreating Europe: The European Union's Policy towards Central and Eastern Europe*, Cambridge University Press, Cambridge.

North, Douglass (1990), *Institutions, Institutional Change and Economic Performance*, Cambridge University Press, Cambridge.

Pierson, Paul (1996), 'The Path to European Integration: A Historical Institutionalist Analysis', *Comparative Political Studies*, No. 29, April, pp. 123-63.

Pierson, Paul (1997), 'Increasing Returns, Path Dependence and the Study of Politics', Robert Schuman Center for Advanced Studies, Florence, *IUE/RSC working paper*, No. 97/44.

Preston, Christopher (1997), *Enlargement and Integration in the European Union*, Routledge Publishers, London, pp. 195-209.

Sbragia, Alberta M. (1992), *Euro-Politics: Institutions and Policymaking in the 'New' European Community*, The Brookings Institution Publication, Washington, D.C., pp. 1-22.

Scharpf, Fritz W. (1996), 'Democratic Policy in Europe', *European Law Journal*, Vol. 2(2), July 1996, pp. 136-155.

Schimmelfennig, Frank (1999), 'The Eastern Enlargement of the European Union. A Case for Sociological Institutionalism', in Lars-Erik Cederman (ed.), *Constructing Europe's Identity. Issues and Tradeoffs*, Lynne Rienner, Boulder, Colo., pp. 10-12.

Stark, David and Bruszt, Laszlo (1998), *Postsocialist Pathways: Transforming Politics and Property in East-Central Europe*, Cambridge University Press, Cambridge, pp. 1-48.

Wallace, Helen (1997), 'Pan-European Integration: A Real or Imagined Community?', *Government and Opposition*, Vol. 32(2), pp. 215-33.

Zielonka, Jan (1997), 'Paradoxes of European Foreign Policy. Policies Without Strategy: The EU Record in Eastern Europe', *European University Institute working paper*, RSC No. 97/72, p. 8.

Zielonka, Jan (1998), *Explaining the Euro-Paralysis: Why Europe is Unable to Act in International Politics*, Macmillan, Basingstoke, pp. 55-125.

PART VI
Concluding Comments

Chapter 12

The Vertical and Horizontal Dimensions of Regional Integration: A Concluding Note

Walter Mattli

Regional integration has two dimensions: the first I call the vertical dimension of regional institutional arrangements; it distinguishes primarily between two models, the intergovernmental institutional model and the supranational institutional model of regional integration. The second is the horizontal dimension of regional institutional arrangements; it describes the process of delegation of policy tasks from regional intergovernmental organizations to private-sector agencies to achieve faster and deeper economic integration. Most studies collected in this volume focus on the vertical dimension; few discuss the growing importance and promise of the horizontal dimension of regional integration. The purpose of this note is to highlight the key features of the horizontal dimension and illustrate its operation in practice.

The Vertical and Horizontal Dimensions of Regional Integration

The vertical dimension captures the extent to which policy authority and tasks have migrated from the national level to the regional or global levels. At one end of this continuum is the intergovernmental institutional model which holds that integration can best be understood as a series of bargains among the heads of governments of the leading states in a region. These political leaders, jealous of their national sovereignty, carefully circumscribe any sacrifice of sovereignty that may become necessary in order to attain common goals. Big states exercise a de facto veto over fundamental changes in the rules of integration. As a result, bargaining tends to converge towards the lowest common denominator of large state interests (Moravcsik, 1991). Further, member states may agree to establish common institutions to assist them build a single market by mitigating the incomplete contracting problem, monitoring compliance with treaty obligations, and sanctioning defections; institutions may also help to create a shared belief system about cooperation in the context of differential and conflicting sets of

273

individual beliefs that would otherwise inhibit the decentralized implementation of integration treaties (Garrett, 1992). This considerable range of tasks not-withstanding, common institutions in the intergovernmental model serve primarily a technical role, that is, they faithfully implement the collective internal market preferences of the member states.

At the other extreme is the supranational institutional model which describes a situation whereby political actors in several distinct national settings are persuaded to shift their loyalties, expectations, and political activities towards a new and larger center, whose institutions possess or demand jurisdiction over the pre-existing states. The primary players in the integration process are above and below the nation-state. Actors below the state include economic interest groups and political parties. Above the state are supranational regional institutions. These supranational institutions promote integration, foster the development of interest groups, cultivate close ties with them and with fellow-technocrats in the national civil services. The power of these supranational institutions stems from the fact that the 'leash' between them (the agents) and the member states (the principals) is rather long. Several factors may account for the relative autonomy of supranational agents, including delegated policy-making discretion, differences in policy preferences among member states that supranational agents may be able to exploit, decision-making rules among governments that render it difficult or costly to overturn supranational decisions, dismiss supranational agents, or change the charter of supranational institutions (Haas, 1958; Burley and Mattli, 1993; Mattli and Slaughter, 1995, 1998; Pollack, 1997).

Students of regional integration have debated at great length the relative merits of competing models of the vertical dimension of integration. The horizontal dimension, however, has received little attention. It is concerned with tracing empirically and analytically the process of delegation of policy tasks from regional intergovernmental organizations to transnational private-sector agencies in order to accelerate the process of economic integration.

Frequently, the most successful regional institutional arrangements are those that blend private and public elements of governance; they partake of the virtues of both governance approaches while minimizing their defects. The key advantages of private agents are superior information, technical expertise, and adaptive flexibility. Public oversight and intervention, on the other hand, can help to ensure openness, transparency, and legitimacy of policy-making (Snidal and Abbott, 2001; Mattli, 2003). For example, politicians may chose to move from a strategy of detailed harmonization of economic policies through intergovernmental negotiations to a speedier and more flexible strategy that divides policy work between public and private agents. Governments could focus, for example, on specifying the 'essential requirements' that products must meet in terms of health, safety, environmental and consumer protection, and leave the task of developing detailed technical specifications meeting the 'essential requirements' to private technical institutions.

Careful institutional design is as crucial here as it is in the context of the vertical dimension. Whether independence of private experts and public accountability can be made complementary and mutually reinforcing values depends to a large extent on the way in which the relationship between elected politicians and technical experts is structured. Democratic regimes must allow electorally accountable leaders to override the decisions of experts when such decisions have broad political and economic implications. However, the interference must be transparent; it must follow well-defined procedures and should entail high political costs if it is not objectively justified (Snidal and Abbott, 2001).

An Illustration of the Horizontal Dimension: The EU's 'New Approach' – Moving to Hybrid Regional Governance

Beginning in the 1960s, the EU attempted to achieve market integration by harmonizing national legislation. Governmental elites and supranational bureaucrats would spend years on end drafting highly detailed directives and regulations. In the early 1980s, the old harmonization approach had run its course; it had become excruciatingly slow and cumbersome with the increasing complexity of the subjects covered. Furthermore, with the quickening pace of technological change and the shortening of product cycles, the technical details in directives and regulations were often obsolete by the time the legal acts were finally promulgated. In the 1985 White Paper on the completion of the internal market, the Commission acknowledged that 'relying on a strategy based totally on harmonization...would take a long time to implement, would be inflexible and could stifle innovation.'[1]

In other words, the old approach had laid bare some of the procedural inadequacies and organizational limits of regional public governance, most notably the excruciatingly slow pace of adopting common standards and, in some cases, lack of technical expertise and financial resources to deal with ever more complex and demanding transnational regulatory issues. These institutional failures led to a much greater involvement of private-sector actors in regulatory matters, as illustrated in the EU's New Approach.

The cornerstone of the New Approach was the retreat of the Community legislature from the field of technical specification and the delegation of regulatory functions to private-sector bodies, namely European standardization organizations.[2] However, as explained below, this delegation does not mean that governments have capitulated to these private bodies; instead, governments have redefined their role; they have been (re-)asserting their authority by imposing upon private standardizers important organizational changes to comply with public interest safeguards.

---

[1] Commission of the European Communities, *Completing the Internal Market: White Paper from the Commission to the European Council*, COM (1985) 310 Final, p. 18.

[2] *New Approach to Technical Harmonization and Standards*, Council Resolution, OJ 1985 C 136.1. See also website www.newapproach.org.

Under the 'New Approach', EU legislation is limited to laying down in directives mandatory so-called 'essential requirements' in terms of health, safety, environmental and consumer protection. These directives cover entire sectors rather than single products. The elaboration of the technical specifications that satisfy the essential requirements is delegated primarily to the European Committee for Standardization (or *Comité Européen de Normalisation*, CEN) and the European Committee for Electrotechnical Standardization (or *Comité Européen de Normalisation Eléctronique*, CENELEC).[3] The national authorities are obliged to recognize that products manufactured according to the standards of these private organizations are presumed to conform to the essential requirements specified in directives (EU law); they must thus allow these products to circulate freely in the EU market. European standards, however, remain voluntary. Producers who come up with alternative technical solutions that meet the levels of safety or health specified in directives cannot be excluded from the market. However, these producers have the burden of proving that their standards do indeed reach the required safety and health levels.

The success of the 'New Approach' was no foregone conclusion; it depended on a complex set of conditions, most critically the 'interconnectivity' of the regional and national levels of standardization organizations. That is, for the 'New Approach' to work, the two institutional levels needed to be tightly linked and highly complementary.

In order to understand this interconnectedness of the regional and national levels, it is necessary to examine the organizational structure and the *modus operandi* of CEN and CENELEC.

CEN was established in 1961 as a non-profit regional association producing voluntary European standards in a broad range of areas.[4] CENELEC was set up in 1972 as an association that produces electro-technical and electronic engineering standards. Both CEN and CENELEC are partially funded by the Commission, and their members are the national standardization bodies in Europe.

The institutional structures of CEN and CENELEC are similar. Both have a general assembly composed of delegations from the national members, an administrative board that acts as the agent of the general assembly, a president that chairs the assembly and the administrative board, and a Secretary-General who runs the Central Secretariat which is responsible for the day-to-day management of

---

[3]   The Commission signed an agreement with CEN and CENELEC in 1984, recognizing them as 'European Standardization Bodies.' A third organization is the European Telecommunications Standards Institute (ETSI). It was established in 1988 to develop standards in telecommunications and related fields. ETSI is a non-profit organization that is funded entirely by the subscriptions of its 400 members which are firms and organizations with an interest in the creation of European telecommunication standards.

[4]   These areas include mechanical engineering, building and civil engineering, health technology, biology and biotechnology, quality certification and testing, environment, health and safety at the workplace, gas and other energies, transport and packaging, consumer goods, sports, leisure, food, materials (iron and steel), and chemistry.

the association, including the meetings of all Technical Committees, the circulation of all necessary documentation, the maintenance of up-to-date records of the standardization activities.

A Technical Board is responsible for monitoring, coordinating, and controlling the standards programs. It advises on all matters concerning the organization, working procedures, co-ordination and planning of standards work, monitors and controls the progress of standards work, examines proposals of new projects, creates and disbands Technical Committees, imposes or releases standstill obligations, and organizes technical liaison with intergovernmental organizations, international organizations and European trade, professional, technical and scientific organizations. It also decides, on the basis of national voting, on ratification of draft standards prepared by technical bodies.

The hard work is of course done in the Technical Committees (as well as Subcommittees and Working Groups). At the end of 2000, CEN had 274 active Technical Committees that had issued a total of 6,666 European standards and related documents, and were working on 8842 items. CENELEC had produced a total of 3633 standards. It is worth noting that in the mid-1980s, the total number of European standards was less than 100. In short, the growth of European standards has been staggering.

Does this imply that national standards developing organizations (SDOs) are becoming obsolete? The answer is 'no'. Paradoxically, the trend towards European standardization has not weakened national SDOs but magnified their importance. The national organizations, which for the most part are also private-sector associations – even though they receive state subsidies, constitute the veritable backbone of European standardization; they provide the resources, technical expertise, and main institutional infrastructure to support the production of regional standards.

For example, national SDOs select up to three national delegates to a given CEN technical committee. At the same time, they establish so-called 'mirror-committees' at the national level that are open to all domestic groups interested in a specific standardization item. The 'mirror-committees' then brief the national delegates, ensuring that all national interests affected by European standardization are taken into consideration. During the public enquiry stage, the 'mirror committees' debate the contents of draft standards and prepare comments that convey the national point of view. In the final stage of the process, the 'mirror committees' decide on how the national delegates should vote. After the formal approval of a European standard, national SDOs implement the standards as national standards, either by publication of identical texts or by endorsement; conflicting national standards must be withdrawn (Falke and Schepel, 2000, pp. 135-150; and De Vries, 1999).[5]

---

[5]   The national transposition of European standards is an obligation for CEN members; however, the application of these standards remains voluntary and thus depends on the acceptability of the standards to those who are expected to use them.

In short, national SDOs produce hundreds of national consensus positions each year, and select and instruct thousands of individuals who serve in delegations to promote the national views in the various committees. Further, because CEN itself, with its small secretariat in Brussels, has neither the facilities nor the staff to house committees and working groups, the national bodies house and manage regional technical committees and working groups. For example, if the secretary of a CEN Technical Committee is a German, then the committee will be housed in the German National Standards Institute (DIN). In other words, the actual work of European standardization is done in a very decentralized way, with national bodies keeping a close eye on regional committees; that is, they monitor all regional standardization activities and inform potentially interested parties in their countries of new regional initiatives and opportunities. Finally, national SDOs are the main financial supporters of CEN and CENELEC.[6]

We can thus conclude that, somewhat paradoxically, the trend toward regional standardization in support of the 'New Approach' has in no way weakened national standardization bodies, let alone rendered them obsolete. The progressive deepening of European integration is to some extent premised on the existence of strong, coherent, and centralized national organizations that are capable of aggregating domestic preferences and projecting them with a single voice on to the regional stage. In the area of standards, integration has not undermined national structures but had strengthened them to optimize the interconnectivity between the national and regional levels.

However, the 'New Approach' also leads to a second question: Is the authority of governments being undermined because of the delegation of regulatory power to private-sector standardizers?

In the early years of the 'New Approach', many observers questioned the legitimacy and even legality of the 'New Approach.' It was argued that private standards bodies, dominated by business interests, would be blind to broader social issues, and that the delegation of powers to these private actors would render legislative control over their decisions impossible (Joerges, Schepel, and Vos, 1999). Partly in response to these criticisms, the member-state governments of the EU have (re-)asserted their authority in the last ten years or so by strengthening their control over standardizers and by engineering subtle but critical changes in the procedures and structure of private European SDOs. For example, they have forced these SDOs to accept the participation of consumer organizations and other societal groups. The member states issued a declaration in April 1992, emphasizing that the involvement of 'social partners...at every stage of the standardization process and at every level of [European] Standardization Bod[ies]...– from Working Group to General Assembly – is a political precondition for the

---

[6]   CEN, for example, receives 46 percent of its budget from its Members (primarily national SDOs); the Commission contributes 41 percent; and sales of documents and specific contracts add anther 11 percent.

acceptability and further development of European standardization.'[7] At the end of the same year, yielding to political pressure, CEN introduced a new category of membership, so-called 'Associate Members,' to integrate into the CEN structure 'social partners' such as the European Association of Consumer Representation in Standardization (ANEC)[8] and the European Trade Union Technical Bureau for Health and Safety (TUTB).[9]

Further, the member states have been improving control over standardization by changing the structure of their financial support to European standardizers, gradually cutting back on general lump-sum subsidies and switching to project-based financing. They also have increased the practice of employing independent experts to monitor regional standardization and determine whether European standards satisfy the essential requirements (Joerges, Schepel, and Vos, 1999, p. 23; and Egan ,1998, p. 500).

Last but not least, the member states have adopted a series of EU directives that provide for continuous supervision of the implementation process of standards. For example, the Directive on General Product Safety[10] gives national administrations considerable discretion to impose restrictions on the free circulation of products that they find to be harmful to consumers notwithstanding conformity with European standards. Similarly, the Product Liability Directive[11] offers national courts leeway to determine whether a product meets 'legitimate consumer expectations' and whether standards reflect the latest scientific and technical knowledge.

In sum, 'European standardization [today]…does not operate in a legal vacuum but is in varying intensity embedded into legal frameworks and constantly fed and controlled through networks of non-governmental and governmental actors' (Joerges, Schepel, and Vos, 1999, pp. 49-50 and pp. 59-61). This fusion of private and public elements in a joint form of governance has conferred upon European standardization a high degree of legitimacy that it lacked in the 1980s.

How successful has European standardization been in promoting economic integration? For several sectors, it is too early to tell. 'New Approach' directives must first be adopted and European standardizers have then to produce supporting standards. This all takes time. Nevertheless, preliminary results do suggest that the new technique is overall doing much better than earlier approaches. This explains

---

[7]   OJ C 96 of 15 April 1992, 23.

[8]   ANEC stands for *Association de Normalisation Européenne pour les Consommateurs.*

[9]   TUTB was established in 1989 by the European Trade Union Confederation (ETUC) to monitor the drafting, transposition and application of European legislation regulating the working environment.

[10]   Directive 92/59/EEC, 1992 OJ L 228/24.

[11]   Directive 85/374/EEC, 1985 OJ L 210/29.

the eagerness of the Commission to apply it more broadly. Indeed, in 1995, the Commission issued a 'Communication on the Broader Use of Standardization in Community Policy,' announcing plans to extent the 'New Approach' to areas such as biotechnology, environmental policy, and telecommunications. More recently, it decided to begin applying the new technique in the areas of food safety, defense, and, services.[12]

The overall positive assessment, however, hides considerable variation across sectors in the effectiveness of the 'New Approach.' A detailed account of these differences is not possible here. Instead, I will summarize some of the evidence from interviews and two recent studies.[13]

The 'New Approach' seems to be working best in sectors in which the level of regional trade is already high, where there is a small number of dominant manufacturers, and where economies of scale make it advantageous for firms to cover the entire EU market.

Consider the example of electrical power tools. Before the adoption of the 'New Approach,' most electrical products and especially tools deemed to represent a health and safety threat were governed by a multitude of national regulations, guidelines, and certification procedures. Many of these national rules have now been superseded by three 'New Approach' directives and corresponding European standards.[14] This change was possible, in part, due to the strong support of industry in Europe which is dominated by a very small number of global companies. Significantly, the number of manufacturers of electrical power tools has shrunk considerably in the last ten years as the larger companies, such as Bosch of Germany and Black & Decker of the US, bought smaller firms and consolidated their positions as European and global leaders. Bosch and Black & Decker have an EU market share of 35 percent and 20 percent respectively, followed by AEG with 7 percent and Metabo with 6 percent. These few big players share similar views about the importance of a single market and have collaborated in the production of European standards.

Other areas that are considered success stories under the 'New Approach' for similar reasons include air reservoirs, pacemakers, and gas cookers.

In sectors like cement, however, where again there are few suppliers but the economies of scale can be achieved within national markets, and where other

---

[12] 'New Areas of Standardization,' *CEN Newsletter* 9 (December 2000), pp. 1-3.

[13] The interviews were conducted at the Commission of the EU, the European Association for the Coordination of Consumer Representation in Standardization (ANEC), the European Organization for Testing and Certification (EOTC), all in Brussels, and the Corporate Standardization Department at Philips in Eindhoven, from April 5-15, 2000. The two studies are Atkins 1998 and Pelkmans, Vos, and Di Mauro, 2000.

[14] The three directives are the Low Voltage Directive, the Machinery Directive, and the Electromagnetic Compatibility Directive.

factors, such as high transportation costs, discourage intra-EU trade, success has been more elusive.

Finally, sectors with many small and medium-sized enterprises (SMEs) and little existing trade are difficult to tackle, because there is no concerted industry support, and vested interests tend to put up fights to keep markets apart. The classic example is the carpet market. The European carpet industry comprises hundreds of SMEs. Each country has a variety of regulations for carpets, especially regarding fire safety. Testing methods vary across countries so as to render comparability of results impossible, and local fire brigades are often authorized to make final decisions regarding choice of carpet to be used in public spaces. Under the Construction Products 'New Approach' Directive, carpets have to meet essential safety requirements for fire resistance, impact noise rating, thermal insulation and specific slipperiness requirements. However, very few relevant European standards have been adopted and progress is certain to remain very slow.

In conclusion, member states of regional integration schemes outside Europe would do well to study the institutional features and *modus operandi* of the EU's 'New Approach.' If they are serious about deepening integration, particularly in difficult areas where fully legitimate, non-discriminatory and proportionate domestic regulations impede trade simply because they exist and happen to differ among member-states, hybrid governance as suggested in the 'New Approach' may well offer an effective, efficient, and balanced approach to regional trade liberalization.

References

Abbott, Kenneth and Duncan Snidal (2001), 'International Standards and International Governance,' *Journal of European Public Policy,* Vol. 8(3), pp. 345-370.

Atkins, W.S. (1998), *Technical Barriers to Trade,* Office for Official Publications of the European Communities, Luxemburg.

Burley, Anne-Marie and Walter Mattli (1993), 'Europe Before the Court: A Political Theory of Legal Integration', *International Organization,* Vol. 47 (Winter), pp. 41-76.

DeVries, Henk (1998), *Standards for the Nation: Analysis of National Standardization Organizations,* Kluwer Academic Publishers, Boston.

Egan, Michelle (1998), 'Regulatory Strategies, Delegation and European Market Integration,' *Journal of European Public Policy,* Vol. 5, 487-508.

Falke, Joseph and Harm Schepel (eds.) (2000), *Legal Aspects of Standardisation in the Member States of the EC and EFTA: Country Reports,* Vol. 2, Office for Official Publications of the European Communities, Luxemburg.

Garrett, Geoffrey (1992), 'International Cooperation and Institutional Choice: The European Community's Internal Market', *International Organization,* Vol. 46 (Spring), pp. 533-560.

Haas, Ernst (1958), *The Uniting of Europe,* Stanford University Press, Stanford.

Joerges, Christian, Harm Schepel, and Ellen Vos (1999), *The Law's Problem with the Involvement of Non-Governmental Actors in Europe's Legislative Processes: The Case of Standardization Under the 'New Approach',* EUI Working Paper Law No. 99/9, European University Institute, Badia Fiesolana, San Domenico (Florence).

Mattli, Walter (2003), 'Public and Private Governance in Setting International Standards,' in Miles Kahler and David Lake (eds.), *Governance in a Global Economy: Political Authority in Transition,* Princeton University Press, Princeton.

Mattli, Walter and Anne-Marie Slaughter (1995), Law and Politics in the European Union,' *International Organization,* Vol. 49 (Winter), pp. 183-190.

Mattli, Walter and Anne-Marie Slaughter (1998), 'Revisiting the European Court of Justice,' *International Organization,* Vol. 52 (Winter), pp. 177-209.

Moravcsik, Andrew (1991), 'Negotiating the Single European Act: National Interests and Conventional Statecraft in the European Community,' *International Organization,* Vol. 45 (Winter), pp. 19-65.

Pelkmans, Jacques, Ellen Vos, and Luca Di Mauro (2000), 'Reforming Product Regulation in the EU: A Painstaking, Iterative Two-Level Game,' in G. Galli and J. Pelkmans, *Regulatory Reform and Competitiveness in Europe*, E. Elgar, Cheltham, pp. 1-55.

Pollack, Marc (1997), 'Delegation, Agency, and Agenda Setting in the European Community,' *International Organization,* Vol. 51 (Winter), pp. 65-97.

Chapter 13

International Regimes or Would-be Polities? Some Concluding Questions and Remarks

Finn Laursen

Introduction

The chapters in this book take us around in the world, from Central America, via South America to Europe, West Africa, the Persian Gulf and East Asia. At the same time, the chapters take us through different theories and approaches to the study of regional integration and co-operation.

The different integration schemes in the world vary in various ways. They vary in functional scope, institutional set-up, size of membership and impact. The different factors used to explain this variance also vary, from economic gains over geopolitics to learning processes and creation of new collective identities.

If the integration schemes in different parts of the world are so different, are they all *sui generis*? Does it make sense to compare them? The premise of this book has been an affirmative answer to the latter question.

Degrees of Economic Integration

Most – if not all – integration schemes involve economic integration. Economists distinguish between various stages of economic integration. Bela Balassa's classic five categories of economic integration are given in Table 13.1.

Willem Molle has introduced some further distinctions, giving the following stages of economic integration: free trade area, incomplete customs union, customs union, incomplete common market, common market, economic union, monetary union, economic and monetary union, political union and full union. Political Union is reached when 'integration is extended beyond the realm of economics to encompass such fields as anti-crime policy (police) and foreign policy, eventually including security policy.' Full union involves 'complete unification of the economies involved.' A full union is likely to involve social security, income tax and macro-economic and stabilisation policy. The latter 'implies a budget of sufficient size to be effective as an instrument of these policies.' The end of the continuum thus is 'some form of a confederation or federation' (Molle, 1994, p. 12).

Table 13.1 Balassa's categories of economic integration

	No Tariff or Quota	Common External Tariffs	Free Flow of Factors	Harmonization of Economic Policies	Unification of Policies. Political Institutions
Free Trade Area	X				
Customs Union	X	X			
Common Market	X	X	X		
Economic Union	X	X	X	X	
Total Economic Integration	X	X	X	X	X

Source: Nye, 1971, p. 29.

Applied to the different integration schemes in the world, it is clear that the EU has progressed furthest. The Maastricht Treaty included the plan for Economic and Monetary Union (EMU). Today 12 of 15 Member States have introduced the single currency, the euro. The EU has not gone very far in the fiscal policy area, but the Stability Pact sets requirements for national fiscal policy. Some harmonisation of taxation policies has been tried, but with somewhat limited success. Taxation, including spending for social welfare, remains largely a national responsibility. The EU budget can maximum take 1.27 per cent of the EU GDP.

On the political side, the EU deals with foreign, security and lately also defence policies as well as Justice and Home Affairs Co-operation, the latter including police co-operation. As such the EU has become a political union, but the EU remains rather weak in these political areas where the member states have been unwilling to transfer sovereignty to common institutions. Consensus or unanimity still dominates in 'high politics' areas and the Commission and ECJ get much less involved – if at all – than in economic matters.

In many ways, the EU can be compared with a federal state in economic, but not in political areas, where the institutional set-up remains intergovernmental or 'confederal'.

Looking at integration in other parts of the world, many integration efforts include at least efforts to create free trade. This is clearly the case of NAFTA, Mercosur and the Asean Free Trade Area (AFTA). Many of these efforts began – or restarted as second generation efforts – in the early 1990s and could be seen as responses to the internal market programme in Europe and to some extent to the difficulties of concluding the Uruguay Round of the General Agreement on Tariffs and Trade (GATT). Facilitation of investments is often a part of these schemes, too. But most states have hesitations about free mobility of persons. The EU has realised the four freedoms as part of the internal market: free movement of goods, capital, services and persons. None of the other integration schemes have gone so far in establishing a common market, but at least the Mercosur aims in that direction. A more detailed comparison between existing integration schemes along the stages of economic integration could be an interesting research project. Finding out why some regions go further than other regions remains a central research question. To answer that question we need not only look at the interests of the participating countries but also at the role of the common institutions created during the process and, possibly, other factors such as wider systemic forces, including the process of globalisation.

International Regimes

Integration schemes usually involve a certain degree of joint decision-making and the creation of some common institutions. As such they all involve the creation at the regional level of what political scientists call international regimes.

Back in the early 1980s, Stephen Krasner gave what has become known as the consensus definition of international regimes:

> Regimes can be defined as sets of implicit or explicit principles, norms, rules, and decision-making procedures around which actors' expectations converge in a given area of international relations (Krasner, 1983, p. 2).

Regional integration schemes may well include more that one 'given area of international relations.' As we have seen, they may set out to create free trade, a customs union or a common market. They may move from liberalisation to the creation of common policies in the economic area. They may also include co-operation related to security issues. Usually they affect expectations and political activities. Sometimes economic co-operation is most important, like in Mercosur and NAFTA. Sometimes security related co-operation precedes efforts to create free trade, as we have seen in the case of ASEAN. Sorting out security related issues before economic integration started was also important in the case of Mercosur. In Europe, from the initial plans for a common market to Economic and Monetary Union (EMU), economics have taken a central place. Political co-operation developed slowly in parallel with economic integration, first through European Political Co-operation (EPC) from 1970, later through the EU's second pillar, Common Foreign and Security Policy (CFSP), introduced by the Maastricht Treaty in 1992. But the original Schuman Plan in 1950, which started the process of integration in western Europe, was also very much motivated by security concerns, viz. the age-old Franco-German problem. As the French Foreign Minister Robert Schuman said at the time:

> By pooling basic production and by creating a new high authority whose decisions will be binding on France, Germany and the other countries who may subsequently join, this proposal will create the first concrete foundation for a European federation which is so indispensable for the preservation of peace (Schuman [1950] in Patijn, 1970, p. 49).

Comparing the different integration schemes, one difference remains striking: The EC created stronger common institutions than other regions in the world have done. In the EU's first pillar important powers have been delegated to the European Commission and the European Court of Justice (ECJ) and decisions have increasingly been taken by a Qualified Majority Vote (QMV) in the Council of Ministers. When writing about international institutions in 1989, Robert Keohane argued that institutions affect states in three ways:

1. the flow of information and opportunities to negotiate;
2. the ability of governments to monitor others' compliance and to implement their own commitments – hence their ability to make credible commitments in the first place; and
3. prevailing expectations about the solidity of international agreements (Keohane, 1989, p. 2).

The concept of credible commitments was later used by Andrew Moravcsik in his effort to explain institutional choice in the EU (Moravcsik, 1998). The EU has gone much further in pooling and delegating sovereignty than other integration schemes or wider international regimes such as the General Agreement on Tariffs and Trade (GATT), now embedded in the World Trade Organization (WTO). Is such pooling and delegation of sovereignty necessary to get credible commitments? Political leaders in other parts of the world have shied away from the bold step of delegating and pooling sovereignty. This raises the question of whether classical intergovernmental co-operation can create 'credible commitments'?

In recent years we have seen an institutionalist turn in social sciences. 'Institutions matter' we are told. If so, different institutions presumably matter differently. Neo-functionalists, inspired by Jean Monnet, have tended to be sceptical about the possibility of creating 'credible commitments' through classical intergovernmental institutions.

Keohane suggested 'institutional variation' over three main kinds of institutions, viz. conventions, international regimes and international organisations. 'Variations in degrees of institutionalization exert substantial effects on state behaviour,' he said. Secondly, for an institutionalist perspective to be relevant, 'the actors must have some mutual interests' (Keohane, 1989, p. 2).

Supranational Polities

To apply Keohane's 1989 distinctions to the EU, we need to add some further distinctions. One of the EU's founding fathers Jean Monnet mentioned the 'negative experience of international co-operation, whose institutions were incapable of decision-making.' He therefore proposed 'a joint sovereign authority' for the first European Community, the European Coal and Steel Community (ECSC) in 1950 (Monnet, 1978, p. 295). He also wanted to 'abandon the unanimity rule in favour of a new system in which, to everybody's advantage, the idea of the common interest would replace that of the national interest – or rather, the national interests of six separate countries' (Ibid., p. 353).

None of the other integration schemes in the world have gone so far in the direction of giving common institutions 'supranational' powers. In that sense, the EU is certainly *sui generis*, and some scholars have argued that the EU is more than an international regime (or international organisation), but less than a federal state (e.g. Wallace, 1983).

Writing about the EC in 1991 Keohane and Hoffmann echoed this:

1. The EC is best characterized as neither an international regime nor an emerging state but as a network involving the pooling of sovereignty.
2. The political process of the EC is well described by the term 'supranationality' as used by Ernst Haas in the 1960s (although not as often used subsequently) (Keohane and Hoffmann, 1991, p. 10).

At the same time, Keohane and Hoffmann did emphasise that 'the EC has always rested on a set of *intergovernmental bargains.*'

In comparisons between the EU and other regional institutions, we therefore need to add supranational institutions (or polities) to those mentioned by Keohane in 1989. Further on an institutional axis we could also add federal states (see Figure 13.1). On Keohane's other axis, mutual interest, we could use a rationalist game theoretic perspective, starting with conflicting interests (deadlock) over dilemmas of common interests (Prisoners' dilemmas) via dilemmas of common aversions, especially co-ordination games with distribution problems (Battle of the Sexes) to situations of no conflict (harmony) (see especially Stein 1983, and Krasner 1991, but also Grieco 1988 and Snidal 1991 as well as the editor's introductory chapter in this book) (Figure 13.2).

| Conventions | International Regimes | International Organisations | Supranational Polities | Federal States |

Source: Compiled by the author

Figure 13.1   Institutional capacity

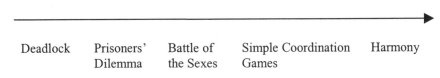

| Deadlock | Prisoners' Dilemma | Battle of the Sexes | Simple Coordination Games | Harmony |

Source: Compiled by the author

Figure 13.2   Common interests

The relation between the two axes is tricky. It may be curvy-linear. In Prisoners' Dilemma situations good institutions are required to get Pareto-efficient solutions. Under the Battle of the Sexes, institutions have to contribute to solving problems of distribution. In the case of Simple Co-ordination Games, there are neither problems of defection nor distribution. So no regimes are needed. When there are fundamental conflicts of interests (Deadlock) no co-operative institutions will emerge. Nor are they needed at the other end of the continuum in situations of harmony.

What this latter axis suggests is that the configuration of interests (or preferences) structures different kinds of situations that affect the institutional requirements if joint decision-making is to take place. The two fundamental situations requiring good institutions are the dilemmas of common interests, where the issue is one of reaching efficient solutions, and dilemmas of common aversions, where the problem is one of distribution.[1]

We have tried to summarise the essentials of the argument in Table 13.1. In pure conflict situations it is limited what institutions can do. Some convergence of interests will have to take place first. At the other end, harmony of interests requires no institutionalisation. 'Parallel unilateral action' as advocated in East Asia and within APEC should be sufficient. The problem for AFTA and APEC is that harmony of interests does not necessarily exist. Domestic pressures have made it impossible for APEC to progress towards freer trade in sensitive areas.

Simple co-ordination problems – like whether to drive on the left or right side of the road – require decisions, but no elaborate regimes. They are basically self executing once decided upon. I suggest that the so-called Open Method of Co-ordination, invented by the EU and applied to employment policy under the Amsterdam Treaty and a number of issues under the so-called Lisbon strategy of 2000, can solve simple coordination problems. The Lisbon strategy set the strategic goal for the EU 'to become the most competitive and dynamic knowledge-based economy in the world, capable of sustainable economic growth with more and better jobs and greater social cohesion.' It is a good question, however, whether these problems are all simple co-ordination problems. So far progress seems to have been limited and slow.

---

[1] For a German discussion of how different game situations structure international relations, see Zürn 1992.

Table 13.2 Nature of issues and institutional requirements

Nature of issue	Conflicting interests/ pure conflict	Dilemmas of common interests. Temptation to defect	Co-ordination problem with distributional issues	Simple co-ordination problem	Harmony of interests
Institu-tional require-ments	Institutions to no avail. Conver-gence of interests required	Pooling and delegation of sovereignty. Sanctions against defection	Pooling and delegation of sovereignty. Side-payments. Budgetary means useful	Open Method of Co-ordination (OMC) sufficient	Institution-alisation not necessary. 'Parallel unilateral action' sufficient

Source: Compiled by the author

Used in a comparative perspective, this raises the question of whether other mechanisms than pooling and delegation of sovereignty can provide for 'credible commitments' when there are temptations to defect from agreements, or distributional inequities follow from integration. The most obvious candidate for such mechanism is leadership (or hegemony) There can be no doubt that leadership is in any case an important variable in processes of integration, as underlined already by Lindberg and Scheingold (1970) and later by Mattli (1999). Thomas Pedersen has studied the role of France and Germany in the European integration process. These two countries have performed a kind of 'co-operative hegemony' he suggests (Pedersen, 1998).

Values and Identities

Do we need to go from the more rational approaches to more social constructivist inspired approaches? If so an axis could start from hostility and go through a no-war zone via a zone of peace to a security community in the sense of Karl Deutsch (1957). The importance of traversing such a sequence of situations was emphasised by Andrea Oelsner in her contribution to this book. Europe has also been going through such a process.

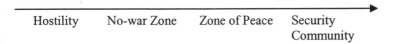

Hostility   No-war Zone   Zone of Peace   Security
                                                         Community

Figure 13.3   The perceptual dimension of integration (sense of community)

We remember that Karl Deutsch emphasised that we find a number of pluralistic security communities, i.e. communities without a common government (amalgamation). The relationship between the perceptual dimension and the more material-rationalist dimension remains unclear. Deutsch's discussion of the relationship between integration and amalgamation was somewhat inconclusive. Sometimes integration precedes amalgamation and sometimes amalgamation precedes integration.

Many of the institutions that contemporary institutionalists are interested in, do not add up to amalgamation, i.e. formation of a new state, either federal or unitary.

If we apply a more sophisticated concept of institutions, there can be no doubt that common institutions can contribute to learning processes, actor socialisation and the shaping of collective identities, which in turn can make the solution of common problems easier. But the shifting of loyalties that early neofunctionalists talked about has not really happened even in Europe, at least among the wider public. Recent problems of ratification of treaty reforms in the EU, from Maastricht to Nice, indicate that national identities are still very strong. Integration in Europe has reached a stage where questions of legitimacy have become problems of great concern for political leaders. The days of the 'permissive consensus' are gone.

An aspect of this is external. Although internally the EU constitutes a security community, the EU Member States still have very divergent views of how to relate to the outside world, especially in 'high politics' areas, as demonstrated at the moment by the different European national approaches to the case of Iraq.

Multi-Level Governance

Since Deutsch contributed to integration studies, the new term 'governance' has emerged. Robert Keohane's presidential address to the American Political Science Association in 2000 was entitled 'Governance in a Partially Globalized World' (Keohane, 2001). International Relations scholars started talking about 'governance without government' in the international system in the early 1990s (e.g. Rosenau and Czempiel, 1992). The term has also increasingly been used in relation to the EU (e.g. Bulmer, 1994; Jachtenfuchs, 1995). Part of this literature puts emphasis on the multi-level nature of the EU polity (e.g. Marks et al., 1996). The literature also discusses the problem-solving capacity of multi-level governance (e.g. Scharpf, 1997; Scharpf, 1999). We shall not review this literature here. Suffice it to say that much of this literature has the 'supranational' EU level as an important level. In that sense, there are some parallels to earlier neofunctionalist theories, which also saw the role of the European Commission and the ECJ as important.

Some of the governance literature puts emphasis on networks. Various scholars have based studies of particular policy studies on networks approaches (see for instance Marsh, 1998). According to John Peterson, the study of networks is particularly useful at the sub-systemic level where policies are prepared (Peterson and Bomberg, 1999). Such networks also play a role in other parts of the world.

Business leaders, especially, may form networks and put pressure on leaders to produce integration even where strong common institutions do not exist, such as has been happening to some extent in the case of ASEAN (Eliassen and Børve Monsen, 1999). But will such efforts last short of what Mattli has termed commitment institutions (Mattli, 1999) or undisputed leadership? Douglas Webber discusses the problems of leadership in ASEAN and APEC in his contribution to this book.

The moment the EU polity starts resembling a federal system it can be studied on the basis of theories from comparative politics (e.g. Hix, 1999) and compared with federal systems (e.g. Friedrich, 1969; Sbragia, 1992; Nicolaidis and Howse, 2001). It seems to us that such comparisons would not make so much sense for NAFTA, Mercosur or ASEAN.

The EU is currently going through yet another treaty reform. A Convention on the Future of Europe is producing a 'constitution' for Europe (Laursen, 2002). The Convention is preparing another Intergovernmental Conference, which will finalise the new constitutional treaty of the EU in view of creating efficient and legitimate governance in a much enlarged EU. 10 new members have been accepted at the meeting of the European Council in Copenhagen in December 2002. If membership is accepted by referenda and confirmed by national parliaments in the applicant countries, the EU may well have 10 new members from May 2004. This enlargement suggests that European integration has kept moving over the years, with ups and downs, but on balance expanding scope and deepening integration while also widening. The Schuman-Monnet initiatives in 1950 put Europe onto a new trajectory which has now reached the 'constitutional' phase.

Concluding Remarks

Scholarship on regional integration faces the challenge of developing more comparative research designs for additional empirical research. Back in the early years of integration studies Nye presented a comparative study (Nye, 1971). More recently Mattli has done so, too (Mattli, 1999). But most studies, including those presented in this book, are single case studies or comparisons of a couple of integration schemes.

Questions for further research include the role of interests and values, negotiations and institutions, and the impact of integration. More detailed comparative studies of the role of commitment institutions and leadership would especially be useful. Have second generation integration schemes turned out to be as resilient as predicted by some in the early 1990s? Or will they slip back as happened to many integration efforts in the 1970s? On this fundamental question the jury is still out.

References

Bulmer, Simon J. (1994), 'The Governance of the European Union: A New Institutionalist Approach,' *Journal of Public Policy,* Vol. 13(4), pp. 351-380.

Deutsch, Karl W. et al. (eds) (1957), *Political Community and the North Atlantic Area: International Organization in the Light of Historical Experience,* Princeton University Press, Princeton, NJ.

Eliassen, Kjell A. and Monsen, Catherine Børve (1999), 'Institutions and Networks: A Comparison of European and Southeast Asian Integration,' in Erik Beukel et al. (eds.), *Elites, Parties and Democracy: Festschrift for Professor Mogens N. Pedersen,* Odense University Press, Odense, pp. 49-74.

Friedrich, Carl J. (1969), *Europe: An Emergent Nation,* Harper and Row, New York.

Grieco, Joseph M. (1988), 'Anarchy and the Limits of Cooperation: A Realist Critique of the Newest Liberal Institutionalism,' *International Organization,* Vol. 42 (August), pp. 485-507.

Hix, Simon (1999), *The Political System of the European Union.* St. Martin's Press,   New York.

Jachtenfuchs, Markus (1995), 'Theoretical Perspectives on European Governance,' *European Law Journal,* Vol. 1(2) (July), pp. 115-133.

Keohane, Robert O. (1989), *International Institutions and State Power: Essays in International Theory,* Westview Press, Boulder.

Keohane, Robert O. (2001), 'Governance in a Partially Globalized World,' *American Political Science Review,* Vol. 95(1) (March), pp. 1-13.

Keohane, Robert O. and Hoffmann, Stanley (1991), 'Institutional Change in Europe in the 1980s,' in Robert O. Keohane and Stanley Hoffmann (eds), *The New European Community: Decisionmaking and Institutional Change,* Westview Press, Boulder, CO., pp. 1-39.

Krasner, Stephen D. (1983), 'Structural causes and regime consequences: regimes as intervening variables,' in Stephen Krasner (ed.), *International Regimes,* Cornell University Press, Ithaca, pp. 1-21.

Krasner, Stephen D. (1991), 'Global Communications and National Power: Life on the Pareto Frontier,' *World Politics,* Vol. 43 (April), pp. 336-366.

Laursen, Finn (2002), 'Vers un traité constitutionnel?' *L'Europe en formation* (Nice), No. 1, pp. 29-40.

Lindberg, Leon N. and Scheingold, Stuart A. (1970), *Europe's Would-Be Polity: Patterns of Change in the European Community,* Prentice-Hall, Inc., Englewood-Cliffs, N.J.

Marks, Gary, Lisbet Hooghe and Kermit Blank (1996), 'European Integration from the 1980s: State-Centric v. Multi-Level Governance,' *Journal of Common Market Studies,* Vol. 34(3), pp. 341-2378.

Marsh, D. (ed.) (1998), *Comparing Policy Networks,* Open University Press, Buckingham.

Martin, Lisa L. (1992), 'Interests, power, and multilateralism,' *International Organization,* Vol. 46(4) (Autumn 1992), pp. 765-792.

Mattli, Walter (1999), *The Logic of Integration: Europe and Beyond,* Cambridge University Press, Cambridge.

Molle, Willem (1994), *The Economics of European Integration: Theory, Practice, Policy,* Second edition, Aldershot, Dartmouth.

Monnet, Jean (1978), *Memoirs,* Doubleday & Company, Inc., Garden City, NY.

Moravcsik, Andrew (1998), *The Choice for Europe: Social Purpose and State Power from Messina to Maastricht,* Cornell University Press, Ithaca, NY.

Nicolaidis, Kalypso and Howse, Robert (eds) (2001), *The Federal Vision: Legitimacy and Levels of Governance in the United States and the European Union,* Oxford University Press, Oxford.

Nye, J.S. (1971), *Peace in Parts: Integration and Conflict in Regional Organization,* Little, Brown and Company, Boston.

Patijn, S. (1970), *Landmarks in European Unity,* A.W. Sijthoff, Leyden.

Peterson, John and E. Bomberg (1999), *Decision-Making in the European Union,* Basingstoke: Macmillan.

Pedersen, Thomas (1998), *Germany, France and the Integration of Europe: A Realist Interpretation,* Pinter, London.

Rosenau, James N. and Czempiel, Ernst-Otto (eds) (1992), *Governance without government: Order and change in world politics,* Cambridge University Press, Cambridge.

Sbragia, Alberta M. (1992), 'Thinking about the European Future: The Uses of Comparison,' in Alberta Sbragia (ed.), *Euro-Politics: Institutions and Policymaking in the "New" European Community,* The Brookings Institution, Washington, D.C., pp. 257-291.

Scharpf, Fritz W. (1997), 'Introduction: The problem-solving capacity of multi-level governance,' *Journal of European Public Policy,* Vol. 4(4) (December), pp. 520-538.

Scharpf, Fritz W. (1999), *Governing in Europe: Effective and Democratic?* Oxford University Press, Oxford.

Scharpf, Fritz (2002), 'La diversité légitime: Nouveau défi de l'integration européenne,' *Revue française de science politique,* Vol. 52(5-6) (October-December), pp. 609-639.

Snidal, Duncan (1991), 'Relative Gains and the Pattern of International Cooperation,' *American Political Science Review* 85 (September), pp. 701-26.

Wallace, William (1983), 'Less than a Federation, More than a Regime: the Community as a Political System,' in H. Wallace, W. Wallace and C. Webb (eds), *Policy-Making in the European Community,* John Wiley and Sons Chichester, pp. 403-436.

Zürn, Michael (1992), *Interessen und Institutionen in der internationalen Politik: Grundlegung und Anwendung des situationsstrukturellen Ansatzes,* Leske und Budrich, Opladen.

Index